IMAGES OF WAR

IMAGES OF WAR

THE ARTIST'S VISION OF WORLD WAR II

◾

Selected and Edited by
KEN McCORMICK
and
HAMILTON DARBY PERRY

Foreword by
JOHN HERSEY

◾

ORION BOOKS

New York

Staff for Ken McCormick and Hamilton Darby Perry

RESEARCH DIRECTOR
Joan Giurdanella

PICTURE AND TEXT RESEARCH
New York—Bonnie Cutler, Beth Turner
Washington—Connie Runyon, Sybille Millard, Diane Schule
London—Caroline Larken ▪ *Paris*—Linda Gutierrez ▪ *Munich*—Dr. Petra Munte
Rome—Anna Bruno ▪ *Canberra*—Kay Walsh, Sylvia Carr
Tokyo—Okimitsu Ohishi ▪ *Warsaw*—Dr. Grazyna Siedlecka-Orzel

ART EVALUATION
Michael Mendelsohn, Patricia Ollague

SOVIET ART SELECTION
Raisa Klisharova, art historian, Aurora Art Publishers, Leningrad

Designed by Beth Tondreau Design

The illustrations published in this book are used with the
permission of the governments, museums, individuals, and special collections
credited in the captions. Permission credits for previously published text are to be
found at the back of this book.

Published by Orion Books, a division of Crown Publishers, Inc.,
201 East 50th Street, New York, New York 10022.
Member of the Crown Publishing Group.

ORION and colophon are trademarks of Crown Publishers, Inc.
Manufactured in Japan

LIBRARY OF CONGRESS CATALOGING-IN-PUBLICATION DATA

Images of war: the artist's vision of World War II/selected and
edited by Ken McCormick and Hamilton Darby Perry;
foreword by John Hersey.—1st ed.
p.   cm.
1. World War, 1939–1945—Art and the war.
I. McCormick, Ken, 1906–   . II. Perry, Hamilton Darby.
D810.A7I43   1990
758′.994054—dc20   89-72162
                                                         CIP

ISBN 0-517-57065-3
10 9 8 7 6 5 4 3 2 1
FIRST EDITION

BOMC offers recordings and compact discs, cassettes
and records. For information and catalog write to
BOMR, Camp Hill, PA 17012.

Frontispiece: *Pearl Harbor,* Griffith B. Coale (U.S. Navy Combat Art Collection)

For Anne and Margaret,
for encouragement and cheer
■

CONTENTS

■

EDITORS' NOTE

■

T his book does not pretend to be a definitive story of World War II. It was inspired by the war experiences of a variety of people from different countries—and what they chose to remember in their published recollections, and in the paintings and drawings of "war artists" reproduced in these pages.

These war artists were not everywhere, so this cannot be a full story of the war in art. Their total number, from all countries, was probably well under one thousand men and women. But works of some two hundred artists from more than a dozen countries are represented here.

The origins of the various national war art programs differed. But the pictures that were created fulfill a universal purpose that was much the same in each country: to create a historical record of the war as seen through the eyes of these talented participants. Perhaps the special interpretation of an artist recording war is clarified by an explanation written in 1964 by Dr. Noble Frankland, who was then the Director of the Imperial War Museum, London, introducing a catalog of that museum's extensive collection:

> The resulting artistic record naturally tends to conflict in exactitude of detail, and sometimes abruptly so, with the photographic record. . . . It may, because of this, tend to conflict with the image of the war in the eyes of the beholder. If this is so, it is because these works of art have no stereotype. On the contrary, they enshrine the individual imaginative reponses of many artists whose differing impressions were inspired by their having witnessed, and in many cases experienced, the incidents they depicted.

We have endeavored to complement what the artists saw with a wide selection of written recollections. Generally they are from previously published sources, though a number of the recollections come from little-known presses, from unknown writers, and from private collections. Included are the experiences of the great commanders as well as the rear-rankers.

The text of this volume attempts to give you a buildup of vivid, powerful recollections of people who went through that cauldron of experience. We could touch on only a relative few of the major events of almost six years of war, as these were recorded by war artists and writers. In the process, we found that single episodes—such as the evacuation of Dunkirk or the bombing of Pearl Harbor—were more easily captured in the limited range of a single volume than extended military endeavors, such as the island-hopping campaigns across the Pacific, or the hundred-mile-wide carrier battles, or the jungle-shrouded fortunes of the China-Burma-India theater of operations, or the seesaw fighting in North Africa. So we sometimes had to select a single encounter to stand for many: the battle for Guadalcanal is offered to represent the hard struggles for dozens of islands; the eleven-day battle of El Alamein was selected to give the feel of actions back and forth across the great sea of the North African desert.

The book is also meant to be nonpolitical and nonnationalistic, as much as that is possible, without seeming dumbly oblivious to the political and nationalistic aims that drove the machinery of war in all nations involved. The political issues have been well examined elsewhere, and the war crimes have been well explored and are still the subjects of investigations and trials. More practically, the politics of the war and the brutality of the war crimes were often subjects that seemed to defy reduction to a picture—although there are examples in the book of artists who attempted this.

The reader will find an intriguing range of art subjects and styles in the book, we believe. Some of the works collected here are valuable primarily as a unique historical perspective of the war. But perhaps one-third to one-half of the art created was of museum quality. A number of the artists were already famous at the time, and young artists developed by the programs went on to noted careers after the war—though each country also lost promising artists killed in the field.

The book sees the first publication, outside of museum catalogs, of many fine works of art. Certainly in the years to come—particularly during the fiftieth anniversary of the war years—much more of it will be seen and appreciated. In their way, these war-inspired pictures and recollections present an unusual tribute to those who gave their lives in the war, as well as to those who have since worked for peace and a world in which it should not be allowed to happen again.

KEN MCCORMICK
HAMILTON DARBY PERRY

FOREWORD

■

Early on the morning of October 8, 1942, I reported with a couple of other war correspondents to a tent on a slight rise on the marine beachhead on Guadalcanal, to be briefed on a probe the marines would be undertaking that day in an effort to safeguard and enlarge their precarious toehold on the island. I had only recently transferred to Guadalcanal from duty on the USS *Hornet,* and I knew absolutely nothing about jungle warfare.

Chow was being served from a cook tent, and a kindly captain named Donald L. Dickson took me in hand and obliged me to down a huge breakfast of sliced pineapple, baked beans, creamed chipped beef, rice-and-raisin stew, crackers, canned butter, jam, and coffee; he said I wouldn't have anything to eat but cold C rations for at least two days. Then he gave me some basic advice—which I badly needed, and which turned out to make all the difference—on how to look out for myself during those days. Little things: if I refilled my canteen from a stream, be sure to get a medical corpsman to put some drops of iodine in the water before I drank it; how to bed down at night on coral outcroppings; how to care for my tender feet. And big things: above all, how to take cover from enemy fire in the jungle. He refrained from saying that I had no business being there at all.

I saw that although it was barely light yet, Dickson had taken the trouble to shave. He was a lean fellow of middle height who under different circumstances might have been counted handsome, but now, like all the other marines at that grim stage of the fighting, he looked drawn, haggard. He wore sweat-stained fatigues and a plastic helmet shell, over which he would fit a combat helmet when he moved into an action. He was helping to deal with the press for the First Marine Regiment, but during our conversation I learned from him that he was, at heart and by profession, an artist.

At 8:30, to the sounds of a friendly artillery barrage, the column of marines set

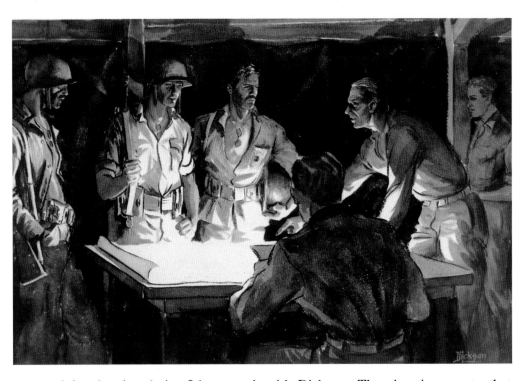

Instructions to a Patrol, Donald L. Dickson
(U.S. Navy Combat Art Collection)

out, and for the time being I lost touch with Dickson. The situation, up to that morning, was this:

Beginning with Pearl Harbor the previous December, the Allies had suffered one humiliation after another at the hands of the Japanese: defeats at Bataan, Hong Kong, Singapore, Wake, Guam, New Guinea, the Solomons. The naval battle of Midway, in early June, had brought a turning point in the Pacific war, and the marines' landing on the obscure little South Pacific island of Guadalcanal two months later had given the first hope that initiative in the struggle might be changing hands.

It was still a slim hope. The marine beachhead on Guadalcanal was only a tiny perimeter around Henderson Field, a crude strip of Marston matting that had been laid down for naval fighter and dive-bomber pilots in a clearing in former coconut groves on Lunga Point. Intelligence had come that the Japanese were reinforcing their troops on the island and had massed twenty thousand men in the jungles around Henderson Field. They had recently moved up in force to the mouth of the Matanikau River, eight miles west of the beachhead, and had begun to cross to the near side of the river. There had been two aborted attempts, neither of them in large enough strength, to force the enemy back away from the river. Considering the continuing Japanese buildup, this third try would be a vital one.

It took most of the day to march out, through rugged terrain of jungles and grassy ridges, to a treeless hill on the near side of the Matanikau. On the way, during a rest break in the march, one of the officers, Lt. Col. Julian Frisbie, described for me the marines' intentions for the next couple of days. He said they would expel the snipers and advance patrols on the near bank of the Matanikau, make a feint at crossing the river at its mouth, and then actually cross higher up and send through a series of three encircling forces to attempt to trap the enemy beyond. He added, with a professional soldier's awareness of the lore of his craft: "This is very much like a plan Lee used at the Chickahominy. He had Magruder make a demonstration south of the river, and sent D. H. Hill, A. P. Hill, and Longstreet across at successive bridges, with Jackson closing the trap at the rear. We aren't sending the units in with quite the same pattern, but it's the same general idea. The advantage of our scheme is that Whaling goes in, and if he finds the going impossible, we haven't yet committed Hanneken and Puller, and we can revise our tactics."

The marines bivouacked on the approach side of the bald hill, hidden from the enemy, readying mortars and machine guns and settling on start-off positions for the assault the next morning. It began to drizzle. Wrapped in ponchos, we hunkered down after dark to try—in my case, unsuccessfully—to sleep. In the morning, marine artillery and navy planes began a heavy barrage of the far bank of the river, and afterward huge white birds circled in terror over the jungle across the way. By late morning Whaling's first upriver crossing had been achieved, and I then joined a heavy machine gun company as it threaded down into a jungle valley to support the second encircling force under Hanneken. We moved toward the river in single file. Several snipers were driven out.

Suddenly we were trapped in a hell of greenery erupting in violent explosions. The Japanese, having explored the valley trail, had targeted it with mortar fire, and it was soon clear that the company would have to retreat or be wiped out. As it was, the casualties were horrible. There were not enough medical corpsmen and bandsmen (who during combat had left their instruments behind to aid the wounded on the field) to get those who had been badly hurt back to surgeons and safety, so I attached myself to a group of blasted and bloodied walking wounded, helping them to struggle along the trail and to cross a stream and then to climb— or, rather, to scrabble, stagger, fall fainting, rest, groan, crawl, stand again, and reel—in muddy footing through tangled growth up steep slopes back to the ridge. I had never experienced such a nightmare, but amid my selfish wonder that I was helping them from the valley of the shadow of death, and not the other way around, I realized that the mere trivial shock and fear and pity and outrage that I

Stretcher Party, Donald L. Dickson (U.S. Navy Combat Art Collection)

felt could not even be compared to the agonies—and the courage—of those maimed men.

After a second night on the heights—sleepless again for me, but for different reasons—the force returned to the encampment at Henderson Field. Bodies of the dead were retrieved; the badly wounded were taken out on stretchers and then in jeeps. The action as a whole, which came to be called the Third Battle of the Matanikau—by no means a memorable engagement in the annals of warfare —had been only a partial success: the Japanese had been driven back, but they had mostly escaped the encirclements. There were many similar and many much worse battles still to be fought in the Pacific theater before atomic bombs would bring to an end the sorts of horrors that were now vividly recorded on my retinas and eardrums.

Straggler, Donald L. Dickson (U.S. Navy Combat Art Collection)

Back on the beachhead, in the next few days I became better acquainted with Don Dickson. In 1924, as a youngster studying at the Worcester Museum School of Art, he had enlisted in the army reserve, and three years later had transferred to an organized Marine Corps Reserve unit in Boston. In the next thirteen years, while he worked as an artist in watercolors, oils, sculpture, cast metals, and molded rubber, and while he moonlighted, besides, as a radio and stage actor, he advanced from private to first lieutenant in the reserves and devoted much of his art to the marines. He painted colored covers for the Corps's magazine, *Leatherneck,* working with a primitive printing process that required his making four separate skeletal paintings, in red, blue, yellow, and black; he wrote and drew an illustrated column for the magazine, called "Marine Oddities"; and, with a warrant officer named Frank Rentfrow, he started a newspaper comic strip on a "perfect" Marine, Sgt. Stony Craig. He also illustrated a book—many years before civil rights became a real issue in America—entitled *Negro Combat Troops in the [First] World War,* giving blacks credit for their contributions then. He was influenced in those formative years by the works of Col. John W. Thomason, Jr., a marine artist in that earlier war; of N. C. Wyeth, the first of the distinguished family line of stark realists; and of the illustrator James Montgomery Flagg, who had drawn recruiting posters for World War I. In time, Dickson developed a straightforward, dry, unsentimental yet deeply felt style of his own, attempting in his serious drawings and paintings to represent things as they really were, not as they ought to be.

In 1940, Dickson's unit was called up, and he became a full-time marine. He took part, as adjutant of the First Marine Regiment, in the initial landing on Guadalcanal on August 7, 1942, and by the time I met him, he had gone through two months of fighting as harrowing as any suffered by United States military units in the entire war. And during those months, I soon discovered, he had spent spare time, if it could be called that, filling a number of spiral-bound notebooks with drawings of what he had seen.

Don Dickson was modest about those notebooks, but one day I persuaded him to show them to me, and in a curious way they opened my eyes to what I had been through that day in the valley by the Matanikau. During the action itself, and especially during and after the mortar barrage, I had been in a daze of wonder, fear, and confusion, and now these drawings let me see with clear eyes some of the meaning of what I had seen. A few of the sketches were hastily and crudely drawn; others were more studied.

Here was a rifleman crouching tensely in the jungle, just as I had seen many on that day; an exhausted runner reaching out with a written message; a group slogging across a muddy stream with steep banks; a man cowering under heavy fire in a shallow foxhole; a straggler on his last legs; one of the walking wounded putting a good face on his pain; stretcher-bearers struggling up a tangled slope. These drawings reached—in a way that photographs might never be able to reach —for the truth. These were not recruitment-poster works of art. Dickson had no illusions about the glory of combat. In a 1987 article about him in *Leatherneck* (of which he became editor in postwar years), one of his daughters said, "War was to him an abomination"—a sentiment far more widely shared among fighting men than press accounts and bond-rally speeches of the time dared suggest.

Lt. Herbert L. Merillat, a historian of the marines who had himself fought on Guadalcanal, told years later, in *Marines at War,* what Dickson had said to him about his art there: "I'm not interested in drawing Marines who are spick and span and smartly dressed. I don't want to gloss over life out there. It's dirty and hot and rugged, and that's the way I want to draw it." And he did indeed. A caption of a Dickson watercolor in that book, entitled *Too Many, Too Close, Too Long,* read: "This is a portrait of one of the 'little guys,' just plain worn-out. His stamina and his spirit stretched beyond human endurance. He has had no real sleep for a long time. He hasn't had enough to eat. He wears all the clothes he owns. And he

For a Pal, Donald L. Dickson (U.S. Navy Combat Art Collection)

probably hasn't stopped ducking and fighting long enough to discover that he has malaria. He is going to discover it now, however. He is through."

I have dwelt on the truth-seeking work of one artist because it seems to me to suggest the underlying value of this remarkable book. Dickson's work will not make art history, but it—like that of all the artists in this volume—contributes to the history of the Second World War something that no other form of representation can: a vivid sense of immediacy which gets its power from the individual vision of the artist. His temperament being exactly what it was, Dickson saw the abomination of Guadalcanal, but he also saw, because he had these qualities in himself, the tenacity of those who took part in the fighting, their calm endurance, their deep need to help and support each other, their ability to keep going against what so often seemed hopeless odds—in sum, the simple human urge, felt by so many soldiers all through history, just to survive with a few companions, and go home. Through Dickson's drawings and paintings, we see this one response to warfare, writ large.

During my time as a war correspondent, I saw other artists at work in other terms suitable to *their* particular traits: Tom Lea, on the *Hornet,* for example, with his grand and dramatizing vision kept under discipline by the precision of his hand as it put things down; or George Biddle, in North Africa and Sicily, a sophisticated man of the world, a gentleman walking abroad, seeing the men and women of the services shrewdly and with a touch of irony. Thus each artist brought a unique set of insights to bear on certain experiences of war. Gathered all together, as this book gathers them, these artists show us the astonishing complexity of the entire range of those experiences, all the way from their manifest terrors to—for some, alas—their hideous attractiveness.

This, then, is a harvest of personal responses to episodes of modern warfare. In the din of all the discussion of weaponry in the years since World War II—talk of ICBMs, B-1s, stealth bombers, Soviet XX-25s, MX missiles, Pershings, the hypothetical hardware of Star Wars, and all the rest—we have become inclined to think of warfare as something buyable, abstract, high-tech, mechanized, more or less automated. The images presented here, of moments in the last great war as seen through the eyes of highly individuated artists on both sides of the conflict, remind us that war is not fought by machines, and that the cost is not to be reckoned in dollars of national debt. War, these very human artists remind us, is fought by human beings. The cost is in human values and human lives.

JOHN HERSEY
Martha's Vineyard, Mass.

Too Many, Too Close, Too Long, Donald L. Dickson (U.S. Navy Combat Art Collection)

IMAGES OF WAR

In Memoriam
More than 64,000,000 dead
■

ITZKRIEG IN EURO

I n September 1938, British Prime Minister Neville Chamberlain flew to Munich to meet with Hitler, Mussolini, and Edouard Daladier of France and returned with the famous piece of paper promising "peace in our time." Hitler had promised that if he could take over Czechoslovakia's Sudetenland, his territorial demands would be over. He had already seized the Rhineland and Austria with no opposition—though he had been ready to back down if strongly opposed.

Then finally in March 1939 he would annex Czechoslovakia. Could he still want more?

But pleasant, unwarlike things were happening, too. During the summer of 1939, King George VI and Queen Elizabeth waved their way through a royal tour of Canada, with a visit to the United States. The World's Fair had opened to great crowds in New York, and most of the soon-to-be-warring nations had handsome buildings of peace.

On August 24, 1939, Hitler signed a nonaggression pact with Germany's archenemy, Russia. Britain and France mobilized, fearing the pact would clear the way for Germany to attack Poland "in defense of Germany's vital national interest." Seven days later, Germany did.

In August 1939 Count Ciano, the Italian Foreign Minister, was told in the frankest terms by Ribbentrop, his opposite number in Germany, just what the Germans intended:

"Well, Ribbentrop," I asked him, "what do you want? The [Polish] Corridor? Or Danzig?"

"Not any more," he stared at me through those cold eyes. "We want war."

■

Walter Schellenberg, a principal in the German intelligence service, first heard of Hitler's plan for war with Poland when a colleague came to him in great concern:

Mehlhorn's voice grew more excited as he told me that Heydrich had confided to him one of Hitler's secret orders. Before September 1, an absolutely irreproachable cause for war had got to be created. . . . It had therefore been planned to dress troops in Polish uniforms and attack the Gleiwitz radio transmitter.

■

Adolph Hitler's first "Directive for the War" carried out the fiction of a Germany forced to take action:

MOST SECRET
Directive No. 1 for the Conduct of War:
31 August, 1939
   1. Now that all the political possibilities of disposing by peaceful means of a situation on the Eastern Frontier . . . are exhausted, I have determined on a solution by force.

■

Dr. Albert Speer, Hitler's architect and advisor, remembered how Germany had begun one of the first official combat art programs of the war:

Even during the mobilization Hitler did not forget his artists. In the late summer of 1939, orders were given that their draft records be sent to Hitler's adjutant by the various army districts. He then tore up the papers and threw them away. By this original device, the men ceased to exist for the draft boards. . . .

■

The German army's belief in its own invincibility sprang quickly into being. In less than one month the "Polish War" was over. Gen. Heinz Guderian, who was in the van of the attack, had a visitor shortly afterward:

On 5 September our corps had a surprise visit from Adolf Hitler. I met him near Pievno . . . got into his car and drove with him along the line of our previous advance . . . to Graudenz, where he stopped and gazed for some time at the blown bridges over the Vistula. At the sight of the smashed artillery regiment, Hitler had asked me, "Our dive-bombers did that?" When I replied, "No, our Panzers!" he was plainly astonished.

■

Poland quickly found its enemy had two heads: Hitler and Stalin. After Hitler had "invented" his war against Poland, Stalin— Hitler's ally since the treacherous German-Soviet Nonaggression Pact of August 1939— moved into Poland from the east and swept some one and a half million Poles into his Siberian prison camps. Stalin's treachery was not confirmed until the information was released by the Soviet Union in 1989, from old records dug out under Mikhail Gorbachev's regime in the new spirit of East-West friendship.

■

A survivor of the German persecution in Poland wrote of experiences that would soon be the lot of Jews all over Europe:

Early in the morning the Jewish homes were entered by force, looted, and destroyed. With lashes and blows the Jews were herded together in the marketplace. . . . They were forced to stand at the station for two days and two nights completely naked, without food or drink. Finally they were loaded into cattle trucks and taken to the gas chambers at Belzec, near Lublin.

■

The Russian attack on Finland late in 1939 provided an unprecedented "training exercise"—vast and bloody for the Russians, encouraging for the German "volunteers" who wanted to learn how to fight the Russians. Finnish field marshal Carl Gustav Manner-

heim, an outstanding tactician in the war, listed some powerful conclusions:

The Russian officers were generally brave men who were little concerned about casualties. . . . The Russian infantryman showed himself brave, tough, and frugal— but lacking in initiative. . . .

   The Russians' phenomenal ability to dig themselves in deserves special mention. It seemed second nature to them, and they were masters of engineering. In spite of long military service, the Russian infantry showed a number of defects. Their musketry with automatic arms and rifles was very poor . . . the troops unable to maneuver successfully. . . . But the greatest weakness of the troops was their lack of familiarity with skis . . . the technique of skiing, especially as practiced in war, cannot be mastered in a few weeks.

   In men, our losses were 24,923 killed, missing, and died from wounds, and 43,557 wounded.

   It is unlikely that the exact Russian losses will ever be revealed, but they can at least be estimated in the light of known facts as approximately two hundred thousand killed.

■

Historians Desmond Flower and James Reeves, whose anthology The Taste of Courage *is a monumental collection of eyewitness accounts of World War II experiences and has contributed often to these pages, summarized the ominous "silence" that followed the mechanized avalanche that rolled across Poland:*

For six months after the conquest of Poland, land and air warfare in Europe virtually came to a standstill, with the exception of Russia's campaign against Finland.

■

Overheard in a Blackpool pub:

"Nothing doing yet?"
   "No. Looks like another bloody Hundred Years War."

■

B. H. Liddell Hart, the British military historian and war correspondent, saw early that the "Phony War's" inactivity was largely only phony for the Allies. The Germans were planning:

Those who coined the phrase meant to convey that the war was spurious. . . . In reality, it was a period of ominous activity—behind the curtain.

■

Sumner Welles was President Franklin D. Roosevelt's frequent advisor on international affairs, along with Harry Hopkins and Averell Harriman. As he moved through Europe in 1940, he could report to the president his reaction both to events and to his meetings with leaders. Welles on Mussolini, February 1940:

The man I saw before me seemed fifteen years older than his actual age of fifty-six. He was ponderous and static rather than vital. He moved with an elephantine motion; every step appeared an effort. He was heavy for his height, and his face in repose fell in rolls of flesh. . . . During our long rapid interchange of views he kept his eyes shut a considerable part of the time. He opened them with his dynamic and often-described wide stare only when he desired particularly to underline some remark.

■

Welles on Göring, March 1940:

When our interview was over Göring insisted upon showing me the vast and innumerable rooms of his palace. It would be difficult to find an uglier building or one more intrinsically vulgar in its ostentatious display.

■

German General F. W. von Mellenthin, who toured the German "Siegfried Line" before the attack on France, did not even write down these very sensitive observations until the defeat of the French army rendered the shortcomings of the Siegfried Line immaterial:

I had an opportunity of inspecting the famous West Wall, or Siegfried Line, at firsthand.

I soon realized what a gamble the Polish campaign had been . . . and the grave risks that were run by our High Command. The second-class [German] troops holding the

Wall were badly equipped and inadequately trained, and the defenses were far from being the impregnable fortifications pictured by our propaganda. . . . The strongpoints could have been shot to pieces, without the slightest risk to the [French] attackers.

■

Winston Churchill evaluated the chances of the Scandinavian countries in the event of a German invasion—though he hoped Britain would get to Norway first:

I could not reproach Denmark if she surrendered to Nazi attack. The other two Scandinavian countries, Norway and Sweden, have at least a ditch over which they can feed the tiger. . . .

■

Alfred Rosenberg, Nazi Party foreign affairs expert, suggested in December 1939 just how the followers of Vidkun Quisling, a flamboyant former Norwegian army officer, should be used to further German designs:

These trained men are then to be sent back to Norway as quickly as possible. . . . Several focal points in Oslo will have to be occupied with lightning speed. . . . The German Navy with contingents of the German Army will have to put in an appearance at a prearranged bay outside of Oslo, in answer to a special summons from the Norwegian Government. . . . Quisling has no doubt that such a coup . . . would at once meet with the approval of those sections of the Army with which he now has connections. . . .

■

An entry from Churchill's war journal as a British expeditionary force landed in Norway:

The Cabinet heartily approved all possible measures for the rescue and defense of Narvik and Trondheim. The troops . . . lacked aircraft, anti-aircraft guns, anti-tank guns, tanks, transport and training. The whole of Northern Norway was covered with snow. . . . There were neither snowshoes nor skis—still less skiers. We must do our best.

■

Carl Hambro, president of the Norwegian parliament, was in a position to follow the

German diplomatic negotiations:

On April 8, the rumors and the menaces crystallized into facts. That day the government was almost completely occupied by the British laying of mines off the Norwegian coast. . . .

That afternoon came the first reports that a German action was in progress. The early afternoon papers published a strange story about numbers of German soldiers coming ashore on the southern coast from a transport ship bound for Bergen, which had been torpedoed by a British submarine. . . .

■

Though surprised and outclassed, the Norwegians stubbornly fought back. Success seemed small, but when journalist Halvdan Koht counted the score, five German cruisers—Konigsberg (at Bergen), Emden, Gneisenau, Blücher, Karlsruhe—had been sunk or badly damaged:

The fortress of Oscarborg and the torpedo battery did not open fire until the German ships were very close. . . . Every shell and every torpedo was a full hit. The greatest German ship, the *Gneisenau* (26,000 tons) was hit by two torpedoes, exploding the oil tanks on board and setting the ship on fire. . . . The big new cruiser *Blücher* was sunk by the artillery of Oscarborg. . . .

A German squadron tried to make its way into the port on the night of April 9. But the ships and the land batteries gave fire at once, and the German attack was repulsed with considerable loss to the Germans. . . . The German cruiser *Karlsruhe* . . . was sunk, and the German squadron retired.

■

Tor Myklehost was an advisor to the king of Norway and had a privileged view of the events that would drive King Haakon to defiant exile in England:

Orders were given to have a special train for Hamar in readiness at 7 A.M. The Minister of Finance, Mr. Oscar Torp, took upon himself the vital charge of saving the gold of the Bank of Norway from falling into enemy hands. . . . The same day, April 9, the Storting [the Parliament] held two meetings at Hamar. Of 150 members, only five were absent.

German troops were on their way to Hamar in motor buses in order to capture all the representatives of the nation. At five minutes' notice, the Storting had again to board a train. . . .

In the morning Mr. Quisling had proclaimed himself chief of a new Government.

■

On April 13, 1940, King Haakon addressed his people. The Germans had wanted the king to cooperate with an occupation government, and that he found impossible:

The German forces have engaged in a violent attack on us. . . . High explosives and incendiary bombs and machine-gun fire were used against the civilian population and ourselves in the most unscrupulous and brutal fashion. . . . God Save Norway.

■

A British military affairs expert reconstructed Hitler's planning. His first hurried timetable had called for an attack in the West as early as November 12, 1939. Hitler noted his reasons for rushing:

What must be prevented above all is that the enemy should make good the weakness of his own armaments, particularly in anti-tank and antiaircraft weapons—thereby creating a balance of power. In this respect the passing of every further month represents a loss of time unfavorable to the German power of attack!

■

Christmas 1939 was misty, rainy, and cold. And quiet! Gen. Kurt Student, commander in chief of German Airborne Forces, remembered bad weather upsetting a plan that might have moved German fortunes ahead by at least six months:

On January 10 . . . a major detailed . . . as liaison officer to the 2d Air Fleet flew from Münster to Bonn to discuss some important details of the plan with the Air Force. He carried with him [on orders] the complete operational plan for the attack in the West.

In icy weather and a strong wind he lost his way . . . over the snow-covered Rhine, and flew into Belgium, where he had to make a forced landing. He was unable to

burn completely the vital document. Important parts of it fell into the hands of the Belgians. . . . [It had been] the outline of the German plan for the Western offensive. While Göring was in a rage, Hitler remained calm and self-possessed. . . . At first he wanted to strike immediately, but fortunately refrained—and decided to drop the original operational plan entirely.

■

In winter 1940, General von Manstein wanted the main attack to be through the Ardennes, an area that was generally thought of as difficult terrain for tank operations. That thought would lull the Allies again in 1944 when Hitler launched his desperate December offensive in the Ardennes. Von Manstein sought out tank expert Heinz Guderian:

Manstein asked me if tank movements would be possible through the Ardennes in the direction of Sedan. . . . I knew the terrain from World War I, and, after studying the map, confirmed his view.

■

B. H. Liddell Hart explained how von Manstein had threaded his way through a minefield of military politics to get his plan adopted:

Hitler, once he had swung in favor of a new key idea, was quick to assume that he had conceived it himself. . . .

Said Hitler, "Among all the generals I talked to about the new plan in the West, Manstein was the only one who understood me."

■

Nicolas van Kleffen, a minister in the Dutch cabinet at the outbreak of the war, was in a unique position to evaluate Hitler's desire that attempts for peace would fail:

Now the Germans were massing troops and materiel along our southeast frontier. . . . Munition dumps had been established . . . innumerable pontoons were lying in readiness to assist in river crossings. . . .

An additional disquieting factor was the discovery that all kinds of Dutch uniforms, belonging to the army, the police, postmen and railway conductors, were being smuggled into Germany.

■

Van Kleffen was struck by the way Queen Wilhelmina became a rallying symbol for the Dutch people:

Pins and pendants were made from coins bearing her picture, and many people displayed orange flowers . . . for the name of the royal Dutch line, "House of Orange," as a silent demonstration. . . . To the Germans, the loyalty of the Dutch to their royal family was a constant source of anger. The Dutch attitude toward the cabinet in London was more restrained. . . .

■

Hitler had been pleased with Panzer leader Heinz Guderian for his performance in Poland. And he would depend on him heavily in the Low Countries. Guderian enjoyed having Hitler's personal approval:

Each of us generals outlined what his task was and how he intended to carry it out. . . . On the day ordered I would cross the Luxembourg frontier, drive through southern Belgium toward Sedan, cross the Meuse, and establish a bridgehead on the far side so that the infantry corps following behind could get across. . . . By the evening of the fifth day I hoped to have established a bridgehead on the far bank [of the Meuse River]. Hitler asked, "And then what are you going to do?" I replied, "Unless I receive orders to the contrary, I intend on the next day to continue my advance westward. The supreme leadership must decide whether my objective is to be Amiens or Paris. In my opinion the correct course is to drive past Amiens to the English Channel." Hitler nodded and said nothing more.

■

Gen. Erwin Rommel found that his habit of being up front with his lead units would earn him respect. . . . It would also get him wounded several times. Here, Rommel crosses the Meuse River. His target then was the Channel . . . or Paris:

Our boats were being destroyed one after the other by the French flanking fire, and the crossing came to a standstill. . . . A smoke screen in the Meuse valley would have prevented these infantry doing much harm. But we had no smoke unit. So I now gave orders for a number of houses in the valley to be set alight in order to supply the smoke we lacked. . . . Military vehicles, tanks, artillery, and refugee carts packed high with belongings blocked part of the road and had to be pushed unceremoniously to the side. All around were French troops lying flat on the ground.

■

Paul Reynaud, president of France:

I received a postcard at my address, found on the body of an officer of Corap's army, who had just committed suicide in Le Mans station. He wrote, "I am killing myself, Mr. President, to let you know that all my men were brave, but one cannot send men to fight tanks with rifles."

■

Military expert B. H. Liddell Hart was pushed back with the fast-breaking advance:

By 15 May Sedan had fallen . . . under German bombing and tanks. . . . Once across the Meuse and clear of the strong points there was nothing in the way of the Panzers. The French thought they would advance on Paris. Instead, the Germans headed due west toward the English Channel coast. . . .

After their victorious ride through Poland the previous autumn, the Germans had feared that France would be a tougher nut to crack. They found the going easier. The roads were better, the bridges were stronger. The Germans were desperately short of military maps; instead they took from garages ample supplies of Messrs. Michelin's excellent touring maps. . . .

■

A strange British force, quickly cobbled together, then made what turned out to be a wonderful stand. In the tide of German victories, it is easy to think of the British army as being brushed aside all along the advance. But General von Rundstedt gave them great credit for their fight at Arras:

A critical moment in the drive came just as my forces had reached the Channel. It was caused by a British counterstrike southward from Arras on 21 May. For a short time it was feared that our armoured division would

be cut off before the infantry division could come up to support them. None of the French counterattacks carried any threat such as this one did.

■

British correspondent Richard Collier told the inspiring story of the "Durham Lights" at Arras. They may have surprised everyone— but themselves:

By tradition the maximum height for a light infantryman was five feet two inches. County Durham, at the end of twenty years of catastrophic unemployment in the coalpits and shipyards, had plenty of people small enough and willing to take a job as a soldier. . . . But nobody expected them to have to fight. As miners, they had a reputation for building wonderful trenches. . . . Every single platoon of both battalions was commanded by a second lieutenant—lads fresh from grammar school, or clerks in their forties who had seen service in the previous war. Most platoons had no sergeant. . . .

■

The Germans came away from Arras with new respect for the British . . . and some heavy losses. Rommel suffered a personal one:

The enemy tank fire had created chaos and confusion among our troops in the village, and they were jamming up the roads and yards with their vehicles instead of going into action with every available weapon to fight off the oncoming enemy. . . . We were under very heavy fire during this action, the gun crews worked magnificently. The worst seemed to be over and the attack beaten off, when suddenly Lieutenant Most [Rommel's aide] sank to the ground. . . . He was mortally wounded. . . . The death of this brave man . . . touched me deeply.

■

Correspondent Collier noted the decision by Hitler to let Göring exercise his ego by charging the Luftwaffe to force the British surrender:

On 24 May, with the battle for Boulogne still in progress and that for Calais scarcely under way, General von Rundstedt . . . or-

dered the Panzers to stop their advances. . . . The Air Force, he said, should be left to deal with the Allied troops bottled up in Flanders. Field Marshal Göring, the Luftwaffe commander, said his men could prevent any trouble from that quarter.

■

But the RAF, which had been stretched thin covering targets all across the Low Countries, now had virtually a single assignment: protect the evacuation of the British Army. A German 4th Army communiqué reported:

FOR TWO DAYS NOW THE ENEMY HAS HAD AIR SUPERIORITY OVER VON KLEIST'S [PANZER] GROUP AND SOMETIMES OVER HOTH'S GROUP. THIS IS SOMETHING NEW FOR US IN THIS CAMPAIGN, AND IS CAUSED BY THE FACT THAT THE ENGLISH HAVE THEIR AIR BASES "ON THE ISLAND ITSELF."

■

Correspondent Nicholas Harman reported the low point in the preparation for an evacuation when the British, French, and Belgian commands seemed to move in confusion:

The French retreated in the evening in good order to their defenses along the western canals, and started to plan a counterattack toward Calais. The British knew that the French had orders to stand, fight, and counterattack if they could. The French did not know that the British had orders to get out as fast as possible.

Neither British nor French knew about the Belgians. During the day the Belgian Army gradually gave up the fight. . . .

The King . . . sent a messenger under a white flag to meet the German Fourth Army. They arranged for the surrender to take effect at four o'clock the following morning. . . .

So, as the day ended, the Allies were in desperate straits. The Belgians were out of the war. The port of Dunkirk was blocked, and the town rendered almost impassable.

■

Watching the pullback into the Dunkirk perimeter, Nicholas Harman remembered the old saw that, "The British army loses all the battles but the last." The soldiers seemed exhausted, but not beaten:

Not since Corunna, more than a hundred years back, had a British Army fallen back like this. . . leaving ruin behind it, shocked and in defeat. . . .

Brig. George Sutton, a World War I veteran, was puzzled once by scores of seething orange Catherine-wheels on the horizon: the tires of abandoned trucks, flaming in the night.

■

At top echelons, there was bickering among the Germans. Maybe Göring had claimed his fliers could do too much. Hitler's order stopping the Panzer units short of Dunkirk was not widely known except among top officers. Baron Wolfram von Richthofen, commander of the 8th Flying Corps and a veteran of the Spanish Civil War, where he had headed the Luftwaffe's "volunteer" Condor Legion, bridled at his fliers being grounded by bad weather . . . and had gotten dressed down by Göring in addition. Von Richthofen noted in his diary:

The Luftwaffe's supreme commander has the jitters.

■

When the skies began to clear, von Richtofen had 180 Stuka dive-bombers ready to go. At Beaulieu airfield, Maj. Oscar Dinort gave the signal to No. 2 Stuka Wing:

Clear all decks for Dunkirk. Report to my truck for briefing. . . . They say there are a lot of small craft around—leave them. We're after the big fish, carrying the most troops.

■

Pvt. Arthur Yendall, British army, as he watched the German planes come over:

The sky looked like a pond in springtime swarming so thickly with tadpoles you couldn't even see the water.

■

The confusion in Dunkirk seemed at first to

make the hope of any orderly evacuation impossible. But many were just waiting for someone to exert command. And when a few vital soldiers and sailors began to step into this vacuum, better things began to happen: Royal Navy captain W. G. Tennant sent a drastic signal:*

PORT CONTINUOUSLY BOMBED ALL DAY AND ON FIRE. EMBARKATION POSSIBLE ONLY FROM BEACHES EAST OF HARBOUR. SEND ALL SHIPS THERE.

■

Correspondent Harman reported the first moves to take men off the beaches:

The smoke from the burning town by now gave some protection from sighting by enemy aircraft. There were too few small boats, and those that were available were mostly ships' lifeboats or naval power boats. The big ships could not come close to the shelving beach. In the shallows, where they could maneuver only at slow speed in the fast tidal stream, the risk of running aground was redoubled by the risk of being dive-bombed.

■

German artillery major Hans Sander got into a forward position to direct his guns and was amazed at the crazy array of "little ships" out from England bobbing about as they moved in to pick up troops:

What are the British trying to do—turn this into a circus or something!

■

The French were making a last-ditch stand on their own soil. But when it became clear that the British intended to evacuate their army, an angry tension began between French and British that not only threatened the evacuation, but also promised to break their whole alliance in the war. Adm. Sir Bertram Ramsay insisted on a joint evacuation:

It is vital that they [the French] should be

brought off if we are ever to have any relationship with the French again.

■

On May 31 at one of the final meetings of the Allies in Paris, Churchill reaffirmed the Ramsay order . . . and in the last four days of the evacuation 98,000 French troops were taken off along with 75,000 British:

I intervened at once to say that the British would not embark first, but that the evacuation should proceed on equal terms between the British and the French.

■

The qualities that made many of the "small ships" sailors feisty enough to carry through with the evacuation was just what made them ornery to command during it. Witness the exchange between engineer Fred Reynard of the motor vessel Bee *and Adm. Sir William James, Commander in Chief, Portsmouth Naval Base, when one of James's officers was trying to put a naval crew on* Bee *for the trip to Dunkirk:*

REYNARD: Beg pardon, sir, but what the bloody hell do your young gentlemen [officers] know about Swedish engines? I've been looking after them since 1912. If the ship goes, I go.
    JAMES: We've no guarantee you'll get back—though we've no guarantee you won't. Ever been under shellfire?
    REYNARD: Ever bloody heard of Gallipoli?

■

Most of the rescue ships did much more than they ever thought they could. The following exchange took place between an officer on a destroyer and the piermaster on the East Mole:

LT. R. C. WATKINS: We can take four hundred.
    PIERMASTER JACK CLOUSTON: Come back and tell me when you've got a thousand.

Danzig, September 1, 1939

T here were various claimants for the "honor" of firing the first shots of World War II. But the claim with the most historic importance goes to a tired old German battleship, *Schleswig-Holstein* (LEFT). She was classified only as a training ship when she bombarded the Polish fortress at Danzig. Adolf Bock lent her proper ferociousness. For some of the Polish reservists, the time between call-up and being marched into a hastily constructed prisoner-of-war compound (like the group Elk Eber painted here below) was scarcely a month. (Both, Captured German Art; U.S. Army Center of Military History)

Medlin Barracks, Poland, Fall 1939

One Polish contingent held out for a day in a strong position prepared around an army
barracks in Medlin, Poland, then were wiped out by artillery and bombing. A lone
Polish antiaircraft gun stands under the guard of a German sentry in Elk Eber's
painting. However, the Poles had picked a logical strongpoint. The roof has blown upward
and the floors have buckled, but the stone arches of the building stand firm under the attack.
(Captured German Art; U.S. Army Center of Military History)

Underdog Finland, Winter 1939–40

For the Soviet Union, its war with Finland—launched in the fall of 1939—backfired embarrassingly. The Red Army proved inadequately armed and poorly trained for the winter campaign. Here an unknown Finnish artist has sketched a patrol by what came to be known as "The White Death"—ski troops, well camouflaged against the snow, who could attack and withdraw rapidly. (Sotamuseo of Helsinki)

Brussels, Spring 1940

As the Phony War extended into the winter of 1940, some reservists gained a brief leave during the quiet to settle emergencies at home. The German attack hurriedly brought them back to their units. A Belgian magazine illustrator, Lermansky, painted these reservists at a train station. (New York Public Library Picture Collection)

Plymouth, Winter 1940

One of the few bright spots for the Allies in 1939 was the surprise victory in December of three British cruisers over the German pocket battleship *Admiral Graf Spee*. Seeing a chance to repair punctured British morale, Churchill ordered HMS *Exeter*, one of the victors, back to England for a refit, and a modest victory celebration. Charles Cundall painted the cruiser's arrival at Plymouth, which several papers referred to in a morale reminder as the port from which Drake had sallied to whip the Spanish Armada. (National Maritime Museum)

(OVERLEAF)

London, Winter 1940

Churchill's victory celebration over the *Graf Spee* was held on the Horse Guard's Parade, off St. James's Park. The public loved it, as a good winter crowd showed. Churchill is the civilian-suited figure at the far right of the awards table in the foreground. *Exeter* and *Ajax* crews are drawn up facing each other across the Parade. Sir Muirhead Bone, another artist veteran of 1914–18, is the artist. (Imperial War Museum)

Norway Rescue, Fall 1939

Norman Wilkinson, after talking to British crewmen on HMS *Cossack,* the ship in the right of the picture above, painted the daring rescue of British merchant seamen captured by the *Graf Spee.* On Churchill's express orders, the captain of *Cossack* defied neutrality and Norwegian gunboats to pursue the German supply ship *Altmark* into a Norwegian fjord. Boarding and breaking open compartments below-decks, the British sailors found the captured merchant seamen. *Altmark* had been a tender, in disguise, for the German pocket battleship. (National Maritime Museum)

The Western Front, Winter 1939–40

One of the most famous photographs of the Phony War (and a picture that came to typify it—much to the later chagrin of Allied commanders) showed an aging French *poilu* seated on a kitchen chair in a frontline observation post, puffing on his pipe and gazing sleepily out toward the German Westwall. When the French and British were overrun, that was the sort of picture that made all the second-guessers say "No wonder!" This sketch by Bryan de Grineau was comparable (OPPOSITE). *(Illustrated London News)*

Invasion of Norway, April 1940

The quality of the German warships and crews clearly surprised the British, who had long been used to the idea of the indomitability of the Royal Navy. Most German ships and equipment were new in the 1930s, while the British frequently had to rely on remodeled vessels that dated back to the end of World War I. These German minesweepers (LEFT) escort high-speed troop transports, ostensibly built as peacetime passenger liners but quickly converted to war use. Adolf Bock was the artist. (Captured German Art; U.S. Navy Combat Art Collection)

Troopship to Norway, Spring 1940

With German aircraft securely based in Denmark and along the Norwegian coast, the water route from Germany was safe enough to bring in large numbers of occupation troops. This deck scene on a German transport headed for Norway (LEFT) could have been a picture of troops of any nation: bored, a little homesick already, and probably apprehensive about what was waiting for them. This is the work of an unknown German artist. (Captured German Art; U.S. Army Center of Military History)

Second Battle of Narvik, April 1940

In one of the few actions of the Norway campaign that ended with English victory, the aging battleship *Warspite* and nine British destroyers surprised the Germans by speeding into the narrow, maneuver-constricting German refuge in Narvik's Ofoten Fjord to bombard the Germans there. The action was sharp and heavy, but all the German destroyers at Narvik were sunk. British artist E. Tuffnell painted *Warspite* and *Cossack* in the late afternoon of April 13, 1940. (U.S. Navy Combat Art Collection)

Glowworm vs. Hipper, April 1940

In one notably heroic—and tragic—encounter, the German heavy cruiser *Admiral Hipper* encountered a British destroyer, HMS *Glowworm,* coming out of a fog bank off the Norwegian coast on April 8, 1940. In less than a minute *Hipper* struck her with a couple of salvos at a range of under 300 yards. But *Glowworm* rammed the cruiser before sinking. Adolf Bock painted the *Hipper* opening the one-sided action. (Captured German Art; U.S. Navy Combat Art Collection)

HMS *Exeter* Hero, Winter 1940

Eric Kennington had served as a war artist in 1914–18, contributing some dramatic battle scenes. But when he came back to duty in World War II, he often preferred to convey "the strength of a face." Here is *Stoker Martin* from HMS *Exeter,* whose portrait reminded many Englishmen of the "hearts of oak" of Nelson's sailors. (National Maritime Museum)

Occupation of Norway

German artist Max Ahrens painted a transport unit in Norway that had just unloaded from a freighter. The men are already well trained to do what soldiers do most of: stand around and wait for orders. (Captured German Art; U.S. Army Center of Military History)

Monotony of Norway

This painting by German artist Albert Janesch shows the monotony of occupation duty in rough, cold Norway, which the war would essentially bypass for the next five years. (Captured German Art; U.S. Army Center of Military History)

Pushing to the Waterfront, Dunkirk, June 1

Bernard Villemot did this hurried watercolor of French dragoons who had been forced to abandon their armored cars outside the Dunkirk defense line when their fuel gave out. They proudly carry their arms and will be boarded by the rescue fleet. But after the fall of France, many would choose to return to France as parolees. They had the pull of families, and de Gaulle's "Free French Army" still largely existed only in the general's head. (Musée d'Histoire Contemporaine—BDIC, Universités de Paris)

Dunkirk East Beach, May 1940

These dejected French troops, painted by German artist Rudolf Hengstenberg, are huddled on the beach, supposedly abandoned by the British. An ugly rumor had started that no French would be taken on the ships until all the English had gotten away. But Admiral Ramsay and Churchill blocked such a policy, ordering that French, British, and Belgians should go aboard "arm in arm." (Captured German Art; U.S. Army Center of Military History)

Air Raid, Dunkirk

Artist Edward Bawden painted this incident during the evacuation. His figures almost give the feeling of peaceful city strollers—while the smoke and flames of the doomed port roll in over the heads of the retreating army. Soldiers enter an air raid dugout cut zigzag into the stone of the pier. The German pilots quickly discovered that a ship sunk at the quay did double duty—reducing the fleet and blocking others from loading. (Imperial War Museum)

Café Break, Dunkirk

In this painting by Edward Bawden, British soldiers wait their turn on the quay, having taken shelter in a nearly wrecked pierside café that ironically was named "The New World." Outside, the damage of another raid subsides, as the men crawl out from under the shelter of tables and benches. (Imperial War Museum)

Panzer Targets, May 1940

A French artist, Bernard Villemot, working with the army, did this painting during the retreat of the French rear guard into the Dunkirk perimeter. Small French scout cars slowly pass burning buildings in Valenciennes. The French army had gone to war supremely confident in its massive army. The numbers were there—but often not the combat quality of the machines. (Musée d'Histoire Contemporaine—BDIC, Universités de Paris)

Sands of Dunkirk

Some of the first troops to reach East Beach at Dunkirk were support units who had seen little action in the retreat. The bombing was shattering, but most of them performed like veterans. Casualties were lighter than feared, because bombs buried themselves in the soft sand before exploding and their force was deadened. Richard Eurich was the artist. (Imperial War Museum)

Rescue Fleet, Dunkirk, May 1940

In *Little Ships at Dunkirk* Norman Wilkinson shows the withdrawal at its peak, and all sorts of craft doing the job: a British destroyer (taking a near miss from a bomb), Thames sailing barges, a large yacht in peacetime white, coasters towing crowded lifeboats. (National Maritime Museum)

(OVERLEAF)

The "Miracle" Happening

The action in the painting by Charles Cundall, *Withdrawal from Dunkirk,* shows the rescue ships and small boats packed so closely together that it is easy to see why they seemed "sitting ducks" to the German planes. For much of the time, however, the air fighting that was shown here was actually conducted so high up that the soldiers on the beaches could not see the hard-fighting, often outnumbered RAF planes driving off larger flights of the Luftwaffe. (Imperial War Museum)

Fight of a Queen, May 1940

HMS *Boadicea,* named for the ancient queen of the Britons, was a bit ancient herself when she steamed into the fight off the Dunkirk beaches, moving close inshore to engage German tanks on the cliffs near Veule-les-Roses. In the shallows, she faced the additional dangers of rapid tidal rips that could ground her into an easy target or send her into a mine. Richard Seddon, who had been with the British Expeditionary Force during the retreat, did the painting. (Imperial War Museum)

Death of a Queen, May 1940

Following the action painted at left, German bombers hit HMS *Boadicea*. Other rescue vessels moved in, as portrayed by Richard Seddon, to take off her crew. (Imperial War Museum)

Headed Home, May 1940

At Dunkirk, when the loaded ships pulled out, there was a momentary feeling of relief for most of the men taken off. But safety was still hours away. Soldiers were jammed in far over normal capacity. A bomb hit or a low-level strafing attack could do disastrous damage. Later—hardly lethal but hard to bear—the over-loaded ships rolled drunkenly. Edward Bawden sketched these dazed soldiers below-decks, many already in exhausted sleep. (Imperial War Museum)

Dunkirk Aftermath, June 1940

During World War I, the British had several times blocked strategic harbors and river mouths on the continent by running in ships and sinking them at critical points. But all the sinkings at Dunkirk had been of ships the British had *hoped* to use for evacuation. However, after the evacuation was over they had some satisfaction in knowing the vessels they lost had blocked the harbor. The painting by German Rudolf Hengstenberg might not have passed muster with Hitler and the heads of the German War Art Program; the effect was of a cluttered, useless port—*not* of a scene of German victory. (Captured German Art; U.S. Army Center of Military History)

Survivors, Dunkirk, June 1940

German artist Josef Arens was struck by the sight of these bomb-skittish artillery horses turned loose when the gunners headed for the ships. The animals were soon pressed into German service; in spite of its "Panzer" reputation, the German army probably used more horses and mules than any army in the world. (Captured German Art; U.S. Center of Military History)

29. Destroyed portions of destroyed French units
City wall of Boulogne.

Mont St. Michel, 1940

German artist Josef Arens sketched this heavy field howitzer moving up to the ancient and historic Mont St. Michel (ABOVE). Unlike many other historic French tourist sites, Mont St. Michel sustained virtually no war damage. (Captured German Art; U.S. Center of Military History)

Boulogne, 1940

Josef Arens found this wreckage of French civilian and military vehicles (OPPOSITE) caught by a bomb, along the city wall of Boulogne. A fire also started, but no firefighting equipment could get through. City services, water, and gas were completely out. (Captured German Art; U.S. Center of Military History)

Beauvais, 1940

erman war artist Heinrich Amersdorffer did this somber watercolor (ABOVE) of an almost miraculously spared church in an otherwise wrecked Beauvais. (Bavarian Army Museum)

Amiens, 1940

udolf Lipus, with the German armies, painted the great cathedral at Amiens (OPPOSITE), which also survived the destruction of the surrounding city. (Bavarian Army Museum)

Retreat, Northern France, May 1940

This tumultuous scene is perhaps reminiscent of Picasso's famous painting of the bombing of Guernica during the Spanish Civil War. The French artist Jean Delpech emphasizes, by the tight confines of his work, the boiling confusion of the rearguard action that let more than 338,000 British and French soldiers escape from Dunkirk. (Musée d'Histoire Contemporaine—BDIC, Universités de Paris)

Refugees, Fall of France, June 1940

In addition to becoming a major block to Allied military movement, the civilian refugee exodus led to tragedies that stayed with French, Dutch, and Belgian families all through the war. Family members were separated and disappeared. The dangers of being machine-gunned or bombed or killed in some other way on the road often surpassed the immediate threat of occupation by the German army. In these two paintings, Frederic Pailhes conveys the oppression of harried refugees; they might break into panic at any difficulty—from a stalled car to German planes overhead. (Both, Musée d'Histoire Contemporaine—BDIC, Universités de Paris)

Waiting for Rescue, June 1940

Bernard Villemot painted these French tankers taking refuge in the dunes at Malo les Bains, waiting for embarkation. It would be four long years before these soldiers could fight for France on her own soil again. (Musée d'Histoire Contemporaine— BDIC, Universités de Paris)

Horse Casualties, France, June 1940

French artist Henri Plisson's work conveyed the jarring impact of the war as it erupted on soldiers, lulled till then by the Phony War: *Versigny, 12 June '40, Wounded Horses and Footsoldiers.* (Musée d'Histoire Contemporaine—BDIC, Universités de Paris)

Human Casualties, France, June 1940

Versigny, 13 June '40, The Battery Gives Rapid Fire, also by Plisson. The technique was wildly untraditional for war art—but certainly woke up the viewer. (Musée d'Histoire Contemporaine—BDIC, Universités de Paris)

Old Equipment, New Year

German artist H. Kaspar sketched this vintage British destroyer (ABOVE), its bow blown off by a German bomb. Destroyer construction and repair were being pushed to their utmost in British and Canadian yards to overcome the losses. Against the heavy, high-speed German Panzer tanks, the French were often throwing little "whippets" (like those Jean Clauseau-Lanauve has painted at left). As in World War I, it seemed that the courage of the French army could be stout enough in the best units—but mistakes before the war and behind the lines had not served them well. (Above, Bayerische Staatsbibliothek; left, Musée d'Histoire Contemporaine—BDIC, Universités de Paris)

Refugee Transport, France, June 1940

French artist Roger Schardner walked for a time with the refugee columns and was fascinated by French ingenuity—particularly when gas gave out and they had to abandon their cars, as in this scene in the town of Rozoy-en-Brie. (Musée d'Histoire Contemporaine—BDIC, Universités de Paris)

The Face of War, France, June 1940

Schardner caught the hollow stare of shock in the faces of these French civilians. The artist described this picture as "a young girl with face blackened by a fire caused by the fighting." (Musée d'Histoire Contemporaine—BDIC, Universités de Paris)

Dover, June 1940

Sir Muirhead Bone captured this somber scene of Dover Harbor in early June 1940, as the rear guard from Dunkirk disembarked. These men were the last to arrive in England. (Imperial War Museum)

BRITAIN STANDS ALONE

The period between the Dunkirk evacuation and the end of the Battle of Britain embraced some of the darkest days of the war for the British. Nearly everybody was "on the front line" more or less. The Luftwaffe's blitz of England began on September 7, 1940, and continued with raids every night for almost two months. British merchant ships were being sunk by U-boats at an alarming rate, convoy escorts were few, and some convoys were arriving with half their ships missing. Between September 1939 and the end of 1941, the Royal Navy lost a number of important capital ships. Hong Kong was overrun after stubborn but brief resistance, and the "impregnable fortress" of Singapore surrendered, sending 70,000 Empire troops into prison camps. British forces were run out of Malaya, Burma, Greece, and Crete, and they were having a bad time in North Africa. The brightest light of this dismal period may well have been the combination of the courageous performance of the British people during the bombings, the tenacious defense of the RAF against the bombers, and the stoic determination of the Royal Navy and the Merchant Navy to keep the supply lines to Britain open.

The British leaders knew they were all very lucky to have ended the dismal defeat in France with the "miracle of Dunkirk." It had been brought about with a large measure of skill, courage, and resourcefulness—but also because of some serious German mistakes. But Churchill warned that wars are not won by evacuations and thus began his enormous effort to bolster Britain by "marshalling the English language and sending it into the battle":

We are told that Herr Hitler has a plan for invading the British Isles. This has often been thought of before. When Napoleon lay at Boulogne for a year with his flat-bottomed boats and his Grand Army, he was told by someone, "There are bitter weeds in England." There are certainly a great many more of them since the British Expeditionary Force returned.

◾

Shortly after the Dunkirk evacuation ended, the Luftwaffe began to step up its night raids on England and daytime sweeps along the south coast, particularly at the fighter airfields and the radar stations, which they knew were important, but not quite how they worked. The Battle of Britain can be said to have started in early July. Flight Officer J. E. Johnson, who would score thirty-eight victories, remembered his first, near the opening of the Battle of Britain:

Ahead of me, not more than 300 yards away, three Messerschmitts climbed steeply as if they were being hauled up three sides of a pyramid. Their prey at the apex of the pyramid was a solitary Spitfire flying straight and level, and although I didn't know his call sign I shouted to him: "For Christ's sake, break!"

The combined fire of the 109s smashed into his belly, and exploding cannon shells ripped through his port wing. . . . The wing drifted down, lazy as an autumn leaf, but the crippled Spitfire fell into a vicious spin.

The Messerschmitts stayed to fight. . . .

Suddenly a 109 arced up in front of me at two o'clock. . . . I was very close to him and could see the square wingtips and tail struts of a 109-E. . . . I swung my Spitfire to get behind him and thought: This is it. Nail him, and get out . . . I was dead line-astern of the Messerschmitt and hit him be-

hind the cockpit with the eight machine guns.

◾

In 1942, the British Ministry of Information prepared a modest paperback: Front Line, 1940–1941, *the story of Civil Defense in Great Britain during the "Blitz," as most of the public called it. The descriptions of the battle that follow come from* Front Line *and the people who spoke out for it:*

The first bomb fell on Hoy in the Orkneys on 17th October, 1939. The first civilian was killed at Bridge of Waith, Orkney, on 16th March, 1940, a half-year after the outbreak of the war. The first bombs on the mainland of Britain in twenty-two years fell near Canterbury on the night of 9th May.

◾

Before September, four-fifths of London's Auxiliary Fire Brigade members had never fought a fire. One auxiliary told of his formidable baptism at Rum Wharf, East India Docks, the night of September 7:

Most of us had the wind-up to start with, especially with no barrage. It was all new but we were unwilling to show fear, however much we felt it. You looked around and saw the rest doing their job. You couldn't let them down. You just had to get on with it. . . .

Occasionally we would glance up and then we would see a strange sight. For a flock of pigeons kept circling around overhead almost all night. They seemed lost, as if they couldn't understand the unnatural dawn made by the fire. It looked like sunrise all around us. . . .

When the real dawn came about five, the Germans eased off their blitz. The All Clear raised a weary cheer.

◾

Section officer Louis Albert "Tug" Wilson was an Auxiliary Fire Brigade member who was a motor mechanic before the war. But it had always been his ambition to be a fireman. He was 37 and married, with two young sons, when he and his squad of six men responded to the fires in the London docks area caused by German incendiary bombs dropped in the first great daylight raid of Saturday, September 7, to start beacon fires for the night bombers to target on:

At the Pageant Wharf station they ordered us off to Gate L. As we turned in at Gate L the dockside was aflame. The water itself seemed alight. But that came from burning barges. Across the water an island jetty was blazing, and from left, right, and all around, the heat waves struck us in the face like a blow. . . .

Eddie was the newest member of my squad. . . . He flung himself head first on a hose branch which had broken loose and was flailing crazily about. . . . If the nozzle end hits the men, it can break their legs. . . . A lot of people treated us as a joke. Later, after they had seen us at work, the jeering turned to cheering.

◾

A man who was probably closer to the explosion of a large bomb than anyone else—and survived—gave his story to doctors:

My head was jerked back due to a heavy blow on the dome and rim of the back of my steel helmet. . . . The missile bent up the front rim of my steel helmet and knocked it off my head. The explosion made an indescribable noise . . . and was accompanied by a veritable tornado of air blast. I felt an excruciating pain in my ears and all sounds were replaced by a very loud singing noise, which I was later told was when I lost my hearing and had my eardrums perforated.

◾

The British were surprised but delighted by the German tactic of switching bombing targets just when it seemed the repeated raids were about to overwhelm London. In this pattern, the bombers turned to the port cities in early 1941:

Naval tradition had one interesting effect on the civil defense services. Senior officers of these services would tell you that elderly men were of more value . . . in Portsmouth than almost anywhere else. "You get an old warden and he seems to be nothing wonderful in exercises or his routine jobs, but when the bombs start, he's a sailor again."

◾

Every person, every city, every section of the country had its favorite story; the Ministry of Information knew their value and circulated them throughout Britain. Copies of Front

Line *were passed from hand to hand, to "read the chuckles":*

When a rescue party [in Cardiff] set to work to see who might be buried in the debris of a demolished house, they were guided to their mark by the notes of "God Save the King" sung at the top of his voice by a little boy of six. . . . He told them: "My father was a collier, and he always said that when the men were caught and buried underground they would keep singing and they were always got out in time."

■

A woman in Clydebank, the shipbuilding center, commenting to a neighbor after cleaning up the broken glass from a heavy raid:

"Well, there's one thing about these raids, they do make you forget about the war."

■

Some of the recollections that follow, gathered by Tom Harrison for his book Living Through the Blitz, *prove the reaction of the rank and file Briton to the German bombings was not all humor, pluck, and "we'll muddle through." Especially when the raids first started and there was a strong element of the unknown, there was natural foreboding and terror. But a fatalistic humor did come through often enough to be a real element of support—as would prove true also in Berlin, Moscow, and Tokyo. Civilian populations were not easily intimidated. A Stepney woman:*

That 'itler!—Giving us the all clear when we was settled. Now what are we going to do . . . ?

■

In London, the extensive and deeply buried Underground stations presented an ideal network of bomb shelters. To Londoners, these were natural places of retreat. At first, authorities were concerned that the sense of security would result in a "deep shelter" complex, and people would not want to come up after the raid was over and "carry on." The problem did not occur with any impact. In fact, the first experiences in the Underground were often more frightening than the bombs:

A porter stood up on the escalator rail and began yelling instructions. He was a leader and kept the crowd in a good humour throughout:

"Now, listen, everyone," he yelled, "this escalator isn't going, but the one going up is. Now platforms 4 and 6 aren't working but platform 5 is. Number 5, Tottenham Court Road, and that's where you're all going!"

There were no protests—the crowd seemed to like being told where it was they were going, to feel that someone was in charge. . . .

By the middle of September, half the population of Stepney was gone. Notes fixed on battered front doors gave new addresses: in Becontree, Chadwell Heath, Dagenham, in Stratford and East Ham—farther out, but still "in London." Few had left altogether. . . . The pressure outlets became West End shelters and soon the huge shelters and the Underground. Those who stayed totally "put" tended to be of "tougher" calibre.

A sturdy, cheeky sort of attitude was growing. . . . The women in particular were growing tougher; even crying was becoming rare.

■

A London mother of two described the painful "indoctrination" many people went through when they knew they just had to bear up . . . or "go barmy":

Suffered agonies of fright at the time of Munich, and again at beginning of present war. Lay awake nights with visions of appalling devastations. Before war started, fled with children to Scotland to escape from the horrors expected immediately. . . . Convinced of being most utter and complete coward—very ashamed. Sure I was bound to panic and lose control if things got hot. . . . Now find myself almost completely proof against fear and jumpiness. . . .

But casualties were significant. Tom Harrison summed up:

Beyond all questions of adaptation lay the shadows of those 13,596 Londoners killed by enemy action before the end of 1940, plus another 18,378 consigned to hospital.

■

Many Americans got their most vivid pictures of the London Blitz through the words of two brilliant reporters, Edward R. Murrow on radio and Mollie Panter-Downes. Her reports were gathered and published in her book London War Notes, *excerpted here:*

SEPTEMBER 14: For Londoners, there are no longer such things as good nights; there are only bad nights, worse nights, and better nights. Hardly anyone has slept at all in the past week. The sirens go off at approximately the same time every evening, and in the poorer districts, queues of people carrying blankets, thermos flasks, and babies begin to form quite early outside the air-raid shelters. . . . The amazing part of it is the cheerfulness and fortitude with which ordinary individuals are doing their jobs under nerve-racking conditions. Girls who have taken twice the usual time to get to work look worn when they arrive, but their faces are nicely made up and they bring you a cup of tea or sell you a hat as chirpily as ever. . . .

SEPTEMBER 29: . . . Plans to improve accommodations in air-raid shelters by the addition of bunks, heating, and better sanitary arrangements were announced . . . to the relief of physicians who had been figuring out that if winter comes, a really first-class epidemic can't be far behind. This announcement was also welcome news to Londoners who use the shelters nightly and are ready with fight and staying power so long as the authorities do the right thing by them. . . .

OCTOBER 27: Last week, Londoners had reason to be grateful for their famous climate. With the hunter's moon waning and what the laconic official communiqués describe as "unfavorable weather conditions" settling down over the capital, the raiders decided not to risk it en masse.

■

As the Blitz grew more intense, a strong rumor went around London about a British "death ray" that would be attracted to the heat of an enemy plane's engines . . . and would destroy the aircraft. After the war, there was speculation that the rumor came about because of the security surrounding "radar"— strongly protecting England just then:

It was perhaps unfortunate that the reprisal

raids on Coventry should have coincided with the appearance in certain sections of the press of the cheerful statement that a defence against night raiders had been found. Citizens of Coventry, wandering among the ruins of their homes and public buildings, may well have felt that they might have been let in on the secret sooner. Air Marshal Sir Philip Joubert told the public that there was no single remedy for night bombing . . . thereby dispelling the popular dream of some Wellsian or Jules Verne-ish machine that would intercept and cripple raiders by the pressing of a button.

■

Mollie Panter-Downes told of Britain's despair when the Japanese attacked Hong Kong and Singapore . . . and soon after, sank the powerful HMS Repulse *and* Prince of Wales, *which had been sent to Malaya to bolster Singapore's "island fortress."*

On Monday, December 8th . . . suddenly and soberly, the little island was remembering its vast and sprawling possessions of Empire. It seemed as though every person one met had a son in Singapore or a daughter in Rangoon; every post office was jammed with anxious crowds finding out about cable rates to Hong Kong, Kuala Lumpur, or Penang. . . . There was gloom which culminated in the stunned silence that met Wednesday's news of the loss of the *Prince of Wales* and the *Repulse.* For sheer mass misery, this was probably England's blackest day since the collapse of France. . . . It was as if some enormously powerful and valuable watchdog which had been going to keep burglars away from the house had been shot while exercising in the front yard.

■

The Air Ministry's Harold Balfour was supposed to concern himself with the large issues of the war. But like many Britons, some of his most vivid wartime experiences concerned small events . . . and the stories of the individuals caught up in them. In the Battle of Britain, his thoughts went often to the RAF men. He knew them too closely to regard them as ciphers on a casualty report:

I flew to Hornchurch, landing just as a formation of Hurricanes were returning from a patrol over the Channel. I joined the boys at

tea in the mess. There were gaps at the table. Suddenly all heads turned to the door. Into the room swayed a young man, very drunk, wearing long sea boots, a filthy sailor jersey and perched on top of his head a far too small naval petty officer's cap. His appearance drew a roar of welcome. His story was that he had been shot down over the sea about 7 P.M. the previous night but not before he had accounted for two certain and a possible third German aircraft. He had bailed out and luckily hit the sea fairly near one of our destroyers, which picked him up, wet, cold and shaken. Naval rum in large and frequent doses was prescribed by the ship's doctor. As he thawed out between blankets the patient happily and steadily absorbed his medicine. He had been landed that morning, lorry-hopped back to Hornchurch but still clutching a bottle of his medicine, which he had not neglected to take. . . . In a bunch of casualty telegrams I looked through a week later this boy's name was marked "Missing, believed killed."

■

An RAF fighter pilot, Squadron 249:

It is not easy to record accurate impressions of events, however momentous, which took place forty-two years ago. Of one thing one can be sure: all the emotions were there, excitement, boredom, eagerness, fear. We knew that an invasion was on the cards. . . . Victory was not in sight, yet the thought of defeat never entered our young minds.

■

Strategists said that when Göring abruptly redirected the German air attack away from the RAF fighter bases that he had savaged severely and sent his bombers at the cities, he gave the British fighter pilots a respite, time to repair their aircraft and fields. One interesting anachronism favored the RAF: many of the fighter airfields were still grass, which made the whole field a "runway," and bomb craters could be quickly filled and tamped down. Air Commodore A. C. Deare of the Royal New Zealand Air Force remembered the pressure:

There was a desperate shortage [of pilots] throughout the Command. Not so fighter aircraft. The miracles worked by Lord

Beaverbrook at the Ministry of Aircraft Production were being felt at squadron level, where replacement aircraft arrived virtually the same day as the demand was sent. . . . All night long, lights burned in the shuttered hangars as the fitters, electricians, armourers, and riggers worked unceasingly to put the maximum number on the line for the next day's operations. . . .

The pilot picture was not so rosy. Not only was the replacement problem serious, but this growing strain on those who had been in action continuously, with only brief rests, was also beginning to tell.

■

After the war, journalist John Willis set out to talk both with "Churchill's few"—RAF fighter pilots—and the German aircrewmen who had survived. In many instances, their stories seemed interchangeable. Flight Sergeant Bam, RAF:

We never had a single briefing. No one said, "You are all in II Group, this goes from here to here." I never saw a map of the Channel; no one showed me where the enemy forces were. It was just my job to get the plane up and see what happened. . . . I had no idea we were in the Battle of Britain. The impression the public had of scores of enthusiastic pilots was wrong. If we scrambled, we knew our heads were on the block.

■

Pilot Officer Ulrich Steinhilper, Luftwaffe:

You rarely acknowledge the fact that you have killed a human. It blunts the senses. I didn't like the feeling of the victim having an identity, a name.

■

In the course of his interviews, Willis found that many of the airmen on both sides seemed to feel more comfortable with the recollection that had an unexpected turn of humor— rather than just another tale of machine gun bullets and planes on fire. It was perhaps the aviator's way of keeping the terrors of the air war at a safer distance:

At 5:00 A.M., Flight Officer Geoffrey Page, RAF, had only just slipped into bed and fallen asleep when the phone rang. Hardly awake, he rushed from his bed at dispersal and clambered into his Hurricane. He had been airborne a few minutes before he noticed that, although he had on his lifesaving jacket and his flying boots, in place of his flying suit was a pair of summer pajamas. It was too late to turn back. . . .

■

Jean Wood was a young music hall entertainer when the Battle of Britain began. Her memories of the bombings indicate that life on tour equipped her to try a bit of everything. She told oral historian Studs Terkel:

I never thought I could sit and read to children, say, about Cinderella, while you could hear the German planes coming. Sometimes a thousand a night came over, in a wave. . . . You'd hear the bomb drop so many hundred yards that way. And you'd think, Oh, that missed us. You'd think, My God, the next one's going to be a direct hit. But you'd continue to read: "And the ugly sister said"—and you'd say, "Don't fidget, dear." And you'd think, My God, I can't stand it. But you bore up. And I wasn't the bravest of people, believe me. . . .

I did fire-watch. And that's frightening. You got up on the roof with a steel helmet on. You're supposed to have a protective jacket. The fire bombs were round balls. They'd come onto roofs and start fires. So the government gave you a bucket of sand and a shovel. Charming . . .

A lot of flowers grew on the bombed spaces, especially one in particular. It was a stalk with a lot of little red spots. It was like a weed, really. It was called "London pride." . . .

■

Psychologists in Britain—and large numbers of young mothers whose husbands were away in some sort of war work—were worried about a whole generation of young boys "growing up wild." To many of them, the war seemed little more than a wonderful excuse to get out from under all that adult control. John Baker was one of these boys for whom much of the early part of the war was an exciting experience. He told Terkel:

When World War Two broke out, I was in Ipswich, about forty miles from London. I was seven. We kids were fascinated by aircraft recognition. They gave out these

charts of what German planes looked like. The charts were called "Know Your Enemy." We instantly memorized them all . . . to me it was all exciting and sort of a game. . . . There was a terrific flurry of building shelters in early 1940. . . . Being in the shelter was like having a little den. You'd go down there and have secret meetings and take candy and chocolates. You'd pretend you were hiding from something. It was fun. . . . It was like living in a boy's adventure story. We really wished something would happen. When the siren went off and nothing happened, we were disappointed. When the all clear was heard, we were doubly disappointed.

They issued gas masks. . . . I don't think they would ever have worked. We'd make faces with 'em. When you breathed into 'em, they made funny noises. . . . We'd do that a lot, being small, laughing boys.

■

The Dieppe raid was complex from the beginning because very little like it had been tried. But it was meant to test the feasibility of a full-scale invasion: Could a usable port be taken and held? Or would the invasion and all its supplies have to go in over the beaches? Terrance Robertson reported on the bizarre foul-ups at two top secret briefings. Major General Roberts addressed select Canadian army officers:

"Gentlemen, we have waited over two years to go into battle against the Germans. The time has now come for a party. This scale model is the target. . . . I must emphasize the need for complete security. . . . "

The name of Dieppe was avoided deliberately, but while the officers were crowding around the model, examining the incredibly minute detail in construction of houses and streets . . . an amazed murmur broke through the silence with the impact of a physical blow.

"Good God, I know that place!"

The room suddenly became tense, while Roberts gazed furiously in the general direction of the voice and said: "I'm not going to ask who said that. But forget it right now. . . ."

■

Later the same day, Rear Admiral Baillie-

Grohman assembled the naval officers who would be involved in the raid, to reveal for the first time the target and dates:

. . . As the Admiral rose to his feet on a dais at one end of the conference room, an elderly reserve officer stood up at the other end and said: "Excuse me, sir, but . . . " Admiral Baillie-Grohman cut him short with a furious glare and interrupted curtly: "You will listen to what I have to say first. Then you can ask questions." Then he proceeded with the briefing. . . .

When Baillie-Grohman had finished, the secret was out—that the navy were to land the army at Dieppe. . . . The elderly officer was allowed to say: "Thank you, sir. That was an exciting briefing. But I think you should know that I'm not part of the operation. I am commanding officer of an anti-submarine trawler waiting to join a Channel convoy . . . and I was ordered to attend the convoy sailing conference. I thought this was it."

On Baillie-Grohman's orders the errant convoy skipper was locked in a toilet and a sentry placed outside the door while staff officers tried to fathom a way of keeping him incommunicado until after the raid.

■

One Canadian officer scheduled for the raid had already gained a reputation for the flamboyant combat gesture. Terrance Robertson remembered him disembarking in charge of a unit that included a token squad of U.S. Rangers who had volunteered for the raid:

Leading the ninety-six Commandos and six U.S. Rangers in the five boats was Capt. R. L. Wills. . . . It worried him not at all. . . . A year before, during the raid on the Lofoten Islands off Norway, he had captured a post office and written out a telegram addressed to Adolf Hitler, Reichchancellery, Berlin. It had said: "You said in your last speech that German troops would meet the English wherever they landed Stop I am here Stop Where are your troops? . . . Wills 2d Lieutenant." He had waited with tommy gun dangling nonchalantly in the crook of his arm while a German Army postal clerk had dispatched it "At urgent rates, please."

■

Lucien Dumais was a French-Canadian who had risen to sergeant-major in a historic Canadian regiment. It was one of the first in action at Dieppe, August 19, 1942. There was considerable personal—and regimental—tradition to uphold . . . and a rigid German defense, somewhat unexpected:

When I woke up it was 0400 and our landing craft was gliding over a calm sea. . . . The men were sleeping like children, without a care. As I looked at them before going into action for the first time, I wondered which ones would be killed. . . .

In a few hours we should be landing in France; this arrival would be very different from the arrival I had dreamed of as a young man. . . . Then, of course, there would be Paris! We French-speaking Canadians loved France as the land of our forefathers. . . .

The eastern sky was beginning to lighten. . . . Wherever we looked now, there were ships . . . a vast flotilla . . . like some great peacetime review.

Then we heard the first shots of the raid. This was the first time any of us had been under fire and we all ducked. . . .

I began to get everyone busy. We had to shave and wash in sea water; I tried to convince the men that sea water was very good for the gums! In the best tradition, we could not die without a shave and shiny boots. . . .

Quite suddenly, we emerged from the fog and smoke into a bright, strange and sunny world. We had picked up speed and were getting rapidly closer. As the smoke cleared, we could see Dieppe. . . . Dieppe beach extended for about a mile, and then there was the harbour with rocky cliffs both behind it and beyond it on the extreme left. Intelligence reported that there were guns and machine guns on the cliffs to our right, in the harbour, and also on the high ground to the left of the harbour; and machine guns all along the esplanade and in the hotels facing it. . . . A heavy smoke screen began drifting slowly seaward. . . . About a hundred yards from the smoke screen, our flotilla put on full speed. Then all hell broke loose. . . . Every enemy gun must have been trained on it, and it seemed crazy to go in. The smoke was being twisted into a variety of shapes by the exploding shells and bombs. There was a continuous roar.

A burst of machine-gun fire whistled past our heads; instinctively I ducked. I had a very curious feeling of self-pity. I began to think the enemy was definitely unreasonable to be doing this to me. . . . One's normal sense of being under the protection of the law was suddenly withdrawn, and left one feeling terribly vulnerable. . . .

I was in my position on deck and very exposed; I should have much preferred to have been with the men down in the boat and below the waterline. For a man who had crossed the Atlantic just to fight the enemy, this seemed a curious reaction. . . .

The whole thing was like being in the middle of a very busy intersection with traffic from four directions at once, and it made one dizzy. It seemed impossible to make the 200 yards of beach without being killed. . . .

Yet we could not stay on the beach in the open, in full view of the enemy. It was only a matter of time before they killed every one of us. The nearest cover was the Casino; so we had to make for that and take it over. . . .

Of my forty-five men, there were four with me. That was all; the others were scattered all over the place. . . .

■

South Saskatchewan rifleman Haggard was prepared for the din of battle—but not for a "secret weapon"—the pipers of the Cameron Regiment. He warned his sergeant:

"Listen! Horsedrawn German artillery coming up! Listen hard, you'll hear the squeaking of the wheels. Take cover!"

■

Many Canadian tanks were disabled on the beach—both from the steep grade of small rocks that caused tanks to throw their tracks and from water swallowed on the way in. Black Watch Sergeant J. W. Marsh saw one apparently stalled tank helped to its attack by German artillery:

Our third tank, which was towing the scout car, seemed to get stuck—half on the beach and half on the ramp. Our captain reversed the boat and so pulled the ramp from under the tank. But at the same moment a shell burst on the ramp and broke the winch ca-

bles. The tank, now released, rapidly pulled the scout car through the barbed wire and also tore through the sea wall. The last I saw of the scout car, it was tearing like hell up Foch Boulevard.

■

The scene under the scant protection of the seawall reminded Lt. Jerry Wood of "a Hollywood bloody movie":

What I looked at was quite as fantastic a scene as the Confederate hospital church in the movie *Gone with the Wind.* The medical orderlies moved unobtrusively . . . in the worst shambles of their experience.

■

The story of Sergeant-Major Dumais was comparable to the experience of many in the raiding party. It wouldn't be until his release from a German prison after the war that he would know how valuable the lessons learned in the raid had been for planning future amphibious operations:

I staggered on through the rain of bullets, and suddenly found myself in the shelter of a burning Troop Landing Craft. . . . The sea was coming in and would soon reach us. The enemy were still firing in a leisurely way at any group showing activity on the beach. . . .

We could hold out for a little longer, but what would be the point? It would not be for glory, because nobody would ever know anything about this last stand. Would it be for a soldier's honour? It would not be an honour to let these wounded men drown. I was responsible for their lives; was I to sacrifice them for the sake of my personal pride?

I picked up a rifle with a bayonet on it and tied my handkerchief to the end. It was an old khaki handkerchief that had turned yellow with age, so I did not even capitulate under a white flag, but under a yellow rag, the colour of cowardice!

One of the Germans was yelling at me.

Then he gestured to me to throw down the rifle and raise my hands. I took the handkerchief from the bayonet and threw the rifle down onto the shingle . . . raised my hands above my head and turned towards the town.

Coventry, 1940

Barrage balloons had been used during the First World War for artillery spotting, and pilots trying to shoot them down were always apprehensive about getting tangled in the dangling handling lines and cables. So at the start of World War II, they were employed for the defense of British cities. Dame Laura Knight, known for her peacetime pictures of ballet, music halls, circuses, and the theater, painted the launching of a barrage balloon in Coventry. The predominantly female crew is under the direction of a female sergeant who has clearly learned stance and command from an old British Army–type. (Imperial War Museum)

Scenes from Embattled London

The evacuation of young children from London at the start of the war is depicted by Ethel Gabain, who recorded this departure scene (LEFT) at a London station—with some faces showing excitement at the outing . . . and others already tightening with stomach-churning homesickness. (Imperial War Museum)

Feliks Topolski views the nightly scene (LEFT) of Londoners taking refuge on the platforms of an Underground station. Families and neighbors settled into regular places night after night. Story-telling groups and singalongs sprung up, tea was brewed, a rigid code of privacy was generally adhered to, and the British began to "muddle through." (Imperial War Museum)

British Air Raid Precautions officials had detailed procedures prepared for the raids because of several earlier war scares. Some of the plans were a bit outlandish, but others were practical, simple, and ingenious. This Evelyn Dunbar painting (LEFT) shows a train, staffed with medical personnel from a London hospital, as it waits on a siding outside the city, ready to roll into the bombed area as soon as the bombers leave. A beautifully simple solution, it kept these valuable "flying squads" safe until they were needed. (Imperial War Museum)

London, 1940–41

Henry Moore, already a major figure in the British art world when the war broke out, had volunteered to learn the making of critical precision tools for the war effort—the only way he could see that his skill might be usefully put to service. But Sir Kenneth Clark, then head of the National Gallery, persuaded him to join the fledgling War Artists Scheme. Moore was immediately struck by the difference in the somewhat standoffish Londoners when they went into Underground stations for shelter, and their generally cheerful willingness to make the best of it. He began a series of "shelter paintings," often using chalk and children's colored wax crayons as his medium. His *Women and Children in the Tube,* below, was a favorite and was picked for a show that toured the United States and Canada to build support for Britain. (Imperial War Museum)

The Face of War, Over Europe, 1939–40

Paul Nash, who titled this painting *Follow the Führer,* had won distinction as a fighting-soldier-turned-artist during the First World War, painting the hard-pressed British Tommies who suffered such staggering losses in the seesaw battles between the trenches. This time, Nash became fascinated with war in the air. And even though he made little attempt to paint technically accurate airplanes (a fact that annoyed some RAF-types immensely), he gained a reputation for achieving in his paintings the powerful feeling of the loneliness of the air war. Another artist might have painted this work as some sort of broad political cartoon, with its "double-take" Hitler-faced shark. But critics felt Nash had created something powerful and threatening. And the British public loved it. (Imperial War Museum)

RAF Base, Southeast England, 1940

The Spitfires, painted here by Eric Ravilious at Sawbridgeworth Airdrome near the North Sea, were the stars of the Battle of Britain, along with the Hurricanes. Ravilious had come into the War Artists Scheme with the rank of honorary captain in the Royal Marines—bringing with him a reputation as a respected painter of rural landscapes, a highly sought-after book illustrator, and a top ceramic designer for the 200-year-old pottery firm of Josiah Wedgwood & Sons. He did almost eighty paintings and drawings of wartime subjects, favoring Royal Navy and RAF scenes. Sadly, he lost his life in the fall of 1942 when an RAF patrol bomber in which he was riding disappeared off Iceland during an emergency hunt for a downed Coastal Command pilot. (Imperial War Museum)

German Ace, France, 1940

Fighter ace Werner Mölders emerged early not only as a great antagonist in plane-to-plane dogfights, but also as an able air commander. By the end of 1940, when Wolf Willrich painted him, he had a record German score of forty-five planes shot down, and was Germany's most decorated soldier. Mölders was himself shot down by RAF Squadron Leader A. G. ("Sailor") Malan. Mölders made it to a German hospital—which was just what Malan wanted. He believed it was more of a drain on German morale to send air crews home shot up than to have them just disappear in combat. (German War Art Program)

Clyde Bank Yards, Scotland, 1940

To replace the heavy loss of British ships, British and Canadian ship-yards developed crash building techniques that saved American yards valuable learning time when the United States entered the war. This painting by Sir Stanley Spencer (OPPOSITE TOP) is one panel in a giant mural painted as a tribute to shipbuilders along the River Clyde in Scotland. (Imperial War Museum)

Replacing the U-Boat Kills, Clyde Bank Yards

Sir Stanley Spencer did almost 140 sketches in Port Glasgow for his "Clyde Paintings" of the massive shipbuilding effort in Scotland. Here (OPPOSITE BOTTOM) he paints what are apparently apprentice welders. (Imperial War Museum)

Bomb Disposal, London

Clive Upton painted the ticklish work of getting a 250-kilo bomb (ABOVE) out of the hole it has dug for itself. If the bomb squad men have not been able to get at the detonator, there is the chance that even a slight slap of the swinging projectile against the boards shoring up the hole will set the whole thing off. (Imperial War Museum)

The Blitz, 1940–41

Devastation in the City was Graham Sutherland's title for this painting of the aftermath of a firebomb raid, with steel girders of a wrecked building twisted and bent by the heat of the fire, and still glowing red as the blaze continues in the rubble of brick behind them. The abstract quality of Sutherland's paintings defied the realistic traditions of war art. And his work was unique among the art from some of the countries involved in the war, where the unspoken rule was to shy away from depicting bad things that were happening at home. But Britons began to consider these pictures of air-raid damage as proud badges of resistance, rather than emblems of discouragement. (Imperial War Museum)

English Channel, 1940–41

William Dring served in the Royal Navy and ended the war in a German prisoner-of-war camp. But among all the heroic paintings of destroyers, cruisers, and battleships in action, Dring's old side-wheeler (ABOVE) stands out in a viewer's memory, proudly flying her white-and-red Royal Navy ensign as she charges down the Channel in the defense of a coastal convoy. (Imperial War Museum)

U-Boat at Sea

The real life of the submariner at sea is reflected in this painting by Claus Bergen. The men were constantly wet on deck, and nothing ever dried below. Mold grew on clothes, food, bedding. And the boat always smelled of too many people, diesel oil, and dirty bilge water. (Captured German Art; U.S. Navy Combat Art Collection)

German E-Boat

The high-speed wooden patrol boat that artist Johannes Buchheim painted was a deadly weapon for the German navy in the fierce fighting in the North Sea, the Channel, and the Mediterranean. Designated *Schnellboots* by the Germans and E-boats by the Allies, they carried two torpedoes under the deck forward, depth charges, and 20-millimeter cannon. At night, they could creep up on a convoy quietly with engines muffled, fire their torpedoes, then dash away at close to forty miles an hour. (Captured German Art; U.S. Army Center of Military History)

E-Boat Signalman

The German navy signalman (RIGHT) is also the work of Johannes Buchheim. E-boats frequently sent lightning-fast blinker signals that appeared to be a friendly response to an enemy challenge, in hopes of getting closer for a torpedo shot before the enemy opened fire. (Captured German Art; U.S. Army Center of Military History)

Arctic Convoy, Winter 1942

The ferocious U-boat and aircraft attacks in the winter of 1942 called for every defense the British could improvise—including the odd-looking CAP rockets at right. The initials stood for "Cable And Parachute." The two rockets were shot into the air with a thin steel cable trailing between them. Then each blossomed a parachute and floated down. The cable between them was meant to entangle attacking planes. The weapon was not very effective, but it gave the seamen some feeling they were fighting back—certainly better than firing pistols, which some did in frustration. Peter Whalley painted the CAP launching gear next to the 20-millimeter gun tub of a Murmansk-bound freighter. (National Maritime Museum)

Temporary Refuge, Kola Inlet

Once in at Kola (RIGHT), out of the stormy Barents Sea, incoming convoys to Murmansk had some respite from the weather. But moored along the shore waiting for quay-space to unload, or for the make-up of a return convoy, the ships were tempting targets for enemy bombers and torpedo planes. James Morris painted the nervous waiting period. (Imperial War Museum)

The Attack on St.-Nazaire, France, April 1942

Norman Wilkinson painted HMS *Campbeltown,* a World War I American "four-piper" transferred to the Royal Navy under the destroyers-for-bases deal, leading the attack to destroy the massive dry dock and submarine berths in St.-Nazaire harbor. *Campbeltown* had been cleaned out below-decks forward and five tons of explosives were concreted into her hull. She would drive at flank speed into the gates of the great dry dock and a time-charge would blow up hull and dock gates. (National Maritime Museum)

On a Canadian Destroyer, English Channel, 1942

Canadian artist Tom Wood painted this night action in the Channel between Canadian and German destroyers. The artist has had to take some liberties to brighten the visibility. Veterans of the destroyer sweeps and the Coastal Forces said often they could see little of what they were firing at and simply aimed back down a line of tracers. But the sure sign of a hit was shells smashing into something in the black night, like water from a garden hose striking a wall. (Canadian War Museum)

(OVERLEAF)

Arriving in Murmansk, Winter 1942

In the late summer of 1941, the British began their Arctic convoys, sailing out of Scotland for the northernmost Russian ports of Murmansk and Archangel. The former was the only harbor in western Russia that was free from ice all winter—but it was not free from German bombers, who could strike it from fields in northern Norway. Charles Pears painted these ice-covered veterans who have made it to the relative safety of Kola Inlet. Now all they have to do is fight their way back. (National Maritime Museum)

Convoy Sailors

Life below-decks in the convoys was recorded by Canadian artists Jack Nichols (OPPOSITE) and Tom Wood (ABOVE) in all its uncomfortable reality. Some men were pragmatists, never taking off their life jackets all through the voyage, like the harmonica player in the picture at left. Others were fatalists and refused to put on virtually useless life-saving gear. In Wood's picture, Royal Navy sailors are climbing into foul-weather gear at the change of watch. The disadvantage of that outfit was that it could pull them quickly under if they went into the water, even with a life jacket. A rubber immersion flotation suit was later developed, but it was largely scorned as hot, awkward to move in—and definitely not for the macho. (Both, Canadian War Museum)

Rounding Them Up

Keeping the convoy together by signaling in bad weather or re-forming it after a night of straggling or U-boat attacks was a slow and often frustrating business. Alfred Leete was the artist. (Canadian War Museum)

North Atlantic, 1940–41

Alfred Leete painted this Royal Canadian Navy officer on the bridge of one of the convoy's escort ships. The escort commander was generally a career RCN officer like the man shown. He would ride in the most powerful navy ship in the escort group. The convoy commodore—the navy's senior man for the merchant ships—was often an experienced officer brought back from retirement and riding in one of the faster merchant ships. He carried aboard a small staff of a few junior officers and radiomen and signalmen. All the merchant vessels essentially got their orders from him. (Canadian War Museum)

Over the Channel, 1940–41

After talks with RAF crew members who survived such attacks, Norman Wilkinson painted this swirling battle when a Sunderland on U-boat patrol was jumped by seven twin-engined German fighter-bombers involved in a convoy attack. It would appear to be an uneven fight—and certainly not one the Sunderland would have sought out. Wilkinson gives the Sunderland credit for one German plane going down trailing smoke, and another hit and burning. The painting was not pure myth. Wilkinson had heard of the big boats driving off such attacks—particularly when the Germans had taken some losses over a convoy and were short of gas and ammunition. (National Maritime Museum)

Escort Carrier, North Atlantic

Stephen Bone, the son of First and Second World Wars artist Sir Muirhead Bone, painted this "baby carrier" (OPPOSITE) in the inhospitable waters of the North Atlantic. The daily operational problems were significant: Take a landing area not much longer than a parking lot in a suburban town's shopping mall, arrange to have it bounce up and down unpredictably, then try to operate a group of high-speed aircraft in and out of it as if it were moving around at about twenty miles an hour—then you see the problems. The baby carrier crews made it work and helped win the Battle of the Atlantic. (National Maritime Museum)

Approaching Dieppe Beach

While training for the Dieppe raid, troops were repeatedly told not to panic if flares or star shells were fired. Even distant flares can seem so bright that soldiers feel they are bathed in light, are easy targets, and will be quickly picked off. The tendency is to start firing in response—giving their position away, when many times the enemy has failed to spot anything. Canadian artist Alex Colville, a lieutenant of Canadian infantry, painted this scene at another landing, but it clearly conveys the trapped feeling of being caught under the German flares. (Canadian War Museum)

Dieppe, August 1942

The Dieppe raid of August 1942 is remembered by Canadians for the valor of their units that went into action on the raid, for the first time in the European war. Canadian artist Charles Comfort painted the assault moving up the pebbled shingle beach in front of Dieppe's Casino. Conspicuous are tanks with improvised "pitchfork" exhaust stacks to bring them through the surf. But the stacks proved too short for the high water encountered. And the rough shingle and steep grade of the beach caused many of the heavy tanks to throw their treads and become helpless targets. (Canadian War Museum)

Churchill at El Alamein, Peter McIntyre (New Zealand National Archives)

STRUGGLE IN NORTH AFRICA

In the Mediterranean, British seapower provided a critical advantage in the fight for North Africa, but the supply route through Gibraltar and across the Mediterranean to Egypt meant convoys would have bitter encounters with Italian and German ships, planes, and submarines. The desert war boiled around tank and armored car battles—first against Italians from Libya . . . then against crack, combat-wise German units sent in to support the hard-pressed Italians. But several British commanders, concluding with General Montgomery, hammered the British Empire troops into the tough, battle-hardened army that called itself the "Desert Rats" and whipped General Rommel's Afrika Korps in costly victories at Tobruk and El Alamein. In November 1942, U.S. forces landed in Algeria to an early and punishing baptism of fire, but were able to provide critical pressure on the German rear. In May 1943, the Germans surrendered at Cape Bon, forced by a true "allied" fighting machine of British, Americans, Australians, New Zealanders, South Africans, Indians, Free French, and Free Greeks.

*A*t the end of World War I, strategists in all of the countries involved determined that if they were ever drawn into war again, they should avoid the terrible, grinding stalemate of trench warfare, which destroyed hundreds of thousands of men for gains that were often no more than a few hundred yards. If, in World War II, the generals were looking for a classic "war of maneuver," they found it in North Africa. Fred Majdalany, an officer of the Lancashire Fusiliers, served in North Africa with both the British and the Americans and took part in a number of the actions that he describes in the pages that follow. The recollections that are not signed otherwise reflect the experiences or interviews of Majdalany:

For practical purposes that part of North Africa in which the campaign of 1940–42 was fought may be defined as a stretch of 500 miles embracing the western two-thirds of Egypt and the eastern half of Libya, the then-Italian colony of Cyrenaica.

If men have to fight wars there could be no more suitable place anywhere in which to do so than this hard-based northern plateau of the Western Desert: an empty nothingness large enough and mostly firm enough to exercise a million tanks and trucks and guns . . . a boundless void in which all the infernal engines and explosive frightfulness of modern war could be deployed. . . .

■

The Italian army ran patrols and reconnaissance—but remained in two fortified camp areas. Early in December, a British and Indian force numbering 36,000 men attacked a gap in the Italian center at dawn, taking them by complete surprise. In swift advances and swirling fights over nine days, British successes caused Hitler to decide he must send a German force to Tripoli. It was labeled a "special detachment." But as wars have a way of drawing enemies in deeper, the special detachment soon became the Afrika Korps. Rommel wrote of their meeting:

In the evening the Führer showed me a number of British and American illustrated papers describing General Wavell's advance through Cyrenaica. Of particular interest [to both of them] was the master coordination these showed between armored land forces, air force, and navy.

■

Rommel quickly saw the potential for victory in Africa that would have helped in other theaters:

The German High Command . . . still failed to see the importance of the African theatre. They did not realise that with relatively small means, we could have won victories in the Near East which, in their strategic and economic value, would have far surpassed the conquest of the Don Bend [in Russia]. . . .

■

Though the British had invented the tank in World War I and used its surprise reasonably efficiently, it was the Germans who perfected tank tactics between the wars. Majdalany, with some experience in tanks, explained one British disadvantage—its aristocratic cavalry tradition:

It was not surprising that hussars, dragoons, lancers, and county yeomanry regiments . . . experienced some difficulty in adjusting an inherited cavalry tradition. . . . Small wonder that they clung to the last to their cavalry terminology . . . resisting as long as possible the process of becoming tank-minded. Small wonder that this over-simplified conception of tanks as horses in armor-plating led . . . to a costly tendency to make cavalry charges as in the past.

■

The desert fighting seemed to bring on a comradeship among one's own unit, and also a strange bond with the enemy:

Out of the shared ordeal came a shared mystique . . . a collective one that began to embrace both sides. . . . It was a remarkably chivalrous campaign, possibly the last in history. Both sides fought to the limit but within the then accepted rules of war. . . . The absence of German SS units was a help . . . but the facts do seem to support the suggestion that in the desert the flower of chivalry on either side brought to twentieth-century armor the knightly bearing of their mediaeval forebears.

■

William Tuit, a British sergeant, remem-

bered a "truce" virtually unlike that seen on any other World War II front:

I still had a Red Cross flag, and when we were about 250 yards from the post, a German stood up with another flag like mine. He shouted what sounded like: "Halten Minen." We could tell we were on the edge of a minefield because we could see the bodies of thirteen of our chaps lying there. . . . [They sent] an electrical mine-detector and guided a lieutenant and a doctor out to us. I told the officer we wanted to pick up our dead and wounded. He replied in English, "Very well, but only one truck and only two men at a time. You must not come closer than this. We will send your wounded out. . . . " [The work was carried out, and then] the lieutenant . . . went back, his men went below. He lowered his flag and I lowered mine. I saluted him, and he saluted back. But he gave me the salute of the Reichswehr [not of the Nazis]. Our armistice was over.

■

Rommel went to the thick of things, and his audacious use of the captured British "Mammoth" command truck almost ended his brilliant career in North Africa in a way that would have brought him lasting fame. General von Mellenthin was with him in a narrow escape:

The Mammoth, now carrying all the most senior officers of the Panzer Group, drove on to the wire fence. Unfortunately, no way through could be found. . . . To make matters worse, they were in an area completely dominated by the enemy. Indian dispatch riders buzzed to and fro past the Mammoth. British tanks moved up forward and American-built lorries ground their way through the desert. None of them had any suspicion that the highest officers of the German-Italian Panzer Group were sitting in a captured command vehicle, often only two or three yards away.

■

Perhaps the lowest point for British morale in North Africa came in June 1942, when, after three weeks of hard fighting in the area, Tobruk fell to the Afrika Korps:

The crucial tank battle having been settled

in his favor, Rommel moved on to Tobruk, which, after two days' hard fighting, he captured on June 21, with 35,000 prisoners and a considerable quantity of materiel.

■

Because it had become such a symbol, the capture of Tobruk was ripe to become a highly propagandized victory. Swedish journalist Arvid Fredborg, in Berlin at the time, was amazed:

The fall of Tobruk made an enormous impression in Berlin and throughout Germany. Public spirits rose at once to a peak not experienced since the conclusion of the Battle of France in 1940.

■

Tobruk would give Rommel one small port closer in his rear. But the tail of his lengthening supply line—the convoy route between Italy and North Africa—was regularly under attack by planes, submarines, torpedo boats, and destroyers from Malta:

The relentless law of desert warfare was now operating against Rommel. The more victorious he was, the more difficult it became to sustain his lengthening supply line. . . . The Panzerarmee Afrika was by now desperately short of gasoline.

■

The escape of the British from Dunkirk, the Germans felt, could be blamed on a period when the enemy had superior air coverage. General von Mellenthin could see that happening again in Africa—regularly:

Our advance on 24/25 June met with little interference from British ground forces, but was exposed to heavy and determined attacks by the Desert Air Force; the pace of the advance was outstripping our available fighter cover and we had to pay a heavy toll in casualties; indeed from the moment we entered Egypt, the writing was on the wall as far as air support was concerned. . . .

■

Then in July 1942 Rommel's advance was stopped by a jury-rigged British defense system running south into the desert from near the little railway station of El Alamein—only

sixty miles from Alexandria. The position had been picked with care. It had two well-defined and secure flanks: the sea to the north—and the so-called Qattara Depression to the south, a giant 200-foot-deep sinkhole of salt marsh and quicksand:*

[The British] had carried out peacetime maneuvers there [the El Alamein area]. They knew it well. When General Auchinleck became Commander in Chief Middle East in 1941, therefore, one of his first actions had been to give orders for the El Alamein line to be strengthened. . . . When he stopped Rommel there a year later he was only doing so in the area long recognized by the British Army as the one where a last-ditch stand against an invader of Egypt would inevitably take place. . . .

■

On August 15, 1942, after Rommel had been checked in the so-called First Alamein, Churchill flew to Egypt to change his commanders. The new commander of the Eighth Army would be Gen. Bernard Montgomery, a tough, stern, Bible-reading, not very popular soldier whose own heroes were Moses and Cromwell. Brig. Howard Kippenberger of New Zealand described Montgomery's first visit:

I saw him first when he called, unannounced, a few days after his arrival. He talked sharply and curtly, without any soft words, asked some searching questions . . . and left me feeling very much stimulated. . . . Now we were told that we were going to fight, there was no question of retirement to any reserve positions or anywhere else. . . . We were delighted, and the morale of the whole Army went up incredibly.

■

On the night of August 30, 1942—after waiting for stocks of gasoline that did not come—Rommel launched his attack on the southern sector of the El Alamein line. He confided his thoughts in one of his almost daily letters to his wife:

Dearest Lu: Today has dawned at last. It's been such a long wait worrying all the time whether I should get everything I needed together to enable me to take the brakes off again. . . . But I've taken the risk, for it will

be a long time before we get such favorable conditions of moonlight, relative strengths etc. again. If our blow succeeds it might go a long way toward deciding the whole course of the war. . . .

■

Lieutenant Schorm of the Afrika Korps wrote an evaluation of the enemy in his journal:

Our opponents are Englishmen and Australians. Not trained attacking troops, but men with nerves and toughness. Tireless, taking punishment with obstinacy, wonderful in defense. . . . The Australians are extraordinarily tough fighters. . . .

■

The Australians resisted "Aldershot discipline." The apocryphal story was told of a British captain inspecting Australian barracks, commenting: "There is a cigarette on the floor." The answer: "You have it, mate. You saw it first." But they were good fighters. Major Bellerstedt of the German 115th Motorized Infantry Regiment particularly respected Australians:

The Australian is unquestionably superior to the German soldier: 1) In the use of individual weapons, especially as snipers. 2) In the use of ground camouflage. 3) In his gift of observation. 4) In using every means of taking us by surprise.

■

A brigade commander, Brig. G. P. B. Roberts, described the beginning of the second day of Alam el Halfa, a scene colleagues said was "like a Hollywood film":

Now I can see the enemy myself through my glasses. They are coming straight up the line of the telegraph posts which lead in front of our position. There is some firing by their leading tanks, presumably at our light squadrons, so I instruct these squadrons to come back—but to take it wide so as not to give our position away.

On they come, a most impressive array . . . like a snake . . . ready to strike. . . . And now they all turn left and face us and begin to advance slowly. . . .

I warn all units over the air not to fire until the enemy are within 1,000 yards; and then in a few seconds the tanks of the

County of London Yeomanry open fire and the battle is on.

■

Montgomery, with new access to U.S. air strength, was determined to keep the pressure on:

Every single night RAF *Wellington* bombers added to Rommel's already considerable supply difficulties by bombing the shipping and the port installations at Tobruk. While the long-range *Liberators* (98th Bombardment Group) of General Brereton's U.S. Air Forces in the Middle East, later renamed the U.S. 9th Air Force, did the same to Benghazi and Tripoli. . . . Montgomery liked making full use of the air forces, and the RAF [to which seven U.S. squadrons were attached] responded eagerly to the requirements of a general who seemed to understand so well what an air force can and cannot do.

■

Inside the German lines, word was going around of a loss that many viewed as more serious than the 2,940 men killed, wounded, or taken prisoner at Alam el Halfa, or the 751 tanks, armored cars, and other vehicles destroyed. Rommel was suffering from a liver and blood pressure condition, and Hitler had personally ordered him home:

Field Marshal Rommel's departure was a considerable disappointment at a time when his army needed all the boost it could get. His hold over the imagination of German and Italian troops alike was by this time so complete that to fight without him was unthinkable.

■

By the fall of 1942, Rommel could see victory in Egypt opening up a southern pincer movement to meet the hoped-for German advances through the Caucasus. In Berlin, he stressed the importance of the African theater—and pushed for support. Majdalany explained:

[Rommel] needled Göring by graphically describing the dominance of the Royal Air Force in the recent battle, its devastating new tactics of carpet-bombing, the huge buildup that Montgomery was receiving, and how the influence of America's great indus-

trial war potential was now beginning to be felt. Hitler soothed him with promises of new shallow-draft ferries (that would be less vulnerable to torpedoes) for his North African supply fleet, and the latest Tiger tanks and a brigade of the new multi-barreled mortar called a *nebelwerfer*. . . . The desert campaign was only a sideshow [in Berlin]. All that really interested them was their coming offensive in Russia, about which they were all tremendously optimistic. . . .

■

At the start of the attack, a code word signaled Churchill in London, and Churchill signaled Roosevelt:

The battle in Egypt began tonight at 8 P.M. London time. The whole force of the army will be engaged. . . . All the Shermans and self-propelled guns which you gave me on that dark Tobruk morning will play their part.

■

Enemy troops hated the sound of the Scotch pipers. It was such an outlandish sound for a battlefield that it suggested to some a "supernatural force." Fred Majdalany remembered the Scots moving forward—and other odd facets of the battle:

There is something incongruous and magnificently tribal about the pipers of Scottish regiments piping the riflemen into battle in the most mechanized of modern wars. The pipers were vulnerable targets and several were killed. . . . One assault company of the 51st Highland Division reached its objective under the command of the company clerk, all the officers and the sergeant major having been killed or wounded.

■

Even faithful and extensive newsreel coverage of the battle—and its openness and rapid maneuvering of machines was ideal for the camera—could not give the true feel of it. Sometimes a few words from veterans did best. Gen. R. M. P. Carver of the 7th Armored Division had a parallel:

There were masses of vehicles all over the place, and the marking of routes and gaps was very hard to see [as night wore on]. It needed only a vehicle or two to stray off to

the side to remove all the signs and lead everybody behind into confusion. . . . The tanks and other vehicles ground along at a snail's pace in the billowing clouds of dust. . . . The whole area looked like a badly organized car park at an immense race meeting held in a dust bowl.

■

The second attack on the evening of October 24 got off in a muddled manner that made Montgomery think, no doubt, about the missed opportunities of the old Eighth Army he had taken over:

The advance, timed to begin at 2200 hours, got off to a late start attended by various misfortunes. A minefield-gapping party was withdrawn in error on a false report that an enemy attack was imminent. The minefield was more extensive than anticipated, and though four gaps, each two tanks wide, had been intended, only two were completed. A bombing attack by a small number of enemy aircraft managed to hit a column of gasoline and ammunition trucks and within seconds twenty-two trucks were blazing and continued to do so for the rest of the night. . . . The fire gave the enemy gunners an admirable mark. . . . They stepped up their shelling of the area where the minefield-gapping parties were working and in which the tanks were painfully crawling along the just-cleared lanes nose to tail and two abreast. . . . On the morning of October 25, the third day of the battle and, as it happened, a Sunday, Montgomery and Middle East Commander in Chief Alexander could feel reasonably satisfied with how things were going. XXX Corps had blasted a gap six miles wide and five miles deep into the strongest part of the enemy mine belt. A total of five armored brigades were now out in front of this gap trying to provoke the counterattacks which they were well placed to smash.

The German counterattacks began soon after dawn. . . . In addition to having to run the gauntlet of the well-sited British armored divisions, the Panzers had to withstand repeated attacks by Royal Air Force bombers and fighters and the full weight of the artillery of both the armored and the infantry divisions. . . . By nightfall the German 15th Panzer Division had only 31 out of 119 tanks serviceable. . . .

Rommel was badly missed. His deputy, General Stumme, had gone to tour the front; his car was taken under heavy fire, his aide killed, and as Stumme jumped to take cover, he was dragged by the car . . . and died of a heart attack. When Berlin got the word of Stumme's death—and the resulting headquarters confusion of the Afrika Korps, Rommel, under medical care, was called. Hitler was on the line:

The news from Africa sounds bad. The situation seems somewhat obscure. Nobody appears to know what has happened to General Stumme. Do you feel capable of returning to Africa and taking command of the army again? [Rommel returned at once.]

■

On the night of October 25, the Australians attacked with great spirit and success, capturing one of the few bits of high ground in the area . . . and opening up new potential for the offensive. Montgomery planned his next move:

The next day, October 26, Montgomery withdrew to his house trailer to consider the situation in solitude. It was one of his great qualities as a general that he could detach himself in this way from the fury of a battle and think over his problems in calm isolation. Undoubtedly he was greatly helped in this by his deep religious conviction and the genuine comfort and inspiration he derived from his Bible reading.

■

On the German side, in spite of the return of their "miracle man," things were not going as they wanted—particularly in the eyes of the miracle man. Rommel wrote his wife:

Unfortunately, the attack gained ground very slowly. The British resisted desperately. Rivers of blood were poured out over miserable strips of land which, in normal times, not even the poorest Arab would have bothered his head about. . . .

■

Majdalany described Montgomery's radical midbattle solution for the fatigue of his fighters:

That night the regrouping began, and the 2d New Zealand Division gratefully moved back from Miteirya Ridge of abominable memory to a location a few miles back by the sea. For a day or two the men could refresh themselves with the only two pleasures available—bathing and sleeping. For forty-eight hours or so they could forget the moldering corpses crawling with flies, the charred remains of burnt-out tanks, the stench of unburied dead so infinitely more nauseating in the scorching desert heat.

■

Fortunately, as General Brooke recalled, Churchill unloosed his criticisms of Montgomery on General Brooke in London—rather than sending them flying off as signals to the battlefield, as was his wont. Churchill complained:

He [Montgomery] has done nothing now for the last three days, and now he was withdrawing troops from the front. Why had he told us he would be through in seven days if all he intended to do was fight a half-hearted battle? [To calm Churchill, Brooke took the tack of explaining that Montgomery was really creating "new reserves" by resting his men. It did have a Churchillian logic to it.]

■

Rommel was still convinced he could put up a stout enough resistance to cool the British attack and gain some time. On October 28, he wrote his wife:

Today there is still a chance. . . . Perhaps we will still manage to be able to stick it out, in spite of all that's against us—but it may go wrong and that would have very grave consequences for the whole course of the war.

■

On November 1, Churchill was sent a summary of Eighth Army casualties: more than 10,000 killed, wounded, or missing. But Rommel was in worse shape. Majdalany wrote:

Rommel, ruefully conscious that his tank strength had been reduced to 90 German and 140 Italian tanks compared with Eighth Army's 800, found little comfort in a message from Marshal Ugo Cavallero:

"The Duce authorizes me to convey to you his deep appreciation of the successful counterattack led personally by you. The Duce also conveys to you his complete confidence that the battle now in progress will be brought to a successful conclusion under your command."

■

Rommel's daily letter home carried his latest disappointment:

Dearest Lu: It is sometimes a misfortune to enjoy a certain military reputation. One knows one's own limits, but other people expect miracles and set down a defeat to deliberate cussedness.

■

Montgomery knew British soldiers were prepared to die to achieve a vital objective—yet the importance of this one would be hard to explain. Majdalany described the briefing:

At his final conference before SUPERCHARGE, Montgomery stressed the importance of what Currie had to do and told Freyberg that he was prepared to accept 100 percent casualties if the brigade succeeded in breaking the iron entrance to what he was convinced was Rommel's last defense. Freyberg passed this on to Currie, who in turn confided it to his regimental and squadron commanders but with instructions that it should go no further down. Not all soldiers can be entrusted with the knowledge that 100 percent casualties are acceptable. . . .

The activities of the previous nine days had churned the desert battlefield into a mattress of dust a foot deep and the impenetrable dust fog churned up by each tank and projected at the one behind was aggravated by a strong head wind. Tank commanders with torches floundered forward on foot, trying to guide their drivers, who were completely blinded. Signs and lamps marking mine-free lanes were obliterated; collisions could not be avoided, and more than a dozen tanks were lost on mines.

■

A delay in the start of the attack sent them off just as the dawn was up—rather than half an hour before:

As the eastern sky lightened, the British tanks, sharply silhouetted, found themselves "on the muzzles of the powerful screen of antitank guns" on the Rahman Track instead of beyond it, as planned. A massacre of the tanks now began. Almost entire troops and squadrons began to go up in flames. Instead of being through the guns, they were right among them. The only thing they could do was to charge, and a fearful close-quarters battle now took place. . . .

■

Typical of his unflappable approach to the battle—and of his devotion to his wife—Rommel took time on November 2, as on each day, to send off his regular letter to Germany:

Dearest Lu: Very heavy fighting again, not going well for us. The enemy, with his superior strength, is slowly levering us out of our position. That will mean the end. You can imagine how I feel. Air raid after air raid. . . .

■

On the following day, Rommel began his withdrawal:

Dearest Lu: The battle is going very heavily against us. We're simply being crushed by the enemy weight. I've made an attempt to salvage part of the army. We are facing very difficult days, perhaps the most difficult a man can undergo. The dead are lucky, it's all over for them.

■

On the Eastern Front, German generals were receiving Wagnerian fight-to-the-death orders from Berlin. In North Africa, Rommel had never been bothered by Hitler's tactical meddling in the campaign. But on November 3, the day Rommel ordered withdrawal, he got Hitler's telegram:

To Field Marshal Rommel: . . . The German people and I are following the heroic struggle in Egypt. In the situation in which you find yourself, there can be no other thought but to stand fast, yield not a yard of ground and throw every gun and every man into battle. . . . Your enemy, despite his superiority, must also be at the end of his strength. It would not be the first time

in history that a strong will has triumphed over the bigger battalions. As to your troops, you can show them no other road than that to victory or death.

■

Hitler's message forced Rommel to reverse his withdrawal orders—briefly. (Twelve hours later Hitler sent a message authorizing the withdrawal.) On November 4, Rommel ordered a general retreat; it was the only measure that would save his strongest troops. Majdalany reported:

Because of the shortage of transport, Rommel's retreat meant abandoning the Italian infantry to save the remnants of his motorized German formations, the strongest forces he had left. . . . Montgomery and the British Eighth Army had completely defeated Rommel's Panzerarmee Afrika and put it to flight.

■

It was fitting that in a battle where the British forces were composed of so many Empire units (plus Free French and Greek volunteers), the Indian Brigade made the decisive breakthrough early in the morning of November 4. Then, as Majdalany reported, "decisions were taken Elsewhere," ending the fighting:

It was a totally unexpected—but undeniably *British*—ending to the Second Battle of El Alamein—that heavy rain, good *British* rain, should have stopped the action.

■

The casualties for the thirteen-day (and thirteen-night) battle were significant. (British losses at El Alamein were 13,500 killed, missing, and wounded.) But strategists and historians pointed out they were not too great for a victory of its impact. Britons remembered that on the first day alone of the Somme in 1916, casualties were some 60,000! And the whole Somme Offensive accomplished virtually nothing. From Majdalany:

This battle was the turning point of the British conflict with Hitler's Germany. It was to be followed two months later at Stalingrad by a complementary turning point on the Russian front. Both were parts of the same swing of [taking] the initiative from Ger-

many and can be considered as one. The ten weeks of Alamein–Stalingrad were the most momentous in modern history, for it was then that the tide of war turned against Nazi Germany on two unrelated . . . fronts. At Alamein and Stalingrad Hitler lost the war.

■

The retreat of the Afrika Korps after the battle of El Alamein was perhaps the closest a Rommel command ever came to a rout. Rommel wrote:

With the Afrika Korps broken through [at a point] between the 15 and 21 Panzer Division and no more reserves left, I gave orders—with a heavy heart . . . for the withdrawal to Mersa Matrûh. . . . It was a wild helter-skelter drive through another pitch-black night. . . . Of the formations, only the transport echelons were on the coast road, choking it with their traffic as they slowly trickled west. . . . Conditions on the road were indescribable. Columns in complete disorder—partly of German, partly of Italian vehicles—choked the road between the minefields. Rarely was there any movement forward and then everything soon jammed up again. Many vehicles were on tow and there was an acute shortage of petrol. . . .

■

As admiring Eighth Army desert soldier and Lancashire Fusilier Fred Majdalany happily summed up:

Montgomery understood the imponderable mechanisms of morale. . . . It was that, coupled with a coldly precise comprehension of the limitations as well as the potential of the citizen soldier, [that] enabled him to revitalize the main British field army after three years of tentative and mostly inadequate performance. . . .

■

After the war, Churchill looked back:

It may almost be said, "Before Alamein we never had a victory. After Alamein, we never had a defeat."

Sketch Under Fire, North Africa, 1941

To bolster national morale, Milan's world-famous *Corriere della Sera* had a painting on the cover of each Sunday magazine that depicted an event in the war. The newspaper's pictures were generally done in a studio in Milan. Marco Casedei's war paintings, however, were done from sketches in the field. At Bir El Gobi (ABOVE) Italian soldiers waited for an attack. Casedei thought them "scarcely older than schoolboys." Casedei sketched this gun crew of an Italian light field gun in action at Sidi Kerek (LEFT). With no formal government war art program, Italian artists who recorded the war generally did it on their own. (Both, Milano Museo Raccolte Storiche del Comune di Milano)

Ambush in North Africa, Spring 1941

Helmut Georg paints an armored column (ABOVE) with infantry riding atop the tanks, which comes under fire from troops hidden in the wadi sides above them. This prolific German war artist adopted a hazy technique that conveyed all the heat, dust, and smell of North Africa. British artist A. A. Gregson painted a scout car of the 5th South African Reconnaissance Regiment (LEFT) acting as point for a heavy armored column behind them. The first sighting was usually a funnel of dust. (Above, Captured German Art; U.S. Army Center of Military History; below, Imperial War Museum)

Night Firefight at Minqar Qa'im, 1941

Peter McIntyre of New Zealand described his *The Breakthrough at Minqar Qa'im* (ABOVE): "Surrounded by the Panzers, the Division fought its way through the German lines. . . . Streams of fire came from both sides until the scene was lit by the burning trucks. It was one of the most *desperate* moments in the Division's history." (New Zealand National Archives)

Commanders took care to bring their men into combat as fresh as possible. Peter McIntyre painted the 28th New Zealand Maori Battalion riding into action (RIGHT). (New Zealand National Archives)

Bombing Up, North Africa, 1942

Certain planes, ships, and machines of the war became favorites with fighting men because they were rugged, dependable, and did what they were supposed to do. They often seemed to give back an almost human personality and response. The American-built Curtis P-40 fighter was one such piece of equipment. Anthony Gross did the painting. (Imperial War Museum)

"Cropdusters," North Africa, 1942

Frank Norton, an Australian artist, depicted a flight of P-40s taking off in a scramble in line-abreast from a field in the western desert. It called for leveling a landing strip seventy-five to one hundred yards wide. If they had taken off in single file, the flight leader would likely have been trailed by a wing of wounded, sand-coughing fighters. (Australian War Memorial)

The Mutual Enemy: Insects

The soldiers on both sides particularly hated the way the flies attacked the dead and the wounded, like fanatic little aircraft circling to strafe. Edward Ardizzone, who combined a fast reportorial art technique with a frequent sense of humor or satire, sketched these two British artillery spotters (ABOVE). One has improvised protection around his head. The other sits and takes it. (LEFT) A battery of New Zealand guns gets ready to open fire at the command of their spotters. Anthony Gross was the artist. The most devastating fire came "over open sights," i.e., simply aiming down the top of the barrel, hardly more sophisticated than a cannoneer at Waterloo. (Both, Imperial War Museum)

"Brew-Up" in North Africa, 1942

For both morale and health reasons, burial had to be quick. Name, rank, and serial number of both enemy and Allied dead were noted and passed to the Royal Army Medical Corps, who sent on the names of German and Italian casualties for forwarding through the International Red Cross. In Edward Ardizzone's picture, the burial party has stopped for tea—a three-times-a-day ritual in the British North African Army. Strictly non-regulation truces were sometimes arranged to allow the recovery of dead or wounded, with the enemy guiding the other side's burial party through their own mine fields to recover the bodies. (Imperial War Museum)

The Wail of the Pipes, Egyptian Desert, 1943

From all accounts, the Germans hated the music of bagpipes. It usually denoted an approaching attack. Jack Chaddock painted Scottish infantry going into battle with their piper in the lead. The casualty rate of pipers was high. The authority that their pipes seemed to give them resulted in several cases where Scottish troops reached their objectives with all officers and noncoms wiped out—and the piper in command. Because pipers couldn't play at a double-time pace, the Scots usually advanced in a sinister, slow march, with an impervious look about it that was not encouraging to the German and Italian defenders. (Imperial War Museum)

The Butcher's Bill, Egyptian Desert, 1942

Anthony Gross was moved by the sight of this long, quiet ambulance train ready to move out for Alexandria from a spur not far from the battle line. There the most seriously wounded transferred to hospital ships for England. The voyage home was still a dangerous one, with threats of air attack all the way through the Mediterranean to Gibraltar, then the long Atlantic route home through U-boat-patrolled waters. Even a brightly lit hospital ship with international markings was no guarantee of safety. Too many accidents could happen. (Imperial War Museum)

Soldiers of the King

New Zealander Peter McIntyre sketched his countrymen in Tunisia. At left is one of the men who made the drive on Takurna, a "Kiwi." McIntyre showed the tough little fighter ready to move out to take the next hill. There was always one more.

The British forces fighting in North Africa were made up of a powerful cross section of the British Empire—Australians, Indians, New Zealanders, South Africans, Egyptians, Canadians—supported by Free French, exiled Poles, and Greek soldiers who had evacuated with the British when their country was taken. The British artist William Coldstream did a series of powerful portraits of Indian army officers and men in North Africa, including (CENTER) Rifleman Mangal Singh.

This helmeted Britisher (RIGHT) has finished his soldiering. He was sketched by German artist Wilhelm Wessel, headed for a prisoner-of-war cage. Veterans of the desert war said they saw little of the atrocities that had befallen prisoners of the Germans in Europe. For one thing, Rommel was in charge. Also, there were no Nazi-oriented SS units in North Africa. (Left, New Zealand National Archives; center, Imperial War Museum; right, Captured German Art; U.S. Army Center of Military History)

Saturation Drop in Crete, May 1941

A number of the British and Australian units that performed exceptional service in North Africa had the dubious distinction of having gone through the defeats in Crete in 1941. This painting by Peter McIntyre shows German paratroopers descending around the British General Hospital at Canea. The German paratroop saturation drops in Crete were among their most perfect airborne operations. All the lessons learned during the Blitzkrieg of the Low Countries were put into effect in Greece and Crete, with virtually the total German paratroop force involved. (New Zealand National Archives)

Advance Toward Alexandria, 1942

Running along much of the eastern end of the desert battlefield was the Qattara Depression, where the sunken terrain was rougher. To the west there were hills and gullies and mesalike high ground in the Qardibiyah. The cover was welcome—but it changed the cavalry-like tactics of the desert. Helmut Georg's picture shows a Panzer column advancing into one of these depressions—cautiously. (Captured German Art; U.S. Army Center of Military History)

Combat Alert, Egypt, 1942

Buttoned-up German tanks proceed into combat. With the desert sun coming down outside and the engine heat within, the tankers boiled but were protected from all but heavy fire. Sand and heat made treads and engines wear out quickly, and the desert was dotted with hulks of tanks abandoned because of battle damage and breakdown. The artist is Helmut Georg. (Captured German Art; U.S. Army Center of Military History)

Reserves for Rommel, Tripoli, 1942

Helmut Georg painted Afrika Korps units leaving Tripoli for the battle front in this colorful East-meets-West scene, concentrating on one of the German army's troop carriers. General Rommel's men had become familiar with sand and heat before arriving. He had found a training site in the Baltic with comparable sandy terrain. Soldiers and vehicles were tested hard, with the men living in overheated barracks and subjected to the discomforts and mechanical breakdowns that temperature and sandstorms would give them later. (Captured German Art; U.S. Army Center of Military History)

(OVERLEAF)

Losers Who Turned Winners

Ivor Hele's painting *Disembarkation from Greece* has often been compared to the scene in Atlanta's railroad station, crowded with Confederate wounded, in the film version of *Gone with the Wind*. The parallel is more than visual. Hele's British troops had also been heavily shot up, and suffered badly wounded morale. Yet in a relatively short time these sturdy survivors were reequipped mentally, physically, and militarily and were part of the army that would defeat the Germans and Italians at El Alamein. (Australian War Memorial)

Deception at Qattara, Egypt, 1943

In preparation for a surprise tank thrust, the British manufactured their own cover, as depicted above by British artist T. C. Davy. During the night, over a period of a week or more, tanks, scout cars, and trucks from the seacoast were moved down to the "park" on the edge of the Qattara Depression. Before dawn, the vehicles were covered with great tarpaulins. From several thousand feet in the air, the terrain looked to German and Italian reconnaissance planes like just more empty desert waste. Then the tanks suddenly exploded out of their canvas cocoons in the southern desert and roared off in a stunning surprise attack. (Imperial War Museum)

The Common Bond of Africa

Wilhelm Wessel sketched a German desert fighter (ABOVE RIGHT), and a captured British soldier (RIGHT) helping a wounded German. The bond grew between soldiers who had shared common danger and suffering. In 1947, when an English amateur football club lost to one from Germany in an important international match, two opposing players discovered they had fought in North Africa. The winning German player remarked after the match: "Sorry to beat you in your national game." The Englishman replied: "That's all right. In 1943, we beat you at yours." (Captured German Art; U.S. Army Center of Military History)

Psychological "Sally Port," Libya, 1941

Tobruk caught Winston Churchill's imagination in the North African campaign. When the German advance passed it by, Churchill wanted it to be held at all costs, and not to let it become "another Dunkirk." Casting back into his classical history to justify the effort, he characterized Tobruk as "a sally port"—the small heavy-doored entrance in a castle wall used by the defenders for surprise raids. And so this little port took on the mantle of the offensive, at least in Churchillian prose. Some 23,000 Empire troops—Australians, British, and Indians—had been holed up here under siege for eight months when Australian painter Frank Norton painted the beginning of a night raid, with German flares falling. (Australian War Memorial)

Rommel's Fueling Station

I vor Hele titled his painting (LEFT) *Tobruk 1944*. It centered on an Australian gun pit overlooking the harbor, with the city looking amazingly sturdy after its two sieges and much battering from the air by both sides. It had been a critical port for the Germans to take and hold in the summer of 1942—particularly when they were driving toward Alexandria, before the second El Alamein. Rommel's offensive plans often had to be made less on the basis of what the enemy was doing than on how much fuel was available for his tanks and what success the convoys from Italy were having bringing in tankers with additional fuel reserves. (Australian War Memorial)

The Cost of Brief Encounter

On April 22, 1941, the 2/48th Australian Battalion ran into strong Italian resistance at a modest rise named Carrier Hill. Ivor Hele painted the scene (LEFT) in all the condensed fury of a nineteenth-century battle painting. As in World War I, the Australians sent some of their best units to the Mediterranean theater. The Australians were long on fighting and short on military punctilio—which nettled some British commanders. But this was usually forgotten when the firing started. (Australian War Memorial)

"Stand-Down" in the Desert, Fall 1942

These Australian troopers are piled exhausted in the back of a truck, well bundled against the night cold of the desert. They were painted by Ivor Hele as they were being hauled off to one of those endless musters that all armies specialize in when there is no fighting to be done. Though sunrises, sunsets, and nights in the North African desert had all the romantic beauty that travel writers had written about for years, the sunrises and sunsets were principally etched in a soldier's memory as favored times for some officer to order an attack—or for some enemy to attack them. (Australian War Memorial)

Australian Night Action, El Alamein, Fall 1942

William Dargie from Australia painted men of the 2/24th Australian Battalion getting ready to attack during the night of October 25–26, 1942. Casualties have already started to come; a stretcher is being readied in the foreground. Flames and star shells—which generally made soldiers jumpy no matter who was firing them—spook up the night. Odd explosions mushroom and fires break out to increase the apprehension. But no word is passed to the infantryman on what it all means . . . and each man tries to ignore the intimidating things and live a little more tightly within himself. (Australian War Memorial)

Debris of War, El Alamein, Fall 1942

Wilhelm Wessel probably did his pencil studies for this painting of the *El Alamein Battlefield* during one of the days when the outcome was still in doubt. But the sad debris and the pylons of smoke on the horizon say the same thing to any viewer of any nationality: war is a terrible waste. North African veterans often commented on the stench of a littered battlefield: there was the smell of dead bodies that had lain too long in the sun, and the acrid scents of explosives, spilled and burning oil, rotting food, old latrines. Advance or retreat would move the soldiers away from the gutted battlefield. But the taste of the place seemed to stick in their noses and throats for days. (Captured German Art; Canadian War Museum)

Episode at Tobruk

The Ivor Hele painting here is harrowingly reminiscent of the hand-to-hand battle scenes from World War I. It is titled *Bardia Road, Tobruk Perimeter, Action Leading to the Fall of Post 11*. The Australians have taken a German strongpoint, and it is cluttered with casualties on both sides. (Australian War Memorial)

Mine Fields: Mersa Matrûh, Egypt, Summer 1942

Among the most deadly and impersonal weapons of World War II—both at sea and on
land—was the mine, in all its diabolical and rapidly improving forms. Wilhelm Wessel
painted the defense line of tank barriers and wire in front of the British fortifications
at Mersa Matrûh, abandoned to the Germans as the British fell back toward Cairo. The
things that don't show are the carefully buried mine fields, "the Devil's gardens." Most
soldiers feared the blast of a mine far more than the relatively clean wound of a bullet. But it
was a Hobson's choice. (Captured German Art; Canadian War Museum)

"Booby-Trapped" Tobruk, Spring 1943

Here is Wilhelm Wessel's *Tobruk Harbor*—several times fought over and facing a cleanup that would not be completed until after the war. Half-sunk ships rested on the bottom and clung drunkenly to the seawall. When taking over after the Germans surrendered, the British feared that many of the sunken vessels and wrecked buildings had been booby-trapped with hidden explosives that would go up when salvagers started to clear the damage. (Captured German Art; Canadian War Museum)

Russian Winter, 1942, Bruno Azimonti (Courtesy of the Artist)

HE INVASION OF
RUSSIA

O peration Barbarossa," the German invasion of Russia, was to set off the greatest bloodletting of all time. The world was taken by surprise at the sudden turn of events. Stalin had badly misjudged the international situation and ignored his advisors and the warnings that came from his Intelligence Service . . . and from Churchill.

When the showdown came with the first lightning thrusts of the German mechanized divisions in the summer of 1941, the technologically superior equipment of the Nazis seemed a total surprise to the Russian soldiers and officers.

Hitler was euphoric with his successes—particularly since many senior officers had advised against the invasion of Russia; after all, history had taught them to remember a warning of von Hindenburg's: "Any general who fights against the Russians can be perfectly sure of one thing: he will be outnumbered." And as the German supply and reinforcement lines got longer, and as the Russian reserves continued to pour into the defense, the professional soldiers seemed to have been right.

On December 18, 1940—only seven months after Dunkirk—Hitler had issued orders that then made clear why he had grown somewhat reluctant to push ahead with the invasion of England. An attack on Russia at the right time had always been in his plan, and he was not eager to see his air force chewed up over Britain:

For the Eastern campaign the air force will have to free such strong force for the support of the army that a quick completion of the ground operations may be expected and that damage of the eastern German territories will be avoided as much as possible. . . .

■

When invaded by Charles XII of Sweden and then by Napoleon, Russia had relied on its tremendous manpower to see it through disastrous reversals—and had come back strong after heavy losses. But Stalin purged the Soviet army officer corps in the 1930s. Thus in the Russian-Finnish War of 1939 and during the 1941 German invasion the Soviet army was crippled at a most critical time. Historian Alan Clark surveyed the purge:

Whatever Stalin's motives, and whether or not he intended to go as far as he did, the final figures were staggering. Only Budenny and Voroshilov survived among the Marshals. Out of 80 members of the 1934 Military Soviet only five were left in September of 1938. All eleven Deputy Commissars for Defence were eliminated. Every commander of a military district (including replacements of the first "casualties") had been executed by the summer of 1938. Thirteen out of fifteen army commanders, 57 out of 58 corps commanders, 110 out of 195 divisional commanders, 220 out of 406 brigade commanders were executed. But the greatest numerical loss was borne in the Soviet officer corps from the rank of colonel *downwards* and extending to the company-commander level.

■

When the terrible Soviet revenge fell on Germany in the spring of 1945, Germans on the home front might have known what to expect if they could have heard Hitler briefing the officers who would spearhead the invasion of Russia. Historian Leonard Cooper, in his book Many Roads to Moscow, *described the briefing:*

On March 30, Hitler had assembled the service commanders in chief and their senior officers to the number of about 250 and had harangued them for two hours about the "ideological" nature of the coming campaign, making it clear to them that the Russians were to be treated as a distinct species of human—or, perhaps better, sub-human—being and that the normal rules of war did not apply to them. The "Barbarossa Order" had already been published on March 3, and it had laid down that the ordinary proceedings of courts-martial were only to apply to soldiers bearing arms and not to civilians in overrun territory. . . .

■

On May 6, 1941—a month and a half before the start of the invasion—Hitler issued what came to be called "The Commissar Order":

Political authorities and leaders (commissars) constitute a special menace to the security of troops and the pacification of conquered territory.

If such persons are captured by the troops or otherwise apprehended they will be brought before an officer who has disciplinary powers of punishment. The latter will summon two military witnesses (officer or NCO rank) and will establish that the person apprehended or captured is a political personality or leader (commissar). If adequate proof of his political position is forthcoming the officer will forthwith order his execution and will ensure that it is carried out. . . .

■

Examining German files after the war, Cooper found that Hitler soon revealed to the senior officers involved a series of additional instructions he had given, particularly to the SS:

Himmler was charged with the establishment of civilian control of each district and of what was known as "the solution of the Jewish problem," which meant nothing less than the extermination of the Jews. Göring was in economic charge and his duty was to strip the country of everything in the way of food and supplies that was portable, and to send it back to Germany.

■

Field Marshal von Rundstedt, who had the Lower Dnieper assignment for his army group, wrote in his journal:

This war with Russia is a nonsensical idea, to which I can see no happy ending. But if, for political reasons, the war is unavoidable, then we must face the fact that it can't be won in a single summer campaign. Just look at the distances involved.

■

Late in the evening of June 21, the German ambassador to Moscow got instructions from Berlin to destroy all his confidential material and his codes, and to wreck his radio equipment. Then he was to call on Russian Commissar of Foreign Affairs V. M. Molotov. Molotov's staff officer, Ivan Krylov, remembered:

At six o'clock in the morning of 22 June 1941, the German Ambassador, Count von Schulenberg, handed Molotov a Note of the German Government declaring war on the Soviet Union.

Both Count von Schulenberg and Molotov were pale with emotion. The Commissar for Foreign Affairs took the Note wordlessly, spat on it and then tore it up. He rang for his secretary Poskrebichev. "Show this gentleman out through the back door."

■

Stalin seemed immobilized for the first days of the invasion. But when he later issued his orders for resistance, they were clear enough for even the simplest farmer and factory worker to understand:

In the event of the retreat of the Red Army, all railway rolling stock must be brought away. We must not leave a single engine to the enemy, nor a single railway coach. We must not leave a single pound of grain or a single gallon of petrol to the enemy. . . .

■

When the invasion jumped off, "Hitler luck"—good weather, surprise, various turns of fortune that a cautious general would not have depended on—seemed to be holding. General Blumentritt could see differences from the Polish and French experiences, and some problems beginning:

By 2 July the first battle was for all intents and purposes won. . . . A hundred and fifty thousand prisoners taken, some twelve hundred tanks and six hundred guns captured or destroyed. . . . The Russian was as tough a fighter as ever. His tanks, however, were not particularly formidable and his air force, so far as we could see, nonexistent.

The conduct of the Russian troops . . . was in striking contrast to the behaviour of the Poles and of the Western allies in defeat. Even when encircled, the Russians stood their ground and fought. . . .

■

Stalin's purge of the Soviet army's officers corps had been explained in some quarters as a measure "to spur command incentives." It had, in fact, often resulted in squelching initiative in critical areas. Leonard Cooper reported:

Nearly all these bridges had been prepared for destruction and at many an actual demolition party was standing by when the Germans arrived. Yet hardly ever was the bridge blown even when there was a Russian officer present to direct operations.

■

On August 21, Hitler had replied "explosively" to a General Staff Memorandum that warned the Führer that in the opinion of the generals, if the army didn't reach Moscow by the end of September, they might get bogged down in the Russian winter, when guns and vehicles could not move. Guderian, von Rundstedt, and Halder decided to oppose Hitler, asking for a meeting. When Halder and Guderian arrived at Hitler's headquarters, a staff officer said their appointment had been approved—with a stipulation:

I forbid you to mention the question of Moscow to the Führer. The operation to the South has been ordered. The problem now is simply to carry it out. Discussion is pointless.

■

Halder felt the interview would be useless

with those restrictions and left. Guderian promised no mention of Moscow and went in. Then, surprisingly, Hitler brought up the subject, heard Guderian out, but refused his recommendations. Guderian recounted the futile meeting:*

For the first time I heard him use the phrase "My generals know nothing about the economic aspects of war" . . . I saw for the first time a spectacle with which I was later to become very familiar; all those present nodded in agreement with every sentence that Hitler uttered, while I was left alone with my point of view. . . .

■

Alexander Werth—a top-rank British correspondent—had been born in Russia, spoke the language fluently, and most important of all perhaps, loved the country and the people. Shortly after the German invasion, Werth was flown to Russia with a group of top British diplomats and military aides. He was to serve as a correspondent for the London Sunday Times *and the BBC. (Where accounts are not credited otherwise in what follows, they are Alexander Werth's experiences and observations.) He could easily sympathize with the Russians' reaction to their first small victory over the German attackers; it proved that the German army wasn't invincible:*

The Battle of Yelnya, south-east of Smolensk, which went on throughout the whole of August, was not a major battle of the Soviet-German war, and yet . . . here was not only, as it were, the first victory of the Red Army over the Germans; here was also the first piece of territory—perhaps only 100 or 150 square miles—in the whole of Europe reconquered from Hitler's Wehrmacht.

■

Leningrad, only ninety miles from the Finnish border, was a tempting early target for the Germans:

To slow down the German advance on Leningrad, not only were some regular reserve troops thrown in, especially along the River Luga, but also freshly improvised *opolcheniye* units, consisting of workers' battalions, student and even schoolboy battalions, so characteristic of that *lève en masse* spirit

which was to prove stronger in Leningrad than in almost any other Soviet city. Moreover, several hundred thousand civilians had been mobilised, early in July, to dig three lines of trenches, anti-tank ditches, and other, admittedly rudimentary, defences on the approaches to Leningrad.

■

From his good military contacts, Werth was able to follow much of the debate among Soviet commanders on whether the stubborn and costly defense of the "Kiev salient" was worth it:

On 16 September, the Germans closed the bottleneck, and the four Soviet armies were surrounded. . . . The question remains whether Stalin was not perhaps right, after all, to have clung to the Kiev salient for as long as he did. Paradoxically, the [official Soviet] *History* suggests that this German victory in the Ukraine hopelessly upset Hitler's time-table. This, indeed, coincides with the prevalent German view. . . .

■

Leonid Volynsky, a Russian soldier, took part in the Kiev defense and reflected on its value later:

To hundreds of thousands of men trying during those nights to break out of the German ring . . . groping their way through forests and marshes, and under a hailstorm of German bombs and shells . . . all this was nothing but a vast and inexplicable tragedy.

■

Field Marshal von Rundstedt could see that Russia was not going to be anywhere nearly as easy a conquest as Poland and France:

I realized soon after the attack was begun that everything that had been written about Russia was nonsense. The maps we were given were all wrong. The roads that were marked nice and red and thick on a map turned out to be tracks and what were tracks on the map became first-class roads. Even railways which were to be used by us simply didn't exist.

■

The Russians weren't long in discovering the

full meaning of Hitler's Barbarossa and Commissar orders. Werth told of SS tactics:

On the following morning, the "Commissars, Communists and Jews" were summoned to come forward, after the arrival of some fifteen SS-men in black uniforms and with skulls on their caps. Some three hundred came forward, were stripped to the waist and lined up in the yard. Then the interpreter, a young man, speaking with a strong Galician accent, shouted that some must still be hiding; and anyone who denounced a Communist, Commissar or Jew could take his clothes and other belongings [and depart]. So, in the end, four hundred were [denounced and] shot, being taken away ten at a time, and ordered to dig their graves.

■

Else Wendel, a German housewife, heard a soldier friend comment that Germany erred in not taking advantage of the cordial reception the German army had found in the Ukraine, in order to make the Ukrainians "allies":

"I was one of those who marched in to be received, not as a conqueror but as a friend," said Rudolf. "The civilians were all ready to look on us as saviours. They had had years of oppression from the Soviet. They thought we had come to free them. Does it sound absurd? Perhaps it does. What did we do? Turn them into slaves under Hitler. Worse, we deported their women for labour in Germany, and did not bother if they were married or single, had children or not. To add insult to injury we forced every woman and girl to undergo medical inspection. . . . "

■

Heinrich Haape, a medical officer in the German advance, remembered an old Lithuanian outside his little farmhouse entertaining one evening with songs:

Some of the soldiers who had been listening to the old man took the opportunity to have a look at the inside of the farmhouse. The massive stone oven in the centre of the living room amused them; it was about twenty feet square. . . .

"Hey, Uncle!" called one of the soldiers.

"You must have a big family. Why do you want an oven as big as this?"

The old man smiled. . . . "Will you be in Russia this winter?" he asked in his thin voice.

"Perhaps."

"Then you will find out!"

■

Doctor Haape had seen the first snow fall on September 12 and was apprehensive:

But the rain continued—rain such as this part of Russia had never in living memory experienced at this time of year. . . . We marched on, but it got colder and colder and we were soaked through and depressed. The roads became quagmires and we thought bitterly of the winter clothing that had been promised us.

■

After surrender, a Russian soldier from the Ukraine who took part in the Kiev salient told a German officer:

If only you had come twenty years ago we should have welcomed you with open arms. But now it's too late. We were just beginning to get on our feet and now you arrive and throw us back twenty years. . . .

■

The Russians were justly proud of saving their factories. Too little of this story was told during the war—when it might have had a strong positive effect on many Allied home front workers whose feelings about Russia were ambivalent after so many years of being subjected to anti-Russian sentiments—particularly during the Russian-Finnish War. A Pravda *story told of one such nearly miraculous factory move:*

In most places where the new factories were located, living conditions were fearful, in many places food was very short, too. People worked because they knew that it was absolutely necessary—they worked twelve, thirteen, sometimes fourteen or fifteen hours a day; they "lived on their nerves"; they knew that never was their work more urgently needed than now. Many died in the process. All these people knew what losses were being suffered by

the soldiers, and they—in the "distant rear"—did not grumble much. . . .

■

Alexander Werth was able to see firsthand much of this enormous job of "rehousing" Russian industry as it moved to avoid the Germans—and he called it one of the "most stupendous organizational and human achievements of the Soviet Union during the war":

Winter had already come when Sverdlovsk received Comrade Stalin's order to erect two buildings for the plant evacuated from the south. The trains packed with machinery and people were on the way. The war factory had to start production in its new home—and it had to do so in not more than a fortnight. Fourteen days, and not an hour more! . . . Over the charts and blueprints, laid out on packing cases, the blizzard was raging. Hundreds of trucks kept rolling up with building materials. . . . On the twelfth day, into the new buildings with their glass roofs, the machinery, covered with hoar-frost, began to arrive. Braziers were kept alight to unfreeze the machines. . . . And two days later, the war factory began production.

■

With his Russian background, language skills, and sympathies, Alexander Werth was able to develop news sources that touched valuable and sensitive feelings in England:

The impression was that the Russians were rapidly learning all kinds of lessons, were dismissing as useless some of the prewar theories, which were wholly inapplicable to prevailing conditions, and that professional soldiers of the highest order were taking over the command from the Army "politicians" and the "civil war legends" like Budenny and Voroshilov was to be confirmed in the next few weeks.

■

Hitler, in a speech to the German people, carried nationwide on October 3:

I declare today and I declare it without reservation that the enemy in the East has been struck down and will never rise again.

■

General Guderian—in the mud and rain of the Russian autumn—saw it quite differently:

Wheeled vehicles . . . could only advance with the help of tracked vehicles. These latter were having to perform tasks for which they were not intended and rapidly wore out. . . . During the night of October 6 to 7 . . . the first snow of the winter fell. It did not lie long and, as usual, the roads rapidly became nothing but canals of bottomless mud, along which our vehicles could only advance at a snail's pace and with great wear to the engines.

■

When German medical officer Haape saw his first snow, he figured the winter gear was bound to come soon. He slogged on:

The black soil immediately dissolved the white flakes as if sucking them in, but as the later afternoon frost set in and snow fell more thickly, the countryside took on itself a white mantle. We watched it uneasily. . . .

■

General Blumentritt saw more difficulty than just winter. There was a troubling feel to the army:

Now, when Moscow itself was almost in sight, the mood both of commanders and troops changed. . . . One began to hear sarcastic references to the military leaders far away in Germany. The troops felt that it was high time our political leaders came and had a look at the front. . . .

■

But, Leonard Cooper pointed out, the "top political leader" in Berlin wouldn't have seen the need for the trip:

Since Hitler had believed that the campaign was over, he had ordered that industry at home cut down on its production of munitions. Only a trickle of replacements reached the fighting units. Winter was about to begin, but there was no sign of any winter clothing to be seen anywhere. . . .

■

Historian Ronald Seth interviewed survivors of the Russian campaign and found that the

men had no warning of what could happen in such severe weather:

Not only were the soldiers numbed all over but terrible things were beginning to happen to their bodies. All exposed limbs were attacked by frostbite, turned black and then became gangrenous within a few days, and there were no medicaments for their relief. Rifles became so cold that if a man picked his up with his bare hand, his hand stuck to it. . . .

■

General Guderian found by early fall that the combination of late summer rains and heavy travel by the trucks and tanks of both armies on the poor Russian roads had crippled the pace of the tankers' fabled speed at "lightning war":

Travelling along the now completely disintegrated Orel-Tula Road our vehicles could occasionally achieve a maximum speed of 12 miles per hour. There were no "fast-moving units" anymore. Hitler was living in a world of fantasy. . . . The combat strength of the infantry had sunk to an average of 50 men per company. . . . The supply situation was bad. Snow shirts, boot grease, underclothes and above all woollen trousers were not available. A high proportion of the men were still wearing denim trousers, and the temperature was eight below zero. . . . It is frightful, unimaginable. The people at the *OKH* and *OKW*, who have never seen the front, have no idea what the conditions here are like.

■

General Blumentritt reported trouble no one had anticipated:

By mid-November the mud period was over and the frost heralded the approach of winter. Tractors extricated the heavy artillery from the mud far behind the front and one gun after another was towed forward. It happened however that, in the process of dragging these guns out of the ground, into which many had become frozen fast, a number of them were literally torn to pieces.

■

Historian Leonard Cooper noted that "on December 2, reconnaissance units of the 258th

German Infantry Division penetrated the Moscow suburb of Khimi, and from there saw the spires of the Kremlin only five miles away. It was the most easterly point which the Wehrmacht was to reach." The German units had used up all their strength to do it and had nothing in reserve. General Blumentritt wrote of the halt:*

Field Marshal von Kluge now decided to call off the attack, which had become hopeless and which could only result in unnecessary casualties. . . . Within the next few days Marshal Zhukov was to launch the great Russian counter-offensive which began on December 6. . . .

Every soldier outside Moscow knew that this was a battle for life or death. If the Russians succeeded in defeating us here, there could be no hope.

■

On December 19, dissatisfied with his worn-out generals, Hitler took the step he had wanted an excuse to take for a long time, announcing:

This little matter of operational command is something which anyone can do. The task for the commander-in-chief of the army is to train the army in National Socialist ways. I know of no general who could do that as I want it done, so I have decided to take over command of the army myself.

■

Unwinterized vehicles were as useless as vehicles knocked out by the Red Army. General Blumentritt wrote:

The lubricant fluid of the artillery pieces froze, the mechanism of the machine guns froze. It was frequently impossible to open the breach. There was no glycerine nor fuel designed for use in the extreme cold. At night it was often necessary to keep small fires constantly burning underneath our tanks, lest the engines freeze and burst.

■

Guderian never hesitated to face up to Hitler when he thought it was a question of a bad tactical decision or the welfare of his men. Some of his fellow generals wondered how he got away with it. On December 26, falling back from Moscow, his luck ran out:

DAILY ARMY ORDER.

Soldiers of the Second Panzer Army!

The Führer and Supreme Commander of the Armed Forces has today relieved me of my command.

At this time when I am leaving you I remember our six months of battle together for the greatness of our land and the victory of our arms. . . . My thoughts will be with you in your hard struggle.

You are waging it for Germany! Heil Hitler!

(signed) GUDERIAN.

■

Alexander Werth, able to travel all along the Russian line during the war and to examine captured documents later, summed up the German effort to capture Moscow:

In the course of the second German offensive against Moscow (November 16 to December 5), says the [official Soviet] *History*, the German losses were: 55,000 dead, over 100,000 wounded and frostbitten, 777 tanks, 297 guns and mortars, 244 machine guns, over 500 tommy guns; this is a reasonable estimate, not greatly differing from the losses suggested, for instance, by Guderian. . . .

A characteristic of the fighting in winter conditions was the avoidance, as far as possible, of frontal attacks on the enemy's rear guard, and the formation of mobile pursuit units, calculated to cut the enemy's lines of retreat and create panic among them. Such pursuit units [were] comparable to the Cossacks of 1812, who mercilessly harassed the *Grande Armée*. . . .

■

Two German participants who were faithful notetakers, Haape and General Blumentritt, pictured the halt before Moscow:

If only the battle for Moscow had started fourteen days earlier, the city would now have been in our hands. Or even if the rains had held off for fourteen days. If—if—if. If Hitler had started "Barbarossa" six weeks earlier as originally planned; if he had left Mussolini on his own in the Balkans and had attacked Russia in May. . . .

A couple of days later our winter clothing arrived. . . . Sixteen greatcoats and sixteen

pairs of winter boots to be shared among a battalion of eight hundred men!

■

General Blumentritt described the retreat from the lines around Moscow:

Our retreating army marched against a backdrop of flame. Special "scorched-earth commandos" were organized to carry out Hitler's adaptation of Stalin's earlier policy.

Supplies were usually short. Only a few railways ran into the area behind the front. These were frequently cut by the partisans. The water froze inside the boilers of the engines, which were not built to withstand the Russian climate. Each engine could draw only half the normal number of wagons. . . . Yet in order to encourage the soldiers on the Eastern Front trainloads of red wine were shipped to us from France and Germany. . . . At forty degrees centigrade below zero, not an unusual temperature, it had often frozen in transit, burst its bottles, and all that remained were chunks of red ice.

■

Alexander Vinogradov, a Russian soldier in the winter offensive, left a note rolled up in a cartridge case and wedged in a tree trunk:

And now there are only three of us left. . . . We shall stand firm as long as there's any life left in us. . . . Now I am alone, wounded in my arm and my head. The number of tanks has increased. There are twenty-three. I shall probably die. Somebody may find my note and remember me; I am a Russian, from Frunze. I have no parents. Good-bye, dear friends. Your Alexander Vinogradov. 22.2.42.

■

When the German armies were stopped short of Moscow, most of the senior officers privately acknowledged that the war with Russia was lost. The official Soviet History of the Great Patriotic War *reported the winter 1942 campaign quite objectively, good results and bad:*

The moral effect even of the incomplete victory of the Red Army during the winter campaign of 1941–42 was enormous, and decisively strengthened the Soviet people's

faith in ultimate victory. . . .

Thanks to the Russian winter offensive, it was now possible to stop the evacuation of central-Russian industry to the east, which meant that the output of armaments and munitions in the Moscow area in particular could be resumed and intensified; in some cases, plants were brought back from the east.

■

Alexei Surkov, a Russian poet, published in 1941 a prose poem, "A Soldier's Oath," that predicted what would happen in the Russian victory over Germany:

Mine eyes have beheld thousands of dead bodies of women and children, lying along the railways and the highways. . . . Hitler the murderer and his hordes shall pay for these tears with their wolfish blood; for the avenger's hatred knows no mercy. . . .

■

Doctor Haape lived through the winter of 1941–42 and the retreat. His diary entries capsule the disaster of the ill-planned winter campaign. But already Hitler was deep in his planning of a great new summer offensive that would chew up more thousands of German and Russian lives—even though the professional soldiers of the German army all knew the war in Russia had probably been lost:

On 25 March . . . there was a three-hour thaw at midday. Then it became cold again and by evening a blizzard was raging across the wide snowfields . . . but on us, the brief thaw made a great impression—it was the first sign of the approach of a new spring.

And the next day our winter clothing arrived! Huge quantities of fur coats, woollens, fur-lined boots, thick overcoats—all of it collected from the civilians in Germany after a moving appeal to the nation by Goebbels in December. He had told the people at home that we were equipped with warm clothing—we had plenty of it—but it was impossible to have too much in a Russian winter. So the good folk in Germany had sacrificed . . . anything that looked vaguely as if it would keep out the Russian cold. . . . We should all have frozen to death had we not been able to shoot the enemy down and pillage their dead bodies to warm our own.

"Summer Soldiers," Fall 1941

When the invasion kicked off in June, western Russia was broiling under the sort of summer that usually brought rich grain harvests, and the German soldiers were equipped in light uniforms of field gray denim. But fall arrived, and the shipments of cold weather clothing were delayed until the more critical munitions and food for the advance could get through. Franz Eichhorst's *Soldiers* showed the results of the clothing shortage: blanket-clad German troopers occupying a soggy trench. It was a powerful picture—but powerful in the wrong direction for the Nazi propaganda machine. By the time the picture fell into Allied hands, along with a large collection of German war art, only a handful of Germans had been allowed to see it. (Captured German Art; U.S. Army Center of Military History)

Soviet Air Force Casualty, Summer 1941

One of Joseph Stalin's first requests of a British war aid commission that flew to Moscow shortly after the invasion began was for combat planes. Hundreds of Soviet craft like this light bomber painted by K. H. Dallinger, a German war artist, had been destroyed on the ground. Hitler had pulled major Luftwaffe units out of France, Belgium, Holland, and Norway for the attack on Russia. And they struck savagely. (Kaschin Bayerische)

Forerunner of Winter, Western Russia

Through the summer the Germans were moving with almost total air supremacy—which was fortunate. Thomas Scharff's painting shows the advancing columns, slowed by mud and rain, enormously vulnerable to air attack as they funneled down the few poor roads that existed. (Bayerische Staatsbibliothek)

The Invasion Slows, Fall 1941

German commanders found that the Russian maps were often almost useless. And purposely so: it was another Soviet tactic to confuse and delay the enemy. Roads and rail lines were indicated where none existed. In this terrain, old-fashioned cavalry came back into its own. In Hans Alart's *German Cavalry Patrol in Russia* (ABOVE) the soldiers pass the grave of a comrade. The real slowdown of the advance on Moscow came about when Hitler diverted units to the capture of Leningrad, a threat as a raiding base in the German rear. Helmut Georg painted *Fighting in a Pocket South of Lake Ladoga* (RIGHT). (Both, Captured German Art; U.S. Army Center of Military History)

New Lands for the Reich, Western Russia

A German trooper is sketched by O. H. Gerster, slogging through a heavily shelled village, clearly not concerned about a partisan ambush. (Captured German Art; U.S. Army Center of Military History)

A Sign of Stiffening Resistance, Fall 1941

The German medical corps had used the campaigns in Poland, Norway, and France, where the distances back to base hospitals had been relatively short, to hone its quick medical treatment of wounded. In the Russian advance, emphasis was placed on maximum treatment of the lightly wounded in the rear of the fighting zone. It got men back into action sooner, and also cut down on the demoralizing effect on German civilians of the long hospital trains returning to Germany. In Helmut Georg's painting (OPPOSITE) two comrades carry a wounded friend back to an aid post. (Captured German Art; U.S. Army Center of Military History)

Summer Sun, Russia, 1941

The reality of the war comes closer as Soviet resistance grows and stiffens. German infantry advances with tanks and scout cars pass dead animals bloating in the fierce summer sun. Karl Busch was the painter. (Captured German Art; U.S. Army Center of Military History)

Medics, via the Enemy

Red Army prisoners of war have been pressed into service here as stretcher-bearers. The work didn't last for long, but it was a welcome reprieve —since most prisoners had heard they would be shot at once. Long, bedraggled columns of POWs marched to the west, filthy and hungry. Prisoners were shot if they dropped and were often marched till that could happen; it served the Nazi purpose, too. Franz Eichhorst was the artist. (Captured German Art; U.S. Army Center of Military History)

Ambush Country

Friedhelm Froemer underscores the debris of the war that was the background of the fighting in Russia. Half-ruined buildings—as the sieges of Leningrad and Stalingrad conclusively proved— were often better fortifications than any number of Siegfried and Maginot lines. (Captured German Art; U.S. Army Center of Military History)

Harvesting Ahead of the Enemy, Ukraine, 1941

The German invaders intended to live off the captured land as much as they could. In addition, useful goods and machinery taken in Russia would be shipped westward to bolster Germany's economy. As long as there were new countries to conquer and strip, the German homeland prospered and Germans lived well. Mikhail Savitsky painted this moving scene (ABOVE), which he called *The Partisan Madonna,* of Soviet peasants pushing to harvest their crops under the guard of watchful militiamen. It was a crop the German army wanted, too. (Tretyakov Gallery)

Scorched Earth, Battered People: Western Russia

Stalin gave the drastic order to destroy everything wherever retreat was necessary. Vladimir Gavrilov painted these Russians (OPPOSITE) falling back before the invading Germans, titling it *For One's Native Land.* They probably had little to destroy, less to take with them, and there was no real plan about where they should go. (Russian Museum)

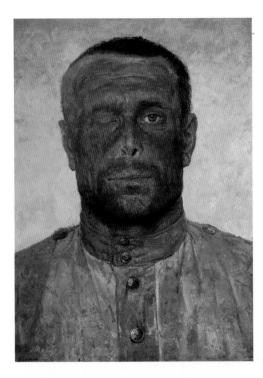

Spirit of a Hard-Pressed Army, Winter 1942

Geliy Korzhev captured this powerful portrait of a Soviet soldier (FAR LEFT), which he called *Traces of War*. This single image of defiance could stand for many. The Soviets lost more fighting men—and more civilians—than any other combatant nation in the war. G. Werner painted Mitka (NEAR LEFT), a boyish Soviet soldier captured by the Germans. Certain Russian units went into action in the summer of 1941 with some men—and boys—unarmed but charged with picking up a rifle as soon as it was dropped by a casualty. (Far left, Russian Museum; left, Captured German Art; U.S. Army Center of Military History)

Another Day . . . Or the Last Day, Spring 1942

Boris Nemenskiy gave his painting an ironic title: *A Breath of Spring*. It is a scene familiar to armies that fought on either side. The tanks are bivouacked in a grove of trees for protection against air spotters. The crews are just waking up in the misty spring dawn. The youngest—to whom the war is both wondrous and frightening—wakes up first. Veterans stay in their blankets until the last minute. By nightfall, all hands know, some of them may no longer be stretching out. Tankers in all the armies were drawn to stay near their "mounts" like old-time cavalrymen, and formed an odd affection for these cranky machines. (Russian Museum)

A Picture That Spoke to All Russia

Fyodor Bogorodsky called this universal tribute *Glory to the Fallen Heroes*. It was not painted until 1945, because in contrast to the assignments of artists in other national art programs, most Soviet painters went through the war with more immediate duties and could only get to their paintings—which tended to be heroic in size—toward the end of the war, inspired by their sketchbooks of wartime drawings. The dead hero is in the uniform of a Soviet sailor. A bemedaled Soviet admiral kneels in mourning. The hero's guard of honor is also a sailor, half hidden in the shadows. (Tretyakov Gallery)

Partisan Combat, Western Russia

Hitler's homicidal "Commissar Orders" and the ruthless programs the SS originated to terrorize the civilian population ultimately had just the opposite effect. Many areas behind the German lines turned into simmering resistance centers that were continually clashing with the invaders. Here Mikhail Savitsky, in a painting of violent combat in a bizarre setting (ABOVE), shows a Soviet detachment that has surprised a German patrol in a wheat field. Boris Shcherbakov painted a Russian soldier (OPPOSITE TOP) looking out over the land, which is burdened with the adornments of war: the broken timbers of a farm building, the naked chimney left from a burned house, and the dying smoke of another burned structure in the distance. Depending on the viewer, the sky is either threatening or hopeful. Shcherbakov opts for the latter, calling his picture *The Invincible Foot Soldier.* The Soviet Government wanted war paintings to give people a story they could understand, a goal they could cling to. And this the war art did. In 1941 and 1942, some Russians had little else for their battered hopes. (Both, USSR Ministry of Culture)

Arena of Giant Tank Battles, Western Russia, 1942

Piotr Krivonogov called this panoramic scene *On the Kursk Battlefield* (LEFT), and it was painted after the war from notes and sketches made there. The Russians faced the invasion in 1941 with tanks that had, over the years, made great newsreel films at May Day parades in Red Square. By the time the war broke out, many were old, slow, and undergunned. The first tank losses were heavy. By late 1942, American tanks coming through Lend-Lease would make up some of the deficit. And then the powerful Russian-designed and -built T-43 began to roll out of the factories that had been miraculously moved eastward to escape the Germans. (Central Museum of the Armed Forces)

Sevastopol, USSR, 1942

Until December 1941, heroic stands by Soviet fighting men—and women—became by necessity a frequent art theme. Aleksandr Deineka, in his painting *The Defense of Sevastopol, 1942,* depicts a Soviet navy shore detachment driving back German infantry. (Russian Museum)

Death March, Moscow, November 1941

On November 7, in preparation for going on the offensive, a grand parade was held in Red Square, reviewing units that would be involved. Konstantin Youn prepared this great painting of the event. It is likely that at the end of the war the survivors from the men on parade in this painting might have consisted of no greater number than compose the military band assembled at middle distance left. (Tretyakov Gallery)

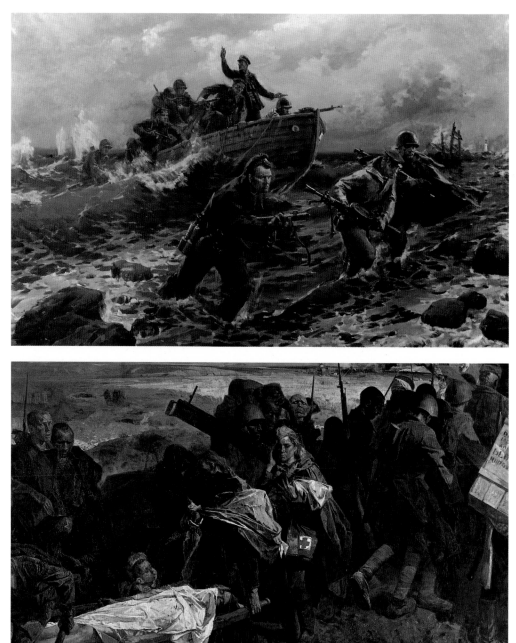

Total Resistance, Ukraine, Fall 1941

Viktor Puzirkov titled his painting depicting a spirited landing party of Soviet soldiers and sailors coming ashore on a raid *Black Sea People* (ABOVE). The picture could represent the resolve of the Russian fighting man to band together with any other resisters he could find and carry the war to the Germans as long as he was able. Soviet partisans followed a tradition of bringing out their wounded (BELOW) that was based perhaps as much on practicality as on honor. Capture by the Germans would likely end in death—but probably not before there had been a fierce attempt to force out information for tracking down the partisan band. Viktor Safronov called his painting *Hard Times*. (Above, Museum of Ukrainian Art; below, Union of Artists, USSR)

No Place for a Wounded Man, Winter 1942

An artist's sketchbook was his most valuable possession while at the front. G. Werner, a *Kriegsmaller* with the Panzers in Russia, collected the two vignettes at top left and on the opposite page for future work. The scenes in the railroad yard underscore the difficulties of operating in Russia: much of the track and almost all of the yard buildings are destroyed. Only the German hospital train is intact. The first snows are quickly banking up beside it, and it becomes a bleak place even for well men. Carefully censored letters kept Germans at home unaware for a time of the mounting casualties in the tough campaign on the Eastern Front. (Bavarian Army Museum)

Fall and Winter, 1941–42

Ernst Widmann sketched the infantryman (RIGHT) so heavily padded for winter that he was probably not able to function very well except to be present on the battlefield. The wounded officer (FAR RIGHT), sketched by G. Werner, has "liberated" his flapped fur hat from a Russian. (Right, Captured German Art; U.S. Army Center of Military History; Far right, Private Collection)

AM BAHNHOF
BATAISK

"Blackshirt" Brigade, Winter 1942

Alfonso Artioli, an Italian painter experienced in military subjects, caught up with the Italian soldiers in Russia in the winter of 1942—not a happy time. Here General Reverberi (ABOVE) climbs to the top of a tank to encourage his flagging troops, who are retreating with the Germans after they were stopped outside Moscow. Some of his Alpini soldiers still proudly wear the regimental felt cap with feather of the mountain men. (Museo Raccolte Storiche del Comune di Milano)

Rest for an Invader, Winter 1942

An Italian soldier (LEFT) finds a few minutes of commandeered shelter in the warmth of a Russian cottage, in this painting by Alfonso Artioli. (Museo Raccolte Storiche del Comune di Milano)

Where Was the Duce? Winter 1942

Andreoni painted machine gunners of the Italian rear guard covering a rickety bridge crossing. In the intense cold, a man touching the metal of a gun with his bare fingers would likely find them frozen there. (Museo Raccolte Storiche del Comune di Milano)

Escape from Leningrad—Defeat at Brest

Hard penalties of war settled equally on civilians and soldiers in the Soviet Union. Aleksei Prokonenko called his painting *Stalingrad Days and Nights* (ABOVE). Civilians are fleeing before the Germans with what little they can carry. Piotr Krivonogov has crowded into a massive canvas (BELOW) a moment in the struggle of *The Defenders of the Brest Fortress.* (Above, USSR Union of Artists; below, Aurora Publishers)

Short Commons, Leningrad, 1942

When the winter of 1942 closed down on Leningrad the only connection that city had with the rest of the Soviet Union was a tenuous supply line—the frozen surface of Lake Ladoga. The truck road, laid over the ice and used mostly at night, had to be changed almost every day to avoid the previous night's bomb craters. Also crossing where the ice was thickest was a shaky railroad track. Through these two lifelines came what few supplies got in. Mikail Larichev painted *Bread of the Blockade,* set under the dim light of a lamp made from a shell casing. (USSR Union of Artists)

Streetcar Soldiers, Leningrad, Winter 1942

I n 1914, French troops went to the Battle of the Marne in Paris taxicabs. In 1942, Russian defenders in the lines around Leningrad could "go to the front" in the city's trolley cars. Anatoley Smirnov captured the scene in *The Last Stop*. Russian soldiers and sailors are moving a heavy machine gun into a new position, after riding the cars to their new post in the defense line. (USSR Union of Artists)

The Red Army's Secret "Reserves," Leningrad, Winter 1942

The women of Leningrad helped dig a massive antitank ditch around the city's edge as the Germans approached—and then began 900 days of duty clearing the debris in the streets from the regular bombardments. In Boris Ugarov's painting *A Leningrad Woman in the Year 1941,* women haul salvaged steel girders from shell-wrecked buildings to a storage site. Across the way, soldiers head for duty on the perimeter. (Russian Museum)

The Battle of Stalingrad, Fall 1942

Dimitry Obozhenko painted an action in the Stalingrad campaign in the winter of 1942–43, *The Attack from the Oranienburg Bridgehead;* Soviets in white clothing blend with the snow-covered debris of the battlefield. (USSR Union of Artists)

The Protective Shambles of Stalingrad, Fall 1942

This Boris Ugarov painting (OPPOSITE) is simply titled *Stalingrad.* The wreckage of the city supplied more protection to the defenders than to the attackers. One of the bitterest lessons of this came when the Germans moved in to wipe out the Warsaw ghetto. What was planned in Warsaw as a simple "police sweep" turned into a full army operation in which the German commander once considered calling for an aerial bombardment. (USSR Union of Artists)

Outside Moscow, December 1941

Historian Leonard Cooper determined that on December 2 "units of the 258th Infantry Division penetrated the Moscow suburb of Khimi . . . and saw the spires of the Kremlin only five miles away." This farthest-east advance had exhausted the invasion, however. These SS soldiers (OPPOSITE), painted by W. F. Gebhardt and better equipped than most regular army units, gaze at country they'll never conquer. (Captured German Art; U.S. Army Center of Military History)

Forerunner of 1945 Germany

For five of the six years consumed by World War II, Germany waged war on other people's soil, with the wreckage taking place far from the Fatherland. But German soldiers often viewed the trials of Russian civilians—particularly village people—with sadness and sympathy. This devastated town (RIGHT) was painted by Hans Herbert Buschhuter, with obvious compassion, in 1942. By 1945, it could have been a scene in his own Germany. (Bayerische Staatsbibliothek)

Winter 1941–42, Russia's Coldest in Fifty Years

An artist with the German army, R. Hanzl, was struck—in the middle of this mechanized war—with the scene of German soldiers on fatigue duty drawing water through the ice of a frozen river, probably for army animals. (Captured German Art; U.S. Army Center of Military History)

Gerster's picture of this young German soldier (RIGHT), not very well clothed for winter, captured the loneliness of any picket for any army in any war. Civil War students may find it reminiscent of Winslow Homer's famous Civil War sketches. (Captured German Art; U.S. Army Center of Military History)

For This Soldier, "The War Is Over," Winter 1942 and 1943

Latvian partisans carry off their wounded on a hastily built litter (ABOVE). If the man was badly hurt, his chances for recovery were slim. Most doctors had been taken by the Red Army. Local care outside the larger towns was minimal and drugs were virtually nonexistent. Gunar Mitrevits was the painter. (USSR Union of Artists)

Russians Learning of "The New Order"

Sergei Gerasimov's painting titled *Partisan Mother* (RIGHT) may reflect a symbolic occurrence as well as a specific incident. But it probably served as harsh propaganda when it was painted in 1943, with the pregnant Russian woman about to receive Nazi indoctrination. (Tretyakov Gallery)

Also "The Workers' War," Moscow, 1941–45

Polish-born artist Feliks Topolski, who covered much of the globe on his assignments for the British War Artists Scheme, traveled to Russia in a Murmansk convoy to see what Allied aid was accomplishing. Here he sketched *The Military Training of Moscow Factory Workers* marching in close order through the factory gate, which is topped with a portrait of Lenin. The workers could claim a strong military tradition that began in the 1917 Russian Revolution. (Imperial War Museum)

A Folk Hero at the Front, Western Russia, Winter 1943

The painting *Rest after Battle* became a great favorite with Soviet soldiers because the storyteller in the center of the group represents a Russian folk character who joked his way through tight situations. The artist subtly makes the point that the Red Army was well equipped for winter fighting—in contrast to the Germans. The Soviet knowledge of how to fight a winter war came the hard way, in the war with Finland. When Germany invaded Russia, some German officers anticipated fighting "a 1939 Russian Army." They faced instead an army that had learned by its mistakes. U. M. Neprintsev was the painter. (Tretyakov Gallery)

St. Anthony's Lighthouse, Newfoundland, John Platt (National Maritime Museum)

In the Atlantic, German submarine raiders—first adventurous single boats and then "wolf packs" that attacked convoys from all sides at once—owned the ocean from 1939 though much of 1943, eventually sinking ships even in sight of American shores. Russia's need for materiel to resist the German invasion created the "Arctic Run" to Archangel and isolated Murmansk, the only ice-free port in the USSR during the winter. The Arctic convoys had to run the gauntlet of German air attacks from fields all along the coast of Norway and were exposed to the threat of submarines and surface ships darting out of the fjords.

But there were some bright spots: the British sank the brand-new battleship *Bismarck*—but not until after *Bismarck* had blown up HMS *Hood,* "the most powerful ship in the world." British, American, and Canadian shipyards pushed crash production of newly designed subhunters: corvettes, frigates, and destroyer escorts. But it was not until late spring 1943 that Allied U-boat "kills" became, for the first time, greater than the output of German U-boat building yards. It was then, Adm. Karl Dönitz would say later, that he knew Germany had lost the Battle of the Atlantic.

The twenty-five days that elapsed between Churchill's elevation to prime minister and the end of the evacuation of Dunkirk set the scene for the sustained sea action that some historians were coming to regard as "the greatest struggle of the war"—the Battle of the Atlantic. Historian Dan van der Vat established the odds against Britain:

"Operation Dynamo," whereby a third of a million British and French troops were rescued from Dunkirk, became the greatest evacuation of them all. Another 200,000 troops were brought back from French ports farther south in "Operation Aerial." The main naval burden of these dashing salvage operations fell on destroyers, already diminished by Norway. The Royal Navy was left with forty-three battleworthy destroyers and fifty-one under repair in home waters. With the coast of Europe from the North Cape to the Pyrenees under German control, Britain now faced the double threat of invasion and of rapid intensification of the enemy submarine campaign against the transatlantic trade route.

■

The popular image of German fighting men reacting to the start of World War II is of tigers straining to be unleashed. Werner Schuaneman, one of the crew of the new German cruiser Emden *(named for a famous World War I raider), experienced it differently:*

We were assembled aft and the *Emden*'s Executive Officer told us that England had declared war on Germany. It was not a happy moment. We recalled that our fathers had told us how they cheered on the declaration of war, but nobody knew now what to say. We all thought, "Now we're in a mess."

■

The agreements of the Hague Convention were "humane" ones . . . and their very "humaneness" worked against the tactics that could make submarine warfare its most effective. The Hague Prize Laws said:

It is illegal to sink a ship without having first placed passengers, crew and ship's papers in a place of safety. For this purpose the ship's boats are not regarded as a place of safety unless the safety of the passengers and crew is assured in existing seas and weather conditions by the proximity of land or the presence of another merchant vessel which is in a position to take them on board.

■

When hostilities were first declared, German U-boats were directed by the German Foreign Ministry to "stick to the rules." A signal was sent to U-boats:

Troop ships and merchant ships carrying military equipment are to be attacked in accordance with the Prize Regulations of the Hague Convention. Enemy convoys are to be attacked without warning on condition that all passenger liners carrying passengers are allowed to proceed in safety.

■

On this and the following two pages are quotes gathered by Terry Hughes and John Costello telling of the bitter sea war. But on Sunday, September 3, the day England declared war on Germany, the 14,000-ton Donaldson liner Athenia *was headed west in the Atlantic, bound for New York. Her captain had assured her passengers, including a number of Americans, that noncombat ships had nothing to fear from submarine attack. Around 7:30 P.M. she crossed the patrol of a U-boat, which had received at 11 A.M. that morning the general order: "To Commanders afloat: Great Britain and France have declared war on Germany." Tom Connally, with his wife and three sons, was grateful to be getting away from war-threatened Europe and heading back home to New York:*

We were all in our stateroom, but the youngest child was in bed, when without warning the explosion occurred. Without being told, we realized what had happened.

■

Josef Goebbels tried to sell the world the story that the liner had actually been sunk by a British submarine as part of a British plot to draw America into the war. All U-boat captains were warned by a signal signed by Hitler. The next day the steamer Royal Sceptre *was stopped by a sub in the Bay of Biscay, and executive officer Reinhard Suhren told of the problem of trying to follow some of "the rules":*

We let the people get off into their lifeboats and then torpedoed the ship. Minutes later another vessel had been spotted, the British steamer *Browning*. Schultze asked me what we ought to do: "Let the people get off and then sink this ship?" It was a difficult decision, for *Royal Sceptre*'s lifeboats were many hundreds of miles out in the Atlantic with little hope of rescue. The *Browning*'s crew were abandoning ship and people were already in the lifeboats. . . . We told the officers [of the *Browning*] to take their boats back to their ship, then to pick up the survivors from the *Royal Sceptre*. We made one condition: they were not to use their wireless.

■

Escorting convoys in World War I had been handled at first most effectively by destroyers—but later it was decided their speed, gun, and firepower was superfluous. So the Allies experimented with smaller escorts: subchasers. In the fall of 1941, with Britain's destroyer fleet hard hit, Churchill took the lesson of World War I and called for the construction of "corvettes," scaled up from the design of rugged, sea-kindly whalecatchers. Almost 300 would be built and they would account for fifty U-boat "kills." Churchill was realistic about their aesthetic appeal to old Royal Navy salts:

These will be deemed the "Cheap and Nasties" (cheap to us, nasty to the U-boats). These ships, being built for a particular but urgent job, will no doubt be of little value to the Navy when that job is done—but let us get the job done.

■

After the fall of Poland, when Hitler had extended an offering of peace to Britain and France, Chamberlain rejected it, saying that after all "it was no longer possible [for the world] to rely on the unsupported word of the German Government." Hitler was furious, and the daring U-boat sinking of the Royal Oak *in Scapa Flow served to show his anger. U-boat commander Gunther Prien described the attack:*

The whole bay is lit up. . . . Two battleships are lying at anchor, and, further inshore, destroyers. Cruisers not visible, therefore attack on the big fellows. Distance apart 3,000 metres. Estimated depth 7.5 metres. Impact firing.

0116: One torpedo fired on the northern ship, two on southern. . . . A torpedo detonates on the northern ship; of the other two nothing is to be seen.

0121: Torpedo fired from stern; in the bow, both tubes are loaded; *three torpedoes from the bow.* After three tense minutes come the detonations on the nearer ship. There is a loud explosion, roar and rumbling. . . . The harbour springs to life. Destroyers are lit up, signalling starts on every side, and on land 200 metres away from me, cars roar along the roads.

■

Arming merchant ships was a controversial move. It certainly gave U-boat skippers every excuse to torpedo without warning. Sometimes the freighters showed a real ability to fight back—with both guns and guile. Capt. Ernest Coultas won a round with the SS Clan MacBean *in the Bay of Biscay:*

I maneuvered the ship, which is very responsive to her helm, so as to continually point at the submarine, following each of her turns—or rather anticipating them—with the net result that, although the submarine was feinting, I constantly managed to close her. . . . The submarine opened fire with her gun, firing three rounds but registering no hits. . . . When we had closed to within 100 feet of the U-boat she realized the danger of being rammed and dived. She apparently left the gun crew in the water, for almost immediately after we heard loud cries of distress.

■

When the convoy system went into effect, each one was assigned a Royal Navy officer as "Convoy Commodore," usually sailing on one of the merchantmen. There was traditional antagonism between the naval officers and the merchant captains—which grudgingly turned to respect on both sides, as Rear Adm. Kenelem Creighton acknowledged:

The masters struck me on first acquaintance as being ordinary, unpretentious people, but I soon found that there was something which set them apart from their contemporaries ashore, a compact, self-contained, confident and calm simplicity. . . .

■

The British merchant marine had languished between wars. World War II started with Britain having 2,000 ships less than she had in 1918—and a population four times greater. Storekeeper Urban Peters told of the antiquity of a passenger ship he was assigned to just after she had been taken out of retirement:

We had a gun mounted aft which was just about the most antiquated thing I had seen up to then. It was a Japanese 4.7″ which was laid and trained by hand. Directly underneath the mounting was the crew galley. . . . When they had practice firing the galley funnel would get blocked with coal smoke. . . .

■

Peters experienced one of the strange incongruities of war when his ship moored alongside a German ship in a port in neutral Chile:

The amazing thing was that, instead of clashes between the two rival seamen, we all used to go aboard each other's ships, sampling the beer and having a good time. Valparaiso was full of Germans, including the crew of a training ship manned by cadets. . . . The whole thing seemed ludicrous at the time.

■

In late 1939, under cover of the worst winter weather in forty years, the Germans began massive sowing of mines off the English coast. The ships the mines began to sink gave Admiral Dönitz a "cover" for unrestricted U-boat sinkings—they could be blamed on British mines. Dönitz ordered:

You are to sink *without warning* all ships in those waters near the enemy coast in which the use of mines is possible.

. . . We must be hard in this war. The enemy started the war in order to destroy us, and thus nothing else matters.

■

In The Battle of the Atlantic *Terry Hughes and John Costello wrote of the gradual introduction of food rationing. The British made it a point of pride that all during the war, its citizens ate better than the Germans. In fact,*

at the end of the war Britons were in better health than ever in history:

By January 1940 only ham, bacon, butter, eggs and sugar had been restricted to 4 ozs. per adult per week. The Home Secretary confidently told the nation "this is only a precautionary measure as there is no real shortage of either. Whereas in Germany weekly rations are: meat 1½ lbs., fat 8 ozs., sugar 8 ozs., milk 2 pints, tea ¾ oz. a month. Coffee, tapioca, clothes, soap, boots, shoes and lighting are all rationed."

■

When the submarine warfare zone was extended to 100 miles off the shores of Britain and France, Hitler specifically ordered that U.S. ships and those of the "friendly neutrals"—Italy, Japan, and Russia—should not be fired on. Nevertheless, Captain Ohrn of the U-37 described his attack on a freighter —without too much concern about her nationality:

The distance apart is narrowing. The steamship draws in quickly, but the position is still 40–50. I cannot see the stern yet. Tube ready. Shall I or not? The gunnery crews are also prepared. On the ship's side a yellow cross in a small square, dark blue ground. Swedish? Presumably not. I raise the periscope a little. Hurrah, a gun at the stern, an A/A gun or something similar. Fire! It cannot miss.

■

After the fall of France, Admiral Dönitz, a top scoring U-boat ace from World War I (who had a son who was a submariner in World War II), ran Germany's submarines. He chose Paris as his base of operations—but not for its glitter. It was closer to Atlantic U-boat bases. Dönitz's staff captain, Meckel, described a dedicated man:

Only on special occasions would he stay up late and go to the Opéra or celebrate his birthday or [present] an award to one of the senior commanders. . . . If an alarm occurred or a convoy came under attack and we happened to be out during the evening, couriers would arrive to bring him and the staff back to the operations room.

■

Dönitz fumed at Hitler's reluctance to order maximum submarine construction during the period of "The Happy Time" successes. The admiral was usually operating only fifteen to twenty boats at sea at any one time. And his total long-range fleet was limited to about forty. Though they now sailed out of French Atlantic ports, giving them more "hunting" time, there were still more good targets than the submarines could attack. Dönitz kept the pressure on the skippers, urging them to stay on the surface during an attack, so they could stay "in command." In the late summer of 1940, he ordered a new tactic of night attacks on the surface. U-boat commander Sclepke delighted in the confusion he could cause his enemies:

About 175 miles from Bloody Foreland, the British SS *Hartismere* was struck on the starboard side underneath the bridge. One minute later the Commodore's ship, the SS *Dalblair,* was torpedoed amidships on her starboard side and sank in 10 minutes. . . . HMS *Gleaner* sighted the explosion and tried to cross ahead of the convoy, narrowly avoiding collision with several ships, which without any commodore and without any orders were scattering in all directions at full speed.

■

Fighting the isolationists, President Roosevelt responded with a unique concept for helping Britain, hatched by a group of unofficial "legal thinkers." It was not going to be the all-out gift Churchill had been looking for— but when adjusted slightly, it set the pattern for a massive flow of U.S. goods to all the Allies. Roosevelt cabled Churchill:

It is my belief that it may be possible to furnish to the British Government as immediate assistance at least fifty destroyers [in return] for the use of Newfoundland, Bermuda, the Bahamas, Jamaica, St. Lucia, Trinidad and British Guiana as naval and air bases by the United States.

■

The success of the night surface attacks on convoys encouraged Dönitz to the deadliest tactic of all: the Rudeltakit—*"wolf pack." It carried a high risk in that he committed multiples of his small fleet of U-boats to one area where a heavy determined escort might de-*

stroy several of them at once. On October 17, 1940, the City of Benares, *carrying some British children on their way to wartime foster homes in America, was torpedoed by a lone U-boat. More than seventy of the children perished; thirteen survived. Fourth Officer Cooper, commanding one of the ship's lifeboats, which saved six of the children, told a story that touched the world:*

Our boat now contained six children, two escorts, one passenger, one cadet, one seaman gunner, the asst. steward, one naval signalman, thirty-two natives and myself. . . . As daylight came I had the canvas hood rigged forward for the children who were quite snugly wrapped in blankets of which there was an ample supply in the boat. . . . At noon I put all the occupants of the boat on food and water rations, detailing the assistant steward to serve out the allotted quantities. . . . About 2 P.M. the flying-boat . . . appeared and dropped a parcel containing food, also a note telling us that assistance was on the way. At about 4:30 P.M. we sighted a destroyer coming guided by the plane. . . . All the children were in good form having, I think, looked upon the whole thing as a picnic. . . . We had already traveled 200 miles and were still 400 miles from land when picked up.

■

Reports by the U-boat skippers—who were certainly not modest about their successes— often made it seem as if the wolf packs were toying with the escort ships. U-boat commander Kretschmer wrote:

0015: Three destroyers, line abreast, approach the ship we torpedoed, searching the vicinity. I went off at full speed on a southwesterly course and very soon regained contact with the convoy. Torpedoes from other boats exploding all the time. The destroyers are at their wits' ends, shooting off star shells the whole time to comfort themselves and each other.

■

A few hours later, the same wolf pack intercepted another incoming convoy of forty-nine ships with a heavier escort. Nine ships were lost to the U-boats. Merchant seaman James Lee was on one of those lost, SS Uganda:

We were thrown about all over the place [by the torpedo explosions] and when we pulled ourselves together we discovered to our horror that all the boats were missing, except one, and it was more by luck than judgment that we managed to get away and clear the ship. . . . About dawn a sloop arrived and stopped. It was a job getting aboard with the rise and fall of the boats. . . . When we got aboard we discovered that . . . she was loaded with so many survivors that she was down by the head.

■

Author (and officer on a naval escort ship) Nicholas Monsarrat knew the quick, "clean" explosion of a torpedo—but also the obscene mess that followed it all:

The first thing you notice when a ship goes down is the hateful smell of oil on the water. . . . But there is always an amazing amount of stuff left on the surface—crates, planks, baulks of wood, coaldust, doors, rope ends, odd bits of clothing—a restless smear of debris, looking like a wrecked jumble sale, on which the searchlight plays. Here and there lights may be flickering: too often they are not the ships you are hoping for, but empty rafts with automatic calcium flares attached to them, burning uselessly, mute witnesses to disaster. . . .

■

For some time, the British had run regular photo reconnaissance flights over the Norwegian fjords near Bergen, checking for any movement of the great new German battleship Bismarck *and a heavy cruiser anchored there. On the morning of May 22, the weather was bad and the flight was not possible. By late afternoon the forecast was showing improvement. A scout flight left the Orkney Islands and streaked low across the North Sea for a look at the German anchorages. That night, Churchill cabled Roosevelt:*

Yesterday, twenty-first, *Bismarck, Prinz Eugen,* and eight merchant ships located in Bergen. Low clouds prevented air attack. Tonight [we find] they have sailed. We have reason to believe a formidable Atlantic raid is intended. Should we fail to catch them going out, your Navy should surely be able to mark them down for us.

■

Burkard Freiherr von Müllenheim-Rechberg was a German naval officer aboard Bismarck, *in charge of fire control of the after guns. He wrote of the ship's first cruise and last battles in* Battleship Bismarck. *In the quotations that follow, where no other speaker is identified, the recollections are those of von Müllenheim-Rechberg. The* Bismarck *was picked up by British cruisers off the Greenland ice and was shadowed by radar. Then the Germans sighted big ships—clearly British—and they seemed to be closing in rapidly for a fight:*

The British ships were turning slightly to port, the lead ship showing an extremely long forecastle and two heavy twin turrets. On the telephone I heard Albrecht shout, "The *Hood*—it's the *Hood*!" It was an unforgettable moment. There she was, the famous warship, once the largest in the world, that had been the "terror" of so many of our war games. Two minutes had gone by since the British opened fire. Lindemann [the *Bismarck* captain] could restrain himself no longer and he was heard to mutter to himself, "I will not let my ship be shot out from under my ass." Then, at last, he came on the intercom and gave the word, "Permission to fire!" . . . The *Bismarck* was in action, and the rumble of her gunfire could be heard as far away as Reykjavik, the capital of Iceland. . . .

■

Bismarck's *navigator witnessed their gunnery closing in:*

"Straddling," boomed out of the loudspeaker. . . . Suddenly, the *Hood* split in two, and thousands of tons of steel were hurled into the air. More than a thousand men died.

■

Bismarck *had taken two hits forward that let 2,000 tons of water into the hull and isolated 1,000 tons of fuel forward so it could not be used. Now speed had to be reduced and the ship was down by the bow and handled sluggishly. Then Adm. Günther Lütjens ordered a course that was clearly for refuge in a French port:*

Before long a British Sunderland flying boat began cruising back and forth over our

wake, beyond the range of our antiaircraft guns. It notified the *Suffolk* that we were trailing oil and kept her informed of the situation. . . . Throughout the morning of the twenty-fourth the *Suffolk* and *Norfolk* hung on and around noon the *Prince of Wales* . . . renewed contact at extreme range. . . .

Some things we did not even have to wonder about. If for no other reason than to make up for the shame of losing the *Hood*, the British would do everything they possibly could to bring an overwhelming concentration of powerful ships to bear on us. How many and which would they be?

■

Late in the evening of May 24, "Swordfish" torpedo-carrying aircraft from HMS Victorious *found* Bismarck. *These antiquated biplanes, each carrying a crew of three, were called "Stringbags" by Fleet Air Arm pilots. They looked pathetically vulnerable:*

Now and again one of our 38-centimeter turrets and frequently our 15-centimeter turrets fired into the water ahead of the aircraft, raising massive waterspouts. To fly into one of those spouts would mean the end. . . . Incredibly, the pilots pressed their attack with suicidal courage, as if they did not expect ever again to see a carrier. . . . All at once the sharp, ringing report of an explosion punctuated the roar of our guns and the *Bismarck* gave a slight shudder. . . . Although I silently cursed what I supposed was a torpedo hit, my immediate reaction was that it had not done much harm. . . .

■

After the war, von Müllenheim-Rechberg found out about the stunned British reaction to the loss of the Hood:

Within six hours of the loss of the *Hood*, the British had deployed against us four battleships, two battle cruisers, two aircraft carriers, three heavy cruisers, ten light cruisers, and twenty-one destroyers. And so there began a chase which, in terms of the area involved (more than a million square nautical miles) and the number and strength of the ships engaged, is perhaps unique in naval history.

■

The critical sighting came from an American-built Catalina patrol boat of RAF Coastal Command Squadron 209, piloted by one British RAF officer and one U.S. naval aviator. The Catalina was one of a group sent to England through "lend-lease," and the American was one of seventeen pilots secretly sent with them to help indoctrinate British crews:

Suddenly, around 1030, a call came from the bridge, "Aircraft to port!" "Aircraft alarm!" All eyes turned in the direction indicated and a flying boat was indeed clearly visible for a few seconds before it disappeared into the thick, low-lying clouds. As soon as it reappeared we opened well-directed antiaircraft fire. . . . For a while, the bridge considered sending our Arado planes up against the Catalina. But because of the risks that would be incurred in recovering the float planes in such heavy seas, Lindemann would not allow them to be launched.

■

On board the Bismarck, *the Germans had watched an airplane with fixed landing gear shadow them after they had driven off the Catalina. The presence of the fixed-gear plane indicated it came from a carrier. When there had been no carrier attack in almost eight hours, they had become more hopeful; then:*

Antique-looking Swordfish, fifteen of them, seemed to hang in the air, near enough to touch. The high cloud layer, which was especially thick directly over us, probably did not permit a synchronized attack from all directions, but the Swordfish came so quickly after one another that our defense did not have it any easier. . . .

The attack must have been almost over when it came; an explosion aft. My heart sank. I glanced at the rudder indicator. It showed "left 12 degrees." Did that just happen to be the correct reading at that moment? No. It did not change. It stayed at "left 12 degrees." Our increasing list to starboard soon told us that we were in a continuous turn.

■

The Bismarck *crew had drilled for the full range of emergencies, including rigging to steer with a hand-controlled rudder yoke. But now, the violent slosh of sea water and oil in* the steering plant compartment made it impossible for the men to rig the emergency rudder yoke. Other solutions were improvised:

One working party volunteered to take off the hangar door and weld it to the starboard side of the stern at a 15-degree angle, which would correspond to a rudder position of 12 degrees. The thought was that this would counteract the effect of the rudders jammed in the port position and make it easier to steer with the propellers. But this plan, too, was rejected because of the bad weather. Sometime after midnight, the word spread that work on the rudder had ceased. . . .

■

Morale on the Bismarck hit bottom on the "dog watch"—midnight to 4 A.M.—when word spread that the rudders could not be fixed:

The older men took the news as a sentence of death for ship and crew. Everyone had to find his own way of dealing with the inevitable.

Later in the night permission was given for everyone to help himself to anything he wanted. This was a clear sign that the ship's command knew the end had come. And the men, above all the young ones, clung more than ever to the radio signals from home, to the promised help, the planes, the U-boats, the tanker, and the ocean tugs.

■

Later an order came from the bridge for Chief Engineer Junack:

"All engines stop." When some time passed and no other order came, Junack began to fear that, after the strains of the past hours, the turbines might be warped by heat expansion. . . . Junack requested an order from the captain for "ahead slow," and was greeted with the reply, "Ach, do as you like." That was not the Captain Lindemann Junack knew.

■

The British suspected they had critically damaged Bismarck's ability to maneuver—but could not be sure; their assumption came from studying her erratic courses, which had

no tactical point. So the British moved in for the final blows. Admiral Tovey sent a final signal to King George V:

To K.G.V. The sinking of the Bismarck may have an effect on the war as a whole out of all proportion to the loss to the enemy of one battleship. May God be with you and grant you victory. JT 26/5/41.

■

HMS Rodney delivered a series of salvos that were supposed to finish Bismarck:

In Bismarck's foretop Schneider was giving orders in his usual, calm voice. He announced that our target was the Rodney, which was off our port bow and heading straight for us. Then, to the ship's command, "Main and secondary batteries ready, request permission to fire." But it was the Rodney that got off the first salvo, at 0847. . . .

■

Some years after the battle, von Müllenheim-Rechberg examined British action reports:

To Tovey it appeared almost incredible that the Bismarck was still afloat. The knowledge that German long-range bombers or German U-boats might appear at any moment made the urgency of sinking her ever more pressing. Moreover, his flagship and the Rodney were running alarmingly low on fuel. Repeatedly he urged Patterson [aboard Rodney]: "Get closer, get closer—I can't see enough hits."

■

It was not until "abandon ship" had been ordered and von Müllenheim-Rechberg was free to leave his battle station in the aft fire control director that he could see all the punishment Bismarck had taken:

The antiaircraft guns and searchlights that once surrounded the after station had disappeared without a trace. Where there had been guns, shields, and instruments, there was empty space. The superstructure decks were littered with scrap metal. There were holes in the stack, but it was still standing. . . .

"Clear ship for scuttling." That was the last order given aboard the Bismarck. . . . Five junior officers and several hundred men were gathered around the after turrets, getting ready to go over the side. . . . A curtain of flame amidships hid from view what was forward of it. All I could see were some dead and wounded scattered about the deck. Our ensign still flew from the mainmast but sea water was spilling over the quarterdeck in the brilliant sunshine and the ship was sinking ever deeper. There was no doubt that the Bismarck was slowly capsizing. . . . Men were running back and forth, trying to find a way of saving themselves. But the service boats, life rafts, and floats had all been long since destroyed. Amid all the devastation on the upper deck, I saw wounded men lying on stretchers. . . . The doctors were scurrying around giving them sedatives. . . . The only thing that could be done for such numbers was relieve their pain by giving them morphine. None of those who really knew what feats were accomplished in the dressing stations and at the collection points lived to tell the story. . . .

"It's that time," I said, "inflate your life jackets, prepare to jump." Just as earlier it was vital not to go over the side too soon, now, it was vital not to delay so long that we would be sucked down with the ship when she finally sank. "A salute to our fallen comrades," I called. We all snapped our hands to our caps, glanced at the flag, and jumped. . . .

When swimmers close to the bow of the ship looked back, they saw Lindemann standing on the forecastle in front of turret Anton. His messenger, a seaman, was with him. . . . Lindemann's gestures showed that he was urging his messenger to go overboard and save himself. The man refused and stayed with his commanding officer until they reached the jackstaff. . . . There [the captain] stopped and raised his hand to his white cap.

The Bismarck now lay completely on her side. Then, slowly, slowly, she and the saluting Lindemann went down. Later a machinist wrote, "I always thought such things happened only in books, but I saw it with my own eyes." The time was 1039.

Convoy Under Attack

Alfred Leete, a Canadian painter, showed these ships under attack by a surface raider. The big, clumsy personnel rafts, which were often hung on slides in the rigging so they could be tripped into the water on either side of the ship, have drifted away from the burning vessel. The convoy plows on—perhaps having been ordered to scatter, a last-resort tactic to save at least some vessels from the raider's guns. Hitler saw his battleships, pocket battleships, and battle cruisers primarily in the "raider" role, not as squaring off against British capital ships. (Canadian War Museum)

U-Boat War: Opposing Views

Anton Otto Fischer was a famous—and very senior—German-born American maritime painter when the war broke out. But before long he was recording the war at sea from the decks of U.S. Coast Guard cutters. Fischer knew how tough merchant sailors could be. These sailors (ABOVE) have lost their ship. But now they would try to sail their way in—and some of them did. The British public delighted in David-versus-Goliath encounters. And when a wheezy North Sea trawler of the Royal Navy Reserve forced a German U-boat to surrender (RIGHT), it made the perfect picture for Charles Pears. A pulling boat has put off, for a chance at U-boat code books. The chance was slim. But in May 1941 the British destroyer *Bulldog* did force the *U-110* to the surface and captured intact a German Enigma encoding machine. The discovery was kept absolutely secret. (Above, U.S. Coast Guard Art Collection; below, National Maritime Museum)

U-Boat War: Victory and Hum-Drum

Norman Wilkinson painted an escort pair that has forced a sub to the surface with depth charges (ABOVE). The angle at which the sub's bow has popped up suggests that it will sink back without the crew escaping. Anton Otto Fischer painted this scene (BELOW) from the deck of the big Coast Guard cutter *Campbell,* as the escorts bird-dog the ships together after a night of attacks and confusion. (Above, National Maritime Museum; below, U.S. Coast Guard Art Collection)

Torpedoed!

Canadian artist Paul Goranson's ship was torpedoed in passage. But the crew was able to get a boat launched in the stormy North Atlantic, and after rescue, the artist painted the incident (ABOVE). Merchant seamen were sometimes the target of criticism for their "war zone bonuses." But on that night they showed Goranson what being an "able-bodied seaman" really meant. This scene (LEFT) by Tom Lovell hangs in the U.S. Merchant Marine Academy at Kings Point, New York. The title is *O'Hara: the Last Five Shells,* and it shows a U.S. Merchant Marine hero who took over when the navy armed guard crew of his ship was gunned down, manning their gun until the end. (Above, Canadian War Museum; left, U.S. Merchant Marine Academy)

Rammed!

U-boat skippers were taught various ruses to make a convoy escort on the surface think the sub had been hit far below and was going down. But lethal damage could force a U-boat to the surface to try to fight it out—or surrender. H. Beaument painted one that came up to fight but surfaced in the path of the Canadian corvette *Ville de Quebec,* which rammed and sunk her. The impact threw overboard one of the gun crew rushing through the conning tower to man the deck gun. (Canadian War Museum)

Lifeboat, North Atlantic

First choice for abandoning ship in the icy North Atlantic were the ships' regular life-boats, kept stocked for the emergency. But they could be hard to get over in rough weather. Canadian artist Jack Nichols painted this crew that got a boat launched, bringing off a few blankets and heavy gear. But what survivors often thought to bring were capricious choices made under pressure: 500 cigarettes but no jacket; two suits worn one on top of the other, but no duffle coat. (Canadian War Museum)

The Middle of the Atlantic

Britain went into the Battle of the Atlantic dangerously short of destroyers for the convoys. As an emergency procedure, the British and Canadians arranged a mid-Atlantic "hand over" procedure—with Royal Canadian Navy destroyers, like the bucking little ship that Rowley P. Murphy painted (ABOVE RIGHT), bringing convoys from North America to that point. There they met a west-bound convoy out of England that took them to North America. (Canadian War Museum)

A Raft in the Atlantic

The conventional lifeboats that merchant ships carried could, if safely launched, give a knowledgeable crew a chance at survival. But getting them launched in stormy weather was chancy. Soon, merchant ships became equipped with assorted rafts that could slide off a sinking ship or, if cut loose, would even float free. H. Beaument painted crew members (BELOW RIGHT) of an escort ship watching their vessel go down from a hastily launched "Carley Raft." (Canadian War Museum)

Night Action, North Atlantic, Winter 1942

At night, U-boats could run relatively safely on the surface, and with their eighteen-knot speed they could catch a convoy, getting good position for attack. Anton Otto Fischer did these paintings: first, a Coast Guard cutter throwing depth charges from a "Y-gun" to bracket a submarine (ABOVE); then the unsuccessful result of the cutter's defense—a ship hit and burning (LEFT). When the Germans developed "wolf packs," or multiple U-boat attacks, the subs could often overwhelm convoy escorts and sink as many as twelve to fifteen ships in a single night. (Both, U.S. Coast Guard Art Collection)

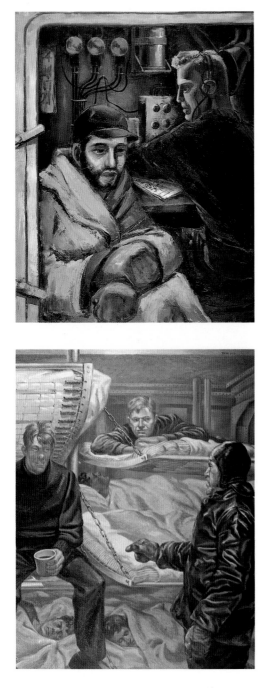

Convoy Life

These three pictures show the wet, cold, uncomfortable life on the North Atlantic. Upper left, Canadian artist Tom Wood painted the radio shack of a merchant ship, with a messenger standing by and hoping no wireless came in that had to be taken to the bridge. Above, Wood captured the officers' wardroom of the tiny Canadian corvette *Drum Heller*. Corvettes were built to supplement destroyers. Corvette speed, under twenty knots, was fast enough for convoy work, though a U-boat could outrun them on the surface in good weather. Lower left, Tom Lea, an American, showed what it was like in the crew's quarters of a U.S. destroyer; in rough weather there were very few places inside a ship that the sea couldn't reach. Wet gear never dried, and damp spread through a compartment. (Tom Wood paintings, Canadian War Museum; Tom Lea painting, U.S. Army Center of Military History)

Harbor at St. Johns, Newfoundland

The little Canadian corvette that centers Tom Wood's painting (and its later sister-type, the "frigate") was developed for convoy work. The corvettes were based on Arctic whale-catchers—stretched out to take a 5-inch gun forward and a 3-incher aft, some antiaircraft guns, and a payload of depth charges. The British corvettes tended to have "flowery" names like HMS *Snapdragon,* and some fierce barroom fights resulted when proud crews went to the defense of their vessels against the likes of sailors from HMS *Furious.* (Canadian War Museum)

Lesson Learned at Halifax

In World War I a munitions ship in crowded Halifax harbor exploded and devastated portions of the town. The disaster was well remembered in Canada. In World War II the government built an underground ammunition storage facility in the hills overlooking the harbor in St. Johns, Newfoundland, which would have confined a blast quite dramatically—but safely. Tom Wood did this striking painting of workers preparing to replenish the magazines of Canadian and Royal Navy ships. (Canadian War Museum)

St. Johns Nightlife

For the younger sailors with the tension and excitement of the voyage still with them and the sap running strong, there was St. Johns's Barrington Street, which in the early 1940s was the center of as much sin as that peaceful city could muster, painted here by Tom Wood (ABOVE). But some sailors just wanted to sleep through a night without interruption, eat fresh foods, and drink fresh milk and juice off a table that did not rock, rattle, and roll. Tom Wood painted this distinctly non-carousing evening (RIGHT) at The Crow's Nest pub in St. Johns. The fire was warm. The last voyage was drifting into history; and the next voyage everyone tried not to think about. (Both, Canadian War Museum)

The Silent Enemy, Western Approaches, 1940–42

In the early stages of the war, before the German navy's long-range U-boat strength was built up, the waters around the British Isles were heavily sown with German mines. They claimed many victims—and also helped the Germans' refute cries of "unrestricted submarine warfare." Berlin's answer to ships sunk without warning: "They probably hit *British* mines." Certainly plenty were out there. Stephen Bone painted minesweeping gear ready to be streamed (ABOVE LEFT), and then the attempt to explode a mine that has cut to the surface (LEFT). (Both, Imperial War Museum)

The Face of the Enemy, English Port, 1944

In World War I, on Christmas Day 1914, after hard fighting in Belgium and France, the British and the German frontline soldiers signaled an informal truce, played soccer between the trenches, exchanged cigars, tinned meats, and bottles of beer, and found out the enemy was just human. The combined General Staffs were horrified: How could you win a war if you did not hate the enemy? Stephen Bone painted a World War II continuation of human curiosity and concern: British servicemen and civilians turning out to look at—not to spit at—captured U-boat crewmen landing from HMS *Starling* at an English west coast port. (Imperial War Museum)

Iceland Anchorage

Bernard Arnest painted a U.S. destroyer- and seaplane-tender at anchor in an Icelandic fjord, with two new U.S. destroyers alongside, plus a smaller one—an old World War I "four-piper" still valuable for convoy duty. A presence in Iceland was highly important to the Allies—giving patrol planes a base for air cover over what had been a mid-Atlantic gap, giving the convoys a halfway harbor to shelter crippled ships and refuel, and providing the Arctic convoys with a route to Archangel and Murmansk that was as distant as possible from German bombers. (U.S. Army Center of Military History)

Patrol out of Iceland

Until the airfield in Iceland was completed, the heavy duties of the Iceland air patrol were handled largely by big, slow, but enormously reliable American flying boats christened "Catalinas" by their southern California builder. Tom Lea painted an observer gunner in one of the side blisters of a patrol plane on a lonely, cold sweep out over the convoy routes. (U.S. Army Center of Military History)

Ocean Rescue

Norman Wilkinson painted this scene (RIGHT) with a Sunderland picking up the crew of a Coastal Command Liberator that had to ditch in the ocean. The Liberator, a four-engined bomber, had one small advantage over most other all-metal bombers going down at sea: if the fuel tanks in the top wing were empty or nearly so, the wings gave the plane a little buoyancy, which gave the crew more time to launch a raft and get into it. Eight or ten men were a lot easier to spot in a bright yellow raft than floating singly in the water. (National Maritime Museum)

Sub Patrol, 1941

Until the arrival of B-24 Liberator bombers from the United States, specially adapted for antisubmarine patrol and able to stay in the air as long as fourteen hours, the rugged, dependable Sunderland flying boats carried most of the responsibility of air support for Royal Navy hunter-killer surface units. Norman Wilkinson painted this situation (RIGHT) after talks with RAF crews: the wolf pack had closed in on the convoy in the background, escorts are twisting and turning in their sonar attacks, and the Sunderland, probably with instructions from the ships on UHF radio, is about to go in on a depth charge run. (National Maritime Museum)

English Channel Dash, February 1942

The fighting in Norwegian waters during the German invasion in the spring of 1940 had proved the claim of airmen on both sides that capital ships without air cover were highly vulnerable. Norman Wilkinson painted this air strike (RIGHT) against the great German battle cruisers *Scharnhorst* and *Gneisenau*. These ships sank some 115,000 tons of shipping in the North Atlantic in 1941. (National Maritime Museum)

Attack on the *Tirpitz*, 1944

The German battleships and battle cruisers lurking in Norway's fjords were ominous threats to the Atlantic convoys—and especially to the ones out of Scotland and Iceland sailing for the Russian Arctic ports. So there were frequent air attacks over these German hiding spaces to try to neutralize the ships. Norman Wilkinson painted these Barracuda bombers (RIGHT) striking the *Tirpitz*. Continuous harassment by air, and by midget submarines, helped the British to sink her with 12,000-pound "Tallboy" bombs. (National Maritime Museum)

Sinking the *Scharnhorst,* December 26, 1943

Shortly before five o'clock in the evening, several hours into the Arctic dark, *Belfast* suddenly lit up the sky with the star shells that Charles Pears depicts in his epic painting of the last battle of the giant German battle cruiser *Scharnhorst.* Some three hours later, the German battle cruiser went down, victim of thirteen hits by 14-inch shells and eleven torpedoes. With her went all but thirty-six of her 1,900 men. (National Maritime Museum)

Escort Carriers

T he small escort carriers at work in the North Atlantic are represented in these three
paintings by Mitchell Jamieson. North Atlantic weather was some of the worst where
carriers had to operate. The planes were essentially the same "hot" combat aircraft
that flew off the big fleet carriers in the Pacific—though the flight deck of a "baby carrier"
was a good deal shorter. Accidents were frequent (ABOVE), and with other pilots waiting to
land after long patrols above the convoy routes and short of fuel, often the only thing to do
with a damaged plane that blocked the deck was to get it out of the way by pushing it over
the side. (U.S. Navy Combat Art Collection)

Carrier at Night

A big Grumman TBF torpedo bomber gets an engine check while lashed down on the deck of an escort carrier in the Atlantic after an all-night repair job in anticipation of heavy daylight patrol schedules. Mitchell Jamieson painted the scene. (U.S. Navy Combat Art Collection)

Graduating Students Depart for the Front, Suzuki Mitsuru (Captured Japanese Art; U.S. Air Force Art Collection)

EXPLOSION IN THE
PACIFIC

With the U.S. Navy badly hurt at Pearl Harbor and Army Air Force units in Hawaii and the Philippines virtually wiped out . . . with Bataan being evacuated and Corregidor under fatal siege . . . with Hong Kong and Singapore captured and Malaya and Burma falling, the western Pacific seemed truly a Japanese Sea. Reports of atrocities on the sixty-five-mile "death march" of surrendered Filipino and American troops were widely circulated in America and colored the U.S. approach to Japan for the rest of the war. The feeling was reinforced by stories leaking out of captured Hong Kong and Singapore of brutal POW and civilian internment camps there. With the sinking of HMS *Prince of Wales* and *Repulse* by Japanese bombers, Allied naval presence virtually ceased to exist in the Far East, and the "battleship era" was clearly nearing its end; air cover was essential to protect big ships. Australia braced for a Japanese invasion and rushed to train new troops; first-class Australian, Indian, and Canadian units had been sent to Hong Kong and Singapore—just in time to be captured. Everywhere in the Pacific, Westerners were hoping just to "hold on" for the time being. Winning the war would have to come later.

The opening moments of the attack on Pearl Harbor were devastating. The torpedo attacks on Battleship Row destroyed within half an hour the myth of "unsinkable battleship supremacy." Several of the biggest quickly took fatal hits . . . turned over . . . or settled ignominiously to the bottom of Pearl Harbor. The U.S. death toll was more than 2,400. In 1944, there was an investigation into why an intercepted warning of the attack had not been acted upon. The conclusion of the hearing was that the White House wanted Pearl Harbor to be attacked. Earlier, Roosevelt had written to Churchill:

I may never *declare* war; I may *make* war. If I were to ask Congress to declare war, they might argue about it for three months.

■

In the half-staffed Sunday quiet of hundreds of American radio stations and newspaper teletype rooms, this is how the first word came in of the worst military disaster in United States history:

FLASH
WASHINGTON—WHITE HOUSE SAYS JAPS ATTACK PEARL HARBOR.

222PES

BULLETIN
WASHINGTON, DEC. 7 (AP)—PRESIDENT ROOSEVELT SAID IN A STATEMENT TODAY THAT THE JAPANESE HAD ATTACKED PEARL HARBOR, HAWAII, FROM THE AIR.

THE ATTACK OF THE JAPANESE ALSO WAS MADE ON ALL NAVAL AND MILITARY "ACTIVITIES" ON THE ISLAND OF OAHU. . . .

AT THE TIME OF THE WHITE HOUSE ANNOUNCEMENT, THE JAPANESE AMBASSADORS KIURISABORO NOMURA AND SABURO KURUSU WERE AT THE STATE DEPARTMENT.

FLASH
WASHINGTON—SECOND AIR ATTACK REPORTED ON ARMY AND NAVY BASES IN MANILA.

■

Every veteran of Pearl Harbor had his own unique experience. Historian Walter Lord interviewed almost 600 survivors to create a finely detailed account of the attack:

The men on the *Arizona*, forward of the *Nevada*, hardly had time to think. She was in-

board of the *Vestal*, but the little repair ship didn't offer much protection—a torpedo struck home almost right away—and nothing could stop the steel that rained down. . . . A big one shattered the boat deck between No. 4 and 6 guns—it came in like a fly ball. . . .

Down in the plotting room—the gunnery nerve center and well below the water line —conditions looked hopeless. Torpedoes were slamming into the ship somewhere above. The list grew steeper. . . .

There was no time for counterflooding on the *Oklahoma*, lying ahead of the *West Virginia* and outboard of the *Maryland*. Lying directly across from Southeast Loch, she took three torpedoes right away, then another two as she heeled to port. . . .

The water rose . . . the emergency lights went out . . . the list increased. Now everything was breaking loose. Big 1000-pound shells rumbled across the handling rooms, sweeping men before them.

■

To many Americans on the scene at Pearl Harbor, the air attack seemed to go on all morning. By tightly cross-referencing the reported incidents, Walter Lord discovered that it probably began at 7:55 A.M. and ended about 10 A.M.—with about fifteen minutes of lull between 8:25 and 8:40 A.M. But Lord also discovered that in spite of weeks of planning and practice, the Japanese task force had gone through an unnerving number of rough moments and unforeseen mistakes:

Admiral Nagumo must have felt even more discouraged when they first tried refueling on the 28th. This turned out to be dangerous, back-breaking work. As the ships bucked and plunged, the big hoses running from the tankers would snap loose and whiplash across the deck. Several crewmen were swept overboard, but nothing could be done about it. . . . The main job was to keep the fleet from being discovered.

■

In spite of the beating the navy had taken at Pearl Harbor, Lord found countless stories to raise American spirits:

The destroyer *Monaghan* and other ships in Pearl Harbor had only morning colors to

worry about. This ceremony was always the same. . . . On the smaller ships a boatswain piped his whistle; on the larger a bugler sounded colors; on the largest a band might even play the National Anthem. . . .

A band crashed into "The Star-Spangled Banner." A Japanese plane skimmed across the harbor . . . dropped a torpedo at the *Arizona* . . . and peeled off right over the *Nevada*'s fantail. The rear gunner sprayed the men standing at attention, but he must have been a poor shot. He missed the entire band and marine guard, lined up in two neat rows. . . .

McMillan . . . kept on conducting. The years of training had taken over—it never occurred to him that once he had begun playing the National Anthem, he could possibly stop. Another strafer flashed by. This time McMillan unconsciously paused as the deck splintered around him, but he quickly picked up the beat again. The entire band stopped and started again with him, as though they had rehearsed it for weeks. Not a man broke formation until the final note died. Then everyone ran wildly for cover. . . .

■

One of the first Japanese prisoners of war was Ensign Sakemacki from a midget submarine that had run aground on a reef off the windward coast of Oahu. His mission had gone all wrong; after the war, Walter Lord was to learn of his frustrating attempts to get into the fight:

Sakemacki dived into the sea about 6:40 A.M.—his watch, which he had loyally kept on Tokyo time, stopped at 2:10. The water was colder than he expected, the waves higher than they looked. They spun him helplessly about as he struck out for shore. Inagaki had jumped with him but was nowhere to be seen. . . . When he came to, he was lying on the beach near Bellows Field, apparently cast up on the sand by a breaker. He glanced up into the curious eyes of an American soldier standing beside him.

■

Thomas Blake Clark, an American businessman in Hawaii, knew he was in the middle of history, and he started taking notes:

There was humor with the tragedy. When the Japanese came over Hickham [Field] the third time, they placed a bomb squarely on the "Snake Ranch," the boys' name for their recently opened beer garden. A first sergeant of a truck company had endured the first two waves bravely enough, but this was too much. He dashed out of his barricade, shook his fist at the sky, and shouted, "You dirty S.O.B.s! You've bombed the most important building on the Post!"

■

Clark and several witnesses saw the downing of one Japanese dive-bomber with a one-in-a-million shot:

"Get out and shoot!" was the command.

A small dive-bomber came in, poised to drop a bomb. The boy [a country boy from the West] had not been trained to handle a heavy rifle, but he had "done lots of huntin' " in his day. He took a bead and fired. One of the freak accidents of the war occurred. Apparently the boy's bullet hit the detonator of the bomb the Japanese was about to drop, for the plane simply burst in midair and disintegrated before their eyes. The boy fainted. . . .

■

The San Francisco Chronicle *got a scoop by accident:*

Eugene Burns, Associated Press correspondent, heard the rumbling of guns, but went on with his breakfast until a bomb burst nearby. In fifteen minutes they reached town from their Tantalus home. . . . On the way down they had seen the fires from Pearl Harbor. . . . Burns dashed into the Mutual Telephone building.

"Associated Press, San Francisco! Number's Douglas 6575!"

"Hello!" he yelled, "the *Chronicle?*" It was. A reporter had come in for his mail. "Swell! Listen, here's a story!"

While he was making his dramatic report a bomb fell on the Schumann Carriage Company a block away, and the explosion was heard over the phone by the reporter in California.

As he left, the Honolulu operator said, "I'll bet the mainland papers are going to exaggerate this!"

■

Maj. J.P.S. Devereux was in Hawaii for another assignment in the fall of 1941, when he was hurriedly sent to take charge of the modest U.S. Marine detachment on Wake Island. On Wake, Devereux received a unique introduction to the enemy:

As senior officer on Wake, one of my duties was to meet the Pan American Clipper and welcome any dignitaries who might be passing through. Thus I met Saburo Kurusu on his way to Washington for those conferences the Japanese kept going as a smoke screen until the day they struck Pearl Harbor. . . . As we sat there chatting over our drinks . . . we skirted around the one topic that must have been uppermost in both our minds. . . .

■

Wake would turn out to be the first American example of "too little and too late":

. . . Commander Keene, who came to Wake to command the navy patrol planes that never arrived, told me that he had seen our radar equipment on the dock in Hawaii. . . . It was not sent to us. . . . We received other equipment during that period. We got a garbage truck, for instance. It was a useful vehicle, but it could not detect Jap bombers coming down on us out of a rain squall. . . .

■

Wake was expecting more planes and the first Japanese flight was easily mistaken for reinforcements:

The gliding bombers were almost on top of us when they broke out of the rain squall at barely two thousand feet. . . .

The entire attack on both islands had lasted only ten minutes. . . . At the airfield, thirty-four men were dead or wounded. Seven of the planes caught on the ground were destroyed. . . . Three-quarters of our air power was knocked out by the enemy's first punch without getting a chance to strike a single blow.

■

Hawaii and mainland America hung on to every report they could get from Wake. Unfortunately, in the absence of news, some commentators began making it up. On the island under fire, some of it made the marines think

they sounded like hick B-movie actors. Devereux noted:

After an especially adjective-studded report, one commentator quoted me as ending a report of a Japanese repulse with the message, "SEND MORE JAPS."

That was news to me. One of the marines said, "Anybody that wants it can sure have my share of the Japs we already got."

■

A soldier in the Japanese invasion force gave an account of the island's resistance. John Goette translated the recollection for his book, Japan Fights for Asia. *Change a few nouns . . . and it could be an American marine going ashore at Tarawa:*

The water was so deep we could hardly walk. Rifles in hand, we desperately fought our way forward. . . . The enemy's tracer bullets which came flying through the dark looked like a show of fireworks. The enemy's position seemed no farther than fifty yards away. . . . An inch at a time we crept toward the enemy. Twenty yards before the enemy, we prepared to charge. All at once a rain of hand grenades came hurtling down on us.

"Charge!" the commander's voice rang out. We jumped to our feet and charged. Huge shadows which shouted something unintelligible were pierced one after another. One large figure appeared before us to blaze away with a machine gun from his hip. . . . Somebody went for him with his bayonet and went down together with his victim.

■

The navy commander sent to Wake before the attack was senior officer on the island. He got first word that the United States had abandoned Wake. And from him, Devereux got his surrender orders:

It was an expensive victory for the Japanese. By their own admission, Wake Island cost them 11 naval ships, 29 planes and more than 5,700 men killed. The American losses were a dozen planes and 96 dead. Our dead included 46 marines, 3 sailors, and 47 civilians.

A long time later I learned that we were right in assuming that an American task force had been on its way to Wake. The task force, built around the aircraft carrier *Saratoga,* was only twenty-four hours from Wake when we surrendered. The force was ordered to turn back. The navy had too little left after Pearl Harbor to gamble the ships on an attempt to retake Wake.

◼

General MacArthur gave an order on December 27, 1941, that he hoped would save Manila from destruction:

IN ORDER TO SPARE THE METROPOLITAN AREA FROM POSSIBLE RAVAGES OF ATTACK EITHER BY AIR OR GROUND, MANILA IS HEREBY DECLARED AN OPEN CITY. . . . IN ORDER THAT NO EXCUSE MAY BE GIVEN FOR A POSSIBLE MISTAKE, THE AMERICAN HIGH COMMISSIONER, THE COMMONWEALTH GOVERNMENT, AND ALL COMBATANT MILITARY INSTALLATIONS WILL BE WITHDRAWN FROM ITS ENVIRONS AS RAPIDLY AS POSSIBLE.

◼

The Japanese landing on Luzon, the island capital of the Philippines, came only twenty-four hours after Malaya had been invaded. Then on December 22 between 80,000 and 100,000 men joined the attack, forcing back outnumbered American and Filipino troops. Carlos Romulo remembered night noises along the lines:

The sounds were nerve-racking. . . . Lauro spoke to me again in a whisper. He explained that these sounds were being broadcast from Japanese sound trucks on the very front of their lines.

Out of the night came a woman's voice, sweet and persuasive. In sentimental words it announced the dedication of a program to "the bravest and [most] gallant defenders of Bataan". . . .

◼

Marine William Martin Camp was evacuated with the remainder of his unit to Corregidor and the tunnels for the final siege. His story of the last days were matter-of-fact and pure "marine":

Down below we can hear the great thunder. The bombs have loosened the ceiling in some of the tunnels, and they have caved in at some places, cutting off any possible escape. . . . Word has been passed that we've

made our last radio contact with the States. It happened about four o'clock this afternoon. No one knows what the last message was, but soon after it was sent a well-placed bomb blew the works all to hell, and the operators with it. . . . Even as they brought around the last of the mulemeat everyone ate it and there was plenty of grumbling. As long as there's plenty of belly-aching, men will not lose heart.

◼

A number of accounts of the "Bataan Death March" appeared after the end of the war. But the report here was made by an American Air Force officer, Col. William F. Dyess, who survived the march, escaped, returned to the United States—and wrote about what he had experienced:

At dawn of the second day, the impatient Japanese stepped among us, kicking us into wakefulness. . . . The sun cast its blinding light in our eyes as we marched. The temperature rose by the minute. . . .

During the afternoon, traffic picked up again. Troop-laden trucks sped past us. A grimacing Japanese soldier leaned far out, holding his rifle by the barrel. As the truck roared by he knocked an American soldier senseless with the gun's stock. Other Japanese saw this and yelled. From now on we kept out of reach if we could. . . .

The hours dragged by, and as we knew they must, the dropouts began. It seemed that a great many of the prisoners reached the end of their endurance at about the same time. They went down by twos and threes. . . .

Skulking along, a hundred yards behind our contingent, came a "clean-up squad" . . . there would be an orange flash in the darkness and a sharp report.

◼

The Japanese had been exposed for years to the world's press, which lionized the Royal Navy as "the world's most powerful." As a result, when the Japanese closed in on the two great British fighting ships that had been sent to protect Singapore and destroy the Japanese invasion force, they felt they might be seriously outmatched. Naval officer Mochitsura Hashimoto remembered:

At 3:15 P.M. the next day two battleships

were sighted by I.165 [a submarine] at a point three hundred miles north of Singapore. . . . The ships were proceeding northwards at high speed; their target was the supply line of our landings. . . . Our entire Malayan naval force, consisting of the battleships *Kongo* and *Haruna,* together with the cruiser squadron and destroyer squadron under the command of Vice-Adm. Nobutake Kondo, was not really a match for the opponents, but our ships forged ahead with all speed. . . .

◼

British war correspondent Cecil Brown reported the Japanese air attack on Repulse *and* Prince of Wales:

The decks of the *Repulse* are littered with empty shell cases. Upon the faces of the sailors there's a mixture of incredulity and a sort of sensuous pleasure, but I don't detect fear. There's an ecstatic happiness, but strangely, I don't see anything approaching hate for the attackers. The facial expression is interpreted by an officer: "Plucky blokes, those Japanese. That was as beautiful an attack as I would ever hope to see."

◼

British correspondent Ian Morrison witnessed a strange exchange. When the escorting British and Australian destroyers darted in to rescue survivors, they expected the heaviest attack. But the Japanese planes sent a surprising blinker signal: "We have completed our work. You may carry on." Morrison thought:

For the first time we had an inkling of what the true balance of factors was in this Pacific War.

◼

Lt. Gen. A. E. Percival, a much-decorated World War I veteran and career soldier, had been posted to Malaya in an almost offhanded way, indicating that London did not feel that area of the war was important. When the flying boat that was to take him to the Far East broke down before takeoff, it was five weeks before the RAF could supply him with a replacement. When he arrived, Percival reported the deficiencies of his position to General Wavell, his superior in the Far East. The report included the discovery of virtually no defenses on the side of Singapore facing the Malay Peninsula, the route of any land attack! Churchill was astounded . . . and memoed the Chiefs on January 16, 1942:

I must confess to being staggered by Wavell's telegram of the 16th and other telegrams on the same subject. It never occurred to me for a moment, nor to Sir John Dill, with whom I discussed the matter on the outward voyage, that the gorge of the fortress of Singapore, with its splendid moat . . . was not entirely fortified against an attack from the northward.

■

British correspondent Kenneth Attiwill heard numerous stories from frustrated military men trying to prepare the defenses, men who had tangled with highly placed civilians in the colony:

Some of the efforts of the military to impose war conditions were met with [civilian] remarks which indicated the refusal in some quarters to understand that there was a war on. . . . When the secretary of the golf club was told that the club was to be turned into a strongpoint, he replied that it required a special committee meeting for approval.

■

To correspondent Cecil Brown, some of the military communiqués about the fighting had an Alice-in-Wonderland quality about them, as if perhaps creative language could change the war:

18 December: Japanese troops are now fourteen miles from Penang. This news came as a terrific shock to everyone in Singapore. . . . The usual official communiqué . . . said, "We have successfully disengaged the enemy and are south of the River Krain."

I stared at that phrase—"successfully disengaged the enemy" . . . Then it suddenly occurred to me that someone had coined a beautiful phrase of defeatist optimism.

■

Flight Officer Donahue, an American volunteer with the RAF, remembered the frosty reception that dismayed some of the pilots who rushed in to try to save Singapore:

Some of the boys went for a dip in the hotel swimming pool. . . . One grumpy old codger staying at the hotel came snooping around and tried to chase them out, saying they couldn't swim there because they hadn't been introduced. . . .

Brownie . . . rose nobly to the situation. "Well, my name's Browne. I guess that introduces me!" The others followed suit, bowed, and dived back into the pool.

■

Correspondent Ian Morrison filed one early story, which would be echoed later from all over the South Pacific, about the superior adaptability of Japanese troops:

The Asiatic appearance of the enemy . . . enabled him to masquerade as a native. The British troops would not have been able to distinguish between Chinese, Japanese and Malays if they had been wearing their respective national dresses, let alone when they were all wearing sarongs.

■

The weakness of the Singapore defenses became apparent, all in a rush, to most of the civilians on the island who had gotten used to seeing soldiers in uniforms from all over the British Empire moving purposefully about: Australians, Canadians, Indians, Malayans. . . . The sad truth was that many of the units were not ready to fight. Correspondent Attiwill explained:

It must be remembered that every . . . soldier in Malaya, except the Malay Regiment, was on foreign soil. . . . They had no great love for Singapore, no devotion to Malaya Command. All they had was pride of race, pride of regiment, loyalty one to another. And some of them did not even have that.

■

With the Japanese clearly showing they would soon take Singapore, most civilians found that "staying to the bitter end" was not only a empty gesture but one that would impede the military manning of defenses. A British soldier told of seeing his wife off on a ship and being presented with a chance to make his own escape, too. The gangway guard advised:

"Take your wife's luggage up . . . and take my advice and stay up there. You won't be the only one."

I was in my khaki uniform, equipment on and rifle slung over my shoulder. I said: "I don't think I can do that."

"It's up to you," he said. "Go on board, anyway. Please yourself whether you come off. . . . We've had it."

■

An eleven-hundred-yard causeway linked Singapore Island to the mainland. The causeway was blown up when the last defenders were across—but not very effectively: the explosion threw a seventy-yard section into the water. But at low tide, only four feet of stream covered it. Royal Artillery Gunner Marshall watched Australians come in:

It is the most vivid memory I have of the Singapore campaign. . . . They came moving at a half-trot. . . . I've never seen anything like it. It was pouring with rain and most of them were clad only in shorts. Few were wearing boots, and some of the men's feet were cut to ribbons. . . . Among them was one Aussie soldier fully equipped: rifle, ammunition, cape, shirt, shorts and boots. He came across the road to three of us who were standing watching. "They're finished," he said. He was quite calm. He was a boy of about nineteen, a private. He seemed sorry for his mates. "Can I join up with you blokes?" he asked.

■

Signalman Fred Mutton of the 28th Indian Brigade remembered the "lift" of the pipers:

The rumbling of the mechanized army subsided and died away. The causeway seemed empty for a little while; and then the infantry began to march across. You couldn't see them very clearly and the tramp of their feet on the asphalt was the only sound in the stillness. It was a tired tramp. . . . And then, as the Gordons marched out on the causeway, a single piper began to play. You could hear every note. It covered the tramping of feet. I didn't leave the terrace until the sound of the pipes had died away. The Gordons had passed. It was daylight now. I signalled to the boat points, "Finish." . . . Their present task completed, the Argylls marched across the causeway led by their two remaining pipers—Stewart and Maclean—for all the world as if they were a hundred pipers and all.

■

On February 11, Japanese planes showered leaflets on the Singapore defenders, signed by General Yamashita. They began:

I advise immediate surrender of the British forces at Singapore . . . to the Japanese Army and Navy forces, which have already dominated Malaya, annihilated the British Fleet in the Far East, and acquired complete control of the China Sea and the Pacific and Indian oceans, as well as southwestern Asia.

■

General Percival marched out to meet General Yamashita for a peace parlay, to be held in a large Ford assembly plant outside the city. It was badly damaged, but the Japanese general had picked it because all the Japanese reporters and cameramen he wanted present could easily be accommodated there . . . and because the plant would be easy to defend. He suspected the parlay might be a British trick:

YAMASHITA: I approve of the cessation of hostilities at 10:00 P.M. After we have finished firing, all the British troops should disarm themselves, save 1,000 men whom we shall permit to carry arms to maintain order. You have agreed to the terms, but you have not yet made yourself clear as to whether you have agreed to unconditional surrender or not. (General Percival, with bowed head and a faint voice, gave his consent. It was 7:30 P.M.)

TOKYO RADIO: There will be no Dunkirk at Singapore. The British are not going to be allowed to get away with it this time. All ships leaving will be destroyed.

■

Even as the drive for Singapore went on, it quickly got to be Burma's turn. On January 16, 1942, the Japanese surged into Lower Burma . . . on the road to India. Major General Smyth of the British 17th Division was charged with the defense of Moulmein. Smyth knew his problem but he had support from a fine superior, Lt. Gen. William Slim:

On Sunday, 25 January, [General Slim] arrived up from Rangoon and we had a good look round and a long talk on the situation.

It was quite obvious that the morale of the troops was poor. In the first place they felt keenly their lack of training in jungle war, their lack of artillery and air support, and their inability to move where they wanted, owing to our acute lack of transport. The Indian troops had absolutely no confidence in the Burmese and the Burmese had no confidence in themselves.

■

Daily Express writer O. D. Gallagher, who had watched British colonials go through business as usual during the fall of Singapore, reported with amazement some of the same approach in Rangoon:

The empty streets were patrolled by troops carrying tommy-guns and rifles. The only other inhabitants were criminals, criminal lunatics, lunatics and lepers. They had been released from the gaols and institutions on the order of an officer of the Indian Civil Service. He had misread an order sent to him regarding their disposal. The convicts numbered some five thousand. At night they made Rangoon a city of the damned.

■

One of the few bright spots in Burma, however, was the leadership of General Slim, who moved in to extract what was left of the British and Indian armies and regroup them. First of all, General Slim had a big morale-building job to do. He assembled his officers in small groups. It didn't always work quite as he had planned it:

I stepped out of my van feeling about as depressed as a man could. . . . A handful of British officers and the Chinese liaison officers stood there silent and looked at me. All commanders know that look. They see it in the eyes of their staffs and their men when things are really bad, when even the most confident staff officer and the toughest soldier want holding up. And they turn where they *should* turn for support—to their commander. And sometimes he does not know what to say. . . .

"Well, gentlemen," I said, putting on what I hoped was a confident, cheerful expression, "it might be worse!"

One of the group . . . replied with a single word: "How?"

I could cheerfully have murdered him, but instead I had to keep my temper.

"Oh," I said, grinning, "it might be raining!"

Two hours later, it was—hard. As I crept under a truck for shelter I thought of that fellow and wished I *had* murdered him.

■

Along with General Slim, another strong leader came out of the retreat to cause the Allies in the China-Burma-India theater to hope that better things would result from the experience of the defeats. He was Gen. Joseph Stilwell. Slim and Stilwell formed an odd but strong tolerance and alliance. Slim wrote:

He's obstinate as a whole team of mules. . . . But when he said he would do a thing he did it. . . . He had a habit, which I found very disarming, of arguing most tenaciously against some proposal and then suddenly looking at you over the top of his glasses with the shadow of a grin, and saying, "Now tell me what you want me to do and I'll do it!"

■

Jack Belden was with Stilwell on what Stilwell called "that goddamn hike out of Burma" . . . and caught some of the charisma of "a tough old bird":

In about half an hour, however, by a small sandy, gravel beach, the general called a noonday halt. . . .

He began to divest himself of his pants and his shirt, and, with his campaign hat still on his head to protect him from the noonday sun, went into the stream, sat down, and bathed. Others soon roused themselves, lay in the stream, and tried to suck water back into their pores.

■

Back in India, the seasoned British military writers, a number of whom prided themselves on service in the First World War, wanted to talk tactics with Stilwell. He wanted to talk "Stilwell":

I claim we got a hell of a beating. We got run out of Burma, and it is humiliating as hell. I think we should find out what caused it and go back and retake it.

The Invasion of Guam, December 1941

Wake, Guam, and the Midway Islands were splashed out in the western Pacific like lonely point men who had strayed too far from the column of soldiers behind them. By December 8, the column to the rear had already been badly chewed up, with little left to come to the defense of the island outposts. Guam in the Marianas chain was gobbled up by the Japanese by December 10 and provided the setting for this strangely peaceful painting of war in the style of a Japanese silk screen. It was done by Ezaki Kohei, who interviewed some of the returning attackers. (National Modern Art Museum of Tokyo)

Preparations, Pearl Harbor Attack Task Force

Japanese artist Arai Shori was riding one of the big fleet carriers in the task force that launched the attack on Pearl Harbor, and he became fascinated with the preparations for flight and takeoff. The Japanese took great pains to keep the location of the task force hidden, by avoiding traditional commercial shipping lanes and by not jettisoning any debris that might be spotted by an American plane or submarine on patrol. (Captured Japanese Art; U.S. Air Force Art Collection)

Flight Deck, Pearl Harbor Attack Task Force

The pilots are in their cockpits, engines are revving, and the deck crew is ready to pull the blocks away from the wheels, sending the planes on their way to the target. It was a long way to Pearl Harbor, and the planes would have fuel enough to stay over the target only briefly, but if all went smoothly, they would arrive back on board with nearly empty tanks. Any one of a series of small accidents could have jolted the plan, but it worked nearly perfectly. Arai Shori did the painting. (Captured Japanese Art; U.S. Air Force Art Collection)

Carrier Farewell, Pearl Harbor Attack Task Force

The first wave of Japanese aircraft to hit Pearl Harbor—almost 190 planes—had flown off the carrier decks about 6 A.M., December 7, Hawaiian time. They faced a flight of almost two hours to Oahu—and Pearl. The Japanese pilots knew they were still at peace with the United States, but some of the flight commanders had heard that a declaration of war would be delivered in Washington shortly before the first bomb was to fall. Arai Shori painted the spirited farewell that deck crews on the Japanese carriers gave each flight taking off. The crews were convinced this was no sneak attack, but the beginning of a war forced on Japan by the failure of the United States to respond to many wrongs to their country and months of negotiation. (Captured Japanese Art; U.S. Army Center of Military History)

Submarine Commanders, Pearl Harbor

An unknown Japanese artist painted a memorial to eight commanders of midget submarines sent to take part in the attack. Unfortunately for the Japanese, none achieved success. The visionary scene that the Japanese submariners surround is a minutely detailed aerial view of Ford Island under attack, painted from a Japanese pilot's photograph taken during the attack. (Captured Japanese Art; U.S. Navy Combat Art Collection)

Arizona Explosion, Pearl Harbor, December 7, 1941

An unknown artist, probably American, painted this scene of the *Arizona* exploding and about to capsize. The painting appears to follow a famous photograph. Interestingly, the artist gives the picture the added drama of a night attack. (U.S. Army Center of Military History)

Hospital Ship, Approaching San Francisco

Franklin Boggs was one of a group of rising American artists who were commissioned by an American pharmaceutical company to paint a historical record of medicine in the war. These artists were among the first in action from the United States, and they began their work before the country had any sort of official war art program. Boggs did several versions of this historic moment, when American servicemen wounded in the Pacific fighting got their first sight of San Francisco's Golden Gate Bridge from the deck of an American hospital ship. (U.S. Navy Combat Art Collection)

The Sinking of *Prince of Wales,* Off Malaya, December 10, 1941

The strategy for holding Singapore was anchored around defense of the island city by its garrison until major elements of the British fleet arrived. When "the fleet" arrived, it was composed of one brand-new battleship, *Prince of Wales,* one remodeled World War I battle cruiser, *Repulse,* and a handful of destroyers. When Japanese planes attacked, the two great ships were sent to the bottom in less than ninety minutes. This painting, done originally in three panels by an unknown Japanese artist, shows *Prince of Wales* under heavy attack. (Imperial War Museum)

Hong Kong, December 1941

Hoshun Yamaguchi called his painting *General Attack on Hong Kong* and the view is from high ground in Kowloon behind the wharves. Across the bay, the buildings of Victoria are burning at several points. The big, modern building at far left in Victoria is apparently the headquarters of the Bank of China, still prominent in the city's silhouette. (Captured Japanese Art; U.S. Army Center of Military History)

Nurses Tend the Injured

Suzuki Tsuguo painted this Japanese medical unit in action, perhaps in Burma. It shows the sad, universal carnage of war that struck every army in every theater. The creases and cracks in the painting testify to a time when it was hidden to try to prevent its capture. (Captured Japanese Art; U.S. Army Center of Military History)

Malay Campaign, 1941–42

Katsuda Totsu, in his painting (ABOVE) of Japanese paratroopers titled *Divine Soldiers Descend on Menado,* gives a quiet beauty to a violent scene. The barbed wire ground barriers laid out by the defenders have obviously been little deterrent to the Japanese troops. And slowly the legend of Japanese invincibility began to build. (Captured Japanese Art; U.S. Air Force Art Collection)

The Surrender of Hong Kong, Christmas Night, 1941

At 9 A.M. Christmas morning, Sir Mark Young, governor of Hong Kong, had received and rejected the last of several ultimatums for surrender sent in by Japanese Gen. Taikaishi Sakai. But when Governor Young saw on Christmas afternoon that he had lost 4,400 men and the next fighting would be in Hong Kong's streets, he surrendered. Usaburo Ihara painted Young and Gen. Christopher Maltby (ABOVE LEFT) signing the documents. (National Modern Art Museum of Tokyo)

Breakthrough at Alor Star Bridge, Malaya, December 1941

The British had built a large air base at Alor Star in northern Malaya, about halfway between Penang and the Thai border. The base was overrun by the Japanese soon after they landed—one more reason for the lack of air cover that resulted in the sinking of *Repulse* and *Prince of Wales*. Konosuke Tamura painted a heroic Japanese motorcyclist who broke through the barrier at the bridgehead, urging on the capture of the airfield (LEFT). (National Modern Art Museum of Tokyo)

Battle of Coral Sea, May 1942

Kobori Yasuo painted the Battle of Coral Sea (ABOVE) with Japanese aircraft sinking an American ship that could be the old four-stack cruiser *Marblehead.* (Captured Japanese Art; U.S. Air Force Art Collection)

The Doolittle Raid, April 18, 1942

Specially modified B-25 twin-engined Army Air Force bombers, flown by crews secretly trained in carrier take-offs, had been carried within reach of Japan on the newly launched USS *Hornet* to bomb Tokyo and other cities. Militarily, the bombing had little significance. But for morale, it was a victory of enormous value. And for the next two and a half years the Japanese home defense force was distracted with the threat that it might happen again. The British maritime artist Norman Wilkinson executed the painting (RIGHT) probably from photographs. (Imperial War Museum)

The Invasion of Malaya, January 1942

In all, the defense of Singapore was an unhappy military bungle, marked by countless incidents of tremendous heroism. Geoffrey Mainwaring, a fine Australian war artist, painted one such incident of tremendous heroism, which he titled *"A" Company 2/22 Battalion in Action at Vulcan, 25 January 1942*. Offshore are Japanese invasion ships, and the first troops landed have already come under fire from the Australians. (Australian War Memorial)

Airstrip at Milne Bay, New Guinea, 1942

William Dargie painted his mates in an Australian squadron (OPPOSITE TOP) getting ready to scramble a flight of Royal Australian Air Force P-40s at Milne Bay in the New Guinea fighting. George Browning painted Australian troops in action (OPPOSITE BOTTOM) during the 2/48th Battalion's attack on Sattleberg, New Guinea, in 1943. (Both, Australian War Memorial)

Brief Respite

An Australian field ambulance unit (ABOVE RIGHT) takes a break on the grounds of a plantation near Singapore. M. Murray Griffin painted the scene. William Dargie painted these two Australians (BELOW RIGHT) at rest on the Kokoda Trail over the Owen Stanley Mountains. (Australian War Memorial)

Battle of Midway, June 1942

Here, Griffith Bailey Coale took on a great battle scene of mural dimensions: the Battle of Midway. Coale paints a hit on one of the great Japanese carriers, with two other carriers and their escorting heavy ships under severe air attack. (U.S. Navy Combat Art Collection)

He Walks Who Can, Kerr Eby (U.S. Navy Combat Art Collection)

SLAND INVASIONS AND CARRIER WARS

After the enormous defeat at Pearl Harbor and the losses of Wake, Guam, and the Philippines, U.S. strategy and morale both demanded some significant offensive blow at the Japanese. It began with the invasion of Guadalcanal, a small island in the Solomon chain that, after hard fighting ashore and afloat, became the first victory of the American "island-hopping" strategy. Tactics of successful amphibious invasion were invented and perfected, as deadly smooth cooperation was hammered out between navy, army, and air-support units. Fighting men, ships, and air groups from Australia and New Zealand linked with the Americans for victories after hard fighting at Rabaul, Hollandia, and New Guinea. With reinforcements coming from U.S. training programs and new ships, planes, and equipment coming from American builders, the pressure against the Japanese increased. Needed morale boosters came early in 1942: sixteen Army Air Force bombers, flying off a U.S. carrier, bombed Tokyo—a forerunner of things to come. Then, the navy won a decisive victory against a Japanese task force at the Battle of Midway—with the Japanese losing four fleet carriers, more than 330 planes, and some of their best pilots and carrier crews.

R obert Leckie served in the South Pacific as a marine and experienced the sort of combat he writes of at Guadalcanal. Where no other name appears, the material that follows is Leckie's research or experience:

Containing the Japanese during the three months beginning with Pearl Harbor had been as easy as cornering a tornado. The Japanese had crippled the U.S. Pacific Fleet and all but driven Britain from the Indian Ocean by sinking *Prince of Wales* and *Repulse*. Except for scattered American carrier strikes against the Gilberts and Marshalls, the vast Pacific from Formosa to Hawaii was in danger of becoming a Japanese lake. . . .

Australia—to which Gen. Douglas MacArthur had been ordered should he succeed in escaping from Corregidor—was threatened by a Japanese invasion of New Guinea. At that moment in early March, as Admiral King knew, the necessary invasion force was being gathered in Rabaul, the bastion which the Japanese were building on the eastern tip of New Britain.

■

Intelligence reported that the Japanese were building an airfield on Guadalcanal from which they could attack convoys to Australia, where MacArthur was trying to build an army. The island had to be captured. U.S. Marines, who would do much of the initial fighting on Guadalcanal, were mostly trained at the famous Marine Corps boot camp at Parris Island, South Carolina, which lies among the marshy southeastern Sea Islands and turned out to be a good training ground for Guadalcanal:

Martin Clemens, the British District Officer on the island . . . thought that Guadalcanal was beautiful. On the outside.

On the inside, he knew, she was a poisonous morass. Crocodiles hid in her creeks or patrolled her turgid backwaters. Her jungles were alive with slithering, crawling, scuttling things; with giant lizards that barked like dogs, with huge red furry spiders, with centipedes and leeches and scorpions, with rats and bats and fiddler crabs and one big species of land crab which moved through the bush with all the stealth of a steamroller.

■

The first landings were deceptively easy. By the evening of August 7, there were 10,000 marines ashore. In another twenty-four hours, they had captured the Japanese airstrip:

By midafternoon they held the highest land on the islet and the American flag was flung to the wind there. But the marines stood atop a volcano. Beneath their very feet were a series of about two dozen impregnable coral caves, and around these a fierce battle began.

Improvising swiftly, the marines strapped explosives to the ends of long poles. They fitted them with five-second fuses and pushed or hurled them into cave mouths.

■

One great stroke of fortune came early, when the Japanese naval landing force that was protecting naval laborers on the island retreated to a defensive position:

Throughout the first day men whose bodies had softened during weeks of shipboard life scrambled up the faces of muddy hills and slid down the reverse slopes. . . . Gasping in humid heat . . . burdened with packs and ammunition loads that were far too heavy, the First Marines moved through dripping rain forests with all the stealth of a traveling circus.

They blundered through fields of sharp kunai grass as tall as a man and sometimes became lost in them or shot at each other there. They forded what seemed to be river after river but what was actually one or two streams doubling back on themselves. . . . If the Japanese had chosen to sit in ambush that day there could have been a slaughter.

But the enemy was absent. . . .

On Saturday morning the First Marines quickly overran the airfield. Here was the prize of the campaign, and it would soon be named Henderson Field in honor of Maj. Loften Henderson, a marine flying hero who was killed at Midway.

■

But on the night of August 8–9, Japanese warships suddenly charged down on the invasion fleet anchored off Guadalcanal, sinking one Australian and three American cruisers in a wild engagement called the Battle of Savo Island. Expecting follow-ups of the at-

tack—and unable to take any such further losses—the Allied warships had to withdraw, leaving the troops stranded ashore:

Colonel Edson lay on his belly, bringing his own artillery in closer and closer to the charging enemy. A corporal named Watson, who would be Lieutenant Watson in the morning, spotted the enemy for him. He marked the Japanese rocket signals and directed redoubled fire to break up the enemy's massing points. . . .

The Ridge shook and flashed. A terrible steel rain fell among marines and Japanese alike. Terrified enemy soldiers dove into marine foxholes to escape death above ground. Marines knifed them and pitched them out again. The night was hideous with the screams of the stricken. . . .

■

By the fall of 1942, the forces trying to hold on to Guadalcanal found they had to deal with another problem that was lining up against them . . . and this was the demand that global strategy placed on limited U.S. resources. Admiral Nimitz, in Pearl Harbor, was concerned:

"It now appears that we are unable to control the sea in the critical Guadalcanal area. . . . Thus our supply of the positions will only be done at great expense to us. The situation is not hopeless, but it is certainly critical."

His grim estimate of the situation came at a time when it was next to impossible for Admiral King in Washington to divert any additional ships or supplies or men to the South Pacific. Operation TORCH, the invasion of North Africa, was gathering. . . .

Nimitz knew that the Guadalcanal situation was critical simply because the Japanese navy was concentrating all its forces there and he had no equal forces to oppose them.

Then, on October 16 . . . Nimitz received a shattering message from Admiral Ghormley.

"This appears to be all-out enemy effort against Guadalcanal. My forces totally inadequate to meet situation. Urgently request all aviation reinforcements possible."

The following day Ghormley came through with an estimate of what he needed. (It seemed to be a list of everything he could think of from submarines to heavy bombers—the material destined for North Africa and desired by commanders all over.) . . . Nimitz, a calm and orderly man, was staggered. Obviously such recommendations did not spring from a hopeful mind. . . . Nimitz sighed and came reluctantly to a decision. . . .

The following day a four-engined Coronado flying boat circled above Admiral Ghormley's flagship, *Argonne,* in the harbor at Nouméa.

The pilot eased back on the throttle and brought the plane down gently on the water's surface. An admiral with a craggy face and tufted gray eyebrows [William F. Halsey] clambered out just as a motor whaleboat drew alongside. The admiral jumped into the tossing whaleboat [and was handed a sealed message by a waiting officer]:

YOU WILL TAKE COMMAND OF THE SOUTH PACIFIC AREA AND SOUTH PACIFIC FORCES IMMEDIATELY.

On Guadalcanal, men who had never once lost hope of victory, who were entering their eleventh week of battle still confident of it, heard the news with shouts of jubilation. A real tiger was taking over.

■

The change of command at the top did much for the morale in the rifle pits on Guadalcanal:

Sgt. Ralph Briggs and his men on outpost hugged the ground, while Briggs rang up Colonel Puller's command post.

"Colonel," he said softly, "there's about three thousand Japanese between you and me."

"Are you sure?"

"Positive. They've been all around us, singing and smoking cigarettes, heading your way."

At 11 o'clock . . . the Japanese came hurtling against Puller's marines. . . .

"Blood for the Emperor!"

"Marine, you die!"

The raggedy-tag marine defenders had decided to holler back: "To hell with you. Blood for Eleanor and Franklin!"

■

On shore, Lt. Comdr. J. E. Lawrence, the U.S. Air Combat Information Officer, re-

membered how the lack of supplies and the pounding from the Japanese big ships were wearing them down:

Our A.K.s (cargo ships) were loaded with the stuff we needed, but every time there was a Condition Red (enemy air raid), they had to up-anchor and get out. First the planes pounded us, and then the battleships. During thirty-six hours on 13 and 14 October, the *Kongo* and the *Haruna* gave us a thousand rounds of 14-inch. But it wasn't that; it was . . . the feeling that nobody gave a curse whether we lived or died. It soaked into you until you couldn't trust your own mind. You'd brief a pilot, and no sooner had he taken off than you'd get frantic, wondering if you'd forgotten to tell him some trivial thing that might become the indispensable factor in saving his life.

■

But in November, the five-day Battle of Guadalcanal—as the last big naval engagement was called—turned the Americans' luck. Admiral Halsey described the victory:

This battle was a decisive American victory by any standard. It was also the third great turning point of the war in the Pacific. Midway stopped the Japanese advance in the Central Pacific; Coral Sea stopped it in the Southwest Pacific; Guadalcanal stopped it in the South Pacific. . . . If our ships and planes had been routed in this battle, if we had lost it, our troops on Guadalcanal would have been trapped as were our troops on Bataan. We could not have reinforced them or relieved them. Archie Vandegrift would have been our "Skinny" Wainwright, and the infamous Death March would have been repeated. (We later captured a document which designated the spot where the Japanese commander had planned to accept Archie's surrender.)

■

A Japanese newspaper, Yomiuri, *described one suicide attack:*

On the eve of the sortie, at midnight, all the assembled men sing the *Kimigayo* ("Your Majesty's reign will last ten thousand and one generations . . .") the sad and solemn hymn to the Emperor, then give three *banzais* (cheers) for his eternal prosperity. The

company bows in the direction of the Imperial Palace. While the American loudspeakers, which are set up above the lines, continue to repeat in Japanese the invitation to capitulate, the two hundred men, including the sick and the wounded who have still survived, rush toward death in a supreme attack. . . .

■

By late 1942, the stalemate at Guadalcanal forced the Japanese to pull some troops out of the fighting against the Australians in the Owen Stanley mountains of New Guinea and send them to the island as reinforcements. This left battered, undersupplied Japanese units in New Guinea alternately trying to hold and then retreat. This first reversal of the war hit them hard. Second Lieutenant Hirano in New Guinea:

It left us momentarily dazed to have to retreat from our present position, after advancing so close to our goal at the cost of enormous sacrifices and casualties.

■

A Japanese army officer who had observed the fighting on Guadalcanal wrote a critique— probably for home front consumption—of the American fighting man:

The enemy has received almost no training. Even though we fire a shot they present a very large portion of their body and look around. Their movements are very slow. At this rate they cannot make a night attack. . . . They . . . fire as long as their ammunition lasts. Maybe they get more money for firing so many rounds.

■

The letter below from a Japanese soldier was not discovered until after the war. But in it, Americans could have seen just "another poor GI" opposite them:

How I wish we could change to the offensive! Human beings must die once. It is only natural instinct to want to live; but only those with military spirit can cast that away. . . . The news that reinforcements had come turned out to be a rumor. All day we stay in the bunkers. We are filled with vexation. Comrades, are you going to stand by and watch us die? Even the invincible

Imperial Army is at a loss. Can't anything be done?

■

One Private Wada of the Imperial Army kept a diary in the jungle that could almost have been written at El Alamein or Stalingrad—or wherever the war came down to soldiers slogging back and forth over the same ground:

24 December—Our troops expect to make a general attack beginning this night before Christmas and lasting till tomorrow morning. I am praying for our complete success. Seems that there will be no rice today. Supper consisted of coconut and octopus. No rice. Ate snakes. . . . Intense enemy artillery fire. . . .

25 December—I suppose the enemy is not having much of a Christmas either. A handful of rice for supper. Our mess area was blown to bits by enemy artillery fire during the morning, and our mess kits were damaged. . . .

1943—1 January—I greeted the New Year. I spent the last days of 1942 in the jungle amid bursting shells. I greeted the New Year in the same way, soaked through and amidst artillery fire.

■

Toward the end of June 1942, Admiral Yamamoto, the architect of the successful Pearl Harbor raid, launched a powerful Japanese naval force toward Midway, America's most westerly scouting base in the Pacific. Admiral Nimitz, helped by the fact that the United States had cracked some of the major Japanese codes, anticipated the Midway strike and had his three carriers—including the patched-up Yorktown, *heavily damaged in the Battle of the Coral Sea, hidden at sea northwest of Midway. Mitsuo Fuchida described the departure of the Japanese fleet for Midway:*

The fleet had formed a single column for the passage through the strait. Twenty-one ships in all, they cruised along at intervals of a thousand yards. . . . As the fleet steamed on, three seaplanes of the Kure Air Corps passed overhead. . . . The planes were on their way to neutralize the enemy submarines which might be lying in wait for us outside Bungo Strait.

■

An American combat report from Midway airfield described the opening of the fight:

The first Japanese air strike—thirty-six torpedo aircraft, thirty-six dive-bombers, and thirty-six fighters, under Lieutenant Tomonaga—was picked up by Midway radar forty-three miles northwest of the island. The alarm was sounded, every aircraft able to leave the ground took to the air, and at 6:16 A.M., when thirty miles out, the Marine Corps fighter squadron, twenty-six aircraft in all, encountered the Japanese van, but was outnumbered and almost annihilated.

■

Mitsuo Fuchida related the activities of the Japanese battle fleet as it came within scouting range of Midway:

Eight minutes after launching [a scout plane] its observer suddenly discerned, far off to port, a formation of some ten ships heading southeast. Without waiting until it could get a closer look, the plane immediately flashed a message to the Nagumo Force: "Ten ships, apparently enemy, sighted.". . . Until this morning, no one had anticipated that an enemy surface force could possibly appear so soon.

■

Theodore Taylor followed the action. After Pearl Harbor, the American public needed a victory:

Down below the blanket of clouds at fifteen hundred feet, unmindful that his fighter cover was not above, [Jack Waldron] rolled Torpedo Squadron Eight northward on a strong hunch. He found Nagumo and the carriers *Hiryu, Akagi, Kaga* and *Soryu*. . . . He rode his torpedo planes in against the carriers without fighter protection; full into the ack-ack and whirling Zeros, hoping to deliver his weenies and pickles. Waldron presented fifteen solid targets to the Japanese gun gallery. Ensign Gay was shot down and hid beneath a floating seat cushion. He witnessed the Battle of Midway from that bobbing seat and was picked up later [as the only aircrewman of Torpedo Squadron Eight who survived]. . . .

As more action reports drifted in, Mitscher informed the *Hornet* crew, "Four Japanese carriers are afire. Direct hits have been scored on their battleships and cruisers."

It was growing dark, and the *Hornet*, blacked out, soon blended into the night. How could her surviving bombers find the flight deck? Two planes angled toward the task force. Then others droned up. None of the *Hornet* pilots had qualified in night carrier landings.

"Turn on the truck lights," Mitscher ordered. The dim red beacons shone out from her masthead but the planes passed over. Mitscher knew the pilots could not possibly spot her deck. "Let's give them more light."

Two search beams climbed into the air over the *Hornet;* a string of lights outlined the flight deck to port. . . .

■

Aboard the aircraft carrier Akagi *in the center of the action, Mitsuo Fuchida was badly wounded. He was transferred to a cruiser before the attack centered on his carrier and looked back proudly at his old ship:*

On *Akagi*'s flight deck all planes were in position with engines warming up. The big ship began turning into the wind. . . .

Visibility was good. Clouds were gathering at about three thousand metres, however, and though there were occasional breaks, they afforded good concealment for approaching enemy planes. At 1024 the order to start launching came from the bridge by voice-tube. The Air Officer flapped a white flag, and the first Zero fighter gathered speed and whizzed off the deck. At that instant a lookout screamed: "Hell-Divers!" Three black enemy planes were plummeting toward our ship. . . . The plump silhouettes of the American Dauntless dive-bombers quickly grew larger, and then a number of black objects suddenly floated eerily from their wings. . . . Down they came straight toward me!

The terrifying scream of the dive-bombers reached me first, followed by the crashing explosion of a direct hit. There was a blinding flash and then a second explosion, much louder than the first. . . . Then followed a startling quiet as the barking of guns suddenly ceased. I got up and looked at the sky. The enemy planes were already gone from sight. . . .

Looking about, I was horrified at the destruction that had been wrought in a matter of seconds. . . .

As the number of dead and wounded increased and the fires got further out of control, Captain Aoki finally decided at 1800 that the ship must be abandoned. The injured were lowered into boats and cutters sent alongside by the screening destroyers. Many uninjured men leapt into the sea and swam away from the stricken ship. . . .

In the next ten minutes the main engines stopped, the steering system went out, and fire mains were destroyed. Crewmen, forced by the flames to leave their posts, had just arrived on deck when a mighty explosion blasted many of them into the water. Within twenty minutes of the first bomb hit the ship was such a mass of fire that Capt. Ryusaku Yanagimoto ordered, "Abandon ship!" It was soon discovered, however, that Captain Yanagimoto had remained on the bridge of the blazing carrier. No ship commander in the Japanese Navy was more beloved by his men. . . .

■

Battle Report, *an official navy history published soon after the war, gives this account from the American side: The victory would mark the turning point for U.S. fortunes in the Pacific . . . and Japanese naval chiefs would privately realize Japan could not win the naval war. The quotations that follow are from Walter Karig and Eric Purdon's* Battle Report:

As a student of naval history, Admiral Yamamoto remembered that shortly would come the anniversary of a battle that made another island kingdom the foremost naval power in the world. . . . Yamamoto wouldn't have an enemy fleet to contend with, he was sure, but his victory would be as far-reaching as Nelson's at Trafalgar. . . . The strategic significance of its [Midway's] capture would change the course of this war.

On June 2, the two American task forces [waiting for the Japanese] made their rendezvous northeast of Midway and Admiral Fletcher assumed command of the joint fleets.

To his eight ships—the patched-up York-town, two heavy cruisers, five destroyers—Adm. Raymond A. Spruance brought seventeen—two carriers, five heavy cruisers and one light, and nine destroyers. Twenty-five submarines under Rear Adm. Robert H. English were deployed in the avenues of likely approach. It was an imposing force, but not quite up to the four carriers, four battleships, seven cruisers and twenty-two destroyers of the Japanese.

An area of poor visibility thickened 300 to 400 miles to the northwest. If the Japanese . . . took advantage of it, the American searchers would not be able to locate the enemy carriers the day before they reached attacking range . . . [and] upon emerging from the obscured area in the early morning hours [the Japanese] would wait for dawn to fix position before launching planes, between 4:30 and 5:00 at the earliest. Midway could, therefore, expect attack about 6:00 A.M. (This analysis proved to be accurate. The first Japanese bomb fell on Midway about 6:30 A.M.)

■

When the three-day battle was over on June 6, 1942—and it was one of the first upturns of fortune that the Americans had seen in the Pacific—the scorecard looked as follows:

U.S. losses: One carrier, *Yorktown*, sunk; One destroyer, *Hammann*, sunk; 150 airplanes lost; 307 lives lost.

Japanese losses: four carriers sunk; One cruiser, one destroyer sunk; 250 airplanes lost; 2,000 lives lost.

■

In the winter and spring of 1942, U.S. morale hit a terrible low. The Philippines fell, MacArthur had to be spirited to Australia under Roosevelt's orders to organize a Pacific offensive when America could stage the effort, and Corregidor surrendered its defenders to what the public already knew (from the Japanese war on China) would be brutal POW camps. There was a tremendous need for some strike or victory to boost the spirit. Out of this grew a bizarre but courageous endeavor. Duane Schultz interviewed most of the survivors for this story. Where no other speaker or source is identified, the words are Schultz's:

The Doolittle raid began with a line painted across a runway in Norfolk, Virginia. . . . Most naval air stations had one to mark off the length of the deck of an aircraft carrier, to help pilots practice short-run takeoffs and landings. . . . On Saturday, January 10, 1942, Capt. Francis Low, a submariner, took a look at the line across the runway at Norfolk and saw in it a way to strike back at Japan. . . .

■

Captain Low outlined his plan:

"I've been to the Norfolk yard, as you know, sir, to see the progress made on the *Hornet*. At the airfield they had marked out a strip about the size of a carrier deck, and they practice takeoffs constantly. If the army has some plane that could take off in that short distance," Low said, ". . . carrying a bomb load, why couldn't we put a few of them on a carrier and bomb the mainland of Japan?"

"Low," King said, "that might be a good idea. Discuss with Duncan [King's air officer], and tell him to report to me."

■

Duncan decided the only plane suitable for the job was the army's new twin-engined B-25 bomber:

It had a wingspan of only sixty-seven feet and required a shorter takeoff run. . . .

Two carriers should be used for the mission, Duncan wrote, one to carry the bombers and the other, with navy fighter planes aboard, to provide air cover for the carriers and their escort of cruisers, destroyers, and oilers. . . .

"Go see General Arnold . . ." King said after reviewing Duncan's plan, "and if he agrees with you, ask him to get in touch with me. Don't mention this to another soul." . . .

On January 17, 1942, Doolittle was called into the air corps chief's office, shortly after Arnold had met with navy captains Duncan and Low. Arnold handed him the assignment that would change his life.

"Jim," Arnold said, "what airplane have we got that will get off in five hundred feet with a two-thousand-pound bomb load and fly two thousand miles?" . . .

While the planes were being readied, President Roosevelt was continuing to press his service chiefs about a way to bomb Japan. At a White House meeting on January 28, with Arnold, King, Marshall, Stimson, and others, the president asked Arnold if any definite plans had been made. Arnold and King were the only ones present who knew about the work of Doolittle and Duncan, and they wanted to keep it that way. . . .

In all, only Arnold, King, Low, Duncan, and Doolittle were aware of the operation. . . . Not the president, the secretary of war, or the army chief of staff. Admiral King appeared to agree. He said nothing about the raid either. . . .

■

The plan to handle the bombers coming into China after the raid seemed logical and relatively simple. What hadn't been considered was the difficulty of working with the Chinese. And the man who could have advised them about that—General Stilwell— had not been taken into the confidences of the planners; they were afraid of a leak through Chiang Kai-shek's devious staff and political advisors:

Arnold told Stilwell only that American bombers would arrive in China at a certain time, and that he should arrange for aviation fuel and oil, English-speaking personnel, and radio homing equipment to be stashed at several airfields in eastern China. . . .

By the end of March, an increasingly frustrated General Arnold had still been unable to confirm the desired arrangements for Doolittle's men. The fliers would have to rely on the Chinese fuel—if it existed—to go on to Chungking, and hope it contained no impurities to foul their engines.

■

On the morning of April 18, when the Hornet *was spotted prematurely by a Japanese picket boat manning the extensive ocean warning line east of Japan, a hard decision had to be made quickly:*

Captain Mitscher of the *Hornet* agreed. "We had to launch them," he wrote. "We weren't

where we wanted to be. We gave them extra gas. It was all a calculated risk. We couldn't risk [the carriers] after the fishing boats had been spotted."

At eight o'clock in the morning, while the *Nashville* was trying to sink the fishing trawler *Nitto Maru,* Halsey issued the order. It was flashed by blinker lights to the *Hornet:*

LAUNCH PLANES. TO COLONEL DOOLITTLE AND GALLANT COMMAND: GOOD LUCK AND GOD BLESS YOU. HALSEY. . . .

Doolittle shook hands with Mitscher and left the bridge. The klaxon screamed, followed by an announcement:

"ARMY PILOTS, MAN YOUR PLANES"

Jack Higler told his crew that they did not have enough fuel to get to China. "The way things are now, " he said, "we have about enough to get us to within two hundred miles of the China coast, and that's all. If anyone wants to withdraw, he can do it now." None of them took up his offer. . . .

Osborn carefully gauged the rise and fall of the deck. When he judged that the moment was right, he brought his arm down in a brisk chop. Knowing the instant to signal the plane to start rolling was critical, Steve Jurika described it this way: "You knew how long it would take them to run down that deck . . . and you wanted to start them as the bow started down because it would take them that length of time to get to within . . . fifty or seventy-five feet of the bow, and then, as the deck started to come up, you would actually launch them into the air at least horizontal but on the upswing, in fact giving them a boost into the air." . . .

When Osborn's arm came down, Doolittle took his feet off the brakes, and the deck crewmen yanked the chocks away from the wheels and threw themselves flat on the deck. The heavily laden B-25 started slowly down the deck. A navy pilot, watching it waddle forward, shouted that it wasn't going to make it. . . .

A few yards before the end of the deck, the B-25 lifted into the air. Doolittle yanked the control yoke back into his stomach. "He

hung his ship almost straight up on its props," Ted Lawson said, "until we could see the whole top of his B-25. Then he leveled off and I watched him come around in a tight circle and shoot low over our heads—straight down the line painted on the deck. . . . I felt a lot better when I saw the wheels leave the deck in less than four hundred feet of takeoff space." In his report on the raid, Doolittle said simply, "Takeoff was easy."

■

The full story of the raid was not known until after the war, when crew members who had crash-landed in Japan and Russia finally came home. In the end, the bombing of the Japanese home islands for the first time had accomplished most of what it was intended to do—in spite of its costs. America was cheered . . . and Japan was alarmed:

The number of fliers accounted for gradually increased, but the more information Arnold received, the clearer it became that part of Doolittle's first message was correct—all the B-25s were lost. Wreckage and debris of the bombers, crashed and burned, was being sighted almost hourly throughout eastern China. . . .

The story continued to be front-page news every day, even though the government maintained its silence, still not admitting officially that a raid had occurred. Finally, one man did say something about it, a comment that delighted the American people and confounded the Japanese. It came to be one of President Roosevelt's favorite stories. He had asked his close friend and speechwriter Judge Samuel I. Rosenman what he should say when reporters asked where the bombers had come from.

"Mr. President," Rosenman said, "do you remember the novel of James Hilton, *Lost Horizon,* telling of that wonderful, timeless place known as Shangri-La?" . . .

Roosevelt called Stephen Early, his press secretary, "and told him that if anyone wanted to know where the bombers originated he was going to say 'Shangri-La.' "

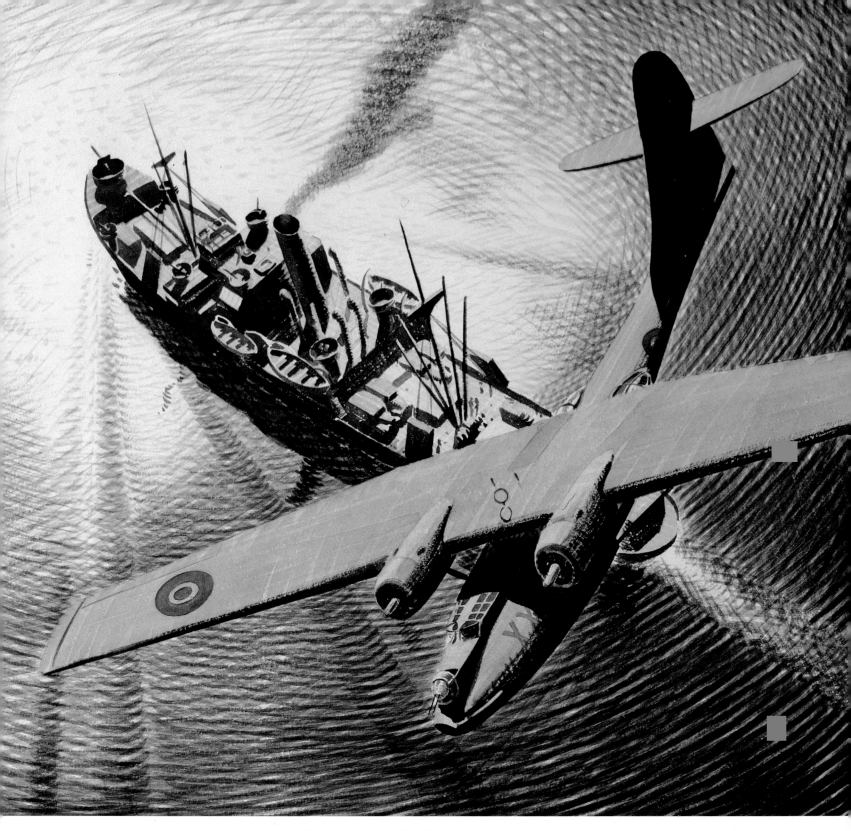

Patrol over the Pacific

New Zealander Russell Clark, flying patrols with the Royal New Zealand Air Force, records a patrol boat swooping low to check the identity of a well-armed freighter—flying no colors—moving among the islands out of convoy. The New Zealanders were flying the dependable, versatile PBY "Catalina," looking for suspicious craft or downed airmen. With over a year of training invested in making a pilot, rescuing one was well worth an extended search in military terms, not to mention the value to morale. (National Archives of New Zealand)

Guadalcanal, 1942–43

Kerr Eby painted *Ghost Trail* essentially in blacks and greens—the colors of the jungle. Guadalcanal veterans said even the jungle rain had a funny rusty color of its own. One of the Corps' basic training centers was Parris Island, carved out of miserable scrub and marsh on the coast of South Carolina. Marines wondered about the Corps' ironic foresight in locating the boot camp in the Carolina boondocks, terrain that would prove so similar to Guadalcanal. (U.S. Navy Combat Art Collection)

Wounded, Island Campaigns, 1942–44

Until the late 1930s, marine landing practice had been carried out from regular ships' boats carried by battleships and cruisers. But they were hard to climb in and out of, could carry little heavy equipment, and were easy to broach in a surf. Then came the first specialized landing craft, of which the LST (Landing Ship, Tank) was the queen. The bow ramp of one of these is the scene for Joseph Hirsch's *Transportation, Latest Mode*. Once an LST disgorged its vehicles, its vast tank deck could be turned quickly into an aid station. (U.S. Navy Combat Art Collection)

Invasion Beach

Jim Turnbull's *Supplies Are Landed* (RIGHT) shows one solution to a gradually shelving beach that could ground a landing craft below the shoreline. The landing craft take a buffeting—but the trucks have to be tough, as well. (U.S. Navy Combat Art Collection)

Prelude to Invasion

One marine saying held that the man who designed the personnel landing craft made them rough and uncomfortable so that troops would be glad to get out of them when they hit the beach—even under fire. Their crashing and banging when loading alongside a transport was described like "being in the middle of a four-car crash." Jim Turnbull painted the ticklish job. (U.S. Navy Combat Art Collection)

Private Moments, Guadalcanal

The "war artists" were not all professionals. Unsigned drawings and paintings from men and women who experienced the hard events of those years are sometimes the most poignant. These two pages are from a battered pocket notebook found on the body of an unidentified Japanese officer at Guadalcanal. He has tried his hand (ABOVE) at both sketching and poetry in a classical Japanese style: "A red lamp fades into waves/White fog covers Shanghai port. . . . /But when the boat with my love arrives/Sad Chinese girl in China's night." (BELOW) He apparently tried in prose to re-create a last meeting with the girl he loved: "In the end of April, I was standing on the bank of the river. . . . It was a beautiful and quiet night. Here there was a beautiful love with a pure heart. Two years have passed since I knew her. A pure love, believing each other." (Courtesy of Anne Zinsser; translation courtesy of Yoshitaka Kamei)

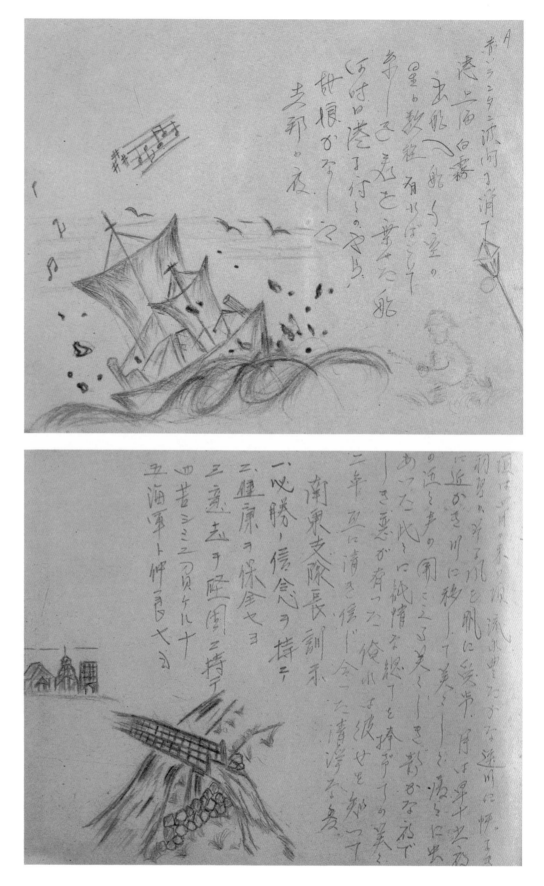

Carrier Landings

William Draper's *Planes Return from Palau* illustrates a time when an aircraft carrier was at its most vulnerable. Planes back from a mission crowd the forward end of the flight deck. The pressure now is to get all planes aboard and quickly down to the hangar deck, refueled, rearmed, and then "spotted" correctly topside for tomorrow's war. No air attack was expected at night, because the Japanese couldn't land on blacked-out ships either. (U.S. Navy Combat Art Collection)

Japanese Carrier Under Attack

Robert Benny talked to navy and marine pilots who had been up against the big Japanese fleet carriers and the best aviators in the Imperial Navy, before painting *The Kill*. A Douglas "Dauntless" dive-bomber swoops up from her bomb drop on a Japanese carrier. In the background, two escorting ships have taken hits. As they came out of their dives, dive-bombers were tempting targets for fighters hovering above. But torpedo planes were the easiest game, having to fly low and straight to launch a torpedo. (U.S. Navy Combat Art Collection)

Solomon Islands, 1942–44

When New York's prestigious Museum of Modern Art opened a modest art show of sketches and paintings by marines and navy men stationed in the South Pacific, the "star" of the show was a rough sketch by an unknown marine found on the floor of an ambulance and which was christened *Stretcher Party.* Surprising numbers of visitors, attracted by reviews and word of mouth, came to see how American fighting men saw themselves. The pictures on this page convey the spirit of that show. Top left, Donald Dickson drew *Naval Gunfire,* with marines sheltering in a palmetto-log dugout. The fire is friendly—but it could kill you. Bottom left, Kerr Eby painted *Gift of Life from Home*—blood plasma flowing from a bottle taped to a rifle butt. Bottom right, Kerr Eby painted *Dentists of Bougainville,* after being struck by the irony of marines preferring frontline foxholes to painful dental work. Top right, Eby's *Say AHH!* Corps regulations said every man got regular care and checkups—and no battle was going to interfere with the regulations. (U.S. Navy Combat Art Collection)

Japanese Prisoners

A nation waging war tries, of necessity, to instill a hatred of the enemy in its citizenry. So it sometimes comes as a surprise to see prisoners looking as worn with war as our own soldiers. These Japanese prisoners on Mono Island, painted by Russell Clark, looked dazed and exhausted—much like prisoners of war anywhere. (National Archives of New Zealand)

Wm. F. Draper USNR
5/16/44

Torokina Airstrip, Solomon Islands

The air war had its start on drafting tables two and three years earlier as nations hurried to design equipment that could outperform the enemy's. The Japanese Zero was the dominant fighter plane in the Pacific until the Allies answered with planes of unprecedented power and range like the Corsair. Russell Clark's painting *Back from Rabaul* shows Royal New Zealand Air Force Corsair fighters on Torokina in the Solomon Islands in 1944. (National Archives of New Zealand)

Carrier Crew

A carrier's flight deck crew, with teams in different colored T-shirts and helmets, performed its duties on the several decks with the speed, grace, and deftness of a ballet saluting the aviation age. When planes were "spotted" topside with engines running, the flight deck could be a deadly place. In William Draper's *Up to the Flight Deck* (LEFT), a torpedo plane, which carried a crew of three, comes up on the elevator from the hangar deck. (U.S. Navy Combat Art Collection)

Round-the-Clock Carrier Work

Perhaps the most important airman on the carrier was the landing signal officer, whom Dwight Shepler painted above. He directed each of the "controlled crashes" of a carrier landing. As the plane got close, the rear of the deck disappeared under the aircraft's nose. You just kept your eye on "the bandleader" and did exactly as he signaled. Mitchell Jamieson was a prolific painter of naval subjects. At left, he sees an early flight of TBF Avenger torpedo planes, on the afterdeck of a new light carrier, being launched for the day's first air patrol. (Both, U.S. Navy Combat Art Collection)

Carrier Ready Room

The tense boredom of the pilots' "Ready Room" immediately below the flight deck inspired this William Draper scene. The ship's position and its intended course were kept constantly updated. The target briefing took place here, with any last-minute information. Navigational problems were often more complicated than the fighting, and there were even cases of lost pilots with drying fuel tanks trying to land on enemy carriers, thinking they were home. (U.S. Navy Combat Art Collection)

Night Repairs on a Carrier

William Draper painted the hangar deck (TOP LEFT) as the mechanics worked late into the night in preparation for the next day's flying. The wear on carrier aircraft was obviously more intensive than on land-based planes. Salt spray and salt in the air could get into every part of the plane in spite of rigorous cleandowns. Even the smoothest carrier landing consisted of a plane dropping to the deck from a height of about twenty feet and then a tremendous wrench on the whole structure of the plane as the arresting hook grabbed the wire and yanked the aircraft to a halt. (U.S. Navy Combat Art Collection)

War Supplies

William Draper was struck with the "appetite of war" as bombs and shells came aboard a heavy carrier (BOTTOM LEFT). The whole point of a preinvasion naval bombardment was saturation—and intimidation. (U.S. Navy Combat Art Collection)

Carrier Defenders

These gun crews (OPPOSITE) are at general quarters during an enemy plane alert. Following are a light carrier, right, and a destroyer in the rear center of the picture. When planes were being launched or recovered, a destroyer cruised astern ready to pick up pilots who overshot, undershot, or went over the side of the deck. William Draper was the artist. (U.S. Navy Combat Art Collection)

Bombs Away, Paul Goranson (Canadian War Museum)

STEPPING STONES TO EUROPE

From bases in North Africa, Allied troops invaded Sicily and Italy in the summer and fall of 1943, putting Allied armies back into Europe for the first time since Dunkirk. The civilian populations often greeted the Allies as "liberators." In their landing at Salerno, the Allies used most of the tactics that would later be used with refinement in northern France: heavy naval bombardment, gliders, paratroops, saturation bombing of landing areas and enemy supply lines. When Italy made peace with the Allies, the Nazis seized Rome and other strategic points to carry on the war. Mussolini was dismissed by the king, arrested, and had to be rescued by the Germans from his hiding place on an Italian mountaintop. The Allies landed at Anzio after the advance from Salerno was bogged down. But with Hitler ordering last-man stands along several defense lines, stubborn German units kept the Allies out of Rome until just before the Normandy invasion in June 1944. Allied bombing took hard measure of various Italian cities and historic sites; air and ground action almost destroyed the ancient abbey of Monte Cassino, with each side blaming the other.

The American soldiers who had first gone into combat in North Africa had faced brutal confrontations with the German units they encountered, often coming out second. The rumor had gone around that the Germans in Sicily might be second-line troops. But when the fighting occurred, there was little evidence of that. American intelligence had failed to pick up the fact that elements of the crack Hermann Göring Division were on the island. Richard Tregaskis had served as a correspondent in the Pacific and had written Guadalcanal Diary, which touched the spirits of thousands of Americans. Unless otherwise credited, the reports of the invasion of Sicily and the incidents that follow are his.

Private Weiherman, the interpreter, explained the hunted look in the pale eyes [of a captured German]; after a few words of conversation with the German, Weiherman translated that the Nazi had been told he would be shot if captured. The German's face relaxed when the interpreter assured him that he would not be killed. . . .

We noticed that a long irregular scar covered one of the prisoner's cheeks. The scar was a large dark area under the right eye, trailing into a narrow red line down the side of his jaw. Weiherman asked if it was a wound, and the German replied, yes, it had been received at Bryansk in Russia, thirty-five kilos from Moscow. "Two of my toes were frozen. I didn't lose them; but I can hardly march." . . .

July 28: Another wounded enemy, a corporal, had the same haunted look as the prisoner who had been interrogated on Hill 1333 yesterday. While Creelman dressed the bullet wound, through the fleshy part of the leg, the prisoner told us that he, too, had been wounded in the fighting in Russia. He had served during the campaign in France.

■

Although armies of the major countries had been experimenting with paratroop units through the 1930s, military traditionalists in many commands tended to be skeptical of what power they could deliver in battle. The skepticism ended within a period of a few weeks in the spring of 1940 when the Germans invaded the Low Countries. Almost the entire German paratroop strength was used.

German units gave Col. James Gavin and other airborne commanders some powerful arguments to be used against opponents of airborne troops they had encountered in Washington and London when the Allies were planning the invasion of Sicily. In the quotations that follow, Gavin tells of confidence justified:

In July 1943 the Allies were to be the latest invaders of Sicily, and we, the 505th Parachute Regimental Combat Team, were to spearhead the invasion. . . . We were gathered in small groups under the wings of our C47s [on July 9, 1943] ready for loading and takeoff. . . . Because of security restrictions, it had not been possible to inform every trooper of our destination until just before takeoff. Then each was given a small slip of paper which read:

"Soldiers of the 505th Combat Team: Tonight you embark upon a combat mission. . . . You will spearhead the landing of an American Force upon the island of SICILY. . . ."

The pilots were revving up their engines and we were ready to roll down the runway [when a messenger rushed up to Gavin]. "I was told to tell you the wind is going to be thirty-five miles an hour, west to east."

There was nothing I could do about it. Training jumps had normally been cancelled when the wind reached about fifteen miles an hour, in order for us to minimize injuries. . . . But we couldn't change plans now.

■

From private to colonel, the jump into Sicily was usually the first combat experience:

After twenty years of military service I was about to meet The Enemy face to face. I stuck my head up over the stone wall. It seemed a long way up, but it was about an inch, just enough to clear my carbine over the top of the wall.

. . . The Germans had scared the wits out of the natives with their stories about the atrocities committed by American parachutists. They spread the news that we were long-term convicts who had been granted our freedom in exchange for becoming paratroopers.

■

The invasion of Sicily was the first time most American soldiers had been in action with British Empire troops. Each had great curiosity about the other. Correspondent Richard Tregaskis reported several of the evaluations on the campaign across Sicily:

The corporal, a sergeant and two other British Tommies stretched out on the floor of the same room. . . . I asked them what they thought of Americans as people, and one of the voices in the dark, in typical chopped, sing-song English, answered, "They 'ave more money than our chaps and take the girls about. Yet," he added, "the Americans 'ave plenty of guts, as we saw at that tank battle at Djedeida."

A column of British Tommies, trudging in step along the grade, passed us. They were whistling a marching tune, in rhythm with their steps, and their strength and plodding patience were impressive. They were sturdy and sun-browned, but short men by comparison with the Americans. I commented on that fact to Hastings, and he said, "The average Tommy is about a welterweight. But he is tough."

■

Tregaskis was with a British column that was among the first to enter Messina. They were ready for stout resistance—but not for what they found:

Miraculously . . . we reached the last bridge before Messina . . . and the bridge did not explode underneath our wheels. We had reached our objective!

We crossed the bridge. My heart suddenly stopped and fell away when I saw something moving in the wreckage of a house. A human form stirred in the darkness and, fascinated, I watched. Suddenly the face of a mad old hag appeared, the gums bared in a snarl. It might have been a smile, but there was no mirth in it. Only strange animal sounds, which could not have been words in any language, came from the toothless mouth. The old woman, the first human being we had seen in this deserted city, had been shell-shocked into insanity.

■

At the start of the campaigns for Sicily and Italy, one of the enemy military advantages that was hardest to overcome was the legend of "invincibility" largely enjoyed by the German air force:

At the height of the fighting the first German Messerschmitts appeared overhead. To my surprise, they ignored us and attacked the small railroad gatekeeper's house repeatedly. They must have thought that was the Command Post. . . .

About four o'clock a young ensign, who had parachuted with me the first night, came up with a radio and said he could call for naval gunfire. . . . We tried to fix our position in terms of the railroad crossing over the road, and he called for a trial round. It came down precisely where the tank had disappeared. He then called for a concentration, and from then on the battle seemed to change. I kept thinking of Shiloh, Bloody Shiloh. General Grant, sheltered under the riverbank, his command overrun, refused to leave the field, counterattacked, and the battle was won.

■

German troops cornered in Sicily—but then withdrawn successfully to fight again in Italy —reminded Gavin of the lesson both sides should have learned as early as Dunkirk: there Göring had promised that his Luftwaffe could finish off the surrounded Allied troops. But they couldn't; Gavin was disappointed:

How did the bulk of the German and Italian forces manage to go scot-free? With the Allies enjoying complete superiority at sea and in the air, it seemed a simple matter to block the narrow Strait of Messina. The airmen were particularly confident that it could be done, but they had not learned the lesson of Dunkirk.

■

Richard Tregaskis witnessed a series of odd scenes—and certainly not the stuff inspiring World War II newsreels were made of—as the Sicilian campaign came to a close:

September 8: Luckily our parking spot happened to be near field headquarters, a first-aid station. We were startled, a few minutes after we dismounted, when two jeeps, arriving amidst clouds of dust, discharged four men wearing stars on their collars. . . .

It was quite a galaxy. We watched, fascinated, while this group adjourned to the first-aid tent. We craned our necks to see as much as we could of the developments inside. The officers were conducting an intense conference. The driver of one of the jeeps waved at the Red Cross flag and said, "I guess they're cuttin' up Italy on the operatin' table right now." . . .

■

Colonel Gavin summed up the paratrooper experiences in Sicily. It had been a proving ground for Italy . . . and a tough one:

Beginning on August 11 and continuing until the occupation of Messina by Patton and Montgomery on August 16, the Germans moved 8,000 men across the Strait daily. Forty thousand Germans and 62,000 Italians, together with 97 guns, 47 tanks, and 17,000 tons of ammunition, were moved across, most of it in the last few days in broad daylight. The airmen blamed the intensity of the antiaircraft fire, and the navy blamed the heavy coastal guns emplaced on both sides of the strait. . . .

The capture of Sicily placed the Allies in a much better position concerning the Axis powers. From Sicily they threatened Sardinia, Rome, and, much closer, Naples and Salerno. . . . Clearly, they now posed a real threat to the Axis forces in all Italy within range of their fighter bomber cover. . . . So the battle of Sicily was not only a military success; the military lessons learned were to prove invaluable to the Allies in the battles that were to come. . . .

The mission to [invade Italy] posed some new and extremely interesting airborne problems. Again, the operation was beyond friendly fighter range, and since enemy fighters were very active, the operation was limited to hours of darkness. The simplest methods of delivering the troops was to airland them on airfields with the cooperation of the Italians. But since our transports were not to enter the enemy fighter range until after dark and they had to clear by daylight, rigid limitations had to be placed on the time that could be spent on the Rome airfields. Parachute troops, of course, require no landing time whatever; a completely equipped fighting force is dropped while the airplanes remain in flight. . . .

[It was discovered that] the Italian troops had little or no gasoline and enough ammunition for only a few hours of fighting, that they could not guarantee that all the airfields would be in Italian hands, and that, anyway, our airborne landings would cause the Germans to take drastic steps against the Italians. Therefore the whole plan as proposed would be nothing less than disastrous. . . .

■

On the night of September 14, at the special request of Gen. Mark Clark, Gavin led two regimental combat drop teams from Sicily to Italy: one to go inside the beachhead . . . and the other far behind the German lines:

I flew with the 505th. After the Sicilian experience we were all quite apprehensive. However, we were in such a rush to get our proper orders out and assemble the necessary arms, equipment, and ammunition that we had little time to think about what was going to happen to us. We took off on schedule. It was a beautiful, clear night with considerable moonlight. Soon after we left the northwest corner of Sicily, the Italian mainland came into view off to the east. We crossed a peninsula jutting out into the Tyrrhenian Sea. In the plane the red warning light came on to tell us that we were approximately four minutes out from the drop zone. We seemed to have been flying over the peninsula forever when a white beach and a river mouth appeared. The scene looked exactly like that in the photos of the correct drop zone. The green light flashed on.

The first parachutes had barely opened when the great T did light up directly under us.

■

Gavin felt one great strength of his airborne units was his aggressive officers, who shared everything with their men . . . and his well-trained, innovative troopers:

The little colonel was up to his ears in battle and seemed to be having a hell of a good time. Altavilla, where the enemy had heavy infantry and tank forces, lay under the hill and slightly to the rear. The little colonel turned to a Greek-American paratrooper named Perici.

"Perici, take six men and go into Altavilla and find out how many Germans are in it."

Resolutely Perici replied, "No, sir, I can't go into that town."

The little colonel, gasping with rage, pulled out his .45. "Perici, why can't you go into Altavilla?"

"Sir," rejoined Perici calmly, "I've been in this army for four years. I done learned that I can't go to town without a pass. The MPs would get me as shore as hell is red-hot."

With a tight smile on his lips, the colonel wrote out a pass for Sergeant Perici to enter the town with six men. Perici, satisfied, went into the town, where he and his patrol got shot up. They found out the German strength, and, although wounded, Perici returned to report as follows to the colonel: "Sir, they's MPs in that damn town with tanks and half-tracks. A rough bunch, sir!"

■

When the Germans were retreating from Naples, Colonel Gavin had the satisfaction—and the nervous responsibility—of leading Gen. Mark Clark into the city. Clark wanted a triumphant entry. But for all Gavin knew, it could be a shoot-out:

"It was midafternoon before we were fully organized and Generals Clark and Ridgway took their place in the column. Finding my way in was not so difficult as I had anticipated, and the streets were ominously empty. . . . I became aware that there was something besides the wreckage that impressed me. I felt that I was riding through ghostly streets in a city of ghosts. We didn't see a soul. . . ."

Gen. Mark Clark later learned that thousands of people had massed at the Plaza Plebiscito about a mile away in another part of the city. It was here that the conquerors traditionally had been received and the people had assumed that that was where the Allied generals would make their triumphant appearance.

■

Churchill didn't want the Anzio landing to develop into another slogging advance; it was supposed to be an "end run." And Churchill peppered the commanders on the scene with suggestions for maneuvers. The action that follows is from Wynford Vaughan-Thomas's Massacre at the Beachhead:

General Alexander signaled to the anxious Mr. Churchill: "We appear to have got al-

most complete surprise. I have stressed the importance of strong-hitting mobile patrols being boldly pushed out to gain contact with the enemy, but so far have not received reports of their activities."

Mr. Churchill replied: "Thank you for all your messages. Am very glad you are pegging out claims rather than digging in beachheads."

But this was exactly what General Lucas was *not* doing. . . . Behind [an eight-mile circle around the port of Anzio] General Lucas had planned to consolidate and repulse the expected German counterattack.

■

The Irish Guards had tangled with the Germans in northern France in 1940, and when they met stiff resistance in Italy at a strongpoint known as "the Factory" they were ready for it:

The fight for the Factory was the first warning to the frontline soldier that the Anzio adventure had lost its early bloom, its promise of boundless opportunity. The Guards had to clear the place by house-to-house fighting, one of the most unpleasant operations that an infantryman is forced to do. It is a deadly game of hide-and-seek, of sudden encounters at close quarters. . . .

■

In spite of air support and heavy artillery, all advances seemed to come down in the end to what the foot soldiers could do. Vaughan-Thomas watched the Sherwood Foresters lead the way:

From a slit trench north of "Smelly Farm" I watched the attack go in. It is difficult to make sense out of a modern battlefield as you look at it from the touchline.

. . . Noise ebbed and flowed over the leafless vines, now rising to a general thunder as the guns cracked out on both sides, now dropping to a treacherous lull. Small figures now appeared, popping up from holes in the ground and half crouching as they ran. There seemed so few of them. And yet everything depended on what they were going to do in the next few minutes.

■

An American tank commander, sent in with his unit to support the British, saw the ferocity of the German counterattack:

I have never seen so many dead men in one place. They lay so close that I had to step with care. I shouted for the commanding officer. From a foxhole there arose a mud-covered corporal with a handlebar mustache. He was the highest-ranking officer still alive. He stood stiffly to attention.

"How is it going?" I asked. The answer was all around me.

"Well, sir," the corporal said, "there were a hundred and sixteen of us when we first came up, and there are sixteen of us left. We're ordered to hold out until sundown, and I think, with a little good fortune, we can manage to do so."

■

The hard fighting brought out strange tactics and unexpected improvisations:

The Irish Guards, digging in on the left of the Albano road, noted in their *War History* that the stillness of the afternoon of 3 February had been broken by the bleating of a thousand sheep. "Like a dirty, ragged wave a huge flock surged over the crest of the Vallelata ridges and scampered crazily through No. 3 Company. Those wise after the event later said that it was a typical German trick to use poor dumb animals as mine-detectors, but at the time no one felt anything but gratitude."

■

A Guardsman wrote of being pinned down in the point of the line that attracted fire from three directions:

After we'd been firing at everything that moved, I was going to open up on a new mob coming out of the smoke, when someone shouted, "Christ, those are our boys!" They were prisoners, shouting in English, not German, "It's hopeless. You'd better join us.". . .

We shouted to the prisoners, "Run and we'll fire on your guards." Some did, others lay down, so we fired. We killed a good many Germans, maybe some of our boys, too. I tell you, that shook me more than anything.

■

The Royal Berkshires took the force of a midnight German attack:

Ammunition was rushed up by cooks, drivers, and anyone else who was available. Sergeant Griffin, the cook-sergeant, stayed with his old company until 2:30 A.M., killing Germans and providing great inspiration to the company. . . . Gradually, as dawn broke, the fighting died down with both sides exhausted. . . .

Back in London the Prime Minister [angered at the slow advance] was still harping away at his wildcat-versus-whale simile—"I thought we were landing a wildcat that would tear out the bowels of the Boche. Instead we have stranded a vast whale with its tail flopping about in the water."

■

General Lucas knew he was going to be sacked; somebody had to be the goat. One of his closest friends in the army, General Truscott, was sent in as his replacement. A visitor to his headquarters observed:

We've got a new head at Anzio, tough, Barrymore-profiled General Truscott, husky-voiced and with slightly graying hair. But he looks . . . like a two-fisted fighter and not like a tired businessman. He was honest, outspoken and completely realistic.

■

Truscott was supported by Britain's General Gregson-Ellis. The two had met in England and felt a mutual trust. Truscott described his fighting companion on the scene at Anzio:

He was fearless. His gaunt figure clad in shorts, his hawklike features topped by a rather silly-looking . . . tin hat, stalking about the front lines with a long staff reminiscent of a shepherd's crook in hand, always brought Ichabod Crane to my mind.

■

Vaughan-Thomas reported some of the life in the battle lines—which was often quite zany:

For days they would be mortaring each other, calling down artillery fire on the slightest movement and sniping at every head that dared show itself a few inches above ground. Then something absurdly normal or pointless would happen—a German would hang out the washing at a bend in the wadis or, fed up with crouching in his foxhole, would stand up on the skyline and stretch his legs. No one would have the heart to fire a shot at him.

So, too, the Germans dealt kindly with the slightly intoxicated GI who had found an Italian top hat in one of the shell-torn villas, put it on and staggered across the minefields of no-man's-land into the enemy lines. The Germans put his silk hat straight, turned him round to the proper point of the compass and sent him back to his comrades with their compliments.

■

In the fall of 1943, the Allied armies were bogged down in rain and mud, still far short of Rome. The Germans were trying to hold along the "Gustav Line," which ran through the old town of Cassino and into the Abruzzi mountains. Troops on both sides felt the abbey of Monte Cassino, occupying a peak above the town and commanding the valley, would be a formidable threat in the hands of the other side. Both the Allies and the Germans had promised to leave it alone—but could either be trusted? Dr. Maximillian Becker, an art enthusiast and amateur archeologist, who was attached to the elite Hermann Göring Division, was fascinated by the abbey, visited it, and became friendly with the abbot . . . and quickly became totally involved with a plan to protect the treasures of the abbey—and perhaps even the buildings—from the destruction that was taking such a toll on historic Italy. The material that follows is from Monte Cassino *by David Hapgood and David Richardson. Where no other speaker is identified, the observations are those of the authors. Dr. Becker was meeting his new "allies" in the plan:*

Becker had led the conversation around to the treasure of the Abbey of Monte Cassino, mentioning the credit that rescuing the treasure would bring to the Hermann Göring Division. The thought that hung unspoken between them was that they would need that credit if the war ended . . . in a German defeat. . . . Becker then said the abbot might ask him to save other valuable possessions. . . . Jacobi then answered:
. . . "But if we're supposed to do all that, there'll have to be something in it for us, too. Just a couple of paintings. Such an old monastery is sure to have enough. Just cut them out of the frames and roll them up."

Becker was dismayed at that suggestion. . . . Jacobi then laughed, made a gesture of dismissal, and said, "Nonsense, forget about my suggestion. I just thought you'd understand a joke." Nothing more was said, but the exchange had left a bad taste in Becker's mouth, a suggestion of trouble to come.

■

With combat obviously about to sweep through the valley, Abbot Diamare, the bishop of Monte Cassino, asked the German doctor what would happen to all his charges—including some thousand refugees within the walls:

The German doctor said he might be able to arrange transportation for the monks, including, if he so desired, Abbot Diamare himself.

At that the old monk drew his stooped figure erect, and, in a suddenly confident voice, said: "Tell me, doctor, would your general leave his soldiers in the lurch in battle?"

"No," said Becker.

"I am the general, the bishop here, the shepherd of my people. I dare not leave them in the lurch in their time of need, even if battle breaks out. I will stay here with my refugees and a few of my younger monks, and we will wait it out, come what may."

■

Becker knew of the concern for the safety of Monte Cassino that had been voiced publicly on the Allied side. But he had also seen the destruction that had fallen on other historic old towns and buildings as the fighting had pushed forward from the beachhead:

The scene at the Abbey of Monte Cassino in those late October days was one of purposeful confusion. It looked more like a military construction site than a monastery. . . .

Each morning German army trucks— marked with the insignia of the Hermann Göring Division—drew up empty at the monastery gate. A steady stream of men carried crates through the cloisters and out the gate to the waiting trucks. Each evening the trucks left, loaded with people and treasures, on the road to Rome 80 miles away. . . .

For the monks the evacuation of their

monastery was a shattering experience. . . .

On the day after the last truck left, two of the monks who stayed at Monte Cassino—Eusebio Grossetti, the artist, and Matronola—began to keep a diary. . . . [The "I" in the diary refers to Matronola.]

FROM THE MONKS' DIARY:
November 4–8: Lieutenant-Colonel Schlegel came to take his leave for the last time. The abbot gave him a bottle of our forty-year-old wine. At our insistent request, he left a document signed by him in which it was declared that the monastery was under military protection and that it was absolutely prohibited to requisition anything without an order from the Division. This was put up on the gate, where there was already a sign saying that soldiers visiting the monastery must be accompanied by a monk.

■

Becker continued to be worried about the German trucks that were headed north to Spoleto, about seventy miles north of Rome, where the Hermann Göring Division had its headquarters. Becker questioned whether the abbey's treasures would be safe there:

The Hermann Göring Divison had taken for its supply depot the Villa Colle-Ferreto, a huge, castlelike country mansion in a pine forest outside Spoleto. . . .

The captain in charge of the depot then told Becker that some representatives of the Kunstschutz, the German art protection bureau, had come to inspect the treasure in early November. He assured Becker that nothing—so far—had been taken from the depot. . . . Becker found a touch of sardonic humor in something he had seen at the depot. Among the paintings taken out of their crates he had recognized Pieter Brueghel the Elder's *Parable of the Blind*. The painting shows six blind men, linked with staffs, groping across a deserted village, gaunt faces turned up to a hostile sky; the first man has already fallen and the second is stumbling over him and falling in his turn. It occurred to Becker that the man in the corporal's uniform might have chosen

the Brueghel for Göring as a silent comment on the current situation of Germany.

■

The unorthodox chain of command that Hitler and the top Nazi party officers had set up within the German armed forces for certain elite units, particularly SS troops, infuriated professional officers and often caused serious military problems. The Hermann Göring Division's favored position even protected it from the orders of the top German army officer in Italy . . . and set up the situation for a raid on the abbey's treasure. One German officer ranted:

"We didn't get that away from the priests just so we could give it back to the church. This stuff belongs to Germany!" The two officers then mentioned the forthcoming birthday of "the Fat One," meaning, of course, Göring. . . .

FROM THE MONKS' DIARY
December 10: From 11:30 on there was one visitor after another, among them Lieutenant-Colonel of Artillery Pollack, commander of the zone. The abbot told him about the military works undertaken in the vicinity and made him understand that the Germans would be showing an ugly face to the world after all the great propaganda they had made about saving Monte Cassino. . . . The Allied artillery is closer, and there is a continual roar of aircraft despite the cloudy, misty weather. . . .

December 19: About 10:30 two photographers came from the German Propaganda Office in Rome: they took some photographs of the monastery because . . . "they could use the pictures to show the barbarity of the Anglo-Americans." We offered them lunch.

In the afternoon about 3:15, while we were saying the rosary in the chapel of the collegio, there was an aerial attack: the explosions were very powerful and close, shaking the whole building; we went on praying. . . .

■

At several points during the removal of the

art treasures from the abbey Dr. Becker was threatened with the power of the Hermann Göring Division:

Becker defended himself as best he could. General Conrath knew what he had been doing at Monte Cassino and, he thought, approved of the rescue operation. . . . "What I did," the young doctor concluded, "I did for European civilization."

At that the chief medical officer's face turned crimson, he jumped to his feet, and he roared at Becker: "If you want to do something for civilization, you're in the wrong place here in Italy. You can do that in Russia. I will see to it that you are transferred to the Eastern Front immediately!" He stormed out of the office, slamming the door behind him.

FROM THE MONKS' DIARY
January 5: The saddest of sad days.
The interpreter for the new Division arrived about 8:30. He asked to speak to the abbot, and he informed him of very painful orders. He declared that by decision of the Supreme Command of the South, the 300-meter zone no longer existed; that all civilians without any exception must be evacuated; German trucks would come for that purpose. . . .

January 20: Aerial bombardment of the center of Cassino in the afternoon. In the evening the [German] lieutenant from the cave came and gave us to understand that soon we would be under the Anglo-Americans.

Around seven o'clock hellish firing started on the plain, which looked as if it were erupting all over; an awful noise shook the whole monastery. I watched the battle for some time from the monks' corridor: the firing did not come as much as halfway up the mountain. This was the first great battle for Cassino. . . .

■

On February 15, 1944, the Allies virtually destroyed Monte Cassino abbey in what the New York Times *called "the worst aerial and artillery onslaught ever directed against a single building."*

North Africa, 1943

The U.S. Army Air Force heavy bomber crews that had come to North Africa for the invasions of Sicily and Italy settled into well-worn airfields along the southern edge of the Mediterranean, often alongside Britons, Australians, Canadians, New Zealanders, and South Africans who had then been in actions going back to Tobruk and El Alamein. Rudolph Von Ripper, an air force artist, painted *Briefing at North Africa*. (U.S. Air Force Art Collection)

Company in the Parlor, Italy, 1943–45

American artist Joseph Hirsch concentrated for a time on medics and surgical teams in their care for the wounded. One touching note: the medics have stashed their plasma bottles in the niche in the wrecked wall that still contains the household crucifix. (U.S. Army Center of Military History)

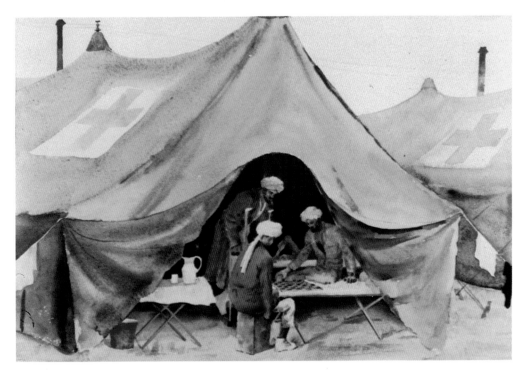

Hospital Tent

A Joseph Hirsch favorite: some of the native North African troops fighting for the Allies. In this hospital scene, three burnoosed warriors have recovered and are waiting for clearance to return to their units. (U.S. Army Center of Military History)

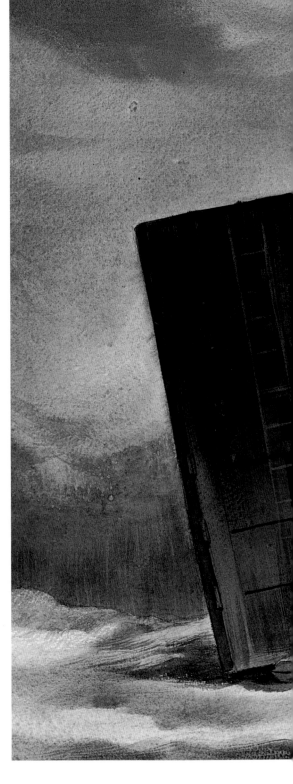

Abandon Ship, Sicily, July 1943

The LST seemed successful in a variety of roles: tank landing ship, floating hospital, traveling machine shop, repair ship for landing craft of all types, seaplane- and PT boat-tender, even "aircraft carrier" for launching army artillery Grasshopper spotting planes on several critical occasions. Before the end of the war LSTs were used by the navies of many of the Allies. In *Inferno,* Mitchell Jamieson records an LST hit and on fire off Sicily. (U.S. Navy Combat Art Collection)

Practice Jump, Italy

Troops on defense found the sight of clouds of paratroopers descending on them an intimidating scene. And as they floated down—in a quite leisurely fashion as it seemed to the men on the ground and like rocks as it seemed to the paratroopers—there was a formidable, unstoppable majesty to them, like the Imperial Guard at Waterloo advancing into heavy fire in measured steps. In his painting *Drifting Down,* Canadian artist G. C. Tinning showed a practice jump in Italy that was held to sharpen up troopers and pilots. The latter normally ferried cargo, and may have received only brief training in combat paratroop operations. (Canadian War Museum)

Evacuating the Wounded

Canadian Jack Nichols titled this painting *First Aid Station,* and it seems to be set in the versatile LST on an Italian beach. The expression of the wounded is pain, anger, and perhaps even the shock of surprise that the enemy is still bombing and shelling them. After all, they are out of play—the match is over as far as they are concerned, at least for the time being. Not so—probably because no enemy could know when an Allied LST stopped being a ship of battle and became a ship of mercy. (Canadian War Museum)

En Route to Sicily, July 1943

Canadian war artist W. A. Ogilvie called this fresh-air briefing of Canadian infantry *Prelude to Invasion,* as an officer uses the teak decks of a once-fashionable passenger ship to make points about enemy shore batteries and fields of fire. Intelligence was vague on some points of Sicily's defense. Among other surprises for the invaders was finding, when they went ashore, that the Axis defenders included the tough, battle-hardened Hermann Göring Division. (Canadian War Museum)

Rendezvous, Over Venice, 1943

This painting by Australian war artist Alan Moore is informally dubbed *The Old and The New*—the "old" because the near-in fighters with Australian markings are the reliable U.S.-built P-40 Kittyhawks that fought at one time or another with most of the Allied air commands, and the "new" because the planes swooping in at right background are American-made A-36 Mustangs that came into action over Italy in 1943. The two groups are probably supplying high cover for bombers below them. And it is clear from smoke rising at the lower right of the painting that the target is shipping in the harbor of the arrow-headed island-city of Venice. The war painters were encouraged to get a firsthand familiarity with their subjects—which accounted for the number of artists who were killed or wounded in action. (Australian War Memorial)

Fighters and Bombers in Formation

A close study of RAF experience and the fire-trial of their own first missions over Europe convinced the American air force of the value of tight formation flying as a protection against enemy fighters. John LaValle painted a flight of B-17s (ABOVE) joined by the distinctive twin-boomed P-38 fighter. The B-17s in their final version had a range of almost 1,900 miles and were armed with thirteen 50-caliber machine guns, each plane protecting others in their "box" formation. (U.S. Air Force Art Collection)

John LaValle depicted B-26 Marauder bombers (BOTTOM) on a run over Leghorn, Italy—in the winter of 1944. Operating from fields in Sicily, Sardinia, and Corsica, and from southern Italy, medium bombers like the Marauder were particularly effective because of their fast turnaround time between missions. At the end of the war, the Marauder had the lowest loss rate of any Allied bomber. (U.S. Air Force Art Collection)

Over Italy

Paul Goranson takes a look at a lonely job (ABOVE): tail gunner of a bomber, waiting in his little "coal hole," where he was likely to be the first target of the bullets from attacking enemy fighters. Tail gunners often said that regardless of all the encouraging chatter they heard over the intercom, they would feel as if they were alone in the plane. (Canadian War Museum)

Graveside, Italy

Fighting men in all countries of the war wrestled with the problem of close friendships made in the services, which could be wiped out in a few minutes of combat. Some men—particularly air crews—steeled themselves against that sort of loss by becoming "loners" who tried to view crew members as parts of the machine that could be replaced —which was what squadron personnel officers had to do. Alan Moore did this moving painting of an Australian Air Force padre, titled *At the Grave of a Bomber Pilot in Italy* (ABOVE). But many men were superstitious about visiting a grave; it might establish a link of fates they did not want to make. (Australian War Memorial)

Firebombs over Pisa, 1943

Airmen sent to bomb certainly wanted to see hits. But many of them had to resist following the second step in the logic chain: the vision of all the people dying down there. Paul Goranson's *Air Raid on San Giusto, Pisa* makes the thought of casualties hard to shut out. With many Canadians and Americans being of Italian extraction, the problem was particularly troubling. Fortunately, the size of the raids in Italy and the types of bombs dropped did not create the "fire storms" that swept through northern German cities in 1944 and 1945 after Allied raids. (Canadian War Museum)

Campobasso, Italy, 1943–44

The Allied troops that landed at Salerno met relatively little resistance, drove inland to cut off the toe of the Italian peninsula, then swung north to drive toward Rome. And then they were stopped by stiffening German lines. The Canadians who advanced on Campobasso in the Appennino Napoletano mountains were struck by the handsome country they might have to shoot up. But before it was done, Canadian war artist Charles Comfort did this striking painting—almost as relief from the war. (Canadian War Museum)

Battleground Near Ortona, Italy, 1943

The fighting in North Africa had been almost like some great, superrealistic war games exercise on a vast military reservation 500 miles long. There were few civilians to force from homes, few cities to wreck. In Sicily and Italy, the worst of the fighting took place in somebody's front yard. And the civilian suffering and the destruction of wonderful old monuments and buildings was depressing to both sides. Lawren P. Harris painted the battered landscape before Ortona, Italy, in a style that almost made the dregs of war look peaceful. (Canadian War Museum)

Canadians Drive Toward Rome, Italy, 1943

Canadian heavy tanks, shrouded with both dust and heavy camouflage mats made of frayed rope, charge across the Italian plain in the drive for Rome in this painting by Canadian artist Lawren P. Harris. Their British comrades had told the Canadians they were lucky they were not fighting in the dust of North Africa—but parts of Italy refuted that. (Canadian War Museum)

Italian Countryside "At Peace"

At first glance, it looks like a harvest going on in this watercolor by Lawren P. Harris. But in fact it's a Canadian tank transporter unit making its way through what looks like a sea of gold in the beautiful Italian countryside. The tank, once repaired, could go back to the business of destruction. (Canadian War Museum)

Dogfight off Ortona, Italy

A dogfight involving aboveground troops would invariably command maximum specta-
tor interest on both sides, though to the average foot soldier, the contest was
actually somewhat academic. He had trouble seeing how one fighter downing another
was going to get him much closer to Rome—and to going home. In Lawren P. Harris's
painting, the aviators' life-and-death struggle seems little more than patterns in the sky for
the men on the ground. (Canadian War Museum)

Mission Outbound, Bastia, Corsica

Corsica, located only sixty miles off the Italian coast from Leghorn and Piambino, was seized by the Allies and turned into a valuable strategic base for American aircraft ranging over the northern portion of the Italian boot. Safe offshore, like a giant aircraft carrier, an air base and a motor torpedo base at Bastia could raid targets on the German right flank. John LaValle did this painting in his documentation of the U.S. Army Air Forces in the Italian campaign. (U.S. Air Force Art Collection)

Corregiano, Italy, 1943

Both the Germans and the Allies attempted, whenever possible, to move themselves into the position where they could take public credit for saving historic buildings—particularly churches. Artist T. R. MacDonald, advancing with the Canadians, recorded the solemn scene as a priest of the Church of San Lorenzo in Corregiano came to see how his building had challenged the bombardment. Some Italians, including churchmen, had advised the Allies not to worry so much about shelling the old buildings—just get the Germans on their way. (Canadian War Museum)

Gliders in Italy, 1943

Gliders wrecked on landing during the invasion of Italy commanded all sorts of unique secondary uses, especially in a country that had been so savagely fought over. These had brought in troopers of the 6th Canadian Airborne Division. A fuselage that cracked apart on landing was not necessarily the sign of a group of men dead. Soldiers walked away from disastrous-looking landings. The armies sent around recovery teams to salvage gliders that could be rebuilt for the next advance. But parts of hulls especially might have long since disappeared to form henhouses and small farm shelters in a poor country. W. A. Ogilvie painted the glider scene. (Canadian War Museum)

A Reward More Valuable Than a Medal, Italy, 1943

Here Canadian artist George Pepper celebrated a happy episode in the Italian campaign (ABOVE LEFT AND RIGHT). It was the sort of attention to soldiers' needs that made the days of dirty living along the battle lines a little easier to bear. The Canadian army operated a system of mobile baths that soldiers ranked right up there with cold beer and hot rations. The accompanying sketches are from a group of about a dozen Pepper made in advance of the painting. W. A. Ogilvie painted the alternative to the Canadian army's mobile baths: a Sicilian stream (BELOW LEFT)—clean, but cold! (Both, Canadian War Museum)

Splendid Quarters, Italy

Most of the Allied invaders were struck by the majesty and imposing historic tradition that surrounded the cities of Italy, particularly when they were often greeted as liberators of those cities and sometimes even ended up quartered in centuries-old abbeys and palaces. G. C. Tinning painted these Canadian army enlisted men (RIGHT) who were assigned this baronial hall as their mess. It had probably seen far more raucous warriors in its history. (Canadian War Museum)

Quiet Quarters, Italy

Canadian artist G. C. Tinning painted this contingent of soldiers quartered in the vaults of a historic cemetery. There was nothing alarming about the atmosphere of the vaults. It was, as one sergeant said, "quiet as a tomb for a change, and we all slept like innocent lads." (Canadian War Museum)

Night Advance, Italy

Any big military movement was liable to air attack from either side, so movements at night were just as prudent as they had always been. George Pepper painted Canadian tanks moving up for a breakthrough. (Canadian War Museum)

Monte Cassino, 1944

Monte Cassino stood at a strategic point on the advance to Rome. From its heights, artillery could command the Italian highway leading north through the Liri Valley. Both the Allies and Germans had promised to avoid shelling the beautiful and historic old monastery that topped the mountain. But when the Allies claimed the Germans were using the abbey as an observation post, it was ultimately shelled and bombed into the rubble that begins to appear in this painting (ABOVE RIGHT) that Herbert Agricola did for the German war art program. (German War Art Collection)

Barrage at Monte Cassino, 1944

New Zealander Peter McIntyre recorded one of the barrages that leveled Monte Cassino (BELOW RIGHT). It took the Allies four attacks over four months to drive out the Germans. The action has been called the biggest battle of the Italian campaign in terms of the number of troops involved, but some historians felt that in the advance on Rome, the monastery need not have been destroyed. (New Zealand National Archives)

Devastation on the Road to Rome, 1944

New Zealanders carried a large share in the battle to take Monte Cassino. Artist Peter McIntyre of New Zealand painted these troops moving on to Rome after it was over. As authorities in Rome read reports of the advance and, more to the point, saw photographs of the devastation to towns along the way, which this painting reflected, the pressure increased to find some agreement that would spare the city. The Germans were unconcerned about the destruction of Rome, and their record of handling Leningrad and Stalingrad showed no promise. As the Allied armies pushed nearer, it looked as if Rome was headed for a wrecking, too. (New Zealand National Archives)

Skywatch, Italy

Around the harbors where the Allies brought in an enormous range of supplies continually, night bombing was a simpler assignment for the Germans, and eluding night fighters looked more possible (RIGHT). So this was where the heavy antiaircraft and searchlight batteries were placed. If a plane was caught in the crossbeams of a couple of lights, more beams would zero in instantly, as has happened here, and then the lights were almost impossible to shake. Fighters or antiaircraft guns would probably make the kill. John LaValle, who specialized in aircraft subjects for the U.S. art program, painted the moment. (U.S. Army Center of Military History)

Rom 15.3.44
Zerstörungen am
Bahnhof Tiburtina.
Prof. Agricola

The Look of War, Italy

German artist Herbert Agricola painted these four scenes in Italy. (TOP LEFT) Barbed wire intrudes on a peaceful beach. (BOTTOM LEFT) Italians take refuge in a tunnel in a scene similar to Londoners in the Underground tubes. (BOTTOM RIGHT) Florence's Ponte Vecchio, one of the most historic bridges in Italy, is hard hit by bombs across its approach. (TOP RIGHT) A view from Rome's Tiburnia Bridge at bomb damage along the Lungo-Tevere de Cenci and in the city near the historic Teatro di Marcello. (German War Art Collection)

Monte Cesima, Italy

George Biddle was one of the American war artists whose work caught the attention of war correspondent John Hersey, who covered the Italian campaign after earning distinction for his reporting from Guadalcanal. Biddle's concentration on the individual swept up in the war may have intrigued Hersey. The correspondent's Pulitzer Prize–winning novel, *A Bell for Adano,* was set in a small Italian town in the path of the war. Most of its characters—Italian and American—performed with distinction, perhaps distinction they never knew they had. In Biddle's painting *German Prisoner on Monte Cesima,* the unspoken question of the surrendering German seems to be: How did I get into this mess? (U.S. Army Center of Military History)

Unreported Casualties

In this stark picture, *War Orphans, Italy, 1944* (LEFT), George Biddle has given the young children almost adult faces. In fact, they almost were adults; they had lived a lifetime in a few years. Yet they would be the heart of Italy as it was rebuilt. (U.S. Army Center of Military History)

Polesina, Italy, 1944

Wilhelm Wessel painted and sketched the Afrika Korps during the fighting in North Africa—then moved back with the remnants of the German army to Italy, where he continued his superb historical record of the war. This painting, *Stragglers in Enemy Searchlights: Polesina, Italy, 1944,* may be one of his most famous. The men seem to have lost their unit in the retreat—and their weapons. Now a searchlight has pinned them down. There is no place to go. (U.S. Army Center of Military History)

Take-Off: Interior of a Bomber Aircraft, Dame Laura Knight (Imperial War Museum)

From African, English, and Mediterranean bases the Royal Air Force and the U.S. Army Air Force combined with air units from the European forces in exile to carry the air war deep into Europe. Prime targets were such enemy oil fields and manufacturing centers as Ploesti, Schweinfurt, Hamburg, Düsseldorf, and Frankfurt. The raids were costly in men and planes—but tactically were judged worth it. The United States and Britain moved to "bombing 'round the clock," the United States by day, the RAF by night. Contrary to the press releases, there proved to be no true "precision bombing." Military targets were heavily hit—but so were civilians. In the destruction, many great European landmarks were obliterated. The Luftwaffe professionals pleaded for the use of a superb new twin-jet German fighter that might be the only weapon able to stop the bombers. But Hitler held back the jets, to be his "secret-weapon bomber." And he held back too long. When the Normandy invasion came, the raids had battered German-occupied Europe so that it was strategically softened up for the Allied entry.

A few months before the opening of World War II, *Illustrated London News, then the journal of record for Britishers around the world, published an impressive double-page spread showing, in a single sky, paintings of each of the aircraft flying at the time for the Royal Air Force and the Fleet Air Arm. Prominent were several combat biplanes that at first glance did not appear to differ much from their 1917–18 predecessors. Relatively inconspicuous in this air armada was a new Hawker monoplane— the Hurricane. It was powerful, sleek, and simple . . . and almost didn't happen. Many influential air officers in England felt the monoplane design was "a bit revolutionary." But innovative designers and builders pushed through the Hurricane and the Spitfire—the latter growing out of a high-speed racing plane that won three world trophies in a row. Prototypes of both had their test flights in the mid-1930s, and the first planes manufactured were in service with a few squadrons when the war was declared. Both carried eight machine guns mounted in the wings— outside the propeller's arc—delivering a devastating cone of fire a couple of hundred yards ahead. They were to be the champions of the Battle of Britain. Enemy airmen still had each other in sight for most of their combat, as in the First World War. And perhaps this gave the war in the air some of the artificial (and unrealistic) "chivalry" of 1914–18. Heinz Knoke was a German fighter pilot who survived all six years of the war, and his experiences were the basis for* I Flew for the Führer:

There are twelve Blenheims. And twelve of us also. One for each. A Blenheim ahead is in my sights and I am ready to fire before he spots me. The Tommy pulls his aircraft up sharply, trying to dodge into the overcast.

I follow him round and keep my sights upon him. Fire! I press both buttons on my stick. I watch my tracers go into his left wing at a range of 150 feet. . . .

■

Suddenly Knoke's plane is hit:

The cockpit is full of flying splinters. Just over my right shoulder there is a large gaping hole. . . . I also notice that two shell holes have appeared in my left wing.

There is the Blenheim again, just ahead.

Once again I open fire. . . . The Tommy in front of me dissolves into a great shadow.

I now notice that my canopy has worked loose. I also smell burning. I gently throttle back and ease the stick forward. A few seconds later the sea is again visible. . . . Still the smell of burning persists. . . . My engine still runs smoothly: revs seem to be normal. According to the instruments there is nothing wrong. . . . The Blenheim has been severely hit; but with a little luck it should reach the coast of England again about the time I go down in flames into the sea.

. . . Land looms ahead. The flat countryside is dotted by a number of lakes behind dikes. . . . I am over the north of Holland. Two minutes later I come down to land on one of the long concrete runways at Leuwarden.

■

Knoke did not get thrown into the Russian caldron, and he used his time dueling with the British off Norway to hone the personal dog-fighting skills that enabled a pilot to survive. Aviation writer Michael Spick related a World War I analysis for fighter pilots that also seemed to apply to World War II: only one in fifteen had a better than even chance to survive his first fight. But if he weathers five encounters his probability of surviving increases by a factor of 20! Pilot Knoke was still looking for his first victory:

I make use of this opportunity to take up a position above him. Apparently he is so intent on his task (taking photographs) that he does not notice me. I am now about 3,000 feet above him.

Then he starts back on a westerly course. I open my throttle wide and check my guns as I swoop down upon him. In a few seconds I am right on his tail. Fire!

My tracers vanish into his fuselage. And now he begins to twist and turn. . . .

He goes into a dive, then straightens out again. He begins trailing smoke, which gradually becomes denser. I fire again. . . .

He is gradually losing speed, but is still flying. . . . The right wing of the Spitfire shears away. Like a dead autumn leaf, the plane flutters earthward. My throat tightens. I had come to like that boy. If he is not dead, why does he not bail out? . . .

I find myself shouting, as if he could hear

me: "Bail out, lad, bail out!"

Then a body becomes detached from the flames and falls clear. A white parachute spreads open and drifts slowly down into the mountains.

A feeling of pure joy is in my heart now. This is my first combat victory in the air.

■

The "Ploesti Raid" occupies a special place in the history of the U.S. Army Air Force. It was a highly radical solution for reaching a target that otherwise seemed to present hopeless odds against bombers achieving success. In any event, losses were likely to be heavy. But of special pride to the flyers was the fact that a number of the tactics of the raid evolved out of what American airmen loved to think of as their talent for "screwball ingenuity." Reporters and historians James Dugan and Carroll Stewart interviewed many of the pilots and later retraced the flight:

Ploesti was an oil boom city at the foot of the Transylvanian Alps, thirty-five miles north of Bucharest. The Arcadian city was incongruously fenced by the source of its prosperity—the smoking stacks, cracking towers, pumping stations, tank farms and noisy rail yards of eleven huge modern refineries, Romania's main economic asset, providing 40 percent of her exports.

■

Though the results of a small trial bombing raid were negligible and the plane survival rate was fine, the estimates of what it would be on the final raid became a big issue of the planning and in determining who would command. But the major planning started:

The Ploesti mandate passed to General Arnold's inner circle, Generals Heywood Hansell and Lawrence Kuter and Col. Jacob Smart. The generals assigned Smart to work up the bombing plan. He was a tall, sandy-haired southerner and a crack pilot whom Arnold often entrusted with viceregal missions to overseas commands. Colonel Smart flew to Britain and enlisted British Intelligence and RAF tactical specialists, the most important of whom was Lt. Col. Lesley Forster, an old Balkan hand who had managed the Astro Romana refinery at Ploesti for eight years. . . .

Forster briefed Smart on the peculiar industrial geography of Ploesti. The refineries did not constitute a single large unit. . . . There were a dozen of them ringed around the city. . . . The entire bomber strength Smart could hope for—perhaps 200 planes —could place all its bombs in the grounds of such a refinery and fail to destroy it. What had to be hit were the relatively small critical installations within the complex—the powerhouse, boiler house, stills, cracking towers and pumping stations. . . .

■

Unlike so much military planning, which was done in distant headquarters by senior officers trying to fight the new war like the one fought years before, planning for the Ploesti raid was done in the field. Colonel Smart— the top man—knew the crews and what they could do, and planned to get himself to the target and back in a manner that gave his crews the same reasonable chance he wanted for himself:

He conceived that the bombers would attack the refineries at very low altitude.

The idea seemed to have everything. It was a cunning psychological trick. Everyone, including the Germans, knew the American monomania for high-level attack by heavy bombers. An unprecedented low-level strike would permit the utmost precision bombing of the vital pinpoints in the refineries and score with the most explosives. It would spare civilians and raise American esteem among the subject peoples of fascism. It would reduce losses of men and planes by affording the flak gunners only low, fleeting targets. By hugging the ground the B-24s would cheat German pursuit planes of half their sphere of attack. . . .

On Saturday morning 31 July, the day before the mission, the five bomb groups went on a full-dress rehearsal on the desert mock-up, using live hundred-pound bombs. It was a spectacular success, the widest, tightest and lowest heavy-bomber front ever flown. Five miles wide, wing tip to wing tip, the Liberators crossed the target and obliterated it in two minutes.

■

To a civilian, the takeoff for Ploesti seemed set at a dramatically early time—like the "dawn patrols" of World War I. It was timed to get the planes over Ploesti opportunely . . .

and get them back in daylight. But the aircrews could have started at 2 A.M. if any generals had wanted it that way. Nobody slept very much that night:

At 0400 Greenwich mean time the flares [for takeoff] went up. At Berka Two, the lead plane of the mission, Flavelle's *Wingo-Wango,* carrying the mission route navigator, Lt. Robert Wilson, started the long and dangerous takeoff run. . . .

Out of seven leagues of dust the lumbering monsters heaved into the air at two-minute intervals and climbed into the five formations circling 2,000 feet up. Through thickening dust they continued taking off for an hour and finding their places in the swarms slowly turning over the airdromes. . . . They took up group order, with Flavelle out front pointing to Corfu, 500 miles away. . . .

The armada now standing for Corfu was the most intensively prepared and most experienced large force that has been dispatched in the history of aerial warfare. Except for the Sky Scorpions, each man aloft had flown an average of fifteen raids, most of them over western Europe in the hardest theater of the air war. Three hundred of them had made more than twenty-five missions and had long since used up their odds on staying alive or out of captivity.

The Germans knew immediately that the force was up from Benghazi. Unknown to Allied Intelligence, the Luftwaffe had recently placed a crack Signal Interception Battalion near Athens. It had broken the Allied code and was reading Ninth Air Force transmissions. Although the attackers were not broadcasting their destination, they had to spread a short, essential message to Allied forces in the Mediterranean theater, simply announcing a large mission was airborne from Libya. . . .

■

The first German "front line" radar unit that picked up the Ploesti armada was sitting in limbo in the mountains, hoping "to get involved in the war someday":

Atop the 7,250-foot pinnacle of Mount Cherin, near Sofia, there was a German Würzburg unit living in wretched boredom. Eight months before . . . they had packed

their tons of equipment a mile up the mountain on muleback and carried it the rest of the way on their backs. All these weary months they had monitored the air without a single trace of enemy aircraft. Suddenly they were talking with soft-voiced airwomen in ops rooms from Vienna to Salonika. "Many wings! Zone Twenty-four East. Sector Eleven. Bearing thirty degrees." . . .

■

In high-altitude missions, navigators had a chance to confirm ground checkpoints by surrounding landmarks that could be several miles away. But everything swept under the low-flying Liberators so fast that there was time for only the most instantaneous decision: had they just roared over the turning-point . . . or was it only a look-alike? Whatever it was, the rear three groups were turning:

Officers behind K. K. Compton were thunderstruck by the turn. Stanley Wertz, the navigator of *Utah Man,* phoned his pilot:
"We're turning too soon."
Stewart said, "There's nothing we can do about it."
Norman Appold broke radio silence. He switched on the command channel and cried, "Not here! Not here! This isn't it!" . . .
A dozen others joined the protest on the open radio, but they had to turn. Potts's twelve planes, for instance, were surrounded by others and could not wheel back on the right course without causing air collisions.

■

On the ground, the defenders were searching the high skies—when suddenly the signals changed. The surprise of the low-level attack delayed some antiaircraft crews for a critical minute or two. And when the big guns started firing, they found that the planes flying low and close by were too fast to track:

Silberg stood by the electric view finder. They heard heavy flak bursts. But the battery sergeant gave no firing order. "I can't see any planes," said Silberg.
Sergeant Aust, in the center of Battery Four, received a signal from Regiment. "They're flying very low. Change your fuse settings for point-blank fire!" Aust put the

Russians to work altering the 88mm shell fuses.

Less than halfway to Bucharest the forward line of the Liberandos walked into a massive ambuscade and the Battle of Ploesti began. The first salvo was dazzling—four enormous blue-white muzzle blasts from 88mm guns.

■

The wrong turn of some of the Liberators gave them some momentary advantage: The trackers on the ground thought Bucharest was a target, too . . . and this drew fighters there:

Ground spotters phoned the German fighter controllers, "They're attacking Bucharest and Ploesti very deep! It's a simultaneous attack on Bucharest and Ploesti!" Controller Zahn said, "Damned cleverly done. They send planes to tie up fighters at Bucharest while the main force hits Ploesti."

Flight Officer Longnecker noted: "An eighty-eight was behind a row of trees at a crossroad. I could see the muzzle flash and the projectile as it came toward us. I forced *Thundermug* under this barrage. The shell removed the left aileron, left rudder and half of the elevator on Captain Roper's ship at my right. I went back into position with him. His plane looked like a junkyard, but he was not wavering a bit. . . . Resistance grew stronger. Our gunners were pounding away steadily. We were going in from the wrong direction at two hundred forty-five miles per hour, sixty-five miles more than our usual speed, pulling emergency power for so long it was a question how much longer the engines could stand the abuse."

Flight Officer Longnecker, coming in to bomb, saw up ahead: "A B-24 sliding down a street, with both wings sheared off. A plane hit a barrage balloon and both disintegrated in a ball of fire. We saw bombs dropped by other planes skipping along the ground, hitting buildings, and passing on through, leaving gaping holes in the brickwork. . . . Suddenly a huge oil storage tank exploded directly in front of my wingman, Vic Olliffe, raising a solid column of fire and debris two hundred feet, waiting for *Let 'Er Rip*. He couldn't possibly avoid it. The next instant I glanced out and saw Olliffe crossing under Roper and myself, barely clearing us, and then going over a pair of stacks like a

hurdler before putting his bombs in a cracking tower.

■

The low-level approach of the Liberators had, as forecast, robbed the defending fighters of more than half their cones of maneuver. The fighters could not come in with a steep dive; there was no room to pass underneath and pull out:

The fighter formation had been dispersed by a new kind of earthbound aerial warfare. The Mizil fighter pilots went hunting in pairs and trios for lone ships, crippled ships and those that were flying too high. Gerhartz and his wingman, Hanz Eder, caught on to a V-pattern of three Liberators departing at an altitude of 300 feet. They ignored one that was dragging and smoking, saving it for later. The Germans drove from behind on their selected victims. . . .

The Circus went to earth and passed out of the fighter zone. The Messerschmitts turned back to Ploesti. The controllers were yelling that new waves of bombers were coming toward the refineries.

Utah Man, the first ship to bomb, was far in the wake of the Circus hegira. The big Mormon pilot could not exceed 150 miles per hour airspeed lest his wreck fall apart. The live thousand-pounders still stuck in the bomb bay sucked closer to their fuse settings. The engineer and the bombardier were in the bomb bay, clawing and hammering to release the ton-weight of death, their labors muffled. . . .

The screeching stopped. The hanging left bay door had torn away in the wind. Now they could hear tools banging in the bay as Cummings and Bartlett worked on the bombs. There was a mighty yelp from the flight deck. Bartlett was hammering the pilot's shoulder. "Walt! They're gone!" The two thousand-pounders bombs were tumbling into a field.

Stewart said, "Get back to crash-landing positions." Now he had a chance to save his men by skidding in. The fuselage men sat in tandem, backs to the bulkhead, nestled between each other's legs like a rowing crew, and padded themselves with their parachute packs. . . . Stewart said, "Hey, I don't smell gas anymore." One of the crewmen said, "We're probably out of gas. Let's set down now." The pilot said, "No, let's not.

Maybe the engines don't know they're out of gas. Watch them like a hawk, Larry, and we'll try to make Yugoslavia, where we have a chance of ducking the Germans." The gunners arose from the crash-landing positions and looked out. There were no other planes in the sky. The feeling came over them that no one else had come through. Shedding fragments of metal, *Utah Man* plodded on.

■

The workhorses for the U.S. Army Air Force's bombing offensive out of England against German-held Europe were the same four-engined Liberators that had bombed Ploesti . . . and the four-engined B-17 Flying Fortresses. Elmer Bendiner was a navigator in the Fortress Tondelayo *flying out of southeast England. He was moved to write* The Fall of the Fortresses, *a powerful account of his time aboard* Tondelayo *that was really a tribute to American airmen anywhere in the war. The observations that follow are Bendiner's own experiences in following the costly American doctrine of daylight bombing:*

The prime minister and the president argued amicably over the war's priorities and perfunctorily approved the recommendations of the Joint Chiefs of Staff concerning the air offensive that was to bear the crisp label "Pointblank."

Issued on May 14, 1943 . . . in the language of the directives we were to "accomplish the progressive destruction and dislocation of the German military, industrial and economic system and the undermining of the morale of the German people to a point where their capacity for armed resistance is fatally weakened. . . ." Despite Pointblank's explicit commitment to terror, we clung to the semifiction that any bomb that fell upon civilians was an unfortunate lapse from technological perfection. . . . Among the specifics in Pointblank was an order for "a very deep penetration at Schweinfurt."

■

After two relatively easy missions, which made Tondelayo's *crew feel like old veterans, they suddenly found themselves being swept up in a briefing that was clearly all about "the real war," a raid on the Schweinfurt ball* bearing works, about eighty miles from the German-Czech border:

The Schweinfurt attackers—230 Fortresses—were to cross the coast at Orfordness and Felixstowe, near the Naze, that estuary which runs inland to Ipswich. We were then to head directly down to those familiar Dutch islands, cross Belgium and enter Germany near Düren. We would turn at Würzburg, and attack Schweinfurt from the south. Because the division bound for Regensburg would be leading the way into Europe it was expected to bear the brunt of the first attack. Most of the fighter escorts—some ninety-six Spits and an equal number of Thunderbolts—were assigned to give them cover. . . .

. . . Once again we fell into bed and rose in the middle of the night. Once again we stumbled through the dark and breakfasted on ink-black tea. I had plucked my poppy from the field. We had heard the Telexes rendered into plain airmen's English, embellished by Rip Rohr's extraordinary explanation of the momentous nature of our mission. It was to be up to us to end the bloody war that Tuesday morning, we were told. . . . We were to take off at 0540.

■

By the time the raiders turned for home, some of the Luftwaffe force that had been drawn off to defend against the Regensburg attackers was heading back to cut off the retreating Schweinfurt bombers:

Again and again they came at us, through us, from dead ahead, from either side, usually from below but sometimes from above. They darted like dolphins amid a formation of plodding tugs.

In England monitors heard the German pilots gathering from all over France and Germany to ambush our homeward flight. . . .

At last we came to the blessed sight of soaring Thunderbolts above the Channel coast. It was 1659 by my watch. The afternoon sun warmed the portside window. Then, with my armor off, I sat down and looked about me. . . . We had been in the air for eight hours and forty minutes. We had been in incessant combat for close to six hours. It had been fourteen hours since we had risen in the predawn. In that time sixty

B-17s had been shot down, six hundred men were missing. The first major strategic air battle of the war had been fought. Did we win? Did we lose?

■

Some bomber veterans who had survived other such heavily-hit "victorious missions" felt the only sure victory of the Schweinfurt raid was announced in a short-wave broadcast picked up from Berlin:

On the morning of August 18, 1943, while a mercifully soggy [no-flying] sky wrapped Kimbolton and let me sleep, the body of General Hans Jeschonnek, Chief of the General Staff of the German Air Force, was found in Berlin with a bullet through his head. A suicide note declared only that the general could not work with Göring and asked that the Reichsmarschall be banned from the funeral. . . . It is not known precisely what Hitler actually said to Jeschonnek after we left Schweinfurt, but it could not have been pleasant.

In the hours and days immediately after the battle our leaders felt so, too. While we were still over the Channel General Anderson had announced that we had achieved our objectives at Schweinfurt. . . . I don't recall that any of us read our notices on the day after our performance, but they were glowing. We had our "pincers" around Hitler's throat, it was reported. The early stories listed our losses as no more than two B-17s. . . . Although the results did not quite measure up to the promise of the raid or to the premature announcement concerning the triumph of strategic bombing, unquestionably we had discommoded the enemy. Albert Speer, once Hitler's minister of Armaments and War Production . . . wrote that Schweinfurt, which accounted for a little more than half of all Germany's ball bearings, suffered a thirty-four percent drop in production.

■

Down through the centuries of warfare, the great Captains have written about the personal pain of committing men to great battles in which the losses would be heavy. Down through the centuries, Rear-Rankers have tended to disbelieve their superiors. Bendiner had heard the story from Ploesti about the general who had said that raid would be "a

success" even if the plane losses were one hundred percent. Bendiner knew which camp he belonged in:

Eaker could not know whether Germany had been given the hoped-for mortal blow by our strategic bombers, but he could and did make a precise count of our losses: 60 planes, 552 men missing . . . but it is certain that it was very expensive.

■

The segregation of the U.S. services in World War II was a historical blunder (as well as a social one) and a diminution of the war effort that might well be blamed for delaying the date of victory by eliminating from many of the combat units black fighting men who would prove their value in Korea and Vietnam. Army Air Force General Ira Eaker caught the problem in backlash—but began a vigorous investigation of the trouble in the all-black air force supply units . . . and found out who was at fault:

To complicate Eaker's life still more, there were problems on the ground of the sort that never troubled combat crews. Bombs and ammunition had to be hauled from depots to combat fields through mud and fog by soldiers who were frequently denied the right to sleep in barracks or eat in mess halls. At night they curled up in their trucks; they lived on K rations. They were all-black outfits. . . . They were officered by whites who did nothing to prevent the "disturbances" that broke out that summer. Eaker found the whites responsible for ninety percent of the trouble. . . .

■

The Duke of Wellington, after Waterloo, was asked to tell the story of the battle and how it felt to be in such a momentous event. He declined at the time, saying a soldier didn't know whether the battle was momentous. All he could see was ten feet on either side of him and a lot of smoke. Bendiner felt the same:

Gen. Robert Williams felt that the first battle of Schweinfurt was the most horrendous engagement ever fought in the air. And so it was if one goes by the statistics. An ordinary soldier, however, judges whether an engagement has been tough by the effects on himself and on the men he knows. He fights in a narrow space barely big enough for his own terrors and triumphs. That other larger battle of gains and losses, victories and defeats, is something he reads about. . . . We did not have to come home alone [from Schweinfurt] and all four of our props were spinning.

■

When the first U.S. Army Air Force units, like Bendiner's, came to England, they knew their equipment and training were superb— but that every enemy they met would have the advantage of experience. TV commentator Andy Rooney, then a young Stars and Stripes *writer, admired their harsh and hurried "learning curve":*

I came to this base often when the bombers were out, and when they returned—if they returned—I talked to the crews about what had happened. Then I'd return to London and write my story. I often felt ashamed of myself for not being one of them. . . .

Often the bombers came back badly damaged and with crew members dead or dying. In April 1943, I was here when they came back from a raid deep in Germany and one of the pilots radioed in that he was going to have to make an emergency landing. He had only two engines left and his hydraulic system was gone. He couldn't let the wheels down and there was something even worse. The ball-turret gunner was trapped in the plastic bubble that hung beneath the belly of the bomber.

Later I talked with the crewmen who survived that landing. Their friend in the ball-turret had been calm, they said. They talked to him. He knew what they had to do. He understood. The B-17 slammed down on its belly . . . and on the ball-turret with their comrade trapped inside it.

■

Before the development of a formation called the "combat box," where the planes protected each other, the Flying Fortress showed its vulnerability. Gunner John A. Miller was one of the lucky ones:

Less than two months after joining my Group, I became at age seventeen the oldest gunner in my Squadron. I was living in the spare gunners' hut . . . and for fifteen days following the March 6, 1944, raid on

Berlin I was alone in that hut. Everyone I knew was either killed or taken prisoner that day. . . .

■

Navigator Lou Bober, a former insurance actuary, figured the statistical odds on his crew completing their twenty-five missions and came up with the wrong answer:

Skipper, mathematically there just isn't any way we're gonna live through this thing.

■

Henry Archer and Edward Pine were RAF bomber crewmen whose squadrons flew by night; the USAAF flew by day. But the survival chances were about the same. There was not much camaraderie between the two nationalities—but the experience was universal as the missions dragged on:

The last trip was always the worst. When you began a tour, risks were part of it, inevitable, natural. In retrospect, the risks seemed suicidal. . . . At the beginning, you did not care; you were full of expectation. Now expectation had hardened into experience. So many of your friends were dead. . . . They were dead and you were alive; and on this last trip, there was so much to lose.

■

Shooting at enemy fighters gave an aircrew a feeling of some control. But flak was something that just burst on you out of an empty sky. The men hated it because it was soulless—and deadly. Airman Ken Stone, Allan Healy, and an unidentified VIII Air Force veteran talked of flak:

You know it's gonna hit somebody, but it's not gonna hit you. . . . The first few missions were an unreality, like a movie you saw but weren't in. . . . You couldn't do a darn thing about it. All you could do was plow through it and figure that it would either get you or it wouldn't.

■

Pat Smithers, a British woman living in the middle of the cluster of Allied bases in southeast England, saw the neat formations of bombers go out day and night—and would also see them straggle back with sometimes

half their number missing. Even a civilian could do the arithmetic:

If you live in Sussex or Kent nowadays you know before getting out of bed and pulling aside the blackout [curtain] if it's a nice day. A clear dawn has a new clarion—the deep and throbbing roar of hundreds of planes, outward bound. . . . But the impressive thing—the thing that makes the Women's Land Army [girls] pause in their stringing of the hopfields and makes conductors of country buses lean out and look up from their platforms—the impressive thing is the numbers. . . . Their courses often converge. . . . As their roar fades with them, another rises until things on the kitchen mantelshelf tinkle and rattle as they catch the vibration. . . .

■

Else Wendel, a German housewife, experienced one of the sometimes terrifyingly beautiful firestorms that the Allied bomber crews could see from 25,000 feet. She wrote of survivors:

When they regained consciousness it was daylight, and they stumbled down into the stream and splashed their faces and hands. The water stung their scorched skin. . . . After a rest they decided to walk back into Hamburg. It seemed suicidal, but they felt they must go and see what remained of the city. It was a terrible walk. They passed through one big square where corpses were piled up.

"All of them were standing in the middle of the square when a firestorm caught them. No one escaped," a woman said. . . .

The woman standing near them shivered. . . . "If there were a God, he would have shown some mercy to them. He would have helped us."

"Leave God out of this," said the old man sharply. "Men make war, not God."

■

The German fighter command became embroiled in a bitter battle with Göring and Hitler over the use of a new twin-jet fighter then in development. The plane would have been a formidable adversary for the Allied bombers. Göring and Hitler wanted to hold it back for use as a "secret weapon" bomber for some mythical "massive raids later."

"Down on the Deck" over Ploesti, August 1943

Historians of air power have differed in their assessments of the strategic results from the U.S. air raid on the Romanian oil refinery complex at Ploesti. Some called it a decisive blow to Nazi war production; some said it was not unlike a twentieth-century "Charge of the Light Brigade"—noble and courageous beyond measure, but accomplishing only a temporary reduction in the production of fuel and sending too many American airmen to their deaths. T. C. Galloway painted *Operation Soapsuds* with 9th and 15th Air Force Liberators atop the target. (U.S. Air Force Art Collection)

Deep Effort to Regensburg

After Ploesti, the pressure came from London and Washington for other deep penetrations into Germany. About two weeks later, the U.S. Army Air Forces sent 146 B-17s over the Alps to hit the Messerschmitt aircraft plants in Regensburg. Frank E. Beresford painted these two Vs flying over the mountains on the way to make their bombing run. (U.S. Air Force Art Collection)

Marshalling "Landcasters" for Stuttgart

Canadian bombers taxi out for a night raid over Europe (ABOVE). The full moon was both an aid and a curse. Ground targets popped out amazingly clearly, particularly if they were on or near rivers, which could shine like mercury trails to the target. But the moon also made it easier for night fighters to pounce. And the Germans—at first lacking an effective airborne detection system—needed the light. Carl Schaeffer painted the takeoff. (Canadian War Museum)

Target: Berlin, 1941

Illustrated London News artist Bryan de Grineau sketched the halting beginning of the Allied air assaults on Europe, with a Royal Air Force Handley Page bomber being loaded up on a winter afternoon in 1941, in preparation for a night raid over Germany. (Illustrated London News)

Ploesti Burning, August 1943

Stanley Dersk painted the return from Ploesti of the U.S. Army Air Force bombers. Some Ploesti survivors who came in at treetop level might say these planes are too high, and the flying looks a good bit more organized than their memories of it. Photographs from some of the planes showed them coming in so low over cornfields that they returned to North Africa with cornstalks caught in bomb bay doors. But the air force gunners welcomed being low; it was the first time their machine guns had been able to fight back at the antiaircraft guns they hated. (U.S. Air Force Art Collection)

Survivors—Who Might Go Back

Despite their suffering, wounded men—such as the U.S. Army Air Force crewmen (OPPOSITE) that Charles Baskerville has painted here—often expressed a desire to get back with their units as soon as they were fit. As military psychologists quickly found out, very few men were fighting for great national ideals. They were usually fighting the war for their buddies on either side of them. (U.S. Air Force Art Collection)

Good Side to Bad Weather, England

Australian servicemen sent to England had a hard time getting used to British "reserve," discipline, and finally British weather. Which was why this painting, *Ballet of Wind and Rain* by Colin Colahan, was a great favorite of RAAF fliers in the U.K. Weather like this meant a day of no operations—and so another day of life on earth assured. (Australian War Memorial)

Plane Crash Near Accra

Single-engine craft and light bombers coming to U.S. units overseas could travel "moth-balled" on the decks of ships. But the four-engine heavy bombers were flown across the Atlantic: Newfoundland to Iceland to England . . . or Recife, Brazil, to Ghana or Dakar, Senegal—and then up to the North African bases. These were arduous over-water flights for relatively inexperienced pilots and navigators. And there were accidents. Samuel David Smith painted this fatal finish in Ghana. (U.S. Air Force Art Collection)

Departure for Germany,
Southeast England, 1943

Lawrence Beall Smith was an early contributor to the American war art collections when he began to paint American medicine working in the war effort. Takeoffs in the first light of morning were tightly orchestrated on a precise timetable. A B-17 loaded with fuel left little margin for error, and the ambulances stood by. (U.S. Air Force Art Collection)

Safe Day, No Mission, England, 1944

Mabel Peacock painted these 8th Air Force bomber crewmen on a chilly, rainy, nonflying day—favoring the little coal stove in the center of their Quonset hut. All the heat hugged the curved ceiling; the floor was cold enough to make galoshes welcome. This was a rare all-black combat crew. It was not until Harry Truman's presidency that segregation and all-black labor units were abolished in the U.S. armed forces. (U.S. Air Force Art Collection)

In from Brazil

Samuel David Smith painted this B-17 undergoing overhaul at Accra after flying the South Atlantic. In the U.K. the B-17's big radial engines were good for about 300 hours between overhauls. But in the dust, sand, and heat of North Africa, thirty to fifty hours called for heavy maintenance work. (U.S. Air Force Art Collection)

They Made Long-Range Bombing Work

Ogden Pleissner painted these husky, reliable P-47s (RIGHT) after their return from escort. The losses suffered in the daylight bombing missions were prohibitively heavy until the arrival of long-range fighters like the P-47 Thunderbolts and the P-51 Mustangs, which could often escort the bombers all the way to their European targets. (U.S. Air Force Art Collection)

Eye-Spy

Intelligence officers in the various Allied air forces made their major decisions in planning bombing raids (and evaluating their results) by a precise analysis of aerial photos. But the analysis wasn't infallible: the Germans baffled the RAF for months by camouflaging the two distinctive lakes that marked the western approach to Berlin. Canadian artist P. G. Cowley-Brown painted RCAF photo specialists (ABOVE) taking linking shots on a "recco run" at 20,000 feet. (Canadian War Museum)

Battle over Malta, 1942, Denis A. Barnham (Imperial War Museum)

ORGOTTEN WARS AN
SILENT SERVICES

With both Churchill and Roosevelt dedicated to Allied reentry into Europe as soon as possible, troops in certain other vital areas felt they fought "forgotten wars." In India, retreaters from Malaya and Burma were now being reinforced and resupplied. Mountbatten was sent to meld the conflicting elements together and build a fighting force of Britishers, Australians, New Zealanders, Americans, Indians, and Chinese. The Japanese invaded the undefended Aleutian Islands, and only a hard campaign in mean weather drove them out. The island of Malta sat astride the Italian-German supply route to North Africa, providing the British with a valuable base for air and surface raiders. The Axis air forces placed Malta under siege, with a bombing blitz heavier than the Battle of Britain—but Malta hung on. A few submarine exploits by both sides during the war were publicized for their propaganda value, but most submariners worked in virtual anonymity. These truly "silent services" played major roles in almost every naval operation of the war, from the blockades on shipping to the great carrier battles. Yet the men knew they faced a casualty rate that rarely claimed just a single submariner —usually a whole boat crew.

Ian Fellows-Gordon served with the British army in Burma and took an active part in a number of the actions he described. Where another speaker is not identified, the words and experiences are those of Fellows-Gordon, from his book The Magic War*:*

The campaigns of North Burma—with Generals Stilwell, Wingate, Slim, and a host of other leaders directing the action—cover a terrible two years of fighting with the Japanese, which finally ended in victory. Many natives joined in to fight the Japanese and became very effective . . . particularly the Chinese "Chindit" Kachin Levies. . . . The battle plan—the denial to the Japanese of key roads and railroads—led to ultimate victory. . . .

For supply in this confused jungle campaign, it was essential to clear landing places for the cargo planes that flew over The Hump. They were, in effect, airborne "freight trains." . . . The story of The Hump and the Burma Road is a book in itself. But the whole struggle of the CBI [China-Burma-India] theatre was enormous and filled with heroic victories and defeats on both sides.

Gen. Joseph Stilwell was friendly with very few American or British officers and was judged hard to work with or serve under. . . . His opposite commander from the British side was Gen. William Slim, whom Stilwell, unexpectedly, liked. They got on surprisingly well.

■

Many of the first stories to come out of the battlefields in Malaya and Burma as the Allied soldiers retreated ahead of the Japanese dealt with the lightly equipped Japanese advancing by bicycle or on foot along native tracks and jungle trails—while the Western troops, who had to carry all the "normal" gear of heavy field packs and gas masks, were baffled by the jungle and kept to the highways. Japanese rations were a bag of rice and some dried protein, while the Western soldiers seemed to need something more elaborate. The Japanese "made friends" with the natives, while no amount of concern by the British seemed to be able to erase the hurt of years of often overbearing colonial rule. The Allied commanders began to try to wipe out the old images. Methods were drastic:

British General Orde Wingate from time to time affected a beard, or hung an alarm clock round his neck by a string "to show the passing of time." He was often unbearably rude. The novelist John Masters was serving under him and his comment is that: "Wingate, above all, is a study in the byways of the human spirit. At what point, and why, did he decide that he would enter the Hall of Fame by the back way? For he was mentally and morally equipped to walk in at the front door. . . ."

General Slim was always struck, when visiting Stilwell's headquarters, how unnecessarily primitive all its arrangements were. Slim commented: "He delighted in an exhibition of rough living which, like his omission of rank badges and the rest, was designed to foster the idea of the tough, hard-bitten, plain, fighting general. Goodness knows he was tough and wiry enough to be recognized as such without the playacting. . . . "

■

Glider forces would come into their own later in Italy and Normady where the terrain was much more suitable for their operation. But one of the most dramatic successes came in the totally unsuitable Burmese country:

Slim knew . . . that the Japanese were shortly to launch a major offensive against Assam. Far from this being, as Stilwell and many others were to regard it, an unforeseen catastrophe . . . Slim had pinned his hopes on this last gasp from his enemy. And, at this moment, Slim needed the Chindits in there, causing trouble behind the Japanese. . . .

■

The "Rail Indaw" airborne operation seemed dangerous and improbable—but it worked:

Apart from the calm, gum-chewing glider pilots themselves, hardly a man had previously flown, and certainly not in one of these flimsy wooden things. But the pilots, unperturbable and unconcerned, seemed to lend calm to their passengers. . . .

Those in the gliders had little idea of what problems the Dakota pilots were facing, though these problems intimately concerned them. Within minutes of takeoff it became clear that a pair of gliders was too heavy for one Dakota. The towplane engines began to

overheat. And with the risk of their seizing up, came the threat of fuel shortage: it was being used at a quite unforeseen rate, getting a too-heavy load to mountaintop height. . . . Within hours, not only gliders, but towplanes, had crash-landed all over enemy-held north Burma, many of them far from their planned destination. Their sacrifice was not in vain: the Japanese were to find themselves hopelessly confused by airborne landings all over north Burma and were to take days to wake up to what was really happening. . . .

■

Now came the most difficult part—a night landing in raw country with no markings and no ground light. Most of the casualties in even the best glider operations came here:

Commanders woke men who were sleeping. One by one, tows were cut, the roar of engines faded. Each glider was now on its own, engineless and at the mercy of air currents and the skill of the young man up front chewing his gum a little faster. . . .

Then, suddenly, there it was, there was Broadway. Definitely not a Great White Way, just a shadowy, sinister, bumpy field, grey in the moonlight.

■

An officer remembered the deadly crunch of wrecked gliders:

"To make matters worse . . . some of the pilots were having trouble judging the correct height to come in, and several gliders crashed into the trees surrounding the runway. . . . Then all would be quiet for a moment until the cries of the wounded men rose up from the wrecks."

One glider, heavy with a bulldozer and other equipment, swerved at the last moment to avoid a tangle of wreckage on the ground, and skidded into the jungle at sixty miles an hour. The wings were ripped off and the fuselage rocketed along by itself until it came to a halt, then the front-facing door opened to let the bulldozer—like a maddened Spanish bull—charge out into the jungle. Pilot and copilot were flung up into the air, the bulldozer rushed on out beneath them and they both landed back unhurt.

"That's all right," said the pilot. "I planned it just that way. . . ."

As dawn broke, the situation at Broadway seemed more cheerful. The American engineers, helped by every able-bodied man, worked nonstop to prepare the Dakota strip. All-round defence positions were dug. And by afternoon, it was ready. That night, fifty-five Dakotas landed at Broadway. . . .

With the arrival of Fergusson's foot-slogging 16 Brigade at its own planned stronghold of Aberdeen nearby, there were now close on twelve thousand Chindits behind the Japanese troops who were facing Stilwell.

■

China-Burma-India theater fighting was often more like the close encounters of the Boxer Rebellion or Clive-of-India days than the sophisticated tactics of World War II armies. Fellows-Gordon describes:

Michael Calvert bellowed, "Charge!"

While men stared, convinced he was mad, Calvert started to run down the slope into the valley which separated him from Pagoda Hill, "praying," he said later, "that the rest would follow."

At first, it was only Calvert, their mad brigadier, and three others, equally mad, who were tearing downhill. Then one by one, others began to follow.

Suddenly, everyone was moving, machine-gunners, mortar teams, the lot. Gurkhas and British troops were rushing past Calvert, "scrambling up the slope as if the whole thing had been their idea and they couldn't wait to get at the enemy's throat."

As they scrambled up, the Japanese, to a man, got to their feet and charged down. In one of the least orthodox battles on record: ". . . Everybody slashed and bashed away at the enemy with any weapon that came to hand, yelling and shouting as they did so."

■

Charlton Ogburn, one of the officers in the advance of the 16 Brigade who came in on foot, was amazed at the endurance of the pack mules:

The saw-toothed ridges would have been difficult enough to traverse when dry. Greased with mud, the trail that went over them was all but impossible. On the steeper descents the mules simply sat down, sliding fifty yards at a stretch, on their haunches. Going up, we hacked steps out of the steeper slopes to give them a foothold. Time to do this was sometimes lacking, though, and in that case the fatalistic animals, realizing that momentum gave them their only hope, would take it at a run, bounding up the grade like monster rabbits. . . . The battle of the mules was unending and, I think, took more out of the men than anything else, more even than fighting the enemy and fighting disease."

Behind the whole story there was just one man. Without General Stilwell, the Northern Combat Area Command could never have existed, this strangest of wars would never have been fought. . . .

■

The value assigned to the Burma Road was a frequent point at issue between the Allies. But Ward Beecher, an OSS sergeant on his way to an intelligence assignment behind the Japanese lines in China, gave the Road—and its "custodians"—high marks:

I believe the Hump Cowboys were basically part of an engineering regiment whose job was to maintain the road, supply those working on it, and generally keep it open for Allied traffic. Most Cowboys were black. They were colorful in what they wore and the way they wore it—bandannas, jewelry, ornamented side arms and sawed-off rifles that looked like very long six-shooters were all part of their style. . . .

If someone ran out of gas because of theft or bad planning, the Hump Cowboys would come to their assistance. On the other hand, if a driver lost a load over the slippery, slimy side of a cliff, the Cowboys would rescue him—but the cargo, once lost, became free game for the Cowboys, who knew how to recover it and then convert it into the native jewelry they loved, a wife or a girl or two, whiskey, or whatever was valuable and needed way out in their wild territory along the road.

Having watched them work, and [having] heard a lot of stories, I think it is reasonable to guess that without the Hump Cowboys, the part of the war requiring support for the Allied Forces in China would have lasted a lot longer. . . .

■

American and Canadian troops headed for the Aleutians had generally gone through training for either South Pacific fighting or conditions they would encounter in North Africa and Europe. The Japanese landings in the Aleutians—though recognized for a feint —caused hurried movement of troops into the North Pacific island chain. In his wartime account, Bridge to Victory, *Howard Handleman followed the reconquest of the Aleutians:*

Bundled to the ears in fur flight clothes, handsome young Lt. Frank Rasor stamps his feet as he awaits the order to get into his sleek Billy Mitchell medium bomber for the twenty-minute run to Kiska.

"This goddamned war business sure isn't what it's cracked up to be. In every damn war movie or dime novel you ever heard of a pilot takes off, has a whale of a fight, knocks down a Messerschmitt or something and then flies back to a bottle, a girl or both. . . .

"And what do we fly back to? This muddy island, some warmed-over macaroni and some cold stewed tomatoes."

■

The best officers were not always West Point–trained. Howard Handleman tells of an accountant named Hartl, commissioned into the army, who applied the same thoroughness that he had employed in his civilian job to sometimes archaic army administration:

Hartl held nothing back. He pointed to a huge map of Attu as he spoke.

"The Japanese are strong here at Holtz, where we're going," he said, "here at Chichagof, where we hope to cut them off. . . . Our job is to move into Holtz Bay as quickly as we can. . . . There has been complaint that we are not carrying our water-repellent clothing with us. . . . It will keep rain out, yes, but after you walk awhile in that country you will be soaked with your own sweat. . . .

"The first shock of combat may pose problems for you. It is your responsibility to watch out for any signs that any of your men are breaking under it. If any do, it will be your responsibility to talk to them and straighten them out or send them back to the medics. . . .

■

During and after the war, armchair strategists would often claim that American units

—matched soldier for soldier with the Germans or the Japanese—were not equal fighters and needed the overpowering edge of superiority in equipment and firepower. But to the private soldier hitting the beach, there was little interest in setting up "an all-even sporting proposition":

There was no answering fire from the Japanese. It was nice to think of the Japanese scurrying for foxholes, leaving their guns, helpless to fight back. That's the way we should fight wars. Throw so much at them they haven't a chance.

■

For the first few days, few Japanese were seen . . . but when they were, they usually looked as cold and miserable as the American GIs. Handleman remembered a few bright spots:

Whoever picked this beach for the landing should have a medal, a big medal.

This was a rotten, rocky beach, completely hemmed in by a cliff 800 feet high. The waters were so rocky no one would ever believe an army could be landed on its shore. Obviously the Japanese didn't think it possible. . . .

The landing party was funneled into a tiny area in which machine guns could have mowed the men down. But the Japanese didn't need to defend the beach as long as they were certain we couldn't land there.

■

Some of the men on Attu thought that frostbite and trenchfoot were their most dangerous enemies:

Captain Natzke had been in the gully with his men all day.

"Lots of them are still up there in the gully. They can't walk. Their feet are frozen. . . ."

That was the first word of the boots, the worst mistake of the expedition. The men were equipped with fine, heavy, black-leather boots, the best hunting boots made. Aleutian soldiers wear them, too, on dry days. But on ordinary days the soldier in an Aleutian garrison wears rubber, the only thing that can protect his feet against the eternal wetness of the islands. . . .

When the casualty figures came in at the end of the battle, they showed fewer men

were wounded in battle by gunfire and bayonet than were forced out of action for varying periods by trenchfoot. . . .

■

The capture of a Japanese supply dump brought a measure of physical relief to some of the American units in need of supplies . . . and also gave them a surprising look at their enemy—in very human terms:

There were . . . heavy wool Japanese Army blankets, brown with a blue star in the corner. They were too short, too, but there were plenty to go around, so every man had two to line the bottom of his confiscated foxhole and another to stake in the sand above as a roof. . . . There were huge stockpiles of ammunition, guns, oil, coal, canned salmon, canned tangerines, canned heat, rope, rice, potatoes, carrots, spinach, medicine, clothing, blankets, paper, pencils, pens, and other items. . . .

■

Japanese huts and dugouts had been abandoned just as quickly . . . and offered all sorts of souvenirs. These were quickly grabbed up. Only later did some Americans feel a strange uneasiness about taking personal things; it made them think of the shoe's being on the other foot:

Through the litter in the Japanese camp they learned something about the men they fought, learned how they lived. . . .

The pictures were strange to our soldiers, every one of whom carried a photograph of his wife or girlfriend. The Japanese soldiers carried pictures of other soldiers, and pictures of Japanese women movie stars or entertainers. . . .

By noon the soldiers blossomed out in Japanese clothing: heavy dry clothing they found in a warehouse. They wore . . . mittens, sleeveless goatskin coats, . . . socks, the fur-lined leggings, the fur-lined shoes, fur-lined felt helmets, itchy woolen scarves. A few of the smaller soldiers found trousers that would fit them, and one got the best piece of clothing of all, a pair of . . . officer whipcord riding breeches.

■

Toward the end of the campaign, the Americans experienced a Japanese tactic that sur-

prised them—but won grudging admiration, and would become all too familiar in the South Pacific:

Here were the first Japanese suicides. . . . Dozens of [the enemy] who met the fierce opposition of American riflemen turned to death as a way out of their misery and defeat.

They turned to the grenades they had tied to their jackets like deadly boutonnieres. They pulled the grenade pins, armed the black and red cans of destruction by tapping them against their helmets, and then held the grenades to their chests and blew themselves up.

■

A look at the map of the Mediterranean indicates the strategic importance of Malta and Gozo, the neighboring island, which was one-fourth its size. Malta sits sixty miles south of Sicily, two hundred miles east of Tunisia. The war of maneuver in North Africa was controlled by the availability of gasoline, and Rommel's letters note again and again the restriction of his strategy as a result of a dwindling fuel supply.

This account of the siege of Malta was written by Ernle Bradford, a retired Royal Navy officer who first saw the island from the bridge of a destroyer that had fought through a convoy. Where no other attribution is made in the comments that follow, they are the words of Bradford.

George Hogan, a British army officer, had not welcomed a posting to Malta. But he was won over—typically. The Maltese were clearly a race apart from the British in their bloodlines and heritage, but British and Maltese history had been interwoven for several hundred years:

When the Hampshires [Hogan's regiment] arrived in Malta early in 1941, after settling in and getting to know the people, we felt that we had somehow suddenly slipped back in time; that everything about us was some twenty-five years behind our known civilization. . . . We discovered the "Not to worry, Joe" attitude with which the Maltese produced a happier, easier way of life.

■

Many Royal Navy men had strong feelings about the Maltese being good allies in the hard time to come. Admiral Cunningham described arriving at the island in HMS Warspite:

It was our first visit since May, and news of our arrival had been spread abroad. As we moved in with our band playing and [our] guard paraded, the Barracas and other points of vantage were black with wildly cheering Maltese. Our reception was touchingly overwhelming. . . . I went all over the dockyard next morning with the Vice-Admiral [Sir Wilbraham Ford] and was mobbed by crowds of excited workmen singing "God Save the King" and "Rule, Britannia." . . . It was a very moving experience.

■

The British navy started World War II with its aircraft carrier strength largely built around a collection of ungainly looking— but surprisingly efficient—carriers that had started life as battle cruisers. Except when close to Malta, from which fighter support could be added, a Royal Navy carrier in the Mediterranean put up its planes against faster land-based enemy aircraft. Admiral Cunningham describes such a fight:

At 12:30 a jagged thickening on the screen of the early radar aboard *Illustrious* indicated a large group of aircraft to the north. No one aboard the ship had ever seen anything like it before. Usually a few "indentations," as it were, would disclose the arrival of a reconnaissance plane or—as recently— the approach of a few bombers. This was something different—a large group of aircraft coming down from Sicily. . . . These were the Junkers 87s and Stukas, forty in all, and behind them a further wave of Junkers 88s. . . . The attacks were pressed home to point-blank range. . . .

■

Joseph Attard, a Malta resident, described an early raid. The inhabitants were to undergo a "blitz" comparable, on their small island, to what the British experienced in the south of England:

The shaking of the shelter, as bombs were hitting the dockyard part (which was beneath the bastion where the shelter stood, only fifty yards away) was tremendous. I

felt the strong wave of blast in the shelter and pressed myself to the wall in the first cavity I found. Women and men alike, screaming prayers, were toppled on each other. . . .

■

Mabel Strickland, editor of The Times of Malta, *which published throughout the siege, wrote of her constituents:*

These people, most of them miners, stonecutters and farmers, are among the most courageous and confident one can be privileged to meet. They have dug shelters, carried away to other villages the most valuable portions of their furniture and household goods, and they continue to live and work there, notwithstanding the severe punishment the village has had to submit to at the hands of the enemy.

■

The Air Battle of Malta, *an official British government record, emphasized one great difference between the Battle of Britain and the bombing of Malta: the concentration of targets in such a confined territory. Over an island not as long as Manhattan and only a few miles wider, the British juggled a maze of friendly air traffic:*

Not only were the airfields within the gundefended area, but it was usual for aircraft to arrive either from Egypt or Gibraltar nightly, for bomber flights to take place almost nightly, or for the Fleet Air Arm to carry out strikes or reconnaissance. Night fighters were usually up, and the enemy was almost invariably present. . . . The problem of dealing with all these factors (of which the most difficult were the arrival of strangers from Gibraltar inadequately briefed as to our plans, and the return of damaged bombers from Sicily, who were not always able or willing to comply with the rules) necessitated very clear-cut instructions to the guns and searchlights, as well as to the air defences. . . .

■

It was well proved in World War II by both the British civilian population being bombed by the Germans and by the German civilian population being bombed by the British and Americans, that the bombing of cities proba-

bly solidified civilian resolve to resist, rather than breaking it down:

In every air-raid shelter of any size there was always a priest, an altar, a lamp burning, and the rites of the Church available. . . . Holy Malta, as the old people had always called their island . . . was in itself a very real presence, helped and preserved by the many saints as well as the Holy Family.

■

The British defenders of Malta knew something about going into a fight with inferior equipment because of some of the outmoded equipment for land, sea, and air with which they had begun the war. And here, strangely enough, some of the career military men sympathized with their Italian enemies:

Their fighters were not the equivalent even of the old Hurricanes, and their bombers were slow and lacked armor. Worst of all, aircraft production in Italy was not geared for the rate of loss incurred in all-out war. . . .

■

The defenders of Malta felt an invasion attempt was bound to come, no matter how well they fought off the air raids. Ernle Bradford told of an odd pact between Mussolini (who wanted to invade) and Hitler (who wanted first to clear up Africa). It bought Malta some time:

Perhaps Hitler felt that by diverting Luftwaffe forces and U-boats to the Mediterranean theater he had done as much as he could then afford. Let Rommel get his major offensive, code-named Theseus, under way in the desert and then, presuming on its success, there would be time to consider Hercules again. . . . Rommel was eager to continue the advance right into Egypt, but the Italians were more cautious . . . and a compromise was reached. If all went well, the desert offensive should halt on the Egyptian border before the end of June, after which everything was to be turned against Malta.

■

The statistics of the defense of Malta are stirring and the stuff of history. And in the end, they earned the island a rare honor:

During March 1942 there were 275 air raids, 90 of them at night, and during April there were 283, of which 96 were at night. Malta suffered 154 days of continual day and night bombing, whereas the longest number of consecutive days on which London was raided only amount to 57. In the blitz on the city of Coventry (which gave a temporary verb to the language, "to conventrate") it is reckoned that 260 tons of bombs were dropped. In contrast, 6,700 tons of bombs fell on the towns and installations around Grand Harbour during six weeks of March and April. In the latter month the airfields alone received twenty-seven times as great a weight of bombs as that which fell on Coventry in October 1940.

■

Dr. Paul Casser, a British Public Health official who had long service on the island, told about Malta's somber preparations for the terror of the air raids:

Before the opening of hostilities it was anticipated that the people would react to the horror and havoc of modern warfare in an exaggerated and abnormal manner. It was consequently forecast that the number of psychiatric casualties would be high and beds for "cases of war neuroses and psychoses" were prepared in special wards at the Mental Hospital at Attard. Subsequent experience, however, showed that this precaution was unnecessary. . . .

On April 15 King George VI made the unique gesture of awarding the George Cross to the island of Malta—the highest honour, equivalent to the Victoria Cross in military terms, that was his to bestow.

■

The drain on Malta's fighter defense force was enormous. The Air Battle of Malta *(the official government account of the siege) described the speedy turnaround of planes flying in for relief:*

The turnaround of the Spitfires was accomplished in six minutes in some cases. . . . Each Spitfire was met and directed by a runner to a dispersal pen, which was a self-supporting unit. . . . A supply of petrol was put up in tins for refuelling by hand. These tins, together with oil, glycol, and ammunition, were waiting in each pen. Two airmen,

assisted by soldiers, fell upon each Spitfire as it reached the pen. The moment their work was done a Malta pilot took over the machine, though in some cases newly arrived pilots went straight into action.

■

Damage caused during the bombings of Malta is still visible at some points around the island today. But rugged construction helped the islanders withstand the siege then . . . and build back later. A war correspondent wrote:

Malta's buildings are made of very solid blocks of stone and it takes a direct hit to destroy a house. The traveller arriving at Valletta might, at first, think that the damage was comparatively slight, but let him just walk to one high vantage point and look down and he will see that almost every building is nothing but an empty shell. . . .

■

The "War Diaries" of the U-boats were written in a formal style and evaluated by commanders ashore. (U-boat exploits were widely publicized. But Americans subs were truly a "silent service.") The German prose was generally sparse—but still forceful enough, with descriptions of action to suggest when decorations might be in order. U-boat officer Herbert Werner also kept his own log for a book after the war, and some of his entries describe the sophistication of a U-boat hunt:

PROCEED AT ONCE INTO AK 50 [coordinates for an area to be patrolled]. CONVOY EXPECTED. ANTICIPATED SPEED NINE KNOTS. COURSE EAST-NORTHEAST.

At once Paulssen [the U-boat's captain] swung U-557 around in a lazy sea. Spring had returned to the North Atlantic. For the first time since our departure we enjoyed being on the bridge. Bearded, palefaced machinists stole a few minutes to look at the sun and the sky, to fill their lungs with clean, fresh air. Inside the . . . stench of 51 sweating seamen, diesel oil, rotting food, and moldy bread mingled with the noisome odors that emanated from the galley and the two tiny washrooms. The overbearing smells and the never-ending rocking made the men in the narrow drum of the U-boat dizzy and numb. . . .

"Alarrrmmm!" The dive went like clockwork.

Paulssen, swinging himself onto the seat of the scope in the tower, gave his order: "Prepare tubes three and four for firing fan shot." . . . A swishing sound came from the bow compartment, accompanied by an increase in air pressure. The compressed air, which had activated the large pinlocks that expelled the torpedoes, was released into the boat instead of the water. . . . Meanwhile the torpedoes, examples of a new type powered by batteries, followed their fixed course toward the doomed ship. . . .

Two powerful detonations from the freighter rocked our boat.

"She's hit, she's sinking!" shouted Paulssen.

■

The U-557 had experienced a maiden patrol that seemed to include a little bit of everything —which was what Dönitz's training schedule was designed to prepare them for. With a "wolf pack" attacking a large convoy, U-557 was located by an escorting destroyer:

Four hellish eruptions threw the boat around like a toy, forced her deeper into depth, made her sway and tumble. Men skidded along the deck plates. In the flicker of emergency lighting, I saw the needle of the depth gauge waver at the 125 meter mark, then move rapidly to 140, 160, 180 meters. The thrashing sound of a destroyer came nearer, and the footsteps of its racing screws seemed to drum loudly against the steel of our hull. All eyes looked upward. The swishing of propellers reached a crescendo as the destroyer passed over our boat.

Three charges exploded, seemingly just above the conning tower. After each shattering roar, the hull moaned, the floor plates jumped and kicked our feet, wood splintered, glass disintegrated, food cans flew through the boat; then all was black for long seconds until the emergency lighting came on again. . . .

Two hours later we surfaced, shaken and exhausted. The fresh air speedily revived the crew, then we inspected the damages. They were greater than we first assumed. The starboard motor was knocked off its foundation, the aft ballast tank was ruptured, and the starboard shaft was bent. This meant the end of our patrol.

The Siege of Malta, 1941–42

The Italians and Germans began their siege of Malta believing that if the native population took heavy punishment in the bombings and suffered shortages of food from the blockade, they might be goaded into some sort of action against the British that would at least hamper the defense of the island. But the Maltese, while suffering severely in the bombings, saw the British undergoing the same trials, and the two peoples moved closer together. A local artist, P. W. G. Maloba, lent a morale boost with this spirited interpretation of a heavy bombing raid. (Imperial War Museum)

Turnaround Under Fire, Malta

The delivery to Malta of new fighters from England often drew simultaneous attacks on the convoy bringing them in and the airfields at Malta, giving the German and Italian fliers two chances of knocking out the planes before they could join the island's defense. The RAF on Malta, however, worked out a fast turnaround system. When a new fighter landed from one of the "ferrying" carriers, it was immediately waved into a revetment, where fuel was topped off (often by a bucket brigade operation using five-gallon cans), fresh ammunition boxes were locked into the wings, and an RAF pilot experienced in Malta climbed into the cockpit. The plane could be airborne again in fifteen minutes. Leslie Cole painted an enemy attack on the field while this sort of changeover was probably taking place. It was a spirited baptism of fire for the ferry pilots. (Imperial War Museum)

Attack on a Carrier, Mediterranean Sea

The *Ark Royal,* similar to the ship in the center of the action in this Charles Pears painting (ABOVE), was sunk there by a U-boat in November 1941, and the *Eagle* was also caught by torpedoes in August 1942. Often the carriers were used to bring fighters to Malta. The British marine painter Norman Wilkinson had also worked as an artist in the First World War. Here (LEFT) he shows the *Ohio,* a plucky merchant ship, with her naval escort and sister ships pushing through to Malta at a time when the blockade had left the island critically short of almost everything. Though badly damaged, *Ohio* made the dock in Valletta—then settled a few feet to the bottom. But most of her cargo came off high and dry. (Both, National Maritime Museum)

Medical Corps of the Imperial Army, Burma, Fall 1944

In the spring of 1944, the Japanese launched an offensive of some 100,000 men from Burma into northeast India. But the British and Indians stalled the Japanese at Imphal about fifty miles inside India, in a series of ferocious fights that lasted from March to July. When the Japanese withdrew, more than 13,000 Japanese and 17,000 British and Indians were dead. Ryozo Suzuki painted medical corps specialists assisted by Burmese volunteers, tending to Japanese who had been wounded during the British advance into Burma that followed in the fall of 1944. (National Modern Art Museum of Tokyo)

Hospital Ship

Joseph Hirsch did this scene (OPPOSITE) called *Mercy Ship*. International agreements called for hospital ships to be painted white with large crosses and hull markings, and to be brightly illuminated. But the confusion of war and the fact that hospital ships had to move in and out of combat areas made the danger of an accident always present. In practice, the Allies often placed wounded on regular troop transports and counted on heavy convoy protection to get them through. (U.S. Army Center of Military History)

Jungle Operating Room, Burma

American painter Howard Baer was commissioned to record the work of the Army Medical Corps. While assigned to American units in Burma, he painted this tent (ABOVE) in the jungle that served as an operating room. Blackouts were the rule, but emergencies took precedence. Baer admired the tough kindness of the Chinese stretcher-bearers (RIGHT) bringing a litter through the jungle. The men were fast, strong, and gentle, and had tremendous stamina. At each aid station in succession behind the lines, the care got better. The most seriously wounded would be flown out. (Both, U.S. Army Center of Military History)

Burma—Jungles and Mountains, 1944–45

These four paintings by Anthony Gross resulted when he moved from North Africa to the action in Burma. At top left, a British officer, identified only as "Captain Howard who is in command of native levies," waits to ambush a Japanese patrol. Gross's picture at top right shows the kindly camouflage of the growth covering the slopes of the Arakan Mountains, where Sikhs of the 7th Rajput wait for orders; judging from the colorful "liberated" parasols, the Japanese are not near. Bottom left, the Lincolns take up position, fast learning jungle fighting from the Chin levies. Bottom right, artillery spotters are working out the coordinates of Japanese positions. (Imperial War Museum)

Burma, 1945

Leslie Cole's assignments for the British War Artists Scheme took him to Gibraltar, Malta, Sicily and Italy, North Africa, Greece, Burma, Singapore, Borneo, and Germany. These paintings are from the Burma fighting in 1945, as the British gained back the territory from which they had been ejected so disastrously in 1942. Burmese irregulars—well equipped now with no-nonsense British automatic weapons—hurry the departure of retreating Japanese (ABOVE). Cole's *Battle of Sittang Bend* (RIGHT) follows the action of a detachment from the Queen's Own Royal West Kent Regiment in the van of the advance. (Both, Imperial War Museum)

Burmese Village

Leslie Cole called this deceptively sleepy scene *The Guerrilla Headquarters.* His description explains that the Britisher is a Sergeant Brierly, who had been with the Maquis in Occupied France. He is planning an attack on the Japanese who hold the next village. His men, who look peaceful enough but are fierce fighters, are Burmese members of Reindeer Force 136—an exotic Arctic code name for troops in the Burma theater. The sergeant pleases his men by wearing the wraparound "dhoti" of the native soldiers—but also a good stout pair of paratrooper boots. (Imperial War Museum)

Seabees, Aleutian Islands

All that wind, snow, and cold provided a formidable proving ground for one important new innovation, the navy's Construction Battalions—Seabees. They were primarily organized to land with the first waves of invasion forces to improve the beach for equipment coming ashore, construct airstrips, roads, communications centers, and strongpoints. William Draper painted these Seabees (ABOVE) bolting together watertight steel "pontoon" cubes, which had been developed so they could be linked together in untold combinations like a Lego set to build dry docks, piers, floating landing fields, and fuel storage depots. (U.S. Navy Combat Art Collection)

Supply Ship, Aleutian Islands

William Draper's painting (OPPOSITE) shows the organized confusion of a landing. Some unfortunate early experiences in the South Pacific, with material needed first on the beach coming last out of the hold of the ship, resulted in a precise manual for loading (and unloading) that gave the navy "beachmaster" what he needed when he needed it. (U.S. Navy Combat Art Collection)

Rising Sun over Attu

Ogasawara Osamu painted these Japanese bombers over Attu (LEFT). It would have been a chilling propaganda picture had it appeared in the United States. It was not seen in America until the end of the war, however, when the picture was seized with a rich collection of Japanese war art, as material that might inflame the rebirth of anti-American feeling in Japan. Most of the art was returned to Japan. (U.S. Air Force Art Collection)

Pitching Camp in the Aleutians

Air force mechanics and armorers (LEFT) camp alongside a landing strip where bombers are coming in and fighters taking off. The painting is by William Draper. The men stationed in these remote, barren, treeless islands developed a bitter joke: "There's a woman behind every tree in the Aleutian Islands." (U.S. Navy Combat Art Collection)

Preflight Briefing, Alaska

In his early days as an RCAF artist, Paul Goranson spent time with units preparing for the invasion of Kiska, planning to drive out the Japanese, who had taken possession of this Aleutian island in June 1942. Here (OPPOSITE), Goranson painted the briefing that preceded a reconnaissance flight over Kiska. (Canadian War Museum)

Kiska Patrol

Edward John Hughes painted so you could almost feel the cold coming out of the picture. It was hard to keep alert on long patrols. A unique Canadian law—brought about by the terrible loss Canadian regiments took in the stalemate battles along the Western Front in World War I—specified that Canadian soldiers had to volunteer for overseas duty in the Second World War; there was some lingering feeling that the British had squandered Canadian troops in such fruitless battles as Vimy Ridge in 1917. But Kiska was considered home territory. (Canadian War Museum)

Kiska Scout Car

The distinctive art style of Edward John Hughes of the Canadian army, who covered the occupation of Kiska, gave a strong personality to the soldiers, the climate, and the terrain. The soldiers in *Armored Car in White* probably didn't mind working on a vehicle at night since they all complained that Kiska was resoundingly dull. (Canadian War Museum)

On the Conning Tower

The crewmen on duty in the conning tower (LEFT) in this picture by Georges Schreiber are each scanning an assigned quadrant of the sky and sea. They could clear the bridge and take the boat underwater in just a matter of minutes in a crash dive. (U.S. Navy Combat Art Collection)

Royal Navy Sub on Patrol

Stephen Bone painted this scene (LEFT) in an S-class submarine on patrol, emphasizing the tightness of submarine life, which called for the stiffest screening of sub crews—both for their skill and for their attitude, confidence, and personality. Bone's painting looks from "Officers' Country" into the "Ratings' Mess"—and it is clear the distinctions were limited pretty much to the lettering on the brass plates above the hatch doors. (National Maritime Museum)

Torpedo Room

The crewmen in the background (OPPOSITE) are getting ready to fire the torpedo tubes (in the depth of the picture). Strapped between the bunks are two more torpedoes ready to be muscled into the tubes by the men standing by. Georges Schreiber's treatment of the men makes it clear this is not a combat situation. (U.S. Navy Combat Art Collection)

Sub Life—the Silent Service

Thomas Hart Benton had served briefly in the U.S. Navy in the First World War, mostly around Norfolk, Virginia, making drawings for official navy use. Between the wars he exploded as a muralist who worked large and ferociously, often executing wildly controversial works that generally pleased him enormously—provided he had been left alone. In World War II, Benton was persuaded to do a series of paintings and drawings of the navy, the most famous including the submarine pictures shown here. Above, Benton captures the intensely crowded life aboard a sub on a long patrol, with off-watch sleep always difficult as the watch on duty worked the boat. At right, a crewman grabs a cup of "Joe" between alarms. Black sailors in subs had volunteered as officers' stewards, but were trained, as were all the crew, to be able to take over the jobs of various other sailors in an emergency. Submariners often got little "press" for their sinkings, in order to prevent suspicion that the navy was reading Japanese codes—hence "the silent service." (U.S. Navy Combat Art Collection)

Score One for the Subs

In his unmistakable style, Thomas Hart Benton depicts his sub bagging a lone merchant ship. Surface attacks were often favored against merchant ships; for a long period during the war, torpedoes ran erratically and often failed to explode on hits. Benton's sub was later sunk with all hands (although he wasn't on it). (U.S. Navy Combat Art Collection)

Wartime Traffic on the Thames, John Platt (Imperial War Museum)

HOME FRONTS, RESISTANCE FRONTS

As the invasion of Europe neared, the annoyance value of the local resistance movements was manipulated by the Allies for real tactical value. After France fell, the resistance was helpful in sheltering escaped prisoners and downed fliers and channeling them back to freedom. When the Allies landed in France, the resistance could be counted on to disrupt the German rear. The Germans had to spend heavily in reserve troops, time, and energy guarding against resistance movements in all the occupied countries. The power and dedication of the Jewish revolt in the Warsaw ghetto was a tragic story of great courage, with no hope of winning. The form resistance took in the concentration camps ranged from dogged adherence to the code "Simply to refuse to die is to resist," to futile revolts in some camps. Finally, the story of Germans who resisted Hitler is still coming to the surface in long-hidden diaries and letters and sealed records. Widespread bombings of civilians in both Axis and Allied countries resulted in parallel situations: Civilians all shared the common perils of shortages, compulsory war service, government restrictions and oppressions, and the terrible events of the bombings. In many ways, the recollections from both sides might be hard to identify by country.

*L*ife on the home front was hardest, of course, in the countries of Europe, Africa, and Asia where bombing was a threat or civilians were caught in the steam-roller of the ground fighting. But life was hard almost everywhere, because of shortages, rationing, government restrictions, crowding, mixed news from the fighting fronts . . . and casualty lists. For families, these translated the awful cost of the war into harsh strips of telegram tape: "We regret to inform you . . ." A reality of the war often became most apparent in letters from the fighting fronts. Here were the often halting, usually censored descriptions of the war from someone you knew. Quotations from letters of participants in the war appear frequently in this book. But there follow some letters from German soldiers in North Africa and in Russia that seem remarkable for their power, their perception, and their compassion. They are translated here for the first time from private and archival sources in Germany:

Twenty-year-old medical student Robert Röhlich arrived in Tobruk at the end of June 1942 and was part of the last advance of the Afrika Korps. Here are the final entries in his diary before he died in front of El Alamein:

July 5: For the second day now we are in the midst of heavy gunfire. . . . We didn't eat anything yesterday. We are lying in foxholes and English guns are firing down on us. We happily received a canister of coffee. We are desperately awaiting our dive-bombers [to attack the English]. It is noon . . . what will the evening bring?

July 8: The climax of our misery is near. We are hardly able to get our noses out of the dirt for more than five minutes. I got five splinters; thank God nothing serious. My only way out now is the holy mother of Maria-Zell. Me, the old sinner become God-fearing! I haven't prayed as many times in my entire sin-filled life as in the past few days.

■

A letter from Martin Penck, a German trooper who died October 26, 1942, near El Alamein:

Africa, October 21st, 1942—Some days the [air raid] alarm comes so often that it is impossible to lose consciousness for just one minute. Today there was no alarm at all. One notices the American relief supplies. They are mostly aircraft, some of them with four motors. . . .

It is all right that you put my African mineral collection in the protected area [from the Allied bombs]. . . . If there is any room left, put all the rest in the wardrobe. . . . More than likely I won't be sending any more items to Stuttgart.

■

Harald Henry was a Ph.D.-holding infantryman from the University of Berlin with the German army in Russia. These excerpts are from a diary written in the summer and fall of 1941 as the German advance slowed down and the rain and snows of fall blew up. Henry died on December 22 near Moscow:

Russia, July 4, 1941: Endless are the hours of the advance, along 25 or 30 kilometers of crushed and burned-out tanks, skeletons and completely destroyed and burned-down villages. . . . A few lilies bloom sinisterly in the little garden. One senses an odd smell, which for me will stick to this campaign forever. It is a mixture of fire, sweat and the cadavers of horses. . . .

October 20, 1941: Hell is fermenting in all pots. It borders on ghastly visions of lashed-up fantasy. We see the misery of the captives and finally we will live through it ourselves. The weather is bad and we have come to rest, because it is impossible to walk any further. The accommodations get worse daily. Thirty men lie on the floor in a farmhouse parlor. . . . All of us have diarrhea and stomach pains as well. The amount of horror and sadness which are gathered by such a war doesn't accumulate for tortured people like us in a lifetime. . . .

■

On December 19, 1942, twenty-year-old Horst Ulrich from Berlin wrote to his parents from Stalingrad, which he referred to as the "mousetrap":

Dear Mom, dear Dad, in a few days we celebrate Christmas. To be honest—I don't really feel like celebrating Christmas. It is horribly cold. . . . I am broadcasting in the tank at the moment . . . sitting in this refrigerator with the headphones on my ears all day, without covers and without moving. . . . Horsemeat has gotten more seldom; besides, one can't eat it rare, and in the midst of this treeless prairie there is no burning wood. I hope things will change soon. . . .

■

In the middle of December 1941, Christoph Faulhaber wrote of an encounter during a breakthrough by the Russians in the area of Charkow:

Wounded men struggle by me. Only the drive of survival keeps them on their feet, in spite of heavy wounds. An old, bearded private sits in the snow and begs me for food. He has both his hands wrapped in bloody, dirty bandages. I open one of my cans filled with meat and feed him. "Comrade, don't leave me here," he pleads. "Help me or shoot me," he begs. There is no vehicle to be seen around anywhere. What shall I do? The gun firing comes closer. It seems to me as if I am giving myself up, while I am looking into the bearded face of the old man. I try to make him stand upright. He must have been sitting in the snow for a long time. His joints are stiff and he keeps falling back.

■

Fragment of a letter written by an unknown German soldier at Stalingrad:

Fortress Stalingrad, December the 18th, 1942: . . . Everything suffers body and soul. I have had to tackle a lot of emotional and physical reserves. . . .

In the big bunker there is a piano. . . . Our commander plays the piano in the bunker underneath the ground. The acoustic reflected by these walls of dirt is strange. How can you listen to music underneath the earth? There are pieces from Bach, Handel, parts of the concert in A-flat by Mozart, Beethoven's *Pathétique* Sonata, and Chopin. The commander plays so well. Everyone is taken by this music. Then [a sergeant] comes in from the midst of the battle. He tells us of the suffering experiences that his troops endured. . . . The commander starts to play again. The walls are shaking from gunfire and bombs.

■

Trooper Kurt Reuber wrote this Christmas letter from a Russian POW camp near Jelabuga. Reuber died about a month later, but a fellow captive brought the letter out with him when he was released at the end of the war:

Russia, December 1943 (shortly before Christmas)—We should remain silent about how heavy the mutual misery weighs on us, especially this year. Even living the existence of a captive of war—I know that I am still alive. But you have been told in an objective manner that I am missing. I feel the misery of your uncertainty, especially now during Christmastime. Do you search among the hundreds of thousands of deaths of Stalingrad or do you still hope that I am alive? . . . If only I could get some message to you that I am alive—alive for all of you.

■

In Stalingrad, an anonymous German officer, who sensed the end of the battle, wrote this last letter to his wife:

I say good-bye to you, because the decision has been made this morning. I want to neglect the military side in this letter completely. It is a one-way matter on the part of the Russians and the only question that remains is how long we will still be part of it. It can only last a few more days or even hours.

■

At the end of 1942, Mathilde Pfitzinger was appointed as secretary of a German agricultural program operating in the Ukraine. On January 8 she traveled to her new post there and soon had to take a very courageous stand:

One of the leaders mentioned that it wasn't possible to get more food from the Russian farmers. The following incident had happened to him: when he attempted to get the last cow from the stall of a farmer, the farmer went and got his youngest child and offered it in lieu of the cow. The leader said: "I should have left him the cow; it was the only thing which could keep them alive." He was horrified by the obvious misery of the population.

At night I sat down and addressed letters to Göring and Hitler stating that I went to the East in order to develop and not to de-stroy. I accused the German administration of high life, while the population went hungry and they were only able to fight back by turning into partisans. My letter was received openly, and the administration in the Ukraine was told to speak to me. . . . I received an invitation from the chief of administration, Dorgel, who welcomed me with the words: "If you had been a man, you wouldn't be sitting here now."

■

Lt. Bernhard Rademacher wrote in his diary at Lygow, in the area of Kursh in Russia, as the great German defeat at Stalingrad was approaching:

Unfortunately we have to also include some of our most talented artists and most splendid human beings and soldiers with the victims of Stalingrad. Again and again our thoughts sway to the catastrophe of the 6th Army. . . . 200,000 Germans slaughtered! There are many who speak of it as the deed of a maniac. The worst and most cruel reality is that the faith in our highest leadership is vanishing. . . . Again and again our discussions consist of the fearful question: whether Hitler is really the great, universally talented leader and creator of a new imperium? Or is he only a phenomenon like Napoleon, rising like a comet? . . .

■

On the other side of the battle lines, in the Russian towns and cities caught in the crossfire, civilians were as hard-pressed as the Soviet soldiers. Elena Skrjabin lived in besieged Leningrad, which was under assault for two years, during which time she kept a tragic diary:

September 5: We have regressed to prehistoric times. Life is a simple formula. It consists solely of a search for food. . . .

September 9: Yesterday, around five o'clock in the evening, we stood on the balcony. . . . Suddenly our attention was drawn by bright spots in the sky, which flew toward us with tremendous velocity. . . . The sirens started to wail. We had to go to the air-raid shelter. . . . The children lament loudly and press against their almost unconscious mothers. With every new tremor the women, many of whom were communicants of the Church, make the sign of the cross. . . . In moments like these it seems that the antireligious propaganda [of the Soviet government] has been forgotten.

■

In November, starvation in Leningrad claims more and more victims:

November 15: Death lives in the city. . . . When I was walking along the street today, a man stumbled in front of me. He could hardly stand on his feet. When I caught up with him, I looked capriciously into his ghastly, pale face. . . . Here one could really say that death was written into a person's face. After a few steps I turned around, stopped and watched him closely. He sat down on the steps, rolled his eyes, and slowly sank onto the ground. When I reached him he was already dead.

■

Many German soldiers who had experienced quick victories in Poland and the blitzkrieg into France knew that in war that moved so fast, the devastation was relatively light. In Russia, however, the destruction was terrible—both from German bombardment and Soviet "scorched earth." And much German war art reflects this. Jergerij Petrow, a soldier in the Red Army outside Smolensk in 1941, described his country's destruction:

Again a new day started under the sounds of guns. . . . Sunrise was incredibly beautiful. . . . My heart said nothing. During the war there is no beauty. . . . On the first day of peace, the people will again understand how beautiful nature is that surrounds them. That long, pale hill that shimmered feverishly in the sunrise was suddenly struck by the sun and looked lemon-yellow. But in reality this is no hill. It is Height Number 117. From there the enemy can see Smolensk; and over the possession of this height there has been a vicious fight for two weeks. . . . The little stream isn't a stream but a border. And the end of the forest isn't the end of the forest but a good location for putting guns. The war took everything away from nature. . . .

■

After the war Victor Nekrassow, a Russian author, was asked whether there was a differ-

ence between the Russian and the German soldiers. He answered:

I lay in adjacent foxholes with the Germans at a distance of 60 to 100 meters for five and a half months, but only after the Germans were captives of war did I have contact with them. I have seen that these are the same people, the same soldiers who were forced into their army to defend some idea. But that wasn't the official idea. To say that we fight for Stalin or communism are only empty phrases. . . . We fought for our houses, our families, and our mothers and fathers.

■

When the French surrender was signed on June 22, 1940, one of the most galling provisions in it called for the majority of the French fleet to be collected in certain ports, decommissioned and disarmed. Loyal crews decided to carry out "a massive act of resistance." Yves Fargo tells the story:

Friday, November 27, at three o'clock in the morning, motorized columns coming from the west set out on the coast road that leads to the center of Toulon. With perfect timing, German tanks appeared on the quays and fired the first shots, intended, it would seem, to intimidate the crews. . . . Then [at five o'clock in the morning] . . . the order to scuttle the fleet was given. Most of the testimony gathered from those who watched the fight from shipboard or on land agree on one point: A formidable explosion awoke Toulon at about five o'clock in the morning. It came from the blowing up of the turret of the *Strasbourg*. . . .

Other explosions followed. The French fleet was being scuttled. . . . At Cap Brun, the explosions died away. The [protective shore] batteries had been put out of action. A mighty chant arose—"The Marseillaise," in which the voices of the gunners mingled with those of the civilians massed along the road to Le Pradet. . . . The work was finished. Toulon had ceased to be a great naval port.

■

Underground newspapers—some quite sophisticated—were published throughout the Occupation years. They performed a valuable service of letting Frenchmen, largely re-

stricted by German travel prohibitions to the areas where they lived and worked, know that they were not alone in the experiences they suffered under Occupation rule . . . and how and where successful resistance had taken place. A. J. Leibling gathered scraps of this highly dangerous reporting for a book, The Republic of Silence:

February 1944: *Nantau-Oyonnax*. On December 6, 1943, two patent collaborationists, a hotelkeeper and his wife, were covered with swastikas and paraded through the streets of Nantau and Oyonnax by the boys of the *maquis*. In reprisal, on the 13th, SS detachments, sent from Paris, surrounded Nantau and arrested one hundred and sixty men from eighteen to sixty years old. . . .

Nice. In December three patriots were executed after having been forced to dig their own graves. Six others were found in the quarries with their eyes gouged out. . . . During this same period, Courbet, printer and bookseller; Joseph Ross, aged forty, lawyer; Spolianski, professor of literature; and Fresco, aged nineteen, a student in the trade school, were either shot by the Gestapo or died as a result of torture. . . .

■

Far from ending Resistance activities, the return of Allied armies to French soil spurred the underground fighters to more frequent and more dangerous strikes. George Millar was a young British officer who escaped after capture by the Germans in North Africa and was parachuted into France to assist a French maquis *group:*

[A] great fan of railway lines gleamed before us. Philippe slid away to guard us from the station end. Buhl, icy in action, his Sten against his leg, watched Control Post No. 3, and gallant Pointu stood over the *Bahnhofs'* [railway workers'] hut, ready to intimidate or to kill if need be. Maurice and I worked across the points from opposite sides. Frisé . . . dealt with his target, the main through line to Belfort and Germany. Pointu, Sten in both hands, had gone into the control post, and before we left the area the loud hailer hissed and a metallic voice said, "All *cheminots* leave this area. Urgent. *Vive la France!*"

The charges had been set on half-hour

detonator time pencils, and we were clear . . . when they began to go off. . . .

The [switching points] we had destroyed were difficult to replace.

Boulaya propagandised our sabotage effort in a message passed to the centres of respectable town opinion: "The *maquis* have today saved Besançon from Allied bombing [by destroying the roundhouse so there was no need to bomb].

■

London had learned to be careful with its supply drops, with the knowledge that everyone fighting the Germans did not have compatible ends. One basic rule was, "Keep the guns from going to the cities," which was where the Communists were strong. Whoever had the authority to pick a dropping area and order it supplied, as George Millar did, had great leverage among the Resistance:

Jacques Painchaux had provided himself with good cover; he was food administrator for his district. His genius lay in organised resistance of the type that some . . . called gangsterism. He was an excellent planner, and studied detail. From the initiatory days of our friendship, when I got him allocated a dropping ground, he produced anything required for our *maquis*—money, tobacco, boots, sugar, petrol. All those he "took" from the Germans in Besançon. He also gave me a beautiful car, a black Citroën, a motorcycle, a lorry, and a pickup van. Berger, delighted, brought all these to Vieilley . . . against the day when we would motorise ourselves. . . .

When our young men had truly blocked the Ognon valley railway, a mouth-watering target appeared . . . one of the few heavy-duty mobile railway cranes left in France. It set to work near the Dardel establishment, clearing the bombed and wrecked locomotives. . . .

I climbed to the railway and set charges. The crane's locomotive would initiate the lot by running over camouflaged fog signals, and it would plunge into a gap, pulling the crane off the embankment. We waited until dark. Nothing came. . . .

Early morning. Still no crane had passed. Georges and I, carrying hay-rake and scythe, went down to the railway. The station master at Merey-Vieilley told us that two railwaymen walking in the early morning had seen my charges on the line and had reported them, fearing they would derail the 8:10, the passenger train that was our morning friend. . . .

Georges and I pedalled off at top speed. While he pretended to scythe some damp grass I got up on the lines, took off the activating fog signals, and laid them well clear. The 8:10 passed safely. . . . [The] charges were dismantled by experts and the crane chugged down the valley with its carriage-load of armed guards. On the far side of Besançon . . . it was blown up by another Resistance joker code-named Pedro, who had buried a big artillery shell between the lines. . . .

■

One of the dangers the Resistance and the maquis *groups feared most had nothing to do with their own safety, but concerned the German tactic of taking revenge on the people of a community at random or as a whole when an act of sabotage took place. But sometimes a very tempting target could urge ignoring the reprisal threat:*

While investigating the Doubs valley on my bicycle I saw a train of petrol tankers . . . drawn up near Roches, where there was a refinery that I had been forbidden to sabotage. . . . The notion of a bazooka rocket penetrating a petrol tanker set me aflame, and I hurried back to Vieilley, where Colonel Maurin, in his usual half-grumbling manner, said he was sure it was a trap. . . . We attacked before dawn. I had not previously fired a bazooka. Working from the instruction card, I launched five or six rockets, singed my eyelashes and eyebrows, and scored hits on tankers. They did not explode. . . .

Overtired (I had been walking most of the night), I was obsessed with that tanker train. I had determined that in soft shoes and complete darkness I could crawl the length of it, fixing a "limpet" [a magnetically held charge activated by a sixty-minute detonator time pencil] to each tanker. No more walking. . . . I saw that young Nono was nearly in tears at the thought that I was bound to take one of the seasoned men, and I told him to pack our haversacks. . . . We had gone perhaps four kilometres on the main road when we topped a rise and saw travellers close ahead halted at a German

army roadblock. . . . As we whirled round our bicycles and pushed on the pedals to gather speed away and downhill there were cries of "Terrorists!"

It was an ambush. Marksmen in field-gray uniform rose from concealment on either side of the road. . . .

The explosion was shattering in my right ear, but I felt nothing. Perhaps that shot hit Nono, for I saw no more of him. I careened downhill. . . .

On my second day in hiding both Dardels went to Nono's funeral in his home village. It seemed that he had been hit while beside me on the road, and had then tried to make across the wheat field, left-handed, for our forest, Chailluz. He had died on the edge of it.

■

Hitler always distrusted Berliners, finding them too sophisticated, too arrogant. Berlin Jews also felt their treatment would surely be more favorable than that of Jews elsewhere in Germany. In the end, out of humanity, a dislike of Hitler, and a refusal to turn their backs on years of friendships, Berlin "Aryans" were responsible for hiding an estimated 10,000 Jews through the end of the war. Here are some of their stories. Alice Stein-Landesmann relates her story of survival in Eric Boehm's book about the hidden and hunted people of Nazi Germany, We Survived:

Dark velveteen curtains shut out the hostile world; books—scores of books—line the walls. There is a low tile table with tea glasses and flowers. . . . Claire was alone and in tears. She clung to me. I had never seen her so desperate. Finally she told me the story. The previous fall the Gestapo had forced their way into the Kochan family's flat, hoping to arrest [her friend] Richard Kochan. He was not there. . . . When Richard turned up one day quite unconcerned, [his father] implored him to flee, but Richard felt sure of himself, called the whole thing a ridiculous mistake, and went immediately to the Gestapo to clear it up. He never returned. . . . After Christmas his father heard that Richard had been taken to the Plotzensee prison, where he could see him but rarely. . . . Everywhere he was told, "Secret matter of the Reich, keep your hands off."

Weeks went by, and now the old man learned that Richard Kochan had been sentenced to death for high treason. . . . So Richard had already been in prison when Claire had taken me into her home! She must expect them to shadow her and to search her apartment.

■

When Claire's apartment became dangerous, Alice Stein-Landesmann tried to find refuge with Hanni, a friend of Claire's. This was unsuccessful. But she did discover that a network of supportive people existed:

Hanni sighed. She leaned forward and said with effort, "I am sure Claire expects me to take you in, Frau Riebe, and I would be willing to do so—if it weren't that—that—I mean—there is somebody—I also have—" She smiled helplessly, with a gesture toward the kitchen.

Claire clapped her on the back. "Good for you, Hanni, you're a sport, though it's bad for us. . . . We must get going. It's very late as it is." Hanni took us downstairs. It seemed that she had promised her guest not to let anybody in on the secret. She merely told us that the woman had been hiding in a coal cellar for the past three weeks, thanks to a kindhearted janitor who let her slip in there. . . .

Finally the day came when white sheets were hung from the windows and we knew that the nightmare was over.

We stepped out into the daylight, not daring to believe the good news, and raised our eyes as if expecting the long-desired freedom to shine upon us from the sky. We stood, a crowd of beggars in dirty rags amid the chaos of a world that was breaking to pieces.

■

Moritz Mandelkern was a Polish Jew who came to Berlin after World War I to find a better life. And at first, he told Eric Boehm, he was sure he had found it:

I am a tailor, and even though I have to walk with two canes because I have been paralyzed since childhood, still I can do my job well. I married my good Henriette in 1922. We were very happy when our boy Siegfried was born. . . .

A persecution of the Jews in Germany

broke out in November 1938. They wanted to deport me. But I was at the synagogue. . . . That was my salvation. . . . [Almost a year later,] on September 13, 1939, the day before Rosh Hashana, the Jewish New Year, they came for me in the morning at half past five. . . . At the police station there was a kind man. He had pity and said, "This man is unfit for arrest." So I was discharged, and our Rosh Hashana was a very happy one, and we thanked God for his intervention. . . .

■

Later their son Siegfried was arrested by police. They did not know where he had been taken. Then:

A day came which started like all the others: I was tailoring, and my wife was working in the kitchen. She often did the ironing for me because it was hard for me to stand. We heard three knocks at the door, the way our boy had always knocked. I dropped everything, but then I said to myself, "Moritz, you are a fool!" And again the knocking, three times, the sound of knuckles on wood.

Then I shouted out and went into the hall . . . my boy held me in his arms. . . .

■

In a short time the boy knew he had to move on for his safety:

He found work with the Jewish Council in Tarnow in Poland and was not badly off. But early in 1942 Tarnow also had pogroms. . . .

Our uncertainty did not last much longer. On November 8 a card came, written in the Gestapo prison in Lemberg. We didn't know how it was smuggled out. Only a few lines, illegible and blotted. But we could make out that the boy had been betrayed by acquaintances and that he had little chance of getting out.

■

When the arrests and deportations were stepped up throughout Berlin, Mandelkern went into hiding in a garret, with the aid of friends. But when the building was badly damaged in the air raids, he had to find something else:

I stumbled along as fast as I could. I had a little money in my pocket and took the subway to another part of town. . . . What should I do now? There was only one answer: go to my wife. She was in the village of Schonebeck near Berlin. So I went to the station and bought a ticket. . . . But the relatives were afraid to keep me for good. We went back to Berlin and found a place for me to stay with a family of mixed marriage.

On April 25, 1945, the Russians came. . . .

And our boy? Should one believe that God will perform another miracle for us? He has done it before.

■

The July 20, 1944, attempt to assassinate Hitler had been several years in the planning —long enough to recruit conspirators in many critical positions, from the top German commander in France to the head of the Berlin garrison, whose men would have the responsibility of taking over the telephone exchange, the radio stations, and the other machinery that would allow the conspirators to secure their position in the first hours of confusion. Eugen Gerstenmaier was one of these plotters, who was quickly arrested. Hitler ordered total retaliation against the plotters and their families. But Gerstenmaier, a churchman, survived and told Eric Boehm his remarkable story:

The plan of the coup d'état . . . called for the assassination of Hitler, Himmler, and, if possible, Göring. Then detachments of the Reserve Army were to march on Berlin and occupy it, to furnish military strength against the SS. Meanwhile, the Berlin Guard Battalion was to surround government buildings and protect the War Ministry. Similar plans had been made for the Reserve Army through all of Germany. The code word was "Walküre," the signal of army headquarters to all its subordinate commands that a state of emergency existed. . . .

To the original Walküre code, which was merely the signal for an emergency program, the conspirators in the Reserve Army had added further sealed orders, including provisions for the establishment of martial law, the cessation of all political activity, and

occupation of all public buildings. . . .

Further orders were to be given to the military forces abroad, who were to arrest SS officials under their command. Once the orders had been issued, General Beck was to announce on the *Deutschlandsender* [the official state radio station] that Hitler was dead, that he [Beck] was now Chief of State and Interim Commander of the Armed Forces, and that there would be a three-day state of emergency during which Nazi resistance would be liquidated and a cabinet formed. The new cabinet would start armistice negotiations immediately.

Stauffenberg had volunteered to place the bomb. . . .

Finally it was decided to carry out the assassination on July 20, even though Hitler might be alone. Carrying the briefcase containing the bomb, Stauffenberg entered the barracks in Rastenburg which was used for the briefing at about 12:30 P.M. He placed the briefcase on the floor.

Shortly after the briefing had started, Stauffenberg's adjutant, Lt. Werner von Haeften, called him out on the pretext that he was wanted on the telephone. Before leaving, Stauffenberg pushed the pin of the bomb in the briefcase. Then he hurried to his car. One hundred seconds later, before they had reached the car, they heard a loud explosion. A few moments later they were on their way to the airfield. They flew to Berlin-Adlershof.

■

Stauffenberg arrived in Berlin to find that Hitler was not dead and that the conspiracy was coming apart. A number of the plotters had been hesitant to act—particularly when the rumor began to circulate that the assassination had been unsuccessful. Nazi loyalists surrounded the building the plotters were using as their headquarters, arrested everyone, and immediately shot a number of these men in the building's courtyard, by the light of automobiles. Stauffenberg was one of these. Others met terrible deaths strangled by wires and hung on meat hooks, in executions that were filmed for Hitler's amusement. Gerstenmaier, miraculously, defended himself so eloquently in "People's Court" that his life was spared.

Scrap Drives and Home Guard Music, Britain

Michael Ford titled this rich and happy picture *War Weapons Week in a Small Town*, and its figures and details suggest dozens of stories, much like the narrative paintings of the old Dutch masters. The British War Artists Scheme ensured that heroic engagements and fighting men would be well recorded. But Ford's picture was a spontaneous salute to the home front. (Imperial War Museum)

Graveyard Shift, Canada

After the sacrifices in World War I, Britain had undergone a traumatic "general strike" in the 1920s that could trace some of its impetus to the anger that many returned servicemen felt about their meager work opportunities. Some people had predicted after the strike that it would take several generations for industry to recover. But British production records, and those of other Commonwealth countries, were astounding. B. F. Taylor's painting, *Early Morning* (OPPOSITE), of a predawn shift change at a Canadian war plant, was typical of war workers' round-the-clock schedules. (Canadian War Museum)

Proud Talk, Britain, 1940–41

Ruskin Spear painted this "cheeky" wall slogan (RIGHT) on a bombed building in the East End, after many of the children—evacuated in 1939—had slipped back. Neighborhoods vied with each other for how much they were "taking it." (Imperial War Museum)

All-Too-Familiar Scene, Britain, 1941–42

During the Battle of Britain, most people in every British community had roles in some committee, drive, or volunteer service. This Kathleen Guthrie painting, *Bombed Hospital Ward* (RIGHT), certainly qualified as heavy propaganda against the German bombing, but it was a true scene of the home front—and one that British bombers were also creating in 1941 by their reprisal raids over Germany. (Imperial War Museum)

"Move It! . . . uh, Mum," Britain

The Atlantic convoys brought large numbers of ships into ports on the British and Scottish west coasts—far removed from German bombers and the prowling grounds of submarines. There, British trains took over. Like all British industries, railroads were short of male workers. William Roberts painted this largely female depot crew—with some good humor all around. (Imperial War Museum)

"Don't Worry, Dearie," Britain, 1941–42

Grace Golden shows the quiet tragedy of *The Emergency Food Office* (in a converted music hall) where bombed-out people arranged for emergency food and new ration books. The pleasant irony of rationing was that the British public ate more healthily during the war than at any point in their previous history. (Imperial War Museum)

"War of the Worlds" Drill, Britain, 1940

Between the wars, the picture press frequently suggested that "the next time" there would be mass gas attacks on civilians. The British were determined to be prepared, and the entire population was issued masks—and told to carry them everywhere. This Dorothy Coke drawing (ABOVE) suggested a mass burial, as members of the Women's Auxiliary Transport Service took cover from "strafing" RAF aircraft in a gas mask drill on the south coast. (Imperial War Museum)

Light Work, Britain

Organizers of volunteers (ABOVE) found that "bandage rolling" was a valuable first assignment for women who discovered they wanted to do more. Ethel Gabain showed Red Cross and St. John's Hospital volunteers at "bandage drill" in Bath. (Imperial War Museum)

War Work, Embattled Isle

Women's Royal Naval Service members (ABOVE) were barred from duty afloat. But a WREN flag secretary to the head of all convoy escorts made a name for herself by beating the admiral several times in simulated war games at Convoy Escort School. Robert Sargent Austin rendered WRENs at a supply base. (Imperial War Museum)

The camouflage netting that these convalescence nurses are working on (ABOVE RIGHT) was a real confuser when viewed from the air. Identifiable lines and forms of streets and buildings were broken up, disorienting navigators and bomb aimers. Evelyn Dunbar's fine attention to detail shows how simply the nets were prepared. (Imperial War Museum)

Ethel Gabain showed women workers "locking in" the turret of a heavy tank (RIGHT) . The war plants even contributed an authentic British "cover girl." Ruby Loftus, a lathe worker in a plant making heavy field guns, became something of a national celebrity after being painted by Laura Knight. (Imperial War Museum)

U-Boat Lairs, Bay of Biscay, 1942

The occupation of France enabled the German U-boat offensive to move bases (OPPOSITE) to French Atlantic coast ports, cutting hundreds of miles off the dangerous North Sea route to the convoy hunting grounds. But the French bases invited RAF bombings. The Todt Organization, the massive German semimilitary construction group, got the assignment to fortify the French Channel coast and strategic spots along the Atlantic where commandos might be expected to land. They also built these hulking U-boat pens—with thirty-foot-thick concrete roofs—that German artist T. C. Spreng sketched in two stages of construction. (German War Art Collection)

Morale Work, Southern England, 1942

Because of his Polish birth, Feliks Topolski frequently visited the training camps of exiled Polish fighting men, following them through their drills and on pass. At top, Topolski's scene in a music hall at Plymouth captures the excitement of the theater —particularly for men who may never have seen it before. Performers headed for retirement found excited new audiences in the Forces. Below, Topolski pictures a Salvation Army band "entertaining" in a heavily bombed section of London's East End. The big British shows to raise troop morale were obviously not coming there. (Imperial War Museum)

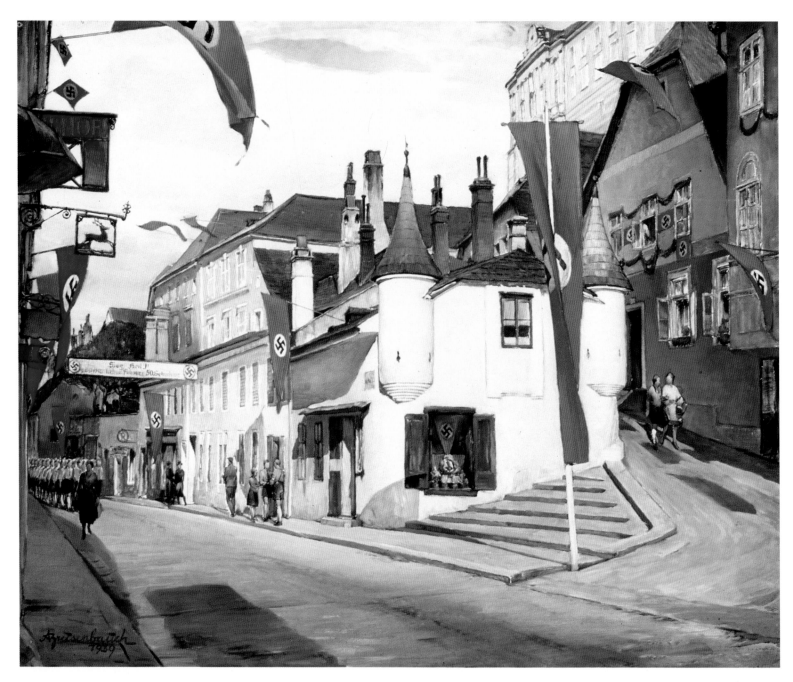

Far Cry from Prewar Rallies, Germany

This painting by an unknown German artist was catalogued in the German art collection as the celebration of Hitler's birthday in a small German city. As the local Hitler Youth troop marches in the distance, the artist has cleverly—or unconsciously— shown the indifference of townspeople, who ignore the parade. (German War Art Collection)

Berlin Under the Bombs, 1943–45

This forlorn scene by Wilhelm Wessel (OPPOSITE) is titled *Bombing Raid on Berlin, 1943* and reflects the devastation that occurred when the British began intensive, systematic raids on the city. In spite of the wreckage of the building in the painting, the traditional massive apartment blocks typical of Berlin (with their secure basement "shelter" areas) and the city's wide streets (less likely to be blocked with rubble) made Berlin safer in an air raid than London. (Captured German Art; U.S. Center of Military History)

"On the Thailand Railway"

Australian artist Harold Abbott so titled this tragic picture (RIGHT). Abbott painted the plight of too many Allied POWs who were worked until they dropped, then neglected to die slowly . . . or shot to hasten their end and the costly maintenance of prisoners who could not work. Protection by the Geneva Convention and the International Red Cross was a weak reed to count on in the Far East. (Australian War Memorial)

Dreamed-Of Meals Must Wait, Singapore, Fall 1945

Leslie Cole obviously painted this scene of Changi jail after the arrival of the British liberators, so the conditions in the jail hospital ward have been substantially improved. Severely ill men are gone to army hospitals. The job then was to nurse the remaining survivors to health on a restorative diet—gradually. After three years of dreaming of sumptuous meals, overeating by starving prisoners could result in a painful death from stomachs that exploded. (Imperial War Museum)

Survivors, Singapore, Fall 1945

Leslie Cole described this picture as "limbless officers checking out of Changi jail, Singapore, after liberation." Changi was the main prisoner-of-war center for Singapore. And through it passed some 70,000 prisoners who were taken when the great city and its naval base fell. (Imperial War Museum)

Work for the Emperor, Korea, 1943

Sinichi Yamada, a Japanese war artist, painted British and Australian POWs at work in Inchon, Korea. These men were fortunate, from the look of them, in getting better food and working conditions than the prisoners Leslie Cole painted in Malaya. The Japanese were ambivalent in their attitude toward prisoners, and a man's future depended largely on the philosophy of the local camp commander. (National Modern Art Museum of Tokyo)

A Small Partisan Victory, Yugoslavia

The war-shattered remains of the Yugoslav village in the foreground would seem little to celebrate about. But Ismet Mujezinovic has shown much joy in *The Liberation of Jacje.* In the years following the war, small numbers of former Allied airmen made their way in ones and twos back to Yugoslavia to hunt for partisan fighters who had helped them. These ex-servicemen, shot down over Yugoslavia, had made contact with the partisans and had been hidden for the duration or guided to safety in Italy or Greece. (Yugoslav People's Army Club)

Real War—and Fantasy, Yugoslavia

These two works by Yugoslavian artists were generally considered the most dramatic paintings in a show of Yugoslavian war art at London's historic Imperial War Museum. At top is Vasko Taskovski's *Riders of the Apocalypse,* in which every viewer can find his own terrifying meaning. Below is *October 1944, the Day of Liberation* by Milic Stankovic. (Both, Yugoslav People's Army Club)

The Defense of Moscow, 1941

Yevsei Moiseenko's painting of somber farewells (ABOVE) is titled *Mothers, Sisters,* and it is the view soldiers would have had from the rear of a Red Army truck as they pulled away for the battlefront. The women have pressed close to the tailgate for good-byes. The scene of Nikolai Osenev's painting (RIGHT) is the outskirts of Moscow. The Red Army has fallen back, and the Russian commanders are preparing for the last great German offensive against the city. Artist Osenev titled this *Komsomol Youth Building Defensive Lines Near Moscow.* The builders are all women, working under the direction of Soviet engineers, their rifles stacked beside them. (Both, Tretyakov Gallery)

Saving Factories to Save a Country, Western Russia, Fall 1941

One of the most enormous combined efforts of Soviet workers and the state in World War II was the movement of whole factories from the path of the German invasion. Machinery, raw materials, work in progress, and workers were transferred hundreds of miles into central Russia—and factories started producing again in the space of a few weeks! As the factories moved east, the troops moved west toward the front, passing through villages like this one soon to be deserted—and probably burned by the advancing Germans. Soviet artist Ovanes Lusegenov called his painting of a ghostly column of troops, trailed by a soldier saying farewell, *I Shall Return*. (USSR Union of Artists)

One More Last Stand, Western Russia, Fall 1941

The city of Vitebsk stands about twenty-five miles from the eastern border of Belorussia, astride one of the main railway lines connecting Moscow to the Baltic ports of Riga and Gdansk, and therefore a prime German target. Mikhail Savitsky calls this *The Vitebsk Gate*. Civilians and walking wounded leave the city and Red Army units move in. Each face that can be seen is a picture of determination—but also an indictment of the human suffering in war. (Belorussian Museum of Decorative Arts)

Startling Defense, Western Russia, Summer 1941

This painting by Gely Korzhev was apparently inspired by a story, circulated along the front, of an incident where German troops placed Soviet hostages on the parapet of a trench to stop fire. True or not, the picture, *People's Shield* (OPPOSITE), made powerful propaganda. Certainly proven was the sustained brutality of German tactics against civilians, encouraged by orders Hitler and the SS had issued. (USSR Ministry of Culture)

The Front May Soon Run Here, Moscow, Late 1941

In the western suburbs of Moscow during November and December of 1941, steel rail tank barriers like these were drilled into the streets and vacant areas between buildings. But the traditional artilleryman's order to "level everything in sight" to get a clear field of fire was not followed. The Soviets had discovered that wrecked buildings provided defensive strong points. Aleksandr Deineka called this grim scene *The Periphery of Moscow, November 1941*. (Tretyakov Gallery)

Small Thanks, Russia, 1942–43

With vast food producing areas of western Russia in control of the Germans and with imports into the country heavily curtailed by the U-boat blockade, the Soviet Union faced serious food shortages as it looked ahead to a long war. Aleksei Zhabsky's painting *The Bread of War* is done in a matter-of-fact way— rather than a pleading one. But it showed a situation encountered all over the Soviet Union in the first two winters of the war. (USSR Union of Artists)

They Have Seen the Worst, Western Russia, 1941–42

Boris Prorokov worked in a style that reminded some art critics of the "posters of exhortation" of the Spanish Civil War. His painting is titled *Near Babi Yar* (a village about ninety miles southwest of Moscow, located on a main railway and highway leading to the capital). The picture was part of a patriotic art series, "This Must Never Happen Again," which has been examined and praised in several published collections of contemporary Slavic artworks. (Tretyakov Gallery)

Beyond Rescue

In *The Partisans Have Arrived,* Tatyana Nazarenko has created a scene that may remind viewers of scenes of the Crucifixion. A German execution squad has done its work and moved on. A partisan band has arrived too late. (USSR Ministry of Culture)

Paying the Penalty, Western Russia, 1941–45

What the partisan rescuers might also discover after a German visit was the punitive burning of the village, or at least the houses of the accused. This grim scene by Aleksandr Deineka shows houses that have been torched as punishment. (Russian Museum)

Dead, Wounded, and Missing, Russia, 1941–45

A look at official casualty figures for the German army issued by their Eastern Front headquarters for the period from June 22, 1941 (the invasion's start), to March 20, 1942, was 1,073,006 officers, noncommissioned officers, and men lost in the fighting. Soviet military casualties of 1,000,000 reported for the same period may not be unrealistic. Mushail Mushailov's *The Black Shawls of Mothers* is one tribute to that terrible loss. The reading of the casualty list, apparently by the woman in the center of the painting, was repeated to stunned women all over the Soviet Union. (Artists Union, Dagestan ASSR)

Starting Over, Western Russia, 1941–45

By the winter of 1943—the time of Petr Ossorsky's grim painting (OPPOSITE)— the German advance had been halted and some Russian villagers, who had left their homes to escape the fighting and punitive enemy occupation, were able to return to what little was left. This work is from a series, "Lifelines of the Motherland." (Tretyakov Gallery)

ASSAULT ON NAZI FORTRESS EUROPE

Dday came in Normandy after uneasy delays because of bad weather that threatened to cancel the whole operation for at least two weeks—and more probably for a whole year. Heavy losses were experienced in the first landing waves and among glider troops and paratroops, but the beachhead held. Then German armor rushed in, with orders from Hitler to drive the invaders into the sea within forty-eight hours—but it was too late. The Allies broke out from the Normandy pocket, south toward Paris and east toward Germany, attacking with armies that included contingents of fighting men from most of Occupied Europe: Poles, Czechs, Belgians, Dutch, Free French, and Free Greeks. Paris was taken—undestroyed, in spite of Hitler's order that the city be burned. Hitler's last big bet, the Ardennes offensive, almost worked; the Germans counterattacked in the snow and fog of December and drove a deep bulge into Allied lines. This last offensive was the largest land battle of the war on the European continent. The wiping out of the "Bulge" began in 1945. The Allies pushed east with power and confidence. It would be the last six months of the European war.

For the Dieppe Raid in 1942, secrecy and space dictated that only a few correspondents could go with the fighting force to report the operation. The Normandy invasion, which was to be the largest amphibious operation in the history of the world, also had the largest press coverage—a record that still stands. What follows are observations by a British correspondent and then by Ernie Pyle, the noted American war reporter. Richard L. Tobin reports first in his Invasion Journal:

Our surge into France in mighty nonstop waves has been going on since dawn. We have now fought our way near Caen, ten miles inside the Normandy coast. . . . To take Cherbourg, Le Havre or Brest means that our troops can be supplied direct from America . . . with no 100 miles of Channel small-boating.

The front has widened at midnight to sixty miles of beach. The first landings were extremely difficult because the wind was force five and coming from the northeastern quarter. . . .

LONDON, June 8: Seven battleships and twenty-six cruisers are standing off the coast of France, covering the invasion. Twenty thousand first-line aircraft cover the sky. . . . The battleships are the *Ramillies,* the *Nelson,* the *Rodney,* the *Arkansas,* the *Texas,* the *Nevada,* and old *Warspite* herself —old *Warspite,* who came right up to the shore at Salerno and spat fifteen-inch venom into the last desperate counterattack the Germans were able to make, an attack that almost succeeded. . . .

■

Ernie Pyle, perhaps the favorite war reporter among American fighting men, wrote from the invasion fleet:

My devastating sense of fear and depression disappeared when we approached the beachhead. There was the old familiar crack and roar of big guns all around us, and the shore was a great brown haze of smoke and dust, and we knew that bombers would be over us that night. Yet all the haunting premonition, the soul-consuming dread, was gone. . . .

As far as you could see in every direction the ocean was infested with ships. There must have been every type of oceangoing

vessel in the world. I even thought I saw a paddle wheel steamer in the distance. . . . [He did . . . and it was a ship that had also helped to evacuate Dunkirk.]

Shells from battleships were whamming over our heads, and occasionally a dead man floated face downward past us. . . .

Angry shells hitting near us would make heavy thuds as the concussion carried through the water and struck the hull of our ship. But in our wardroom men in gas-impregnated uniforms and wearing life belts sat reading *Life* and listening to the BBC telling us how the war before our eyes was going. [Ernie Pyle was killed by a Japanese sniper on Iwo Jima in the western Pacific in April 1945.]

■

General Gavin remembered the preinvasion pressure. Everyone trained almost up to loading time. Even those troops with lots of experience in combat were put through exercises to restore their sharpness. Their commanders endured war games sessions, trying to put themselves into the mind-set of the enemy. As always, there were some prophets of doom:

When our forces were moved to the takeoff areas [Air Vice Marshal] Leigh-Mallory personally called on General Eisenhower to protest the use of the U.S. airborne forces, using the term "the futile slaughter of two fine divisions." In *Crusade in Europe,* Eisenhower states: "[Leigh-Mallory] believed that the combination of unsuitable landing grounds and anticipated resistance was too great a hazard to overcome. . . ."

We studied intently the use of "asparagus" [a spikelike ground defense against paratroopers] for a long time as a possible indication of the Germans' evaluation of each sector from the defensive viewpoint. We believed that there must be a reason for their being especially thorough in the preparation of one area and not of another. . . .

■

General Rommel had studied the British anti-invasion devices and became a "believer" in "asparagus." He wrote:

The construction of antiparatroop obstacles has made great progress in many divisions. For example, one division alone has erected almost 300,000 stakes, and one corps over

900,000. Erecting stakes alone does not make the obstacles complete; the stakes must be wired together, and shells and mines attached to them. The density must be about a thousand stakes per square kilometer. . . .

■

General Gavin was a close observer of combat all through the war, because he jumped into action with his men. In the passages that follow, the observations are Gavin's, usually firsthand, unless they are otherwise credited:

A night jump into combat is not as scary as it might seem. What apprehensions one experiences seem to go away once the commitment is made. . . . Then your total faculties are concerned with survival, and that means carrying out things you have been trained to do as well as you possibly can. . . .

The exit was probably the moment of greatest danger. To begin with, the troopers were all heavily overloaded. Most of them carried an M-1 rifle loaded and ready to use, 156 rounds of rifle ammunition, a pistol with three clips of ammunition, an entrenching shovel, a knife, a water canteen, a first-aid packet, usually four grenades, reserve rations, some maps, and a raincoat.

■

Large numbers of the paratroop carriers and the planes towing the glider troops departed from England at the Bill of Portland, a high point of land shaped roughly like the continent of Africa, that juts out south into the Channel almost directly opposite the Cherbourg peninsula. Dusk came late in the summer evenings, and great waves of these planes, including Gavin's, with their wing lights lit, moved down the coast to Portland, doused lights, and turned for France:

I stood at the door of the airplane to check the navigational aids. By talking to the pilot through the crew chief, I was assured from time to time that all was well and that we were moving on schedule. As we left the coast of England, all was quiet below. We were flying quite low, down near 600 feet, the prescribed jump altitude. That altitude was selected to minimize casualties from enemy fire and at the same time to give us optimum time for the parachute to deploy

■

"The General Patton Deception" was the sort of caper at which the British excelled. Gavin noted one occasion in the invasion execution where the U.S. Army was able to try its hand:

Since General Patton had been brought from the Mediterranean theater to the United Kingdom early in 1944, German intelligence had kept track of him as closely as they could. . . . He was the only general besides Eisenhower they seemed concerned about. . . .

[There developed] an elaborate deception plan intended to mislead the Germans into believing that an Army Group commanded by General Patton was prepared to attack Calais. . . . Part of the plan was for Patton to show himself about London and other areas, where his presence would be obvious and news of it would reach the Germans. . . . Several drops of miniature parachute dummies were also made. . . . They were so successful that in some situations the Germans reacted tardily to the actual landings. . . . A complete field army communications network was laid out across from Calais and regular communications traffic set up to cause the Germans to believe that the army was, in fact, there.

Finally, on August 1, Patton's very real Third Army was turned loose in France. . . .

I remember following his movements in the war room of the 82d Airborne Division in Leicester, England, and to one with combat experience, it was an amazing display of audacity. I asked about the danger of Germans moving up from the south and learned that he had planned to have the Air Corps bomb the crossings over the Loire River and then disregard all Germans to the south.

■

Eisenhower never hesitated to acknowledge Patton's military genius, using it effectively. But controlling his pistol-toting general was a continuing problem. When preparing his account of the fighting in Europe, Eisenhower told editor Ken McCormick how Patton would castigate himself after being "braced" for some "imprudent, hare-brained scheme":

"He'd say he would never do it again—then promptly do so. I had to keep him well under cover when visiting groups of congressmen came to observe. I didn't want him to rile anyone and then have them call him back to the U.S. to answer for it. I needed him for the final push. A lot of his "non-Army" talk was unbecoming of a general. But the troops usually loved it."

■

Col. Charles Codman, Patton's aide, described his boss in action:

The old man has been like one possessed . . . the spearheading armored divisions, following the motorized infantry, have been moving bumper to bumper . . . [Patton was] pushing, pulling, exhorting, cajoling, raising merry hell, he is having the time of his life.

■

The Third Army's rapid drives south into Brittany and then east had created a pocket of German resistance between Falaise and Argentan. Canadians and Poles attacking in the north and Americans and Free French in the south surrounded the pocket—except for a fifteen-mile gap:

By this time five and a half of the seven Panzer divisions in the pocket were committed against the Americans. . . . Hitler could not have played into the hands of the Allies more completely if the Allies had planned it. . . .

The Allies had complete air superiority. This was devastating to the Germans. . . .

Up to now it had been Sicily all over again, with Montgomery making very little progress and Patton making an enormous enveloping movement; the destruction of two German armies was in their grasp. . . .

All day on August 13 Patton tried to get authority to move north and thus link up with the British and Canadians and cut off the Germans. But by the end of that Sunday afternoon, it was quite definite that he was not to be allowed to . . . close the gap. . . . Thus, incredibly, was lost one of the great tactical opportunities of the war. . . . [Some 40,000 Germans escaped. But 10,000 were killed in the pocket and 50,000 taken prisoner.]

■

Reviewing German army documents after the war, General Gavin learned some of the behind-the-scenes snap judgments that brought about the last great Nazi offensive:

It all began a day before we parachuted into Holland, September 17, 1944. The location was the Wolf's Lair, Hitler's East Prussian headquarters. The Führer was conducting a daily conference, and Field Marshal Alfred Jodl was ticking off the depressing statistics: shortages of ammunition, shortages of tanks, German troops withdrawing from southern France. Suddenly Hitler interrupted. "I have just made a momentous decision. I shall go over to the counterattack, that is to say—" He pointed to the map unrolled on the desk before him. "Here, out of the Ardennes, with the objective—Antwerp."

■

Gen. Hasso von Manteuffel described a briefing of top commanders to be involved. General Jodl is speaking:

"Gentlemen, before opening the conference I must ask you to read this document carefully and then sign it with your full names."

The date was 3 November 1944. . . . Each officer present had to pledge himself to preserve complete silence concerning the information which Jodl intended to divulge to us: should any officer break this pledge, he must realize that his offense would be punishable by death.

On 11 and 12 December Hitler summoned all the commanding officers who were to take part in the forthcoming operation, down to and including the divisional commanders. . . .

Facing them was the Supreme Commander of the Armed Forces, a stooped figure . . . a sick man apparently borne down by his burden of responsibility. . . . When he walked he dragged one leg behind him. . . .

■

Field Marshal von Rundstedt was one of a number of officers who felt the offensive was likely just to chew up men and equipment they would need later:

I strongly object to the fact that this stupid operation in the Ardennes is sometimes called the "Rundstedt offensive". . . . It was only up to me to obey. It was a nonsensical operation, and the most stupid part of it was the setting of Antwerp as the target. If we had reached the Meuse we should have got down on our knees and thanked God—let alone try to reach Antwerp.

■

Hitler had briefed his generals for the Ardennes offensive at a secret meeting in a German command post that had been set up originally for the 1940 attack on France but never used. Suspicious of the army since the July 20 assassination attempt, Hitler had the generals bused in at night over roundabout routes to confuse their sense of direction. They entered a briefing room with SS guards surrounding the walls, and each officer had to surrender his pistol and his briefcase before being admitted. Hitler spoke for two hours, concluding with: "A few well-struck blows and this artificial common front [Britain, the United States, and Russia] could come crashing down any moment."

The German attack that opened the Ardennes offensive pushed off with several elements of surprise. The sector was thought of as a quiet area and inexperienced American troops were holding it in only light strength. Bad weather—rain, then winds, snow, low clouds, and fog—had grounded American and British reconnaissance planes. The massing of German troops for the attack had been undetected. General Gavin tells of the start:

. . . Finally, by December 16, all was in readiness, and bad flying weather was predicted for at least forty-eight hours. The attack jumped off at 5:30 A.M., three hours before daylight, with three German armies abreast on the frontage of about seventy miles.

A very powerful [Panzer Corps] force was attacking on a narrow front. It was equipped with about 500 tanks and armored assault guns, including ninety Tiger tanks. It was like a monstrous steamroller. . . .

■

Under the cover of bad weather that kept Allied planes grounded at first, the Germans pushed ahead rapidly. A German soldier wrote to his wife:

We have been on our way through Belgium. . . . No rest or sleep at all. My Christmas present, after twelve days, consisted of washing, shaving, and five hours of sleep, but we are on our way again. The main thing is that the Americans are on the run. . . .

■

General Ridgway encountered a veteran mortar man who had worked out a "convenience" with the enemy:

In that same fight, not long afterward, I came upon another warwise, war-weary G.I. He was a mortar man, down in a hole, with his weapon. He wasn't firing. . . .

"General," he said, "every time we shoot, them S.O.B.s shoot right back." . . .

He took a sight on the opposite ridge top, dropped a shell down the tube. . . . Hardly had our shell exploded on the ridge opposite than there was a tremendous explosion a few yards to our left, and shell fragments screeched through the trees. . . .

"See whadda mean?" he said.

■

When General Gavin looked back at the Battle of the Bulge, he found he particularly admired the way some primarily noncombat units rose to the challenge:

On December 17 an Engineer squad from the 291st was detailed to establish a roadblock at Stavelot. The traffic on the road [to Stavelot] was heavy, and they had difficulty making their way. They arrived at Stavelot about 6:30 P.M., well after dark. They crossed the bridge and ascended the hill on the far side . . . [coming] to a point near the top of the hill where the road made a sharp turn to the right around a rock cliff. Sergeant Hensel decided that that would be a good place for a roadblock. They strung their mines across the road. He sent Private Bernard Goldstein ahead to give the alarm. . . .

At 10:45 Peiper's Panzer column was sighted rapidly approaching from Stavelot. The 57mm opened up and disabled the first Peiper tracked vehicle. . . . It was a Panther tank. The next Panther opened fire, knocked out the gun, and killed all four members of the gun crew. Within seconds

the Engineers blew the first bridge, the bridge over the Ambleve. . . .

The work of the Engineers had been superb . . . and resourceful. . . . Peiper could only sit with leaden heart and face the fact that time and his luck had entirely run out on him. . . . And he could only sit helplessly, pound his knee and swear bitterly, "The damned engineers! The damned engineers!"

■

Lester Atwell was a British soldier spending Christmas with his unit in their segment of the battle line near a Belgian village, as the line began to hold:

"Mass! Anyone here going to Mass? Fall out!" The tiresome routine of putting on ammunition belt, gas mask, helmet, rifle—and out on to the road. Men were coming up the street in groups, all armed. . . . The church bells were ringing. . . .

When the bell rang for the start of Mass, the parish priest came out in handsome white vestments, the two altar boys in red cassocks, starched white lace-edged surplices and white gloves. Blasts of frigid air blew in. The children sang hymns in French, but when the priest—stocky, middle-aged and dark—ascended the pulpit, the long sermon, surprisingly, was in German.

■

British trooper R. M. Wingfield had a Christmas experience that was probably just about like the one going on across the battle line:

We discussed the peculiar first Christmas of the First World War when the opposing sides swarmed over their trenches into No-Man's-Land and played football. Later they shelled each other's trenches to hell. We thought it stupid.

Tom gripped my arm. "Listen!"

Faintly, from across the river, came the sound of voices singing "Stille Nachte, Heilige Nacht." [It was the German forward patrol.]

The age-old carol gained in strength as it floated to us on the frosty air. The war was distant, almost stopped.

Dropping In, Normandy, June 6, 1944

British war artist Albert Richards, who did the painting above, *The Drop—Paratroopers,* had trained in that branch before being brought into the War Artists Scheme. Richards jumped with a squad of paratroopers early on the morning of D day, and when the ranking noncom could not be found once they were on the ground, Richards took charge of the group and led the men to their objective. (Imperial War Museum)

Waiting—June 4–5, 1944

Perhaps the most wearing wait, when the invasion was temporarily postponed because of bad weather, settled on the troops that had already been embarked on big transports and LSTs (ABOVE), some of whom had been aboard for several days at that point. Many of the big landing convoys moved up into the Irish Sea, to be farther from German observation planes. The men cleaned their weapons, slept, and staged some dice games that challenged records both for consecutive play and money lost and won. A general low overcast over southeast England and a heavy umbrella of Allied aircraft patrolling overhead kept the Germans from spotting the idling convoys. Mitchell Jamieson, who was in a convoy of first-wave men, did the painting. (U.S. Navy Combat Art Collection)

Headed for France, June 6, 1944

Alexander Baron, on the way to Normandy with men of a British infantry battalion, found that the last few hours aboard ship as they moved toward the coast of France were nothing like he expected: "There was no sentimental talk, no singing or playing of harmonicas, no writing of farewell letters, no men sadly gazing at the distant shore. Three days with nothing to do but eat, sleep, and gamble was an event in the lives of the men of the 5th Battalion. They made the most of it, and thought of nothing else." Alexander Russo, an artist in the U.S. Navy war art program, painted a similar quiet last few moments (OPPOSITE) on the deck of an American Landing Ship, Tank. (U.S. Navy Combat Art Collection)

Coast of England

Dwight Shepler pictured landing craft beached at low tide at Appledore in Devon (ABOVE). Many beaches on both sides of the Channel were rock-hard at low tide, and heavy vehicles could move easily. (U.S. Navy Combat Art Collection)

D Day Rehearsal, Spring 1944

Shepler, one of the most prolific of the artists covering the U.S. Navy operations in the invasion of Normandy, painted (RIGHT) *Attack on Slapton Sands: Invasion Preparation, Devon, England.* He depicts a daytime practice in the spring of 1944 with Landing Craft, Infantry (LCIs) and the small personnel landing barges grounding at Slapton, later the target of a chance pre–D day German raid. (U.S. Navy Combat Art Collection)

Juno Beach, Normandy

These Royal Navy LCIs carrying Canadian troops (RIGHT) head for the beaches on either side of a Normandy resort town. One wave of soldiers is ashore and resistance fortunately seems light. If the shoreline and tide are right, the troops on these craft will climb down gangways lowered from either side of the bow and walk to shore dry—or nearly so. Some Canadian veterans who were going ashore could remember the withering fire they had met on an August morning in 1942 many miles farther up the coast when they had rushed ashore in the Dieppe raid. Canadian artist Tom Wood, who had painted a number of powerful convoy scenes, created this picture. (Canadian War Museum)

Near Gold Beach, Normandy

Aleksandr Zyw was a Polish soldier with talent as a painter who was able to develop that talent in the midst of all the confusion of being a fighting man. On D day he had made his way with the Polish Legion to the shores of Normandy and landed with early waves at Arromanches. The Poles were fierce fighters and many had made their way to England and the D day forces by way of Russia, Turkey, and North Africa (where a unit of Free Poles fought with Montgomery's 8th Army at El Alamein), then through action in Italy, and finally to the Normandy beaches. (Polish Army Museum)

Rhino Ferry to Normandy

Acraft sailors almost invariably described as "ugly as hell, cranky as hell—but efficient as hell" was the Rhino ferry. As O. N. Fisher's painting shows (ABOVE), they could carry enormous loads. Visible on the tops of the last trucks on board is the white star in a circle that was painted on tank and truck tops, on ship decks, and on almost anything else "Allied" that floated. (Canadian War Museum)

Water-borne "Field Artillery," Utah Beach

Dwight Shepler's *Bombardment at Fox Green Beach* (ABOVE) came out of events on the afternoon of June 7, 1944, off the Normandy coast, as a U.S. destroyer moved inshore (to almost grounding depth) to give gunfire support to infantry advancing inland from the "Utah" beachhead. Offshore fire support had been enormous, and included such proud, but rather long-in-the-tooth, battleships as the *Texas* (LEFT) and the *Arkansas,* both planned for World War I. (Both, U.S. Navy Combat Art Collection)

Advance into Holland

This hand-over of territory near Meijel by U.S. troops to a detachment of Highland infantry is apparently one of the last paintings that Albert Richards made before his death. The viewpoint, as from a balloon, was somewhat unexpected from an artist covering ground action. The artists usually tended to view the war through the eyes of the men they were painting. But the unusual angle gave Richards vivid sundown colors in a wet countryside. (Imperial War Museum)

Wreckage in Normandy

*C*rashed *Gliders* is also an Albert Richards painting. A point that rarely comes into the memoirs of fighting men, but which has invariably made a strong impression on them, is the incredible amount of trash scattered on a modern battlefield, from abandoned equipment to shell casings, letters, remnants of food containers, pieces of clothing, and finally the greatest waste of all—bodies and parts of bodies. Albert Richards, unfortunately, became one of those last pieces of debris. He was killed when he went in a wrong direction and drove his jeep into a mine, on his way to cover a night reconnaissance party. (Imperial War Museum)

Overnight Harbors

These Dwight Shepler paintings show the massiveness of the artificial harbors for Normandy that would have to handle the flow of supplies until a regular harbor was captured. *Pierheads for Mulberry* (ABOVE) looks through the stern trestle of one pierhead at another behind it. Once in position, the towering steel legs would be pushed to the bottom and the deck of the pierhead lifted out of the water. Shepler followed the making of the artificial harbors in *Sinking the Breakwater* (LEFT). Great concrete caissons are towed into position, like giant and unwieldy barges. Then water is let in and they settle to the bottom—where their weight was meant to hold them. It did—till the storm came. (Both, U.S. Navy Combat Art Collection)

Gale Down the Channel, June 19–22

Mitchell Jamieson depicted the height of the storm (ABOVE). A coxswain is still at the wheel of the boat on the left—and apparently trying to go to the rescue of a crewman waving from the ramp of the foundering landing craft on the right. The storm came when the chain of sunken freighters and artificial Mulberry harbors formed the only port of supply for the troops on shore. Craft of all sizes were sunk or smashed on the beach. The artificial harbors were largely knocked out, and the supply line to the troops ashore was cut more effectively than the whole Luftwaffe could have cut it. Anthony Law, a Canadian artist, painted the gale near its height (RIGHT). It has driven ashore an LST and an LCT. (Above, U.S. Navy Combat Art Collection; right, Canadian War Museum)

Patrol off Le Havre, Fall 1944

German E-boats and destroyers clashed almost nightly with British motor torpedo boats, "Fairmile" gunboats, and destroyers in the Channel. By the fall of 1944, the invasion forces were firmly enough established in France that these confrontations had evolved into attempts by the Germans to evacuate by sea top rocket scientists and military staff from besieged and bypassed ports. The Canadian artist Anthony Law painted these British MTBs leaving for a night patrol off Le Havre. By 1944, the British torpedo boats had been strengthened by several squadrons of American PT boats. Though adaptations of a British design, these were about thirty percent faster in the cool air of the Channel than the MTBs and were much more heavily armed. (Canadian War Museum)

Searching for Survivors off Le Havre

This Anthony Law painting shows the aftermath of one of the almost nightly English Channel gun-battles between the patrol craft. An MTB has been sunk, the German E-boats have retired, and Royal Navy rescuers are cautiously searching the area off Le Havre for survivors. Both German and British boats carried torpedoes. But since these cost about $25,000 each, the skippers saved them for bigger game. (Canadian War Museum)

Normandy Countryside

Bruno Bobak, a 21-year-old soldier-artist in the Canadian Fusiliers, painted mechanized troop carriers moving forward after dusk in open country in Normandy. The hedgerows were behind them now. (Canadian War Museum)

V-1 Rockets, 1944

In midsummer 1944, Allied troops in France began to be aware for the first time of German "flying bombs" going into England. Leslie Cole painted a V-1 bomb (OPPOSITE TOP) that has been hit by antiaircraft fire near London. This deadly but primitive machine was basically a rocket with wings and a tail. Because the V-1s had no instinct to dodge, they were vulnerable to antiaircraft fire and fighters. The flying bombs forced Londoners back down into shelters again for the first time since the Blitz. In some ways, the V-1 rockets were more devastating—they came singly at any time of day or night, and they came so fast there was not much time for warning. The rocket engine was programmed to shut off after a designated time of flight, then the V-1 went into a dive and crashed into whatever was below. Londoners learned that as long as you could hear its unearthly roar, you were safe. When the noise stopped, you raced for shelter. Frederick Cook painted a V-1 streaking over Tower Bridge, London (OPPOSITE BOTTOM). (Both, Imperial War Museum)

Near Nijmegen, Holland, September 1944

At right are two of a dozen "studies" that Alex Colville, the Canadian art- ist, made for his painting *Infantry, Near Nijmegen, Holland* (ABOVE). Colville might make sketches for a dozen pictures on a trip in the field, then return to a quieter spot where he could paint, turning the best of them into the sort of finished pictures that have generally been selected for this book. (All, Canadian War Museum)

The Bridge at Nijmegen

Alex Colville, probably on the same scouting expedition, was also able to make sketches for this painting of the Nijmegen Bridge, one of the Allies' main objectives in Operation Market Garden, a daring raid that ultimately failed to penetrate into the Ruhr. (Canadian War Museum)

Taking Prisoners, France, 1944

Traveling with a Canadian column, W. B. Deschamps painted the capture of a lightly armed German scouting group (ABOVE) in a small village that seems to have escaped major fighting. The young man at left could be a member of a French resistance group who guided the Canadians to the patrolling Germans. (Canadian War Museum)

Paris, August 1944

Eisenhower knew the capture of Paris would be a great psychological lift—though presenting other problems. The political decision was made to let the Free French forces of General Leclerc enter first. At left, Milton Marx painted the debris of war in the Place de la Concorde on Liberation Day. (U.S. Army Center of Military History)

Liberation of Paris, August 25, 1944

By the summer of 1944, Anthony Gross of the British War Artists Scheme had painted almost every phase of British participation in the war: the training after mobilization, the raid on Norway's Lofoten Islands, the convoys to North Africa and the Far East, the North African campaigns, the fighting in Burma in 1943, and the Normandy invasion. It was natural to find him in Paris on Liberation Day, and the two pen-and-wash works here are (ABOVE) *General Leclerc's Division Entering Paris by the Route d'Orléans, 25 August 1944* and (RIGHT) *Frightened Crowds in the Place de la Concorde After the Attempted Shooting of General de Gaulle from the House-Tops.* (Both, Imperial War Museum)

The Nuremberg Trial, 1946. Dame Laura Knight (Imperial War Museum)

THE END OF THE WAR IN EUROPE

Allied armies crossed the Rhine and faced dogged resistance on German soil. The chance seizure of an old railroad bridge, intact, at the riverside town of Remagen allowed a four-division buildup on the far side, well ahead of the scheduled crossing of any other Allied units. Some German armies were heavily cut up, near collapse. But there were strong rumors circulating that Hitler and the diehards would retreat into one of several "national redoubts" in easily defended forest and mountain areas— to fight to the last. Hitler, however, had retired to an elaborate bunker under the Reichchancellery grounds in Berlin, poring over maps and giving orders to dwindling and ghost armies. The British, French, and Americans slowed, debating the military and political advantages of capturing Berlin ahead of the Russians. But Eisenhower regarded Berlin as being no longer a military objective and maneuvered to destroy the German armies still in the field. Berlin fell to the Russians, with fierce Soviet vengeance on people and property. Hitler committed suicide inside the bunker, and Admiral Dönitz was charged with surrendering the beaten nation.

By the beginning of 1945 only a handful of top Nazi officials, conditioned by years of Party indoctrination, refused to believe that Germany had lost the war. On January 1, 1945, Hitler had quietly moved from his elaborate apartment on the top floors of the old Reichchancellery building into what his staff members had heard called "the safest bunker in Berlin." Fifty-five feet below ground level, it was prisonlike and unfinished, with rough concrete walls that sweated from the cold of the ground around them. The roof was sixteen feet thick, the walls six feet thick. There were some thirty small rooms painted warship gray. It was close and depressing. He would leave Berlin only twice from then until his death, making brief trips out of the city on February 25 and March 15—the last time for a four-hour tour to "the Eastern Front"—then only about sixty miles away at Frankfurt an der Oder. When "the battle for Berlin" began on April 16, he had less than three weeks to live.

Cornelius Ryan, a veteran American war correspondent who had followed the Allied armies from the Normandy beaches to Berlin, tells the story of the capital's last days. The quotes that follow, unless otherwise identified, are from Ryan's book, The Last Battle:

The battle for Berlin, the last offensive against Hitler's Third Reich, began . . . Monday, April 16, 1945—or A day as it was called by the Western Allies. At that moment, less than thirty-eight miles east of the capital, red flares burst in the night skies above the swollen river Oder, triggering a stupefying artillery barrage and the opening of the Russian assault. . . .

At about that same time, elements of the U.S. Ninth Army were turning away from Berlin—heading back to the west to take up new positions along the river Elbe between Tangermünde and Barby. On April 14 General Eisenhower had decided to halt the Anglo-American drive across Germany. "Berlin," he said, "is no longer a military objective." When U.S. troops got the word, Berlin, for some of them, was only forty-five miles away.

■

Ryan, who went to Berlin shortly after its fall and conducted hundreds of interviews, got a vivid picture of the great city's collapse:

[On the morning of April 16] the 314th Allied raid on Berlin was over. . . .

In this wilderness of devastation it was remarkable that people could survive at all —but life went on with a kind of lunatic normality amid the ruins. Twelve thousand policemen were still on duty. Postmen delivered the mail; newspapers came out daily; telephone and telegraphic services continued. Garbage was collected. Some cinemas, theaters and even a part of the wrecked zoo were open. The Berlin Philharmonic was finishing its season. Department stores ran special sales. Food and bakery shops opened each morning, and laundries, dry-cleaning establishments and beauty salons did a brisk business. The underground and elevated railways functioned; the few fashionable bars and restaurants still intact drew capacity crowds. . . .

[But now] all sorts of atrocity stories spread throughout the city. . . . In her private clinic in Schöneberg, Dr. Anne-Marie Durand-Wever knew the truth. The 55-year-old gynecologist, well-known for her anti-Nazi views, was urging her patients to leave Berlin. She had examined numerous refugee women and had reached the conclusion that, if anything, the accounts of assault [by the advancing Russians] understated the facts. . . .

Dr. Margot Sauerbruch also expected the worst. She was appalled by the number of refugees who had attempted suicide. . . . How many had actually succeeded in ending their lives nobody knew—Dr. Sauerbruch saw only those who had failed—but it seemed clear that a wave of suicides would take place in Berlin if the Russians captured the city. . . .

There were some, however, who not only expected the Russians, they longed to welcome them. . . . Hunted and harassed at every turn by the Gestapo and the criminal police, a few hardened cells had somehow survived. The German Communists and their sympathizers waited eagerly for the saviors from the east. . . .

Incredibly, all over Berlin, in tiny cubicles and closets, in damp cellars and airless attics, a few of the most hated and persecuted of all Nazi victims hung grimly to life and waited for the day when they could emerge from hiding. They did not care who arrived first, so long as somebody came, and quickly. . . . They were the Jews. . . .

Another group of prisoners was also living in Berlin. . . . These were the slave laborers—the men and women from almost every country that the Nazis had overrun. There were Poles, Czechs, Norwegians, Danes, Dutch, Belgians, Luxembourgers, French, Yugoslavs and Russians.

In all, the Nazis had forcibly imported nearly seven million people—the equivalent of almost the entire population of New York City—to work in German homes and businesses. Some countries were bled almost white. . . . More than 100,000 foreign workers—mostly French and Russian—worked in Berlin alone.

■

When the war was going poorly, Hitler said several times to his inner group that if Germany didn't win, it was because the German people didn't deserve to win . . . or to live. Albert Speer, for one, was afraid Hitler would be able to make his promise come true: nothing should be left for them:

Reichsminister Speer was facing the greatest problem of his career. All through the war, despite every conceivable kind of setback, he had kept the Reich's industrial might producing. But long ago his statistics and projections had spelled out the inevitable: the Third Reich's days were numbered. . . . "The war is lost," he wrote the Führer on March 15, 1945. "If the war is lost," Hitler snapped back, "then the nation will also perish." On March 19, Hitler issued a monstrous directive: Germany was to be totally destroyed. . . .

Speer, the man who, more than anyone else, was responsible for forging the terrible tools of Hitler's total war, could not face [Germany's] total destruction. . . . Speer told Hitler, "We must do everything to maintain, even if only in a primitive manner, a basis for the existence of the nation. . . ."

Hitler was unmoved. "There is no need to consider the basis of even a most primitive existence any longer," he replied. . . . "Those who remain after the battle are of little value, for the good have fallen." Speer was horrified. . . . As he put it to General Jodl, "Hitler is totally mad. . . . He must be stopped."

■

There had been rumors circulating about the concentration camps, but each man's first en-

counter with them was a terrible shock. Here was General Gavin's:

At dawn the next day I learned that the Mayor of Lugwigslust and his wife and daughter had committed suicide. I was shocked and puzzled. I could think of no reason for their suicide. . . . It was two days later that we discovered the reason.

One could smell the Wobelein Concentration Camp before seeing it. And seeing it was more than a human being could stand. Even after three years of war it brought tears to my eyes.

Wobelein had been a transfer camp built hastily to hold the overflow of thousands of political prisoners who had to be moved west in front of the inexorably rolling Russian armies. Unlike Auschwitz and Buchenwald, it did not have gas ovens and similar killing devices. However, in its own unsophisticated way, it manufactured its own horrors. . . .

The camp contained political prisoners of all ages. . . . The enclosure contained about 4,000 political prisoners, of which, in the final weeks of the war, almost a quarter had died of starvation. As quickly as we could organize it, hundreds of cots were placed in a hangar at a nearby airfield. Doctors were brought in and intravenous feedings began. It was a sad sight, and I went by the hangar almost daily until the people were ready for more solid feedings and movement. . . .

■

In the years following the end of World War II, it is difficult to remember that knowledge of the Holocaust broke over most of the world only at the very end of the war in Europe, when Allied troops advancing in Germany— as General Gavin's paratroopers had been— came upon the first concentration camps . . . or the pitiful columns of former inmates being driven ahead of the armies by SS guards, who had orders to kill all the camp survivors before the Allies found them and learned the whole terrible story. Though Jewish leaders in England and America had tried to break open the story once they were sure the rumors coming out of Occupied Europe were true, there were very few officials who were ready to believe it—and fewer still ready to push for action. The stories that follow, from Voices from the Holocaust, *edited by Sylvia Roth-*

child, are recollections of survivors. The early warnings seem clear enough—now. Sylvia Rothchild prefaces these stories:

Officially, anti-Jewish legislation began in Germany in July 1933. The mass killings in death camps were halted in April 1945. In the years between, the war against the Jews spread into every country occupied by Hitler. . . .

Thousands of Jews in Germany lost their jobs the day that Hitler came to power. Survivors remember when their driver's licenses were confiscated, when they were pulled off a trolley by young hoodlums while the police watched. They remember the day the Gestapo took their factories and businesses. . . . They were shocked by once-polite shopkeepers who became surly and insulting and drove them out of their stores. . . .

The first act of resistance was flight. German Jews fled to the Netherlands, Poland, Hungary, France, Italy and Greece. Some went to England and America. . . . They were the first to bring the news no one wanted to hear.

■

In reading histories of the World War II persecutions of the Jews, it seems that there may have been more people who stepped forward to help the Jews in their worst time of oppression than in the mid- and late-1930s, when the penalties were, at worst, unpopularity. In the 1930s in countries around the world a snide and cynical practice of anti-Semitism happened all too frequently at many levels of society:

(Elizabeth Mermelstein from Viskovo was nineteen when Hitler invaded Czechoslovakia. Her father was deported, her town was turned into a ghetto, and she was sent to Auschwitz and then to Theresienstadt.)

I was walking down the street with my cousin on the way to my aunt's house [when] two German soldiers came toward us and began talking to us. We were too frightened to answer them. . . . But they . . . were telling us about concentration camps, and suggesting that we escape because there *was* really such a thing as a concentration camp and they were actually killing the Jewish people. And we thought, "It's not true. That can't be true."

Then one morning they gave us five min-

utes to dress and line up in fives in the yard. They let us take only what we could carry and took us to the station. They stripped us of everything we had and hustled us into the boxcars. I was still with my mother and sister and her two children. My father didn't make it into our car and was in the next group. . . . And so we ended up in Auschwitz. They unloaded us and there was the famous Dr. Mengele [making his picks for medical experiments] saying, "Left, right, left, right." . . . I was running after my parents and Mengele said, in German, "You there, fatty—you can go to work. You're young enough." I'll never forget that. . . . We hoped our parents were [in the next barracks] and that they were being taken care of. We didn't believe that the whole camp full of people would be exterminated after a few days. The kapo over us was a mean, mean woman. She would point to the crematorium and say, "See, that's where your parents are burning. That's where your kids are burning," and we just thought she was mean. She was Jewish, but she had been there for five years and had become inhuman. . . .

(Jack Goldman, though born in Mannheim, Germany, was jailed with his father as a Polish Jew. He was in Auschwitz during the uprising of September 1944.)

The Germans kept all the Polish citizens [in jail] until the war with Poland was over. The Poles who were not Jewish were then sent home. The Jews were kept in jail until they were sent to camps. My uncle was on the first transport to Buchenwald. The rest of us were sent to Sachsenhausen, near Berlin. . . . In our barrack we put the oldest and weakest men in the center and the youngest and strongest guys in the first row, which was only a step from the door. When an SS man came in he was likely to slap the first guy in his way, so we changed the first guy so that the same one wouldn't get slapped all the time. Then we practiced the domino theory of falling—that means the guy that gets hit falls at the first blow and pulls the others down with him. This made the SS very happy. As soon as they saw somebody falling down they had accomplished what they wanted.

■

One of the shameful controversies of the war was the failure of the Allies to bomb the rail lines leading to the concentration camps, once they had been discovered and identified for what they were. On April 4, 1944, a U.S. Air Force reconnaissance plane photographing the I. G. Farben synthetic oils and rubber manufacturing plant at Monowitz in Upper Silesia, during preparation for a bombing effort, was late turning off its camera after it had passed over the plant site. And when the film was studied it showed three exposures of a strange installation some distance past the Farben works that seemed to be the huts and barracks of an army, prisoner of war, or labor camp. It was not until later that this barracks installation, and two others in the vicinity, were identified as Auschwitz and its satellite camps. This information came with an appeal made in late May by Titzhak Gruenbaum, chairman of the rescue committee of the Jewish Agency, to the U.S. Army Air Force suggesting that "the deportation of Jews would be much impeded if the railways between Hungary and Poland could be bombed." Much time and many lives were lost in indecision. Though the railway tracks to the camps were later hit several times, it was as a result of raids on the industrial facilities nearby. Both the U.S. Army Air Force and the RAF refused to go after the tracks because the results "would not influence the outcome of the war." Marika Frank Abrams was deported on a train to Auschwitz after bombed rail track had been repaired and would appear to have been doomed—but she survived:

The first transport was very lucky. The tracks to Auschwitz had been bombed and they were sent to Vienna instead. My girlfriend was on that one and she said they were treated as prisoners of war, housed in school buildings and assigned jobs in the city. The second transport with the hospital personnel went straight to Vienna. All the people on it came back to Hungary unharmed. The third transport—ours—went straight to Auschwitz. The tracks, by then, had been repaired.

When we arrived we were asked to come out of the boxcars and the men and women were immediately separated. . . . My father said good-bye to us in a very positive way. I was in a row with my mother. . . . As we were walking by the selection officer, he asked me how old I was and I said nineteen. He put his hand on my shoulder and pushed me off to the left. I looked back and couldn't see the others anymore.

■

Much was made by some German apologists that the people of Germany did not know the Holocaust camps existed. But stories of the survivors indicate that it would be very hard for this to be true. Marika Abrams explained:

There were many factories in Magdeburg and about a hundred thousand POWs working in the area. I was in a barrack with three hundred Jewish women. We went on foot to the factory every morning. . . . We were starved, we had no hair and hardly any clothes and we marched in rows of five with the German citizens watching us, as many as twelve hundred coming together from different barracks.

If the German people say they didn't know about the camps, don't believe them. They would have had to have been blind and deaf. The camps were right in the midst of their lives. We worked alongside Germans in the factory. They saw us. They were even good enough to bring us needles, which were very valuable in the camp; a needle was worth a few rations of bread. . . .

I met my first Americans in Zerbst, and I'll never forget the sight of them coming together with the Russians. . . . But it was very dramatic to see young Americans who played baseball when they were kids, who had this loose-jointed way of moving their arms and legs, and the Russians who were tall, straight, very stiff. . . .

The American Army wasn't interested in us, however. They completely ignored us except for two young Jewish soldiers from New York. They searched us out and knew who we were and what had happened to us. One of them spoke Yiddish and was very disappointed because we didn't. But we communicated and they would have given us their hearts.

■

The philosophies of the several German armed forces branches that ran detention camps differed markedly, and at first the only knowledge of this came from word that got out through the International Red Cross from military prisoners. The SS-run camps were the most notorious. Everything that was later discovered from the Holocaust camp survivors confirmed that the SS often carried out great killing sprees when they knew Allied troops would soon overrun the concentration camps. Robert Spitz was arrested in Budapest in March 1944 and was being taken from Bergen-Belsen ahead of the Allied advance:

At the beginning of April 1945, when the British army was eight miles from our camp, 4,800 of us were marched to the railroad station to be taken to Theresienstadt in a suburb of Prague. Several days later we encountered a train heading westward, and for the first time I saw hundreds of German soldiers covered with bloody bandages, torn, tattered, filthy and thoroughly disgusted with war. They were antiaircraft artillerymen, and they confronted our SS escort and insisted on looking into the sealed railroad cars where we were confined. The SS were outnumbered ten to one and were forced to show them their cargo of starved, filthy, lousy Jews. The artillerymen insisted that they leave the doors open and brought us food and water.

(Dr. William Glicksman was thirty-four years old when the war broke out. Czestochowa became the ghetto for the area. His parents were deported and his wife and child killed before he was sent to Auschwitz to dig in the coal mines.)

In Auschwitz I drained swamps. I was sent to dig in the coal mines. I was in solitary confinement for seventy days and beaten to make me tell who made me the false passport. . . . I stayed alive through spiritual strength. We never forgot for a minute that we were Jews. We didn't need the religion. We didn't need the Hebrew school. We kept the calendar in ourselves. . . . We knew the prayers by heart like we knew our own names. . . .

American and English soldiers were coming close [in the spring of 1945], and again they put us on cars.

I remember I was on the floor of the car and we stopped at a station and heard all of a sudden a rat-tat-tat-tat and there was an American tank platoon going by on the highway on the other side of the station. We thought, "The Americans are running away and we are surrounded by German Gestapo, and it is the end of us." And then suddenly the door of the car opened and an American officer was standing there. I couldn't move but I could see the Germans put down their weapons. The officer came into the car and picked me up on his shoulders and carried me out. It was April 30, 1945.

■

With the German resistance ended in many areas, Eisenhower worried about the fast-moving Allied and Russian advances smashing into each other. Gavin remembered the Germans fleeing ahead of the Red Army:

By late morning large groups of Germans began to appear in patches of woods on the horizon. They seemed to be milling about indecisively and to be not particularly desirous to fight. It was an eerie sight for those of us who had fought for more than three years all the way from Africa. . . . So, taking our lives into our hands, we drove right up to them. They wanted to surrender. As we went on, their numbers increased by the hundreds and then thousands. . . .

The movement of the prisoners and refugees continued all that day and all the next day. We had never seen anything like it. We told them just to throw away their weapons and continue to our rear. By day's end we counted more than 2,000 trucks and more than 125 half-trucks and tanks, not to mention thousands of rifles, machine guns, and artillery pieces abandoned in the ditches along the road. Two Hungarian cavalry regiments with splendid-looking horses and equipment came by and offered to fight with us against the Russians.

■

Gavin stopped his advance briefly and sent forward a cavalry scouting unit under Capt. William Knowlton to find the Russians. Knowlton did, and the initial contact was hair-trigger. Then Gavin went ahead himself:

I made my way with a Russian interpreter, a sergeant from the 82d Airborne Division, toward the Russian lines. After we left the front of the 82d, there was absolute quiet; the area was abandoned with no evidence of war except the piles and piles of weapons in the ditches beside the roads. As I approached the small German town of

Grabow . . . I could hear the sounds of a few weapons firing and vehicular movement. As I entered the town square of Grabow, I saw that Russian soldiers had a hogshead of wine in the square. They had fired into it with their pistols, and as the wine spurted out, they caught it in their helmets and drank it. . . .

I continued to the next small town, a couple of miles away. There on the main street were two very prim-looking, Tartar-featured, stocky, tough soldiers guarding the front of a building. They had Russian tommy guns slung across their chests and looked at me rather menacingly. I inquired about the nearest Russian headquarters, and that building turned out to be the Command Post of the Russian division commander I was looking for. I went into the living room of the house and introduced myself. Maps were spread on the table, and we went about explaining our dispositions. . . .

At first they were obviously suspicious of us, but in the next weeks the evening receptions and the vodka seemed to remove all barriers. There was much celebrating and many toasts. However, as the days went by, I noticed that the senior Russian generals were accompanied by their political commissars. The Russians began to behave a bit more quietly and more seriously and, in fact, almost became unfriendly.

■

When Hitler shot himself in the Reichchancellery bunker, the officers who had been with him were free to try to break out through the Russian lines. They met near the bunker in a garage used to store the bulletproof limousines of Nazi leaders. Gen. Wilhelm Mohnke addressed the officers in the bunker:

The news that the Führer is dead . . . must be kept from the troops until at least ten o'clock. Panic and chaos must be avoided at all cost. General Weidling has ordered that active position fighting shall cease at eleven o'clock, whereupon all German troops must be prepared to try to break through the Red Army iron ring now closing around Berlin. We must attempt this in small battle groups, probing for weak links wherever we can find them. . . . Once outside Berlin, our general compass direction will be northwest. . . . This is a general order; there are no more

specific details. . . . Battle groups will simply have to play by ear, probing to find the best march route. No provision can be made for any rear guard. We *are* the rear guard.

■

Ernst-Guenther Schenck, who had run an emergency medical facility in the basement of the Reichchancellery, watched the troops defending the bunker area get ready to pull out:

Now from the dark gangways, there kept arriving, in small groups, both the fighting troops being pulled in from the outside, then the officers and men of the Reichchancellery Group. The troops, many of them very young, were already street-fighting veterans. Other soldiers had stubble beards, blackened faces; they wore sweaty, torn, field-gray uniforms, which most had worn and slept in without change for almost a fortnight. The situation was heroic; the mood was not. The official announcement of Hitler's suicide had not yet reached the lower ranks. But they guessed as much—from the silence of their officers. There was little talk now of "Führer, Folk, and Fatherland." . . . Each man . . . was silently calculating his own chance of survival. . . . What was building up was . . . what I imagine happens at sea when the cry goes out to man the lifeboats.

■

General Mohnke's escape group started out on a unique route that would keep them out of the fighting in the streets at the beginning:

The one organization we were not braced for was the . . . Berlin Municipal Transport Company. Less than a hundred meters after we had passed the Friedrichstrasse station platform, we came to a huge steel bulkhead. Waterproof, it was designed to seal this tunnel at the point where the subway tube starts to run under the Spree River.

Here—and I could not believe my own eyes and ears—we spotted two stalwart, uniformed Transport Company guards. Both, like night watchmen, were carrying lanterns. They were surrounded by angry civilians imploring them to swing open the bulkhead. They kept refusing. One clutched a giant key. . . . I ordered them to open the bulkhead forthwith, both for my group and for the civilians. The guards categorically refused. They cited regulation *this* and paragraph *that* of their . . . "Standing Orders." . . .

The regulation, dating from 1923, *did* clearly state that the bulkhead was to be closed every evening after the passage of the last train. . . . No trains had been running here for at least a full week, but these two dutiful characters had their orders and that was that.

We were armed, of course, and they weren't. . . . I sat for long years in Soviet captivity, quietly cursing myself for my strange hesitancy at this critical moment. . . .

■

When the breakout group was captured, they expected to be shot. Instead they were asked to dinner. A Russian colonel welcomed them:

Welcome in the name of the chief of staff of our army. . . . We pride ourselves on having fought in the field against such valiant opponents. We congratulate you on the soldierly valor your troops often displayed. . . . We are all aware that it has been a long and active day, and now is a good time to relax. Would the German officers and gentlemen like to remove their pistol belts? If so, there is a small table reserved for that purpose.

■

As the fighting died, the rape of Berlin began. An SS officer, to whom harsh measures were well-known enough, held one stark memory for years following the war:

I had been in Russia, so I knew there were two sides to this ugly story, atrocity followed by counteratrocity. Still, it is just not a pretty sight to see a terrified, naked woman running along a rooftop pursued by half a dozen soldiers brandishing bayonets . . . then leaping five or six stories to certain death.

■

General Gavin moved in to surrendered Berlin as one of the Allied military commanders, sharing responsibility with the British,

French, and Russians. The cleanup job had not been part of any of their training:

The occupation of Berlin was a new experience for us. To begin with, as the senior U.S. Army officer, I was also the senior American member of the Kommandantura, the government body for the city of Berlin. Our first task was, of course, to clean up the city, remove and bury the bodies, and feed and care for the living. There were estimated to be more than 3,000 bodies in the subway system alone. It had not only been destroyed by bombing, but had been flooded. It was a tremendous task. Food was rationed, and the old and the children received barely a starvation diet. Plans were made to cut down the trees in the nearby forest to provide fuel for the coming winter.

■

Soviet soldiers had developed a habit of drawing and firing their pistols "to emphasize a point." Gavin made the point that American paratroopers had been told they could shoot in self-defense. Mistaking the Soviet gesture, several paratroopers did shoot. The Soviets wanted to charge murder. But the "emphasis pistols" stopped:

Our relations with the Russians continued to deteriorate. One Russian general I had known in Mecklenburg seemed to go out of his way to be unpleasant when we were together in public. In December I finally received orders to return to the United States with the division. Before I left, he invited me to his quarters. We went out on the porch, where there appeared to be some privacy, for a drink. We talked and drank for several hours. He was a well-read man, kind and intelligent. He told me that he had been embarrassed to have to behave as he had, but that he had strict orders that in no circumstance should he fraternize with us. Because we had been such good friends in Mecklenburg, he felt that he had to lean over backward, as it were. He wanted me to understand that. It was my first encounter with clear evidence of what the Cold War was to be.

■

The end of the war in Europe was one of those days almost everyone who lived through it can remember. A very poignant memory came from a young second subaltern in the Royal Auxiliary Transport Service, Elizabeth Windsor, who could not see all she wanted and moved to a better position to watch the celebration Britain had waited so long for:

I remember the thrill and relief after the previous day's waiting for the Prime Minister's announcement of the end of the war in Europe. My parents went out on the balcony in response to the huge crowds outside. I think we went on the balcony nearly every hour, six times, and then when the excitement of the floodlights being switched on got through to us, my sister and I realised we couldn't see what the crowds were enjoying. My mother had put her tiara on for the occasion, so we asked my parents if we could go out and see for ourselves. I remember we were terrified of being recognised, so I pulled my uniform cap well down over my eyes. A grenadier officer amongst our party of about sixteen people said he refused to be seen in the company of another officer improperly dressed, so I had to put my cap on normally. We cheered the King and Queen on the balcony and then walked miles through the streets. I remember lines of unknown people linking arms and walking down Whitehall, all of us just swept along on a tide of happiness and relief. I remember the amazement of my cousin, just back from four and a half years in a prisoner of war camp, walking freely with his family in the friendly throng. And I also remember when someone exchanged hats with a Dutch sailor, the poor man coming along with us in order to get his cap back. After crossing Green Park we stood outside and shouted, "We want the King," and we were successful in seeing my parents on the balcony, having cheated slightly because we sent a message into the house to say we were waiting outside. I think it was one of the most memorable nights of my life. [Her Majesty the Queen's memories of V-E Day. For a painting of the V-E celebration outside Buckingham Palace, see pages 388–89.]

White Flags: No German Troops Near

Edward Ardizzone, who had painted the war since it started in 1939, serving in France, North Africa, Italy, and Normandy, was with British units spearheading into Germany and recorded these frightened villagers. Since Normandy, German propaganda had warned them of the brutality they could expect from Allied soldiers. But what the Germans generally got was Americans trading wampum—Spam and C-ration Woodbine cigarettes; both items had few American takers. (Imperial War Museum)

One of 20 Million Russian Dead

The Soviet-German battles in 1941 and 1942 were such that many of the Russian dead could not be recovered for burial. The Russian family in Rei Yermolin's painting *Forget No One* (ABOVE) has suffered the loss, but at least they have recovered a body. (Artists Union, Komi ASSR)

Punitive Destruction, 1942

The German retreat from Russia was even more destructive than the advance. The order for the retreat was often to level whatever was left behind. This stark painting (RIGHT) by Mikhail Kupryanov, Nikolai Sokolov, and Probiry Krylov is titled *The Fascist Retreat from Norgorad*. The Soviet attack has overrun the Germans, who are burning the church and falling back. (Tretyakov Gallery)

Saving "Holy Russia's" Treasures

Among the stories proudly told in the Soviet Union about the Great Patriotic War is how the Soviet government rescued the art treasures of the world-famous Hermitage museum in Leningrad, as well as other fine art collections. The Soviet soldiers in this Mikhail Volodin painting (ABOVE RIGHT) are *Saving the Pictures of the Drezhensky Gallery*. (USSR Ministry of Culture)

The Road Back, Western Russia, 1944

Red Army artillerymen move westward through a battered city (RIGHT), pressuring the German retreat. Many Soviet soldiers had last seen their home cities intact when they were called up at the start of the invasion in 1941. Looking at the awful wreckage, the desire for revenge grew hotly. Yuriy Pimenov called this scene *Road to the Front*. (Russian Museum)

"Human Laundry," Belsen, Spring 1945

Doris Zinkheisen was with the British army when it stumbled on Bergen-Belsen. British medics were trained to handle the wounds of battle, but were unprepared to deal with the terribly debilitated survivors in the camps. What Zinkheisen has painted was the arrival of trained medical personnel—which panicked some survivors; white-coated doctors and nurses might mean more Nazi medical "experiments." (Imperial War Museum)

"Who Are These Soldiers?": Belsen

This is a scene of the women's compound at Belsen (ABOVE) as the first British troops found it. Inmates have turned out because of the noise in the yard and see strangely uniformed soldiers. Did it mean that someone else had come to torment them? Leslie Cole was the artist. Eric Taylor painted the stark body pile at right. Many who viewed both photographs and paintings of the camps felt the latter were somehow the most obscene of all. (Both, Imperial War Museum)

The Most Offended Victims, Poland, 1945

Anatoly Tyurin called this *The Liberation of Children from Concentration Camp* (LEFT). The camp was overrun by the Red Army before the SS guards could drive the prisoners westward to try to keep the secret. If these children have survived, they would be nearing their fifties now, with, one hopes, only the dimmest memories of that terrible time. (USSR Union of Artists)

"They Didn't Live to See," Poland, 1943

Luba Krugman Gurdus, artist and now also art historian, was swept into the Majdanek concentration camp in 1942, losing her four-year-old son and her parents to the Nazis in the deportations. For protection in the camp, she had only identity papers with an Aryan name, fluency in German, and ingenuity. The forged papers kept her from the gas chambers. The language made her valuable to the Germans (but could have signaled her educated Jewish background). The ingenuity enabled her to gain release before the war was over. She immediately began to make drawings of all she had seen. These four (OPPOSITE) are from a portfolio of sixteen she made of her impressions and experiences. Clockwise from upper left: *Fighting Ghetto, One of the Nameless, Slaves at Work* (her father was in charge of such a forest detail and secretly dragged out the work to keep his crew alive), and *Before the Execution*. She was reunited after the war with her husband (who had escaped to serve in the British army), now lives in America, and has written and lectured extensively about Holocaust art. (Courtesy of the Artist)

Going Home, Germany, 1945

Some Allied POWs had survived German prison camps since the fall of France in 1940. When they were finally freed by the advancing armies, some launched on a frenzied gorge of rations cadged from liberating soldiers. This was poor fare to the soldiers, but a sometimes deadly meal for near-starved prisoners. Doris Zinkheisen painted a luckier group of recently liberated British POWs, having a supervised meal at a German airfield before finally flying home to England. (Imperial War Museum)

No Spoils of War, Germany, 1945

When the first American soldiers crossed into Germany, no one knew what fanaticism to expect. But the battered towns and dazed civilians seemed just as pathetic as the war-torn survivors in France, Belgium, and Holland. Bernard Arnest painted an officer (ABOVE) warning his unit about proper conduct with civilians. (U.S. Army Center of Military History)

In the last months of the war, the German aircraft industry had been widely dispersed to avoid a crippling blow to a single plant. Julius B. Stafford-Baker, who painted fine pictures of Allied air activity, discovered this assembly line (LEFT) for Focke-Wulf fighters below ground at Berlin's Templehof Airfield. (U.S. Army Center of Military History)

Victory, Berlin, May 1945

Oleg Ponomarenko used one of Berlin's most famous pieces of statuary—the horses and chariot atop the Brandenburg Gate—to salute his Soviet comrades raising their flag in victory. The Brandenburg Gate stands at the entrance of the East German Zone near the edge of the Tiergarten, with scars of war still visible. (USSR Union of Artists)

Soviet-American Link-Up, April 1945

General James Gavin's recollections make clear Eisenhower's concern over the possibility of an accidental clash between the rapidly advancing Soviet and Allied armies. Gavin described his own men encountering the Red Army and experienced the dangerous reality of an unpredictable meeting. But here, British war artist Anthony Gross painted a meeting on April 26 between the armies at Torgau, Germany, with the trappings of a classical military canvas. (Imperial War Museum)

The Beginning of Soviet "East Germany," May 1945

Most Soviet troops involved in the capture of Berlin had little idea of the layout of the city, other than quick briefings about the streets they would advance along. But just as people who have never been to Paris know the look of the Eiffel Tower or Tower Bridge in London, so did many Russian officers have the great columns of the Brandenburg Gate in their minds. They symbolized the road to the East—to Warsaw and Moscow. Aleksandr Lopukhov chose the monument as the background for his painting *Victory Day*. (Ukrainian Museum of Decorative Arts)

Storming the Reichstag Steps, Berlin, May 1945

In the last days of Berlin, when German defenses were breaking and dissolving, those who could escape headed west to surrender to the Allied armies. Or, as rumors were circulating, to try to join one of several "National Redoubts" the Nazis were said to be forming for the last stands in mountain areas. The redoubts turned out to be myths. But in Berlin, the last stands concentrated in some of the famous buildings of the Nazi regime. The Soviets were determined the Reichstag would not be one of these. Piotr Krivonogov was the artist (OPPOSITE). (USSR Ministry of Armed Forces)

A Soviet View of "The End"—Berlin, April 30, 1945

James P. O'Donnell's book *The Bunker* describes in detail Hitler's last hours. The first
outsiders to enter were Red Army soldiers, whose reports helped Mikhail Kupryanov,
Nikolai Sokolov, and Probiry Krylov prepare their version of Hitler saying good-bye to
his officers. According to O'Donnell, Hitler and Eva Braun (who had just become his wife)
emerged from his quarters in the lower bunker, spoke for about three minutes to a group of
some fifteen officers, secretaries, and servants assembled in the corridor. Hitler then gave
them a royal wave of his hand, ushered Eva ahead, and closed the door to his private
quarters behind them. His adjutants had been told to wait precisely ten minutes, then enter.
When they did, both Hitler and Eva Braun were dead. The painting is called *The End*.
(Tretyakov Gallery)

The Tribunal, November 1945–September 1946

When the specifics were laid down for the conduct of the German War Crimes Trials, the oncoming proceedings began to generate certain cautious second thoughts by judicial and historical scholars about the propriety of victors from democratic countries conducting such a tribunal. But as the trials began and evidence was presented, the careful German documentation of atrocities quickly made the debate of trial authority forgotten. Mikhail Kupryanov, Nikolai Sokolov, and Probiry Krylov created this painting, *The Indictment: War Criminals and Their Defenders at the Nuremberg Trials*. It suggested the impact of some of this evidence. Easily identifiable is Hermann Göring, whose face and eyes are diabolically lit by the lamp over his notes. (Tretyakov Gallery)

Parade to End Parades, Bremerhaven, 1946

Soldiers traditionally dislike parades—or at least the spit and polish preparation for them. And they could be certain that if held at the end of the war in enemy territory, there weren't going to be crowds of cheering spectators lining the streets. But most of the parades organized then had a sound military purpose. Edward Payne painted a post-surrender parade of British tankers in Bremerhaven—with an appreciative crowd of mostly off-duty British troops. It was the closest they would come to humorist Will Rogers's suggestion for the ideal end-of-the-war parade: let the soldiers sit in the reviewing stands and have the public march past. (Imperial War Museum)

Women Warriors, Russia, 1985

Sergei Bocharov did not execute this painting until 1985. So by the strictest definition, it is not "Soviet war art." But the elements and occasion of its composition may make it interesting to readers. Fifteen women who had been members of a Red Army aviation unit assembled for a reunion and posed before a mural made of them during the war. The painting is symbolic of the extensive war role of Soviet women. (USSR Union of Artists)

"We'll Meet Again . . . Some Sunny Day"—Favorite English Song, 1939–45

Leila Faithful's cheerful *V-E Celebration Outside Buckingham Palace* seems the perfect end-of-the-war echo of earlier London scenes. The King and Queen are dimly seen on the palace balcony (in the center panel, between the two trees). Winston Churchill and the other British leaders had told the people V-E Day would surely come. And a solid belief in that by Britons through all the worst war years was certainly what made it possible. (Imperial War Museum)

Jeep Turns Ambulance, Kerr Eby (U.S. Navy Combat Art Collection)

CLOSING ON JAPAN

Every Pacific island that had to be invaded and conquered presented its own costly fight. The Japanese last-man defense allowed no easy victories. The U.S. Navy engaged a heavy Japanese force in the Battle of Leyte Gulf—both a carrier and a battleship action, perhaps the last battleship fight that will ever occur. At the battle's end, the American admirals felt the Japanese fleet was finished as a fighting force. A new Japanese tactic appeared during the invasion of Okinawa: "The Divine Wind"—kamikaze attacks: one pilot, one plane, one bomb —and, for the most part, one direct hit on a U.S. ship. The United States suffered a heavy loss of ships in the naval force and in the screen for the Okinawa anchorage; almost 400 ships were damaged or sunk by the kamikazes. Iwo Jima—a tiny, lonely volcanic island, but essential as an emergency landing base for B-29s coming back crippled from Japan—was taken in another costly fight. From Okinawa and Tinian and the Marianas, the B-29s repeatedly pounded the Japanese mainland with shattering tactical results. And the fast carriers roamed deep into Japanese waters.

One of the few lucky breaks in the Pearl Harbor attack had been the absence of carriers in the harbor. From then on, they carried much of the offensive. Ernie Pyle, essentially an "Army man," was awed by them:

An aircraft carrier is a noble thing. It lacks almost everything that seems to denote nobility, yet deep nobility is there. A carrier has no poise. It has no grace. It is top-heavy and lopsided. It has the lines of a well-fed cow. . . . Yet a carrier is a ferocious thing, and out of its heritage of action has grown its nobility. I believe that every navy in the world has as its No. 1 priority the destruction of enemy carriers. That's a precarious honor, but a proud one.

◼

The American public was made well aware of the dangers carrier pilots faced; getting on and off the flight deck was just the beginning. But Father Farrell, chaplain of Yorktown, saw nonflying crews also at risk:

There are a lot of ways a man can get killed on a carrier without ever seeing the enemy or taking off in a plane.

◼

Historian Oliver Jensen, serving as a navy line officer, talked to the carrier men quoted here. Good fighter pilots needed intuition and lightning-quick reactions. And confidence. The last sometimes only came after that first air victory. Hamilton McWhorter of Fighting Five told of his:

Suddenly I was aware of Zekes all around me. There must have been twenty. I didn't see any of my gang around so I headed to join up with three planes from another carrier. Just then it happened; there he was sitting in my sights. So I let go. Just one burst. . . . And I had my first Zeke.

◼

The pilots were well drilled on ditching in the ocean. And considering the vast scope of the carrier battles, the number of men picked up after ditching provided the hope of rescue. James Shearer of Torpedo Nine had faith—and got home:

We got the raft out all right and sat there

watching the fleet steam away fast. Once in a while some Japanese would make a strafing run on us. Sitting there, pitching up and down, you could see columns of smoke all over the place where crashed Japanese were burning. . . . My gunner and radioman were getting worried after the fleet passed out of sight. But I knew they'd be back because they had seen us go in.

◼

Mayo Hadden, Jr., discussed a danger most seamen preferred not to talk about. Sharks were a threat to downed pilots. And not all encounters turned out as well as Hadden's:

It was fairly calm. I hit right near a U.S. destroyer . . . walked out on the wing and stepped off. . . . Suddenly a black shape bobbed up in the water next to me. I kicked wildly, beating the water with my hands and thrashing about to scare the shark away. . . . I swam smack into another black shape. . . . There was a third. . . . Just then the destroyer came by, let down a cargo net, and I climbed up. The boys on deck looked at me with strange expressions. Finally one said: "You looked pretty active down there. What were you thrashing around for?"

"There were sharks all around me!"

"That's the first time I ever saw anybody swim away from a life preserver," [the man on deck answered].

Those life preservers are grayish black. When they get wet they look blacker. The destroyer had tossed eight of them at me, and I had been trying to evade them all.

◼

An unknown torpedo plane pilot said after Midway, where Torpedo Eight lost all its aircrews but for one man:

One of the many troubles with this war is that victory is always too expensive to enjoy.

◼

Masuo Kato was a highly respected journalist with the Japanese news agency, Domei. When Pearl Harbor was attacked, he was stationed in Washington and experienced the weird yesterday-we-were-friends/today-we-are-enemies cartwheel of arrest and internment:

I suppose my own reaction to the war was typical of that of many who considered themselves liberals. . . . However wrong I believed my country to be, it was my country just the same, and perhaps some day it would come to its senses. My biggest misjudgment was during the period when the militarists were coming to power. I was aware of what was happening, but I believed that the Japanese people would have enough common sense at the critical moment to avoid being carried into war. . . .

◼

Some of the best units of the Australian army had already been sent off for duty in North Africa and to the Far East. As a result, a large cadre of experienced officers and non-coms were not available for the critical roles of training called-up reserves and new recruits. Traditional Australian toughness and bravery could not always compensate for inexperience and confusion:

Making every allowance for the state of affairs existing in Australia at the time of the outbreak of the Japanese war, the condition which manifested itself immediately after the arrival of the Aquitania convoy [in New Guinea] calls for severe censure of the persons responsible for the loading of the troops' camp equipment. The troops were of the average age of eighteen and a half years, and had received no proper training. They were in the charge of inexperienced officers who appear to have had little or no control over them. They were inadequately equipped in every way. . . . But no excuse is apparent . . . for the gross carelessness and incompetence which resulted in the stowing of camp equipment at the bottom of the holds. . . . When troops were disembarked there were no facilities to enable them to be fed and encamped. [Barry Report]

◼

Americans and Australians facing the Japanese for the first time in the Pacific campaign had to overcome an initial impression of Japanese invincibility. The Japanese seemed battle-tested, seasoned, almost welcoming the difficulty of the jungle atmosphere. But after the war, when Japanese diaries and letters were examined, it was discovered that the apprehensions of combat troubled both sides almost equally. *Second Lieutenant Hirano of the Imperial Army wrote of an abortive night attack at Kokoda:*

Our formation was faulty, and the rain hindered us. . . . We began the night attack at 10:20 P.M., advancing stealthily on hands and knees. . . .

Corporal Hamada, because of the darkness, was unable to assemble the men remaining. I went to the rear and tried myself to assemble them, but I turned in the wrong direction in the darkness, and with two of my men, suddenly realized that we were within forty metres of the Australians' lines, and grenades were thrown at us. The night attack ended in failure.

■

U.S. General Robert L. Eichelberger, MacArthur's commander in New Guinea, had been sent in with orders, in effect, to bring back a victory—or don't come back. His summary of the enemy was a tribute:

Fortitude is admirable under any flag, and those Japanese foot soldiers had it. They pressed on—ill and hungry. They had no way to evacuate their sick and wounded. Sanitation was wretched, and they suffered from tropical fevers and exhaustion. There is a limit to human faithfulness and fervor.

■

Although the Allied troops in the island-hopping campaigns had encountered suicide charges by Japanese infantry, when the first kamikaze aircraft appeared, their impact was sobering. Admiral Halsey reported one of the first suicide attacks:

The plane that struck the *Intrepid* had not been damaged; the dive was obviously a deliberate sacrifice. Intelligence had warned us that "the Divine Wind Special Attack Corps" had been organized. . . . We could not believe that even the Japanese, for all their *hara-kiri* traditions, could muster enough recruits to make such a corps really effective.

■

Theodore Taylor, an American correspondent, reported the kamikazes off Okinawa in the spring of 1945:

At the end of each day canvas shrouds slipped into the waters off Okinawa. Death was in the air and on the face of the sea. The Divine Wind blew hot and steadily. In April, including both the task force and invasion forces, a hundred and twenty ships received minor damages, a hundred were damaged severely, and twenty-four were sunk. . . . We sent strikes to Kyushu and raked the Japanese airfields in desperation, but the Divine Wind kept coming.

■

Historians Desmond Flower and James Reeves set the scene:

Three engagements made up the Battle of Leyte Gulf . . . : Surigao Strait on the night of 24–25 October, and Cape Engaño and Samar, which both began on the 25th.

The Japanese aim was to draw off the American fleet protecting the Leyte landings and then to smash the [landings] while the covering forces were absent. On the 23d and 24th two Japanese battle fleets began to converge on Leyte. One approached the San Bernardino Strait north of the island of Samar, intending to pass through the strait and sail down the east coast of Samar to its objective. The other pincer made for Surigao Strait to the south of Leyte itself.

■

The British, Germans, Italians, and Americans had all experimented with small, high-speed torpedo boats as an inexpensive defense against big ships: even losing a whole squadron of the smaller boats was cheaper than losing one larger warship. Their last major tactical use in the war was the Battle of Leyte Gulf, where American PT boats were assigned battleship and cruiser targets. In his recollections after the war, Admiral Halsey described the battle:

When the Southern Force pushed into Surigao soon after midnight of the 24th, it pushed into one of the prettiest ambushes in naval history. Rear Adm. Jesse B. Oldendorf, Kinkaid's tactical commander, waited until the enemy line was well committed to the narrow waters, then struck from both flanks with his PTs and destroyers, and from dead ahead with his battleships and cruisers. . . . The Japanese lost both their battleships and three destroyers. The rest

fled, but Kinkaid's planes caught and sank a heavy cruiser later in the morning, and Army B-24s sank the light cruiser.

■

The heroic action of two U.S. destroyers and a destroyer escort (with its largest armament being a couple of 3-inch guns) came the next day, and probably prevented the destruction of an escort carrier task force that had steered into the path of the heavy Japanese ships. The escort carriers were little more than converted merchant ships. They were good for scouting, convoys, and air cover over a beach—but not a fleet action. Nevertheless their planes scrambled:

Sprague immediately turned east, into the wind, launched his available planes, and ordered all ships to make smoke. . . . When the Japanese cruisers had closed to fourteen thousand yards, Sprague ordered his screen to fall back and deliver a torpedo attack. Two destroyers, the *Hoel* and *Johnston,* and the destroyer escort *Samuel S. Roberts* reversed course, ran within ten thousand yards of the battleships, and fired a half-salvo, then fired the other half within seven thousand yards of the cruisers. Smoke concealed the effect of their torpedoes, but it lifted to show that all three of these heroic little ships had been sunk. . . .

Except for the three ships from the screen, Sprague's only loss to the guns was the carrier *Gambier Bay.* . . .

For these first two hours, Sprague's gallant men fought entirely alone, at such close quarters that his CVSs' single 5-inchers were registering hits on the cruisers, and with such valor that his Avengers, their bombs and torpedoes expended, were making dummy runs to distract the battleships.

■

By late evening, the three-day battle was over, and Halsey could claim that the Japanese could not reenter the Philippines, the fleet engaged had been crushed, and the damage had been extensive enough to prevent a new threat for some months. General Eichelberger commented:

After long miles and weary months of The Hard Way Back, all of us had the heartening news that Japan's stolen marine empire had been broken asunder. During the next weeks Allied ships roamed at will from Hong Kong to Indochina, pounding away at shore facilities and shipping.

■

Since the invasion of Malaya, the Japanese had been credited with being instinctive jungle fighters. Actually, it was just fine training. They were "light infantry" in the classical sense. Yet postwar records showed the Japanese had suffered terribly in the jungles. A Japanese soldier in Hollandia kept this diary:

22 April 1944: Resigned to death, I entered the muddy jungle. Enemy airplanes are flying overhead. I am hungry and am beginning to become alarmed about the situation. . . . The vast expanse of the jungle cannot be expressed in words.

2 May 1944: At a small creek. There is no end to this life. We are still roaming aimlessly on the thirteenth day. Perhaps this is part of our fate. . . .

24 May 1944: . . . The jungle is everywhere, and there is absolutely no water in this area. We must reach Kotabaru or we will all die.

■

Later at Wakda, on the northwest coast of New Guinea, the same soldier wrote:

25 June 1944: Under the existing situation, we are helpless. . . . There were about thirty of us wounded soldiers left in the cave. Those who could move assisted others. They all shouted, "Long live the Emperor," before leaving this world. My friend Nagasaka stabbed his throat with a knife, but he did not succeed in killing himself. I finally decided to assist him so that he could rest in peace. I stabbed my own brother in arms. Who could understand my horrible predicament? I still have two hand grenades; one to destroy myself and one for the enemy. . . .

25 June 1944: Long live the Emperor!

■

American submarines enforcing the blockade of Japan and its occupied out-islands worked in relative anonymity compared to the press coverage received by the army and navy and their air wings. Much of the reason for all that secrecy had to do with hiding the fact that

the Allies could obtain advance knowledge of ship movements by reading certain top-secret Japanese navy codes. But George Grider, a U.S. Navy submarine officer, described the sort of encounter that was slowly strangling the Japanese merchant marine in the Pacific:

Motor Machinist's Mate D. C. Keeter was a good man to have on lookout, for he was one of the most alert lookouts I ever saw. He had a habit of freezing every now and then, like a good pointer that has come on a covey of quail, while he studied some speck on the horizon. At first it was distracting; you would forget to watch anything but Keeter, waiting to see him go on point. . . . Keeter froze, pointed, and sang out, "Smoke on the horizon." . . .

We turned toward it in the bright moonlight. . . . It was a freighter of the *Keiyo Maru* class, six thousand five hundred tons. . . .

"Fire Four!"

First came the loud explosion. The breaking-up noises followed, small explosions piling one on top of another, sounds that made you see bulkheads caving in, water pouring through great jagged wounds in the hull. . . .

Now was the time to get quiet again. Every piece of machinery that made any noise, everything we could do without, was cut off. . . .

An exploding depth charge has three noises. First there is a click. Then comes a clang or crashing sound, like someone hitting your hull with a million sledgehammers. Finally there is a swishing noise, as though water is falling over a waterfall or pouring into a cavity the charge has created. The closer the charge is, the more closely together these noises come. When it is very close, you hear one horrible *clang!*

■

Mochitsura Hashimoto, who had been involved in the Imperial Navy's hunt for Re-pulse and Prince of Wales off Malaya at the start of the Pacific war, found tougher hunting when his submarine was sent to help in the defense of Truk Island:

When we got near to Truk we could see the reflection of sheets of flame in the night sky. There were sounds of frequent explosions, and we soon realized that the situa-

tion was hopeless. . . . Eventually we received orders to enter Truk harbour. Finding a suitable route was tricky, for it was difficult to see a safe passage through the remains of our sunken ships. . . .

. . . On this particular day only half the normal number of Japanese search planes had been up due to a heavy storm, and these had already returned to base. The enemy, however, made his approach during the height of the storm. . . . Six warships and twenty-six of our transports were sunk. Aircraft losses amounted to one hundred and eighty planes.

■

The topography of many of the Pacific islands was often no better known than what was printed on British Admiralty charts made after random surveys in sailing-ship days— say fifty or sixty years after Captain Cook and Captain Bligh. Landing craft at Tarawa began to strike uncharted coral reefs and shallows almost half a mile from shore. There was nothing to do then but "get out and walk." Robert Sherrod reports in November 1943:

No sooner had we hit the water than the Japanese machine guns really opened up on us. There must have been five or six of these machine guns concentrating their fire on us—there was no nearer target in the water at the time—which meant several hundred bullets per man. . . . It was painfully slow, wading in such deep water. And we had seven hundred yards to walk slowly into that machine-gun fire, looming into larger targets as we rose onto higher ground. . . . Our casualties had been heavy on the first day. . . .

[Third day:] . . . The bulldozer scoops a long trench, three feet deep. Its Seabee driver pays scant attention to the sniper who fires at him occasionally. The bodies, not even covered by [blankets] are brought over and placed in the trench, side by side, while Chaplains MacQueen and Kelly supervise their identification and last rites. . . . The bulldozer pushes some more dirt into the marines' faces and that is all there is to it. . . .

Tarawa was the first frontal assault on a heavily defended atoll. . . . Yet, for every marine who was killed more than four Japanese died—four of the best troops the Emperor had.

■

The kamikaze units tapped a heroic impulse. Many of the pilots who volunteered were short of training or combat experience, and their dedication was the stuff that wins wars— even against the sort of odds Japan was facing toward the end of 1944. A senior officer of the Imperial Navy who helped form the program drafted its first order:

The Empire stands at the crossroads between victory and defeat. The first suicide unit determined to triumph through the power of the spirit will inspire . . . one unit after another to follow its example. It is absolutely out of the question for you to return alive. Your mission involves certain death. Your bodies will be dead, but not your spirits. The death of a single one of you will be the birth of a million others. . . .

■

The last letter home from Akio Otsuka, a kamikaze pilot who had been assigned his mission of sacrifice:

Contrary to my usual habit, I woke early, at five o'clock. I did my exercises stripped to the waist. I felt extremely well. . . . I do not want a grave. I would feel oppressed if they were to put me into a narrow vault. . . . Keep in good health. I believe in the victory of Greater Asia. I pray for the happiness of you all, and I beg your forgiveness for my lack of piety. . . .

■

The tiny volcanic island of Iwo Jima stood out almost alone in the western Pacific, some 1,000 miles south of Tokyo—500 miles closer to that target than the B-29 bases in the Marianas. Which was why it was needed: an emergency landing spot for bombers crippled in the Japan raids, or hit with engine problems going or coming. The island today seems a barren and disagreeable spot. But in 1945, it seemed worth the lives of some 6,000 Americans to take it—and some 21,000 Japanese to hold it. Theodore Taylor wrote of the attack on Mount Suribachi:

After more than three days of hard fighting the mountain was encircled by noon, 23 February. Four hours earlier, the first

American flag was raised on Suribachi. This was a small flag from a ship's boat, and raising it aloft on a short section of Japanese pipe found on the spot was the idea of some of the men who made the assault to the crest.

■

Perhaps one of the blackest marks in America's World War II history—and one that has been redressed only superficially—is the country's treatment of Japanese-Americans. They were treated by a panicked government as spies, saboteurs, or worse. And in addition to the emotional and economic hardships, which for many lasted most of the war, the young men in these families—though qualified and usually eager to serve in the armed forces—were denied that chance to show their loyalty. Finally, under the manpower pressures of the war, special Japanese-American units were organized, and they performed with great distinction. The stories that follow are from The Color of Honor, *a film produced by Loni Ding and soon to be a book. Harry Fukuhara, who ultimately served a long career in military intelligence with the U.S. Army, relates the sort of incident that generally signaled the start of this national ostracism:*

At the time of Pearl Harbor, December 7, 1941, it was a Sunday, I clearly remember that day. I was gardening on this particular Sunday when the lady of the house came out and told me that Japan had bombed Pearl Harbor. It didn't mean anything to me. I didn't even know where Pearl Harbor was. . . . I said, "Where's Pearl Harbor?" And she said, "It's in Hawaii." I said, "Oh, that's terrible. . . ." And then she said, "I want you to go home." So I said, "Why?" And she said, "Well, this is a terrible thing that Japan did . . ." and she didn't think that I should continue working for them. And so I just . . . left.

■

A nisei woman felt the greatest helplessness came from having no one to turn to:

It seemed like all the authorities were against us. Congress, the army, governors and mayors, newspapers—they all wanted us out. There were so few of us. Our leaders were all taken away; even our own fathers.

■

Senator Spark Matsunaga, Hawaii:

Those who were confined there [in the internment camps] were without any criminal records. . . . As a matter of fact, they weren't charged at all for any crime. . . . There was no indictment, no trial, no hearing, and yet they were taken into these camps and confined . . . for what reason? Just because they happened to be of Japanese ancestry.

■

Judge John Aiso from Los Angeles went into the army as a private, after being a lawyer in civilian life, and immediately embarked on a career of promotions rarely equaled in the army. First they told him he was going to be a student in Intelligence School, then that he was going to be an instructor, then a week later that he was to be Head Instructor of the school! He ended as Academic Director, Military Intelligence Service Language School:

A student came to me and said, "*Sensei* (meaning instructor, professor), I'd like to speak to you but I'd like to speak in private, not here." And he said, "*Sensei*, shouldn't we go over the hill at this time?" And I said, "What for?" and he says, "This may be our last chance," and I said, "But where are you going to go?" And he said, "Can you guarantee that I will not be among those [who might be] lined up tomorrow morning and shot?" I told him that I could give no such guarantee, but that the whole future of nisei and our children in America depended on how we would act on this occasion.

■

Hakubun Nozawa was a private at Fort Riley, Kansas, when Franklin Roosevelt paid a visit. Nozawa and about two hundred other nisei were elated that the president would see them serving. But before the review, all of them were locked up in a warehouse at gunpoint "for the president's safety." Private Nozawa and the others felt "hurt and betrayed." He wrote to the War Department in protest:

[At his court martial in 1944, Private Nozawa said,] "I will fight for this country to protect democracy, as I am a real American. . . . [Nozawa served several years in

Leavenworth, was dishonorably discharged —and was only given an honorable discharge, and back pay, after a Pentagon hearing in 1983.]

■

Rudy Tokiwa served in the army in the 442d Regimental Combat Team, an all–Japanese-American unit that served in Italy and France, becoming the most decorated unit in U.S. military history:

My mother turned around and she went through a one-hundred-pound sack of rice, and she found one rice that still had its kernel on it. And she put that in a little bag and she presented that to me. And she said, "This one rice must be very lucky because [of] all those thousands and thousands of kernels of rice that was in that sack, it was the only one that still had its kernel on. So it's gotta be very lucky, and it'll bring you back."

■

A resident of a liberated French town, remembering the arrival of U.S. troops in the form of the 442d Regimental Combat Team:

When my mother saw the first troops, who was going into the village . . . she was not sure, who was this troops. And she said, "My God, could be Japanese . . . why Japanese here? Japanese have to fight somewhere else, I mean Pacific, you know?" . . .

■

Yukio Kawamoto knew all about "the right way, the wrong way, and the army way." But he fixed it before service in the South Pacific:

The army at that time recognized only three kinds of religion. One was Catholic, one was Protestant, one was Jewish. And if you didn't fit into one of the three categories, they usually stamped you Protestant [on your ID tag]. Well, I told the guy I was a Buddhist, and he said, "We don't have that, so we'll make you a Protestant," and he put a *P* on it. Later, when we were in Angel Island, before we went overseas, . . . this GI was just pounding away on this metallic ID tag printing machine, and I said, "Hey, by the way, I have a *P* on here, but I'm

really a Buddhist; do you think you could put a *B* on there?" The guy said, "Well, I never heard of a *B*, but if you want a *B*, I'll give you a *B*," and—BANG!—he put a *B* on top of the . . . *P*."

■

Kenjiro Akune, a Los Angeles man who ended up in China in U.S. Military Intelligence, felt the nisei soldiers didn't need to view any resounding U.S. Armed Forces Why We Fight film series. They had their own targets:

I think as a nisei being in service, we all had a goal: that we were going to prove ourselves to be loyal and as good a citizen as anybody else. . . . It was sort of a mutual understanding, that no one was gonna let the next guy down.

■

When the army sent nisei from Army Intelligence into combat in the Pacific, a bodyguard was often assigned to be with them at all times, to protect them from being shot by confused soldiers from either side. Harry Fukuhara mostly remembers it as an awkward system:

When it came time for a landing, a combat situation, we were assigned bodyguards. It was very difficult for them, because they had to stay with us twenty-four hours a day. We slept in the same foxholes, we ate together, when we were working they were nearby, and we even went to the latrine together.

■

Minoru Hara, serving with the 6th Infantry Division, in New Guinea and the Philippines, discovered the ways of the American army gave him a strange interrogating advantage:

I was interrogating this prisoner, and all our troops were eager for souvenirs 'cause I had a stack of documents on my side, and I was glancing through them while I was interrogating the prisoner. Then they closed in so tight that I couldn't see my prisoner, so I told them to step back—which everybody did, except one soldier. And I told this

soldier, "Get your ass back 'cause I can't work!" And I looked up there and I saw my commanding general. So the general smiled at me and says, "Okay, Min, I'm stepping back." So the whole GI bunch laughed. And after the general left, the Japanese soldier asked me, "Who was that officer, he had two stars on his collar?" I said, "Well, that was my commanding general. Now I'm telling you in our army, I could tell my general that, and he laughs and he steps back. What would've happened to your army?"

■

Kiofumi Kojima, a captured Japanese navy signal officer, on his first encounter with American soldiers in the Pacific:

American soldiers appeared at the gate; I was surprised to see many different people, all colors of hair, blond, silver, brown, black and gray. Different colored eyes, blue, brown, black and green. Skin, white, yellow and black. We are surrounded by all those people. When I saw those people staring at us I thought Japan was fighting every race in the world. It was beyond my imagination that a nation could consist of different races, for I only knew a homogeneous country like Japan.

■

After serving with distinction in Europe in the much-decorated 442d Regimental Combat Team, Ernest Uno came home to visit his family—in a Department of Justice camp:

My homecoming was a painful one. I had to write ahead in order to get approval . . . to visit my family. . . . Second, when I got to Crystal City, I had to call the camp administration and they had to assign me a time when I could come out to the camp, and according to their rules, sign in at the visitor center. I would meet my family in a visitor's cottage, and would have an hour to visit them. I still have visions of my folks, they were off there, away from where the taxi had driven up. I heard their voices greeting me. And I went up to the fence, touched their hands, my mother said, "*Okairi,*" she said, "I knew you'd come home."

Jungle, Pacific Theater, 1944–45

James Cook painted *Patrol Resting* in a distinctive style. The men are carrying advanced arms and equipment that suggests it is a work about combat in 1944 or 1945. Australian commanders of some of the first units thrown into the Pacific fighting were critical of poorly trained troops, poor leadership, and inferior equipment. (Australian War Memorial)

Ambush, New Guinea, 1943–44

Australian artist Russell Clark shows the miserable territory (LEFT) that both Australian and Japanese troops had to endure. Here, a narrow jungle trail provided natural ambush points at every turn. (Australian War Memorial)

Jungle Trail, New Guinea

When the men were not in actual combat, the rains, the jungle humidity, and the eternally spongy, muddy ground underfoot rotted leather straps, boots, and web belting. Sweaty uniforms would never dry, guns, bayonets, and knives would rust, and ammunition would misfire. In the painting below, Alan Barday Barns-Graham portrays the sense of constant dampness. (Australian War Memorial)

Helping the Wounded, New Guinea

Australian painter William Dargie
caught a memorable bit of action
(ABOVE) in the Owen Stanley mountains with this scene of native guides and
stretcher-bearers helping wounded Australian soldiers back to an aid station. The
bearers were strong, gentle—and could
trot a litter at near dead-level through a mile
of tangled jungle without a stumble, then
head right back to the fighting lines again.
Native guides and messengers also proved
invaluable to the Australian "coast watcher"
networks among the islands who relayed
information about Japanese naval traffic.
(Australian War Memorial)

Bougainville, Solomon Islands, 1943–44

Australian artist Harold Abbott titled
his painting (RIGHT) *Life on Slater's
Knoll.* It showed rest after furious
action in the Bougainville campaign. (Australian War Memorial)

Karako, New Guinea

Villiam Dargie of the Australian war art program showed LSTs in an almost peaceful landing scene at Karako, New Guinea, as material comes ashore for an RAAF wing to be based nearby. The cavernous tank decks of the LSTs (which open out onto the ramp where the men are working) could hold any wheeled or tracked vehicle in the Allied arsenal. (Australian War Memorial)

Native Village, New Guinea

George Browning painted the native village of Uberi on the Kokoda "road." The road was actually only a native track, a couple of feet wide, that led over the Owen Stanley mountains. One Australian described the formidability of the mountain range: "Imagine an area approximately 100 miles long. Crumple and fold this into a series of ridges, each rising higher and higher until 7,000 feet is reached. . . . Cover this thickly with jungle, short trees, and tall grass . . . and figure the 'road' is a treacherous mass of red, moving mud." (Australian War Memorial)

Leaving Okinawa, 1945

Mitchell Jamieson, the U.S. Navy combat artist who created a fine pictorial record of the American invasion of Okinawa, titled this grim picture *Evacuation by Sea* (ABOVE). A "duck" (amphibious truck) takes stretchers of wounded from the beach to an LST waiting offshore that has been turned into an interim hospital ship. (U.S. Navy Combat Art Collection)

Medics, After the Battle

Mitchell Jamieson titled this *Battalion Aid Station*. Working in the middle of the jungle, the medics appear to be treating both Japanese and Allied casualties. (U.S. Navy Combat Art Collection)

Segregation in the U.S. Armed Forces

Through most of the war, there were few black combat units, and the potential of black manpower was basically squandered. Hughie Lee Smith's murallike painting (ABOVE) is entitled *Special Training Unit.* Marion Greenwood titled her drawing (NEAR RIGHT) *Whirlpool Bath,* and this combat soldier is well on the way to recovery after airlift to the rear with shrapnel wounds. Norman Goldberg sketched black sailors and marines (FAR RIGHT) aboard a troopship on the way to Okinawa. (Above, U.S. Navy Combat Art Collection; near right, U.S. Army Center of Military History; far right, courtesy of the Artist)

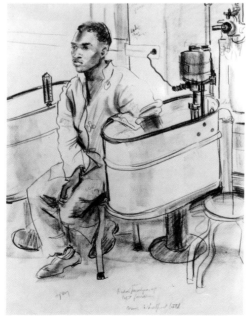

WAVEs Take Over

The navy had experimented briefly in World War I with women volunteers, but the program had no strong plan or direction. In World War II, however, the army, navy, marines, and coast guard enlisted strong volunteer corps of women auxiliaries. In addition, flier Jacqueline Cochran organized the WASPs (Women Airforce Service Pilots) to ferry planes from factory to the front, tow targets for gunnery drill, and handle other flying assignments. The Navy WAVEs, painted here by Howard Baer, are repairing shot-up sea-plane floats. (U.S. Navy Combat Art Collection)

American Naval Base, Pacific Theater, 1945

Titled *Grooming the Dogs of War,* this Howard Baer painting of the gull-winged F4U "Corsair" fighter being serviced by a WAVE ground crew at a Pacific naval base emphasized the distinctive characteristics of this rugged plane. The "Corsair" started out with some reputation as a "pilot killer," but it went on to earn fame as one of the most durable and dependable navy and marine fighters. Its size, large enough to make it something of a problem as a carrier-based fighter, was one of the reasons fliers often referred to it affectionately as "the hog." (U.S. Navy Combat Art Collection)

If Successful, They Won't Return, Japan, 1944–45

Western military men had a hard time understanding the rush of volunteers that answered the call for Japanese air force suicide units. But it drew on an honored Japanese tradition that won for the volunteers great admiration from their comrades and the public. And it turned out to be a formidable weapon against the Okinawa invasion. Usaburo Ihara painted the stirring departure from an airfield in Honshu. (Captured Japanese Art; U.S. Air Force Art Collection)

Over Rabaul, 1944

In January 1942 the Japanese seized and began to fortify Rabaul on New Britain in the Bismarck Islands chain. The harbor was well protected, and an airfield soon built there could be the air cover base for Japanese forces all down through the Solomon Islands. The Australians struck back with flights like these Beauforts. Alan Moore painted this raid of *Planes from Squadrons 8 and 106 Attacking the Anchorage, Rabaul.* The base was cut off to starve out in spring 1944. (Australian War Memorial)

A Brief Lull, Okinawa

Here is one of those strange lulls that come between actions and make fighting men believe—for a brief time at least—that the world hasn't gone completely crazy. U.S. Navy and Coast Guard crews from the LSTs waiting for the tide hunt for snails on the beach at Okinawa (ABOVE). William Goadby Lawrence, a Coast Guard artist, did the peaceful scene. Norman Goldberg, a combat infantryman on Okinawa with a talent to sketch and paint, drew an exhausted fellow trooper (RIGHT) who has fallen asleep propped up against a stump, knowing he'll soon be ordered to move forward again. (Above, U.S. Coast Guard Art Collection; right, courtesy of the Artist)

Kamikaze Pilots, 1944–45

Recruits for the kamikaze missions came rapidly from pilots in training who wanted to get into action and strike a blow for the emperor. Iwata Sentaro made this stirring painting of some of his countrymen who had joined the kamikaze corps, waiting for their orders at their base at Tachikawa. They wear the white scarf, which symbolized the head cloth of the samurai warriors, and each carries a ceremonial sword, which will go down with him in the plane. (Captured Japanese Art; U.S. Air Force Art Collection)

Dejection, Okinawa

A forlorn Japanese infantry officer captured on Okinawa (RIGHT) was sketched by Norman Goldberg as he waited for interrogation. By being captured rather than killed, he felt he had lost face. (Courtesy of the Artist)

Okinawa—After a Smooth Start, April 1944

Mitchell Jamieson's paintings of the Okinawa invasion reflect one of the bitterest running battles of the Pacific war. Initial reconnaissance indicated 65,000 Japanese troops on the island. But on April 1, there turned out to be more than 100,000 regulars and auxiliaries. The first landings were virtually unopposed, with the Japanese retiring to the island's solidly fortified south end. In *Ack-Ack at Sunset* Jamieson shows nervous gunners reacting. (U.S. Navy Combat Art Collection)

Moving Inland, Okinawa

The Japanese losses on Okinawa were staggering. It was a forerunner of what to expect in the invasion of Japan. Mitchell Jamieson caught an early lull in his *Green Beach Two, Okinawa, D Day Plus One*. (U.S. Navy Combat Art Collection)

(OVERLEAF)
Off Iwo Jima, February 1945

William Goadby Lawrence, an artist with the U.S. Coast Guard, whose personnel manned many invasion landing craft and support ships, painted "rocket ships" bombarding the tiny volcanic island of Iwo Jima, in advance of the marines' landing. Capture of the island and construction of an airstrip there that could handle the giant B-29 bombers were responsible for saving almost 24,800 U.S. pilots and air crew members from planes in trouble on the raids to Japan. (U.S. Coast Guard Art Collection)

High Cost of Island-Taking: Men and Materiel, Spring 1945

The battle for Iwo Jima came to represent the worst of the island battles—an abominably costly invasion to take a completely desolate island. Yet, the island was desperately needed by Allied bomber crews en route to and from Japan. William Goadby Lawrence painted the landing (OPPOSITE TOP). Mitchell Jamieson created fine paintings of the Iwo Jima invasion. Iwo Jima was covered by a gray volcanic soil that made the island look forlorn enough before the fighting, and afterward it was totally pockmarked and torn (OPPOSITE BOTTOM). Just carting away the debris of wrecked military equipment after the war was a major job. Jamieson called his painting (ABOVE) *The Beach at Dusk,* with Mount Suribachi looming in the background. His *Two Boys* (RIGHT) might be said to symbolize the strains of combat dissolving the World War II segregation of the armed services. This soldier and sailor, on board one of the assault ships, were waiting to go onto the beach. (All, U.S. Navy Combat Art Collection)

The Swimmers, Okinawa

itchell Jamieson must have done this painting in July 1945 after Okinawa was secured. The wrecked landing craft, still with a shot-up tank inside, overwhelms the whole scene. It was just one small vessel of all those lost in the invasion by the American and British covering force. The Japanese navy losses included the giant battleship *Yamamoto,* which was charging toward the beaches on its own suicide mission when sunk by American carrier planes. Its loss was said to have taken the heart out of the emperor. (U.S. Navy Combat Art Collection)

Military Control Checks, Atsugi, Hans Mangelsdorf (U.S. Army Center of Military History)

By January 1945, the American invasion of Luzon had begun, and the Allies had a foothold back in the Philippines. By the end of February 1945, American marines were ashore on Iwo Jima, only about 1,000 miles from half a dozen important bombing targets in the Japanese home islands. Before the end of March, Americans were in Okinawa—less than 500 miles from the southern tip of Kyushu, the southernmost Japanese home island. Still, most realistic Allied strategists looked in apprehension at what might be two more years of war before final victory in the Pacific. What would an invasion of Japan cost? Only a few highly placed persons knew of the Allied trump card (or so hoped the president of the United States): a bomb so powerful it might end the war. It could hardly be conceived of, yet it had been by a former noncommissioned officer in the Austrian army during World War I, a reject from the Aryan purity of Nazi Germany that Hitler had strived for. Albert Einstein had urged Franklin Roosevelt to consider the possibility of a powerful new bomb. When it came, it might mark the end of one world—but possibly the beginning of a better one.

In the 1970s, Studs Terkel—perhaps America's best-known compiler of "oral history"—finished half a dozen years of interviews and published The Good War, a rich collection of reminiscences of World War II from many of the countries that took part. (The title was a sardonic one; viewed against the war in Vietnam, the Second World War looked like "a simple war with clean-cut issues.") In the pages that follow, Terkel lets Americans and Japanese speak of incidents in the war they will never forget. Yasuko Kurachi, who speaks first, was five years old when the war began:

I was immediately aware of how rigid wartime school was. It was military, even for the first-graders. . . . All the students had to assemble in the assembly hall. The principal gave a speech about the Emperor and the need to support him.

There was a tiny door on the stage, behind the principal. . . . There was another door behind it. He didn't open that one. Behind that second door was supposed to be the Emperor's picture. We never got to see it. . . .

By 1944, some of my father's friends started to go to war. They were physicians. I remember them home on leave, telling stories. The whole atmosphere was one of resignation, or treating the whole thing as stupid. There was no enthusiasm at all.

By this time, Tokyo and all the major cities were being bombed. The capital of the next prefecture, Toyama, was bombed completely flat. Our family was in this shelter in the mountain. We looked out and saw the whole sky over Toyama was bright red, burning, burning bright. . . .

∎

Yasuko Kurachi describes a scene that took place ten years after the war ended. It may have familiar resonances for Americans remembering the Vietnam War experience. The wars you lose you want to forget—along with everyone in them:

As late as 1955, you'd see unemployed, one-legged soldiers at the Tokyo subway stations, begging. This was before the government revised their war-compensation rules. People resented these beggars very much. They were a bad memory, standing there with little tin cans . . . begging. People were so cold, so hostile.

∎

Masuo Kato in The Lost War *remembered everything changing, with the daily schedule built around the raids:*

Satisfactory sleep was almost out of the question in most cities from the beginning of 1945 to the end of the war. Cooking gas had become almost nonexistent, and it was necessary to cook by open fires, which could be seen from the sky at night. As a result, most cooking was done before dusk, so families ate in the twilight and then went to bed. . . .

Almost as soon as the first bombs fell, the fire was out of control, racing crazily through the district as house after house flared up like a torch before the touch of the flames . . . leaping streets, firebreaks, and canals at dazzling speed.

Frantically, panic-stricken residents seized what belongings they could carry and began to flee, some toward Tokyo Bay, some to vacant lots, parks, school grounds, any open space, toward higher ground, to canals, ponds, and the Sumida River. The flames, riding the gale, moved faster. . . .

On the night of May 25 we watched Japanese aerial defenders put up one of their most spirited displays of resistance of the war. . . . The B-29s were clearly visible in the searchlight beams as they floated across the Tokyo skies, and it was even possible to catch glimpses of the smaller Japanese interceptors rising to the attack. . . . That night my wife's sister was staying at our house. A short time earlier she had received notice that her son . . . had been killed off the Philippines in October 1944. Her husband urged her to come out of the dugout for a while to watch. . . . Just as she came out, a B-29 burst into flame high above us and began to cut a slow parabola earthward. Although my wife's sister is ordinarily a woman of great poise and unusually quiet in her manner, she clapped her hands suddenly as she watched. "Banzai!" she cried out, and there were fierce tears in her eyes. "Banzai! Thank God." . . .

In all there were six major raids on Tokyo and a number of minor ones. Official casualty figures for the six raids were 93,956 killed, 59,633 injured, 2,890,000 homeless, and 744,895 houses destroyed.

∎

John Ciardi, who would later become a Pulitzer Prize–winning poet and famous translator of Dante, was one of the more improbable B-29 aircrewmen flying against Japan. Ciardi's transition from a youth with dreams of flying to the chilling reality of air combat with an enemy shooting back was shared by many young men in other countries. Ciardi told Studs Terkel:

I was terribly innocent at twenty-six. . . . I had dreams of being a pilot, so I signed up as an aviation cadet. The army decided I was not pilot material. The army was right. They sent me to navigation school. . . . A year later, I heard that all forty-four men of my graduating class were either KIA or MIA, dead or missing in action.

When we got to Saipan, I was a gunner on a B-29. It seemed certain to me we were not going to survive. We had to fly thirty-five missions. The average life of a crew was something between six and eight missions. So you simply took the extra pay, took the badges, took relief from dirty details. Now pay up. . . .

I think it was a certain amount of pride that kept men from asking to be grounded. The unit was the crew. You belonged to eleven men. You're trained together, you're bound together. I was once ordered to fly [in another plane] in the place of a gunner who had received a shrapnel wound. I dreaded that mission. I wanted to fly with my own crew. . . .

We got to Saipan in November of '44, in time to fly the first raids over Tokyo. Those were long missions . . . normally about fourteen hours. . . .

You got an Air Medal for surviving five missions. If you survived eight more, you got another Air Medal. The next one was a distinguished Flying Cross. I got two Air Medals, so I must have had fourteen or fifteen missions. . . .

This program [awards and decorations] was raided by the brass, so that decorations were pointless after a while. Anybody up to the grade of a captain, you may assume, earned it. Anybody from the grade of major up who has a high decoration *may* have earned it, but you don't have to believe it. . . .

We were in the terrible business of burning out Japanese towns. That meant women and old people and children. One part of me

—a surviving savage voice—says, I'm sorry we left any of them living. I wish we'd finished killing them all. . . . Then you say, Now, come on, this is the human race, let's try to be civilized. I had to condition myself to be a killer. This was remote control. All we did was push buttons. I didn't see anybody we killed. I saw the fires we set. . . .

We had been trained to do precision high-altitude bombing from thirty-two thousand feet . . . except we discovered the Siberian jet stream. . . . We began to get winds at two hundred knots, and the bombs simply scattered all over Japan.

Curtis LeMay came in and changed the whole operation. . . . He said, go in at night from five thousand feet, without gunners, just a couple of rear-end observers. We'll save weight on the turrets and on ammunition. . . . We'll drop fire sticks. . . . After that, Tokyo looked like one leveled bed of ash. . . .

We were playing a lottery. A certain number of planes had to be lost. You were just hoping that by blind chance yours would not be. When news of that atom bomb came— we didn't know what it was—we knew we had won the lottery. Hey, we're gonna get out of here! We may survive this after all. . . .

When you're on a mission and you saw a Japanese plane go down, you cheered. This was a football game. When one of your guys went down, you sighed. It was miserable. One of the saddest things I ever saw, when we were flying wing on a plane that got hit, was the barber's-chair gunner in the big bubble at the very top. He was right there beside us in plain sight, beginning to go down. He just waved his hand good-bye. . . .

You were under a compulsion to say nice things about the guy [who died]. . . . The truth is—the dark truth—you were secretly glad. It could have been you. . . . There were a certain number of blackballs to be passed out. Every time another plane went down, it was taken out of play. Somebody had to catch it, and somebody else caught it for you. . . . That's a dirty, dark thing to say. When we go to funerals of old friends these days, in one corner of our mind we're saying, Well, I outlived that old bastard. . . .

■

Among the plentiful ironies of the war, a list of the most notable must include two critical scientific developments which came to the Allied side but just as easily might have fallen to the Axis: radar and the atomic bomb. Experiments preliminary to radar were undertaken in Germany in 1904 when a "telemobiloscop" on a bridge in Cologne focused on and detected ships in a fog on the river. But the Germans were uninterested. And in 1939, Albert Einstein, who had been forced out of Germany, sent a letter by a trusted contact to President Roosevelt. William Craig tells the story in The Fall of Japan:

Alexander Sachs, a director of the Lehman corporation, an influential economist and a friend to scientists . . . came to the White House with a terribly important message contained in a letter he began to read [to the President]:

"Sir: Some recent work by E. Fermi and L. Szilard, which has been communicated to me in manuscript, leads me to expect that the element uranium may be turned into a new and important source of energy in the near future. Certain aspects of the situation which has arisen seem to call for watchfulness and if necessary, quick action on the part of the Administration. . . . It may become possible to set up a nuclear chain reaction in a large mass of uranium, by which vast amounts of power and large quantities of new radium-like elements would be generated. . . . It is conceivable—though much less certain—that extremely powerful bombs of a new type may thus be constructed."

■

The development of the bomb was so well concealed that none of the combat commanders who were preparing for the ultimate invasion of Japan had any idea that such an experiment was being carried out, or that its use might be an option to the terrible bloodletting that an invasion promised.

But would the bomb work? In Potsdam, Germany, in the late summer of 1945, Truman got word that it did; William Craig quotes the message Secretary Stimson got in Potsdam from his aide in Washington:

TO: SECRETARY OF WAR FROM HARRISON. DOCTOR HAS JUST RETURNED MOST ENTHUSIASTIC AND CONFIDENT THAT THE LITTLE BOY IS AS HUSKY AS HIS BIG BROTHER. THE LIGHT IN HIS EYES DISCERNIBLE FROM HERE TO HIGHHOLD AND I COULD HAVE HEARD HIS SCREAMS FROM HERE TO MY FARM.

Highhold was Stimson's summer place on Long Island, 250 miles from Washington; Harrison's farm was fifty miles away in Virginia.

■

Hurrying home after Potsdam (and having ordered with incredible secrecy the use of the atomic bomb on Japan), Truman got word of its drop. He was often asked later if he regretted his decision. His answer was always a firm "no." He said he was also in the business of saving lives, and the casualty toll for an invasion of Japan would have been staggering. William Craig reported how Truman received the news of the Hiroshima bombing:

Half a world away, Harry Truman heard the news while he ate lunch with men of the cruiser *Augusta* [that was] carrying the President home from Potsdam. An aide handed Truman a dispatch:

"Big bomb dropped on Hiroshima August 5 at 7:15 P.M., Washington time. First reports indicate complete success which was even more conspicuous than earlier test."

■

The B-29 Enola Gay, *which had bombed Hiroshima, had been followed by planes to measure the impact and a photographic plane to record the damage. At the B-29 base in the Marianas, a crew from the 3d Photo Reconnaissance Squadron was standing by to analyze photos of what had been labeled only as "another late-night job." Maj. Hamilton Darby, a former archeologist who had worked to reconstruct ruined ancient cities in the Near East, remembered receiving the photos with no preamble:*

Even personnel immediately involved with certain phases of the first drop were told nothing. Our job in the regular bombing situations was to spot likely strategic targets. . . . Then, following bomb strikes, we were to comb the follow-up photos to analyze damage done and evaluate the success of the mission. But there was nothing about the analysis we were asked to do that night that indicated anything special.

The photos arrived a bit faster than usual, however, and we were asked to put our best interpreters on the work. It would take a good bit of time because of the amount of film involved. When the interpretation report was finished, I was somewhat surprised to see a top-brass general from Washington come into the Quonset hut to conduct some special questioning as to what we considered the noticeable difference in the types of damage. For example, multiple-story buildings were left standing in some cases—but totally "hollowed out" . . . and large riverboats were blown "whole" onto dry land, some distance from the riverbanks. . . .

We thought the massive devastation was caused by a raid of many bombers. Then the general told us the simple truth. The whole awful mess had been caused by one plane, one bomb.

■

President Truman, August 7, 1945, in a radio announcement to the American people:

Sixteen hours ago, an American airplane dropped one bomb on Hiroshima. That single bomb had more power than twenty thousand tons of explosive. It is an atomic bomb. . . . We are now prepared to obliterate more rapidly and completely every productive enterprise the Japanese have aboveground in any city.

■

A Japanese journalist wrote from Hiroshima:

On 6 August there wasn't a cloud in the sky above Hiroshima. . . . At nine minutes past seven in the morning an air-raid warning sounded and four American B-29 planes appeared. To the north of the town two of them turned and made off to the south. . . . The other two, after having circled the neighborhood of Shukai, flew off at high speed southward in the direction of the Bingo Sea.

At 7:31 the all-clear was given. Feeling themselves in safety, people came out of their shelters and went about their affairs and the work of the day began.

Suddenly a glaring, whitish pinkish light appeared in the sky, accompanied by an unnatural tremor, which was followed almost immediately by a wave of suffocating heat and a wind which swept away everything in its path. . . .

. . . By the evening the fire began to die down and then it went out. There was nothing left to burn. Hiroshima had ceased to exist.

■

People all over Japan still remember exactly where they were and what they were doing when they heard about the great explosions in Hiroshima and Nagasaki. A colleague of Masuo Kato assigned to the Domei news bureau in Hiroshima was at his home in the outskirts of the city when the bomb dropped. Kato wrote of the man's experience:

At about 8:20 A.M. Nakamura felt an intense heat which brought with it a sharp aching sensation about the face. At the same instant all the window glass in his house was shattered. He was seated on a tatami, a Japanese mat, and a powerful concussion wave lifted him, together with the mat, a short distance into the air, seemingly pushing up from beneath. . . .

As soon as he reached the open, Nakamura saw in the sky a . . . streamer of smoke, perhaps fifty yards high, rising from the center of Hiroshima, about two miles distant. At the top of the column of smoke . . . was a ball of orange fire, which seemed to him to be about the size of a large oil tank. He was convinced at once that something unusual must have occurred. . . .

Mounting a bicycle, Nakamura started for the Domei office, but before he had gone far the area was swept by heavy wind, much like a whirlwind, and a torrential rain. . . .

Late in the evening he was able to hire a small boat and approach the center of the city along the Ota River. . . . He talked to several persons who had been burned in the explosion, and without exception they reported that they felt no pain from their burns. . . . Here and there reinforced concrete buildings remained upright, but their interiors were smashed and gutted. . . .

Full casualty figures for the bombing probably will never be assembled. . . . Unofficial estimates were that 80,000 persons died on the first day alone. There was a second group of casualties who lived for about a week, suffering from burns and a decrease in white blood corpuscles. A third group of fatalities included persons who lost their hair and suffered from bleeding from the eyes, ears, and mouth. Their deaths occurred about a month after the bombing.

■

The Japanese knew the details of the last days of Germany. Hitler's insane "Last Great Battle" philosophy for destroying the whole nation was also held by many officials at the top of the Japanese government. Perhaps the only person who could hold them back was the Emperor. He advised the leaders of the government:

"Those who argue for continuing the war once assured me that the new battalions and supplies would be ready at Kujikurihama by June. I realize now that this cannot be fulfilled even by September. As for those who wish for one last battle here on our own soil, let me remind them of the disparity between their previous plans and what has actually taken place. I cannot bear to see my innocent people struggle any longer. Ending the war is the only way to restore world peace and to relieve the nation from the terrible distress with which it is burdened. . . . The time has come when we must bear the unbearable."

■

Masuo Kato had a unique opportunity to see what was going on at top government levels as the leaders began to struggle with the problems of ending the war:

I am certain that [Premier] Togo's entire attention was devoted during that period to finding a peace formula. It was a personally hazardous task for him; he found it advisable to change his residence to one place after another because of the danger to himself and his family should the ultranationalistic elements learn of his efforts. . . .

In the fortnight between Japan's surrender and the arrival of the first Occupation troops, most of the Japanese people went mechanically about their daily affairs, partly because there was nothing else to do. . . . Tokyo street scenes in those two weeks reminded me more of China than of the Japan I had always known. Instead of the industrious activity usually to be seen in the streets of Tokyo during the war, there were everywhere idle groups of people, huddling together in the ruins of a once-great city, watching the sky and the passersby waiting for what might happen next.

When the Americans came, foodstuffs and billets would be requisitioned through the Government in an orderly manner and would not be seized haphazardly from individuals. (It was taken as a matter of course by the public and the Government as well that the Occupation troops would expect to requisition food supplies, and this was one of the greatest sources of worry.) The fact that the Allied forces carefully refrained from using any of Japan's meager food supplies gave to the Japanese a surprising and reassuring insight into the nature of the Occupation at an early stage. It probably also prevented mass starvation and food riots. . . .

■

Japanese newspapers urged great caution. Propaganda beamed at the Japanese people during three and a half years of war had nourished the image of Americans as a race of brutal killers with a hatred of Asians. Now many Japanese faced the Occupation with great fear—based on what they had been taught:

"Don't wear conspicuous clothing and don't walk alone, especially at night," one article advised women readers. "Don't go out at all in the evening. . . ." It was pointed out that Japanese had a habit of smiling where there was nothing in particular to smile about, and such smiles on the part of Japanese women might be misunderstood by American troops.

■

Before the Emperor went on the radio to the nation announcing the war's end, most Japanese had never heard his voice:

"We have ordered our Government to communicate to the Governments of the United States, Great Britain, China, and the Soviet Union that our Empire accepts the provisions of their Joint Declaration."

[The language was court Japanese—a stilted, archaic form strange to many of his listeners. Comprehension of his purpose was slow in coming as he next set about exonerating his country for the debacle of the war, William Craig reported.]

"To strive for the common prosperity and happiness of all nations as well as the security and well-being of our subjects is the solemn obligation which has been handed down by our Imperial Ancestors, and which we lay close to heart. Indeed, we declared war on America and Britain out of our sincere desire to ensure Japan's self-preservation and the stabilization of Southeast Asia, it being far from our thought either to infringe upon the sovereignty of other nations or to embark upon territorial aggrandizement. . . . Work with resolution so that ye may enhance the innate glory of the Imperial State and keep pace with the progress of the world."

With this, the voice stopped.

■

Gwen Terasaki, a Westerner married to a Japanese and living in Japan, had asked neighbors and their household servants to listen with her to the Emperor's speech:

As Terry translated [the translation was necessary because of the court Japanese, which most Japanese could not understand] they grasped the sense of what was being said, that it meant surrender, [a] bandaged woman [listening nearby] began to weep—not loudly or hysterically but with deep sobs that racked her body. The children started crying and before the Emperor had finished, all his people there were weeping audibly. The voice stopped. Silently the old men, the women and their children, rose and bowed to each other, and without any sound each went along the path leading to his own house.

■

Maxine Andrews was a member of the Andrews Sisters, the famous 1940s singing group, which performed for thousands of servicemen in the U.S. and abroad during the war years. In August 1945, she told Studs Terkel, they were finishing a USO tour near Naples for a group of infantrymen who were waiting for ships to take them directly to the Pacific in preparation for the invasion of Japan. All the talk in the Naples replacement depot was about the high casualties they could expect. To Maxine Andrews, they looked like a very tough audience:

They hadn't been home for four years, and

it was just their bad luck. We were trying to get them into good spirits

We were pretty well through the show when I heard someone offstage calling me: "Pssst. Pssst." The soldier said to me, "I have a very important message for Patty to tell the audience." I started to laugh because they were always playing tricks on us. He said, "I'm not kidding. It's from the CO."

So I took the piece of paper. I didn't read it. I walked out on the stage, saying to myself, I'm gonna get in trouble with Patty, with Arthur [Treacher, a troupe member], and with the CO. . . . I shoved the note to Patty. She finally said, "All right, I'll go along with the gag."

So she said to the fellas, "Look, it's a big joke up here. I have a note supposedly from the CO." Without reading it first, she read it out loud.

It announced the end of the war with Japan. There wasn't a sound in the whole auditorium. She looked at it again. It was serious. So she said, "No, fellas, this is from the CO. This is an announcement that the war is over, so you don't have to go." With that, she started to cry, Laverne and I were crying. Still there was no reaction from the guys. So she said it again: "This is the end, this is the end."

All of a sudden, all hell broke loose. . . . They yelled and screamed. We saw a pair of pants and a shirt come down from the rafters, followed by a soldier. . . .

A few years later, Patty was working someplace in Cleveland. She checked into the hotel and was in the elevator. The elevator man said, "Don't you remember me?" He was a short, bald-headed guy. She said, "Should I?" He said, "Yeah, remember Naples? Remember the guy that fell off the rafter? That was me."

■

To Americans, one of the most tragic pictures of the war was an oil by a Japanese artist, done for propaganda purposes and widely published in the West. It showed Gen. Jonathan Wainwright, tired and gaunt, seated at a table on the veranda of a tropical house in the Philippines. He is surrounded by Japanese photographers and newsreel cameramen. Opposite Wainwright sits General Homma, taking Wainwright's surrender. Wainwright could not believe his liberation when an

American army group arrived at the prison where he was held. William Craig described the scene:

Several minutes later, the emaciated man appeared. He did not enter. Instead, he waited at the door. He stared at Lamar and whispered, "Are you really Americans?" Lamar nodded, identified himself . . . and said, "General, you are no longer a prisoner. You're going back to the States."

Wainwright thought a moment, then asked the one question that had plagued him for so many long days and nights: "What do the people in the States think of me?" His eyes bored into Lamar's as the major answered, "You're considered a hero there."

■

William Craig reported a potentially explosive situation inherent because of the large numbers of Allied prisoners of war who were in camps purposely isolated on the Japanese home islands and on the Asian mainland. As the victors found later, some prisoners were immediately killed by their Japanese captors because they knew too much about atrocities. Others, prematurely freed, went on revenge rampages in nearby towns and villages:

American army and navy planes had instituted relief measures immediately after the Emperor's broadcast. Drums of food were dropped into prison compounds, where starving men tore them open and ate ravenously. As the day of occupation arrived, thousands of skeletal human beings waited impatiently for the sight of a friendly force at the camp gates.

■

Rumors of various attempted revolts against the Japanese government by extremists and ultranationalists were disquieting to General MacArthur. And though the outbreaks were generally put down quickly, the Americans could not be sure just what awaited the first troops to go in. Japanese correspondent Masuo Kato was witness to MacArthur's arrival:

Although the American public was kept relatively well informed on the progress of surrender arrangements, the Japanese public was not told that a Japanese delegation had been sent to Manila to confer with General MacArthur until after the delegation's return. . . . The dramatic moment of [August 26], of course, was the arrival of General Douglas MacArthur in his private transport plane, *Bataan,* accompanied by Lt. Gen. Robert Eichelberger and Lt. Gen. Richard K. Sutherland. As soon as the big monoplane came to a halt on the runway, a ladder was automatically lowered, and the supreme commander, wearing dark sunglasses and smoking a long-stemmed corncob pipe, stepped out. He moved deliberately, pausing to glance casually about the sunlit airfield as he savored the moment that meant the end of a dogged fight from Bataan to Tokyo. Slowly he descended the ladder, very much like a great actor making a carefully planned entrance down the passage leading to the stage in a Japanese theater. . . .

I was one of four Japanese newspapermen, including two reporters, a photographer, and one newsreel cameraman, permitted to cover the surrender ceremony aboard the battleship *Missouri* in Tokyo Bay. . . . We went aboard an American destroyer at about six A.M. on September 2 and started the half-hour trip to the *Missouri* about an hour later. . . . Presently one of the destroyer's officers brought us some hot coffee in very large cups, which to me was the most impressive event of the day. That coffee was the smell of America, of the whole Western world from which we had been so long cut off, and it symbolized in a concrete way the peace that had come at last. . . .

While I waited for the ceremony to start, I watched the tremendous concentration of naval power, which choked Tokyo Bay on all sides of us. There were more than one hundred British and American warships of all types in that formidable panorama. . . . I thought of the only battleships Japan had had to rival the *Missouri* in size—the *Yamoto* and the *Musshi,* both over 45,000 tons and both now destroyed by enemy action. . . . One bright spot in Japan's gloomy future was that rebuilding the country would be so much the easier without the crushing burden of such expensive armament. . . .

The surrender required no more than twenty minutes. . . .

After Shigemitsu and Umezu had signed the surrender document for Japan, General MacArthur asked General Percival, the British commander who surrendered Singapore to the Japanese, and Gen. Jonathan Wainwright, who surrendered Corregidor, to stand beside him while he signed the document. . . . General Percival showed little sign of having suffered from his experience, but General Wainwright . . . seemed dazzled and bewildered, like a man who had just emerged into the light after long confinement in darkness.

■

Tom Sakamoto, a Japanese-American who had been caught in the nisei internment fiasco, ended the war as a translator for General MacArthur and was also aboard Missouri *for the surrender ceremonies:*

The impression I got of the whole thing was like a huge lion in a cage where it's cornered a tiny, timid-looking mouse. When Foreign Minister Shigemitsu and followers came up the walk in front of all the Allied representatives, there was an uncomfortable silence. . . . If ever the Japanese people suffered hardship from this war, it was today . . . I am sure.

■

Masuo Kato standing on the same deck thought of an odd historic parallel to the surrender:

As he spoke I was thinking of the "black ships" of Commodore Perry and what they had meant to Japan. Would today's ceremony mean that Japan, now reduced to an area of 148,505 square miles—about the size of the state of Montana—after having conquered in the South Seas area alone a territory of 984,965 square miles, experience a second opening to intercourse with the West? When Perry's ships came, the people of Japan did not welcome them, but they had no choice except to yield. Now that the Americans had come again, there was, perhaps, much of the same feeling. How long would they stay?

. . . As the surrender ceremony came to an end . . . the Japanese delegation walked stiffly off the scene and into obscurity without further formalities. Hundreds of American planes in beautiful formation roared overhead as a final reminder of the power that had destroyed an empire. The sky was clearing and the rest of the day promised to be bright.

Clean-Up on the Road to Tokyo, Philippines, Spring 1945

Frede Vidar was struck by these wrecked Japanese and American planes that had to be cleared away to make the Philippines' old Clark Field operational. The airfield had taken its first bombs when the Japanese attacked in December 1941. (U.S. Air Force Art Collection)

Roving Threat, Western Pacific, 1945

Tom Lea, an American artist, was best known for his paintings of U.S. infantrymen. But as carrier strike forces roamed the western Pacific after victory in the Battle of Leyte Gulf, Lea painted their activities. Here, a TBF torpedo plane, which doubled as a bomber and a sub-hunter, circles the *Hornet,* which had seen action at Midway and had carried Jimmy Doolittle's bombers to raid Tokyo. (U.S. Army Center of Military History)

"Divine Wind," Okinawa, April 1945

Dwight Shepler painted this detailed scene of a kamikaze attack on a heavy carrier at the carrier's most dangerous time—its decks covered with fighters that have not yet gotten aloft. The trajectory of the Japanese plane looks as if it might carry the aircraft safely into the sea—but it might pinwheel down to crash into the fighters. The USS *Franklin* was hit this way off Okinawa, partially abandoned, then reboarded by its crew and sailed all the way to New York for repairs. (U.S. Navy Combat Art Collection)

Short-Haul Devastator, 1945

Robert H. Laessig painted B-25 medium bombers (ABOVE) being loaded for a mission in the Philippines. This is the type of plane, heavily modified, that carried out the Tokyo raid from the carrier *Hornet* in the spring of 1942. (U.S. Air Force Art Collection)

"Forked-Tail Devils," Luzon, 1945

Lingayen Airfield on Luzon (RIGHT) showed its scars to U.S. fighters brought in to base there. These P-38 "Lightnings," with their distinctive twin-boomed tails and a range of 1,100 miles, provided strong escort for bombers in the western Pacific. Jim Turnbull was the artist. (U.S. Navy Combat Art Collection)

Long-Haul Devastator, 1945

Mitchell Jamieson shows the tense waiting at a B-29 field on Iwo Jima as the big bombers return from the long round-trip to Japan. Crash teams stand by at a radio request from one of the damaged planes. (U.S. Air Force Art Collection)

(OVERLEAF)

"Scorched Earth," Finally at Rest, Far East, 1945

The legacy of war at so many points around the globe by the fall of 1945 is reflected in Leslie Cole's powerful *Scorched Earth in Burma.* This particular "scorched earth" is the remains of what had once been one of the finest rubber plantations in the world. (Imperial War Museum)

Braced for Heavy Fire, Japan, August 23, 1945

Standish Backus was an artist with the U.S. Navy as the Allies entered Japan, and he covered these events in powerful detail. This scene is one everyone thought would take place under devastating enemy fire—marine landing craft going in to a Japanese beach. In his book *The Fall of Japan,* William Craig closely followed the movements of an American colonel, picked "for the honor" of being the first American to fly in. He thought it might also be a death sentence; his landing spot was an airfield occupied by kamikaze pilots. (U.S. Navy Combat Art Collection)

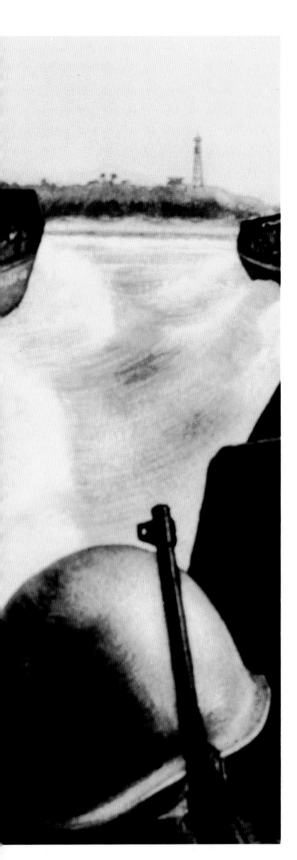

U.S. Colors, Surrendered Land, August 1945

Standish Backus did this quick painting of a historic occasion—the first American flag raised on Japanese soil at the end of World War II. It was an impromptu celebration atop the watchtower of a former Japanese signal station. This appears to be the follow-up to his painting at left, where the tower appears in the picture's upper right corner. (U.S. Navy Art Collection)

Imperial Navy Burial Grounds, Japan, Fall 1945

Backus called this *Postmortem at Yokosuka.* He has painted the harbor, with an Allied warship at anchor—as seen from the wrecked bridge of the Japanese battleship *Nagato.* (U.S. Navy Combat Art Collection)

Japan's Sacred Symbol, Enemy's Landmark, August 1945

More than 170 naval planes had been launched from carriers on a strike over Japan on August 15, 1945, when Admiral Halsey received a signal that the Japanese had agreed to all the Allied terms of surrender. He was able to recall 73 of them before they were into the combat area, but the remaining planes bombed and strafed Japan that day and were engaged by 45 Japanese fighters. It was the last air combat of the war. Standish Backus painted a flight of marine F4U fighters (LEFT) homing on Mount Fujiyama, the sacred Japanese landmark that proved also to be a damaging landmark for incoming planes. (U.S. Navy Combat Art Collection)

"These Proceedings Are Closed"—MacArthur, Tokyo Bay

Standish Backus did this annotated sketch (ABOVE) on the USS *Missouri* on September 2, 1945, in preparation for a formal painting. His notes in the upper left corner of the sketch begin: "Following signing of surrender documents, Japanese delegates start to leave U.S.S. 'Missouri.' At this moment the sky is darkened by hundreds of planes (*all* U.S.)." (U.S. Navy Combat Art Collection)

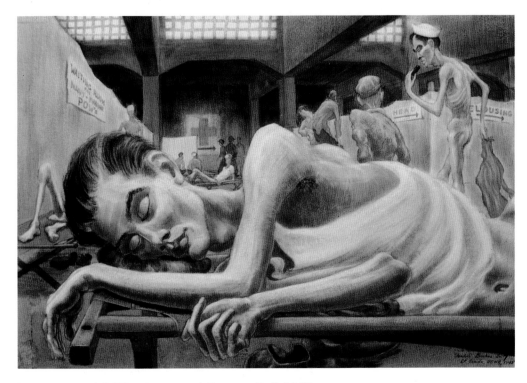

Internees and POWs, Japan and Borneo, Fall 1945

Priority assignment for U.S. medical teams flown into Japan (and parachuted into remote locations where there were prison camps) was to find and treat American servicemen and civilians who were being held. Standish Backus met some of the prisoners and painted *Recent Guests of Japan* (ABOVE). (U.S. Navy Combat Art Collection)

Introduction to the Atomic Age, Hiroshima, Fall 1945

American medical teams were horrified by the strange range of injuries caused by the atomic bombs. Some assumptions had been made, knowing the power of the bomb, about how many people might be killed outright, but the potential for burn and radiation damage was largely unknown. When Standish Backus visited a Red Cross hospital in Hiroshima, he recorded the condition of some of the victims he found there (ABOVE). (U.S. Navy Combat Art Collection)

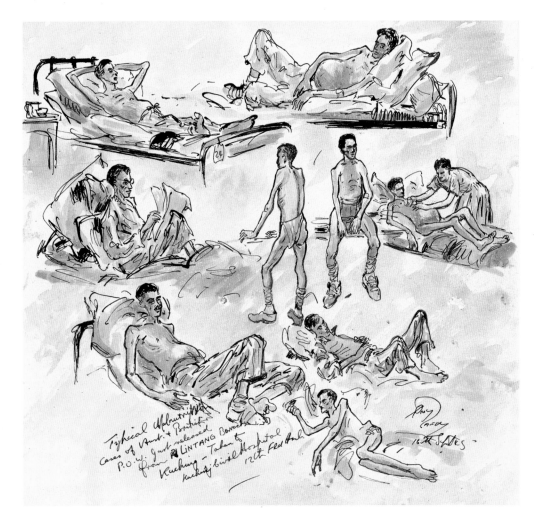

Nine Who Survived

Tony Rafty made these studies (LEFT) for a painting of British and Australian prisoners liberated in Borneo and suffering from extreme malnutrition. (Imperial War Museum)

A Home for Three Years, Singapore, Fall 1945

British artist Leslie Cole distinguished himself with paintings of the Royal Navy, war workers at their jobs, the siege of Malta, and the Holocaust camps. Then he covered the end of the war in the Far East. Cole described this 1945 scene (ABOVE) as "British women and children interned in a Japanese prison camp, Syme Road, Singapore." These people had been in camps since the surrender of Singapore in the spring of 1942. The younger children had never known any other life. (Imperial War Museum)

Liberation Party, Shanghai, Fall 1945

In Shanghai, artist James Morris sketched a joyous occasion (LEFT). The Royal Navy had liberated British women and children interned in Shanghai since December 1941. As soon as they had received the necessary medical care and had regained some of their strength, they were surprised with a party aboard HMS *Belfast*. That battle-tested heavy cruiser, in at the kill of the *Scharnhorst,* is moored today in the Thames off the Tower of London as a museum of World War II. (Imperial War Museum)

Five Years, Eleven Months After the Parades and Bands

Standish Backus painted these two devastating antiwar statements in Hiroshima, titling them *Garden at Hiroshima* (RIGHT) and *Settlers in New Hiroshima* (BELOW). No other explanation seems necessary. (Both, U.S. Navy Combat Art Collection)

Garden at Hiroshima

Standish Backus Jr. '46

War Crimes Trials, Tokyo, Spring 1946

With the five months of experience with the Nuremberg War Crimes Trials to help them, an international panel of judges from the Allied nations began war crimes trials in Tokyo in April 1946. Among the defendants were General Homma, who had defeated the Americans in the Philippines (and was charged with responsibility for the Bataan "Death March"), and General Yamashita, who had humbled the British at Singapore. Julius B. Stafford-Baker is the artist. (Imperial War Museum)

The Amazingly Peaceful Occupation, Fall 1945

Japanese news correspondent Masuo Kato commented on the strange immobility of most of Japan between the time the surrender was announced by the emperor (August 15) and the arrival of the first Occupation troops (August 23). The Japanese did not know what to expect of their former enemy, nor what was expected of them. But in the background of this calm confusion, ultranational elements tried to take over the government and create the stage for a "last great battle." Fortunately, they were unsuccessful. Japanese soldiers turned in their arms and headed for what they hoped were undamaged homes. American army artist Hans Mangelsdorf painted this scene in Tokyo Station (OPPOSITE) after the surrender as Japanese troops from overseas stations came home. (U.S. Army Center of Military History)

—But It Shouldn't Happen Again, London, August 1945

Lt. Molly Lamb Bobak was a prolific Canadian artist serving in the Canadian Women's Army Corps, and the wife of Bruno Bobak of the Canadian Fusiliers of the 13th Canadian Infantry Brigade, who painted *Carrier Convoy After Dark* (Chapter 12). Her *V-J Day Celebrations in London's Hyde Park* symbolizes end-of-the-war enthusiasm all over the world. The lights had gone on full in England for the first time on V-E Day in May . . . after *six years* of blackout. But on Bobak's V-J night, it was still a novelty. (Canadian War Museum)

ART COLLECTIONS

■

Major collections of World War II art are housed in the following museums and galleries. In some cases, these are primarily holding points for the paintings and drawings, and public displays are not always under way. The visitor is urged to call or write in advance to find out what may be seen and to get specific directions to the display rooms and hours when they are open.

Army Art Activity
U.S. Army Center of Military History
DAMH-HSA, Washington, DC 20314-0200

Navy Combat Art Collection
Naval Historical Center
Washington Navy Yard
Washington, DC 20374-0571
(includes the Marine Corps Collection)

U.S. Coast Guard Academy Museum &
    Library
New London, Connecticut 06320-4195
also
Public Affairs Office
U.S. Coast Guard Headquarters
2100 2d Street, S.W.
Washington, DC 20593

U.S. Merchant Marine Academy Library
Steamboat Road
Kings Point, NY 11024

Air Force Art and Museum Branch
The Pentagon
Washington, DC 20330-1000

Canadian War Museum
221 Champagne Avenue, North
Ottawa K1R 7W3
Ontario, Canada

Australian War Memorial
Canberra, Australian Capital Territory
Australia 2600

Imperial War Museum
Lambeth Road
London SE1 6HZ, England

National Maritime Museum
Greenwich SE10 SNF
London, England

National War Art Collection
National Archives
22 Ghuznee Street
Wellington, New Zealand

Musée d'Histoire Contemporaine—BDIC,
    Universités de Paris
Hôtel National des Invalides
75007 Paris, France

Bayerische Staatsbibliothek
D-8000, Munich 34
Federal Republic of Germany

Bavarian Army Museum
Ingolstadt, Bayern
Federal Republic of Germany

Sotamuseo Military Museum
Maurinkatui 1
00170 Helsinki, Finland

Museo Civico di Storia Contemporanea
Milan, Italy

Istituto Nazionale per la Grafica
Milan, Italy

Milano Museo Raccolte Storiche del
    Comune di Milano
Milan, Italy

Museum of the Polish Army
Al Jerozolinskie 1-3
00-495 Warsaw, Poland

State Russian Museum
Inzhenernaya ul. 4
Leningrad, USSR

Tretyakov State Picture Gallery
Lavrushiniski pr. 10
Moscow, USSR

State Museum of Ukrainian Art
Ul. Kirova 6
Kiev, Ukrainian SSR

Military Museum of the Yugoslav People's
    Army, Belgrade-Kalemegdan
Belgrade, Yugoslavia

National Modern Art Museum
Kitanomaru Park
Chiyoda-ku, Tokyo 102, Japan

SOURCES

■

In 1960, Desmond Flower and James Reeves, British editors who had been active in military or home-front services during World War II, published in England *The War: 1939–1945* (Cassell & Company Ltd.). This was an extensive and unusual anthology that not only included war recollections of the great leaders but also, and more importantly, experiences of men and women in all situations and from most of the countries involved. The book was later published in the United States as *The Taste of Courage: The War, 1939–1945* (Harper & Brothers Publishers). We are particularly indebted for the inspiration and information this book gave.

The editors are authors only of the picture captions and the commentary that introduces the quoted material. Commentary identifies all speakers or authors of quoted material where they are known. The chapter by chapter listing of books that follows is provided to indicate the primary sources consulted for that chapter but also as a bibliography for readers. Though some of these books were quoted only briefly, each provides a far greater amount of valuable history that readers may want to explore. The editors wish to express their thanks to copyright owners of those books from which major excerpts were used for permission to quote them in *Images of War*.

CHAPTER I:
BLITZKRIEG IN EUROPE

■

The Memoirs of Marshall Mannerheim, Carl Gustav Mannerheim, E. P. Dutton & Co., Inc. (1954)
They Came As Friends, Tor Myklehost,

translated by Trygve M. Ager. Translation copyright 1943 by Tor Myklehost. Used by permission of Doubleday, a division of Bantam Doubleday Dell Publishing Group, Inc.
Dunkirk, the Patriotic Myth, Nicholas Harman, Simon & Schuster (1980)
The Sands of Dunkirk, Richard Collier, E. P. Dutton & Co., Inc. (1961)
Panzer Leader, Heinz Guderian, translated by Constantine Fitz Gibbon, E. P. Dutton & Co., Inc. (1952)
I Saw It Happen in Norway, Carl Joachim Hambro, D. Appleton-Century (1940)

CHAPTER II:
BRITAIN STANDS ALONE

■

Front Line: 1940–1941. Reprinted by permission of the Controller of Her Britannic Majesty's Stationery Office.
London War Notes, Mollie Panter-Downes. Copyright © 1971 by Mollie Panter-Downes. Reprinted by permission of Farrar, Straus & Giroux, Inc.
Living Through the Blitz, Thom Harrison. Reprint 1988 by Schocken Books.
Churchill's Few, John Willis, Michael Joseph (1942)
Children of the Blitz, Robert Westall, Viking (1943)
The Man Who Went Back, Lucien Dumais, Leo Cooper Company, London (1975)
The Good War: An Oral History of World War Two, Studs Terkel. Copyright © 1984 by Studs Terkel. Reprinted by permission of Pantheon Books, a division of Random House, Inc.
Dieppe, The Shame and the Glory, Terrance Robertson. Copyright © 1963 by Terrance Robertson. By permission of Little, Brown & Company.

CHAPTER III:
STRUGGLE IN NORTH AFRICA

■

The Rommel Papers, edited by B. H. Liddell Hart, Harcourt Brace Jovanovich (1953)
The Battle of El Alamein, Fred Majdalany, J. B. Lippincott (1965)

CHAPTER IV:
THE INVASION OF RUSSIA

■

Russia at War, Alexander Werth. Copyright © 1964 by Alexander Werth. By permission of E. P. Dutton, a division of Penguin Books USA, Inc.
Many Roads to Moscow, Leonard Cooper, Coward McCann (1968)
Panzer Leader, Heinz Guderian, translated by Constantine Fitz Gibbon, E. P. Dutton & Co., Inc. (1952)
The German Generals Talk, edited by B. H. Liddell Hart. Copyright © 1948 by B. H. Liddell Hart and renewals. By permission of Kathleen Liddell Hart.
Moscow Tram Stop, Heinrich Haape, Collins (1957)

CHAPTER V:
SEA WARS

■

The Battle of the Atlantic, Terry Hughes and John Costello. Copyright © 1977 by Terry Hughes and John Costello. Reprinted by permission of Doubleday, a division of Bantam Doubleday Dell Publishing Group, Inc.
The Atlantic Campaign, Dan van der Vat, Harper & Row (1988)

Battleship Bismarck: A Survivor's Story, Burkard Freiherr von Müllenheim-Rechberg. Copyright © 1980 U.S. Naval Institute, Annapolis, Md.

CHAPTER VI:
EXPLOSION IN THE PACIFIC

■

Day of Infamy, Walter Lord. Copyright © 1957, 1985 by Walter Lord. Reprinted by permission of Henry Holt & Company, Inc.

Remember Pearl Harbor, Thomas Blake Clark, Modern Age Books (1942)

The Story of Wake Island, James Patrick Sinnott Devereux, J. B. Lippincott (1947)

Fortress: The Story of the Siege and Fall of Singapore, Kenneth Attiwill, Doubleday (1960)

CHAPTER VII:
ISLAND INVASIONS AND CARRIER WARS

■

Challenge in the Pacific: Guadalcanal, the Turning Point of the War, Robert Leckie, Doubleday (1965)

The Doolittle Raid, Duane Schultz. Copyright © 1988 by Duane Schultz, St. Martin's Press, Inc., New York.

Battle Report, Walter Krieg and Eric Purdon, Farrar & Rinehart (1947)

The Magnificent Mitscher, Theodore Taylor, W. W. Norton & Company, Inc. (1954)

Midway, The Battle That Doomed Japan, Mitsuo Fuchida and Masataka Okumiya. Copyright © 1955, U.S. Naval Institute, Annapolis, Md.

Carrier War, Oliver Jensen, Simon & Schuster (1945)

CHAPTER VIII:
STEPPING STONES TO EUROPE

■

Invasion Diary, Richard Tregaskis. Copyright 1944 by Random House, Inc. Reprinted by permission of the publisher.

On to Berlin: Battles of an Airborne Commander, James Gavin. Copyright © 1978 by James M. Gavin. All rights reserved. Reprinted by permission of Viking Penguin, a division of Penguin Books USA, Inc.

Inside Rome with the Germans, Jane Scrivener, Macmillan (1945)

Anzio: The Massacre at the Beachhead, Wynford Vaughan-Thomas, Holt, Rinehart & Winston (1961)

Monte Cassino, David Hapgood and David Richardson. Copyright © 1984 by David Hapgood and David Richardson. By permission of St. Martin's Press, Inc., New York.

CHAPTER IX:
AIR WAR OVER EUROPE

■

The Fal! of the Fortresses, Elmer Bendiner. Copyright © 1980 by G. P. Putnam's Sons. Reprinted by permission of the author.

Ploesti: The Great Ground-Air Battle of 1 August 1943, James Dugan and Carroll Stewart. Copyright © 1962 by James Dugan and Carroll Stewart. Reprinted by permission of Random House, Inc.

I Flew for the Führer: The Story of a German Fighter Pilot, Heinz Knoke. Translated by John Ewing. Copyright 1953, 1954 by Heinz Knoke. Reprinted by permission of Henry Holt & Company, Inc.

One Last Look, Philip Kaplan and Rex Alan Smith, Abbeville Press (1983)

CHAPTER X:
FORGOTTEN WARS AND SILENT SERVICES

■

Siege: Malta 1940–1943, Ernle Bradford, William Morrow & Company, Inc. (1986)

Bridge to Victory: The Story of the Reconquest of the Aleutians, Howard Handleman. Copyright 1943 by Random House, Inc., and renewed 1970 by Howard Handleman. Reprinted by permission of Random House, Inc.

Iron Coffins, Herbert R. Werner, Holt, Rinehart & Winston (1967)

The Magic War, Ian Fellows-Gordon, Scribner's (1971)

Defeat into Victory, William Slim, David McKay (1961)

CHAPTER XI:
HOME FRONTS, RESISTANCE FRONTS

■

The Republic of Silence, A. J. Liebling, Harcourt Brace Jovanovich (1947)

We Survived: The Stories of Fourteen of the Hidden and Hunted of Nazi Germany, Eric H. Boehm, Yale University Press (1949)

Road to Resistance: An Autobiography, George Millar. Copyright © 1975 by George Millar. By permission of Little, Brown & Company.

CHAPTER XII:
ASSAULT ON NAZI FORTRESS EUROPE

■

Overlord: D-Day and the Battle for Normandy, Max Hastings. Copyright © 1984 by Max Hastings. Reprinted by permission of Simon & Schuster.

On to Berlin: Battles of an Airborne Commander, James Gavin. Copyright © 1978 by James M. Gavin. All rights reserved. Reprinted by permission of Viking Penguin, a division of Penguin Books USA, Inc.

The Young Lions, Irwin Shaw. Copyright © 1948 by Irwin Shaw. Reprinted by permission of Random House, Inc.

CHAPTER XIII:
THE END OF THE WAR IN EUROPE

■

The Last Battle, Cornelius Ryan. Copyright © 1966 by Cornelius Ryan. Reprinted by permission of Simon & Schuster.

On to Berlin: Battles of an Airborne Commander, James Gavin. Copyright © 1978 by James M. Gavin. All rights reserved. Reprinted by permission of Viking Penguin, a division of Penguin Books USA, Inc.

The Bunker, James P. O'Donnell, Houghton Mifflin Company (1978)

The Way We Were. © 1985 by Godfrey Talbot, Radio 4, British Broadcasting Corporation.

Voices from the Holocaust, edited by Sylvia Rothchild. Copyright © 1981 by the William E. Wiener Oral History Library of the American Jewish Committee. Reprinted by arrangement with New American Library, a division of Penguin Books USA, Inc., New York, N.Y.

CHAPTER XIV:
CLOSING ON JAPAN

■

The Lost War: A Japanese Reporter's Inside Story, Masuo Kato. Copyright © 1946 by Masuo Kato, Alfred A. Knopf.

How They Won the War in the Pacific, Chester Nimitz and Edwin P. Hoyt, Waybright and Talley (1970)

Admiral Halsey's Story, Fleet Admiral William F. Halsey and J. Bryan III, McGraw Hill. Copyright © 1947 by William F. Halsey and Curtis Publishing Company

War Fish, George Grider and Lydel Sims. Copyright © 1958 Little, Brown & Company.

Tarawa: Portrait of a Battle, Robert Sherrod, Duell, Sloan & Pearce. Copyright 1944 by Robert Sherrod

The Color of Honor: The Japanese American Soldier in World War II, Loni Ding, producer. Documentary film, 1989, Vox Productions, Inc., San Francisco, Calif.

The Magnificent Mitscher, Theodore Taylor, W. W. Norton & Company, Inc. (1954)

CHAPTER XV:
THE END OF THE WAR IN THE PACIFIC

■

The Fall of Japan, William Craig. Copyright © 1967 by William Craig. Reprinted by permission of Doubleday, a division of Bantam Doubleday Dell Publishing Group, Inc.

The Lost War: A Japanese Reporter's Inside Story, Masuo Kato. Copyright © 1946 by Masuo Kato, Alfred A. Knopf.

The Good War: An Oral History of World War Two, Studs Terkel. Copyright © 1984 by Studs Terkel. Reprinted by permission of Pantheon Books, a division of Random House, Inc.

Bridge to the Sun, Gwen Terasaki. Copyright 1957 by the University of North Carolina Press.

ACKNOWLEDGMENTS

■

Most of the national war art collections we went to for the pictures in *Images of War* had been assembled with great urgency. Immediate wartime uses for certain specialized material—to strengthen morale, sell war bonds, stimulate enlistments—were most pressing. But most of the paintings and drawings that came in from artists in the field were simply cataloged in a rough manner, then put aside as part of each country's historical record of World War II.

Too often after the war, in the rush to resume the rhythms of peace, staffs of the various war art collections were cut, planning was suspended, and some of the smaller, less fortunately funded holdings disappeared from public view. The people in charge of these collections in the 1980s who helped us find our way in this treasure hunt were small cadres of hard-pressed but thoroughly dedicated archivists, curators, and librarians who had inherited these unique caches of art and history, which were growing more valuable with each decade.

The search started close to home. Linda Gutierrez, a writer and researcher based in Spain, had done a preliminary survey of the field in the early 1980s, identifying a number of collections abroad—but suggesting Washington, D.C., as a place to start. German and Japanese war art seized as "war booty" by the Allies had largely been brought to the United States at the end of the war, in order to prevent it from being used to rekindle neonationalistic fervor in Germany and Japan. But by the mid-1980s, there was sentiment in Congress, spurred by petitions from the original painters, to return all but the most severe "propaganda art" to the countries of origin and let them settle ownership.

In Washington we received an indoctrina-

tion from Marylou Gjernes and Verne Schwartz and their staff at the U.S. Army Art Activity, from John Barnett and John T. Deyer, Jr., at the U.S. Navy Combat Art Collection, and from Alice Price and June McHugh and their staff at the U.S. Air Force Art Collection. This aided us in every other source we worked with.

Terry Brown of the Society of Illustrators in New York helped put us in touch with former American war artists. Anne Brodzky of the Society of Art Publications of the Americas directed us to Canadian artists of the war period. Anne Zinsser provided a touching sketch and poetry book of a Japanese officer, which had been found on the battlefield at Guadalcanal. Special assistance in tracking down a fine collection of some 150 Japanese paintings came from Edward Boone, the curator of the Douglas MacArthur Memorial Museum in Norfolk, Virginia. The general had been presented with an album containing color prints of all these paintings, and this enabled us to trace a number of them to the National Modern Art Museum of Tokyo, and in turn to relatives of the painters. (We were politely refused permission to publish in several instances by families of the Japanese painters; the war years still caused rancor in some older people. And in *Images of War* you will see some Japanese art with creased and cracked canvas where the artwork had been rolled and folded in hopes of hiding it from the Americans. Understandable.)

Dorothy McConchie of the Department of Defense and Patricia Tombs of the Navy Department were red-tape cutters in getting first-rate reproduction material. P. H. Johnson, head librarian and museum curator at the U.S. Coast Guard Academy, and Martin Skrocki, Public Information Officer at the U.S. Merchant Marine Academy, guided us through buildings at the two academies to

find art that is on display as a daily reminder to midshipmen of the historic heritage of those services.

In Ottawa, Canada, Rikki Cameron, Fred Fagan, and William Kent at the Canadian War Museum took us to the vaults of Canada's grand collection on the same day they were hosting a group of Soviet naval officers searching for paintings of Canadian seamen on the "Murmansk Run." The Russian comments mirrored our own interests, and we found several paintings both of us could share. Some 75 paintings and sketches of Canadian Army, Navy, Air Force, and Merchant Navy activity were photographed for *Images of War*. And in thanks for permission to reproduce them, these transparencies will be donated to the museum at the end of this project for use by other researchers.

In Canberra, Australia, novelist Morris West, head of the Morris West Trust Fund of the National Library of Australia, helped us locate seasoned picture researchers and put us in contact with Keith W. Pearson, director of the Australian War Memorial. Nancy Tingey, Penny Kerr, and Anne Gray, senior curator of art at the Australian War Memorial, opened that country's superb collection of war art to us. Dame Ann Hercus, New Zealand's ambassador to the United Nations, was particularly helpful in getting us accredited to the corresponding collection in the New Zealand National Archives at Wellington, where its director, R. F. Grover, personally undertook the search and assembled a striking collection of paintings for us to pick from.

James Lothian, a retired British major of artillery with a sense of history, was our sponsor at Britain's National Maritime Museum collection in Greenwich, where Anne Carvell guided us through their holdings; these also included unexpected captured

German and Japanese war art. Jane Astell, royal liaison assistant at the BBC, helped us obtain approval from Buckingham Palace for a recollection about the end of the war by Her Majesty, Queen Elizabeth, and her approval of accompanying paintings by a pair of women war artists from Britain and Canada.

At the Imperial War Museum, London, a distinguished collection of art from World War I had set a pattern for the museum's organization of the vast amount of material that came in from British art programs during World War II. As you have seen, some British artists contributed to both conflicts. Angela Weight, keeper of the Department of Art; Michael Moody, her deputy; and Pauline Allwright, administrative assistant for the Department of Art, gave us valuable advice on the history and quality of the pictures we saw during one of the most difficult selections we had to make. The collection is vast, perhaps unmatched elsewhere. The Imperial War Museum also supplied us with useful leads to war art from Poland and Yugoslavia; both countries had been encouraged to mount shows at the museum long before *glasnost*.

Maurice Varney, a representative of the British Council who is on frequent assignments in Eastern Europe, recommended researchers and sources in areas he knew best. Sergey Nizovtsev, director of Foreign Trade Firm "Aurora," the distinguished Leningrad art publishers, was responsible for getting the help of a knowledgeable group of Soviet curators to gather recommendations of Russian war art; only a handful of the paintings selected for *Images of War* have ever been published outside the Soviet Union. Heyward Isham, an editor experienced with Russian publishing, undertook the translation of picture and museum information for the Soviet paintings. Sibylle Ch.B. Lachner, in Munich, did the moving translations of the "Letters from the Front" written by German soldiers in North Africa and Russia and by their Russian counterparts.

French war art, notably of events in the Blitzkrieg across France, is from the Musée d'Histoire Contemporaine—BDIC, Universités de Paris, where Cécile Coutin arranged for a selection of stark, powerful paintings of those dark days in a variety of art styles that marked the French program. Tadeusz Wiacek, vice-counsel at the Polish Consulate in New York, and Damir Grubisa, director of the Yugoslav Press and Cultural Center in New York, gave us valuable introductions to sources in their countries.

From the beginning we had been apprehensive about the long lead time that would be needed for communications with all these distant sources, but New York printer Luigi Sessa shared with us his own experience in international publishing—*and* his electronic equipment—to help us pass information back and forth to half a dozen countries quickly and efficiently.

Finally, Carl Apollonio at Orion Books first saw the possibilities of *Images of War* and marshaled an understanding editorial, design, production, and marketing team to see us home: Jake Goldberg, Steve Topping, Jim Walsh, Ken Sansone, Beth Tondreau, Jane Treuhaft, Laurie Stark, Jo Fagan, Allan Eady, and James Wade. And Joan Denman pushed a complex book through at full throttle—like the Red Ball Express going to the Battle of the Bulge. It was a heavier cargo than any of us thought it would be to bring in on schedule.

ARTISTS' INDEX

■

SUBJECT INDEX

■